PERILOUS STATES

Late Editions 1

Cultural Studies for the End of the Century

PERILOUS STATES

CONVERSATIONS ON CULTURE, POLITICS, AND NATION

George E. Marcus, EDITOR

The University of Chicago Press
Chicago and London

George E. Marcus is professor of anthropology at Rice University. He is coauthor of *Anthropology as Cultural Critique* (University of Chicago Press, 1986) and was the inaugural editor of the journal *Cultural Anthropology*.

The University of Chicago Press, Chicago 60637
The University of Chicago Press, Ltd., London
©1993 by The University of Chicago
All rights reserved. Published 1993
Printed in the United States of America
02 01 00 99 98 97 96 95 94 93   1 2 3 4 5
ISBN: 0-226-50446-8 (cloth)
         0-226-50447-6 (paper)

ISSN: 1070-8987 (for Late Editions)

CONTENTS

1   Introduction to the Series and to Volume 1   1
     GEORGE E. MARCUS

2   Dirges for Soviets Passed   17
     BRUCE GRANT

3   Returning to Eastern Europe   53
     KATHRYN MILUN

4   Six to Eight Characters in Search of Armenian Civil
     Society amidst the Carnivalization of History   81
     MICHAEL M. J. FISCHER AND STELLA GRIGORIAN

5   Two Urban Shamans: Unmasking Leadership in Fin-de-
     Soviet Siberia   131
     MARJORIE MANDELSTAM BALZER

6   Racism and the Formation of a Romani Ethnic Leader   165
     SAM BECK

7   Working through the Other: The Jewish, Spanish,
     Turkish, Iranian, Ukrainian, Lithuanian, and German
     Unconscious of Polish Culture; or, One Hand
     Clapping: Dialogue, Silences, and the Mourning of
     Polish Romanticism   187
     MICHAEL M. J. FISCHER

8   Greek Women in the Europe of 1992: Brokers of
     European Cargoes and the Logic of the West   235
     ELENI PAPAGAROUFALI AND EUGENIA GEORGES

9   Illicit Discourse   255
     DOUGLAS R. HOLMES

10   The Outlaw State and the Lone Rangers   283
          JULIE TAYLOR

11   A Terrible Commitment: Balancing the Tribes in South
          African National Culture   305
          DAVID B. COPLAN

12   A Preview of Volume 2: Reflections on Fieldwork in
          Alameda   359
          PAUL RABINOW

          Contributors   373
          Index   377

Introduction to the Series and to Volume 1

This is the first in a series of annual volumes that sends anthropologists and other kinds of scholars back to particular sites and situations within areas of previous knowledge and asks them to operate somewhat outside their usual genres of work. They are asked to trade the scholarly treatise or essay with all of its conventions of disciplinary authority and distance, for interviews, conversations, and biographical portraits in a manner more evocative of journalists or correspondents. The impetus for such a project is the desire to provide an unconventional but deep access to emergent cultural formations out of the maturing or exhaustion of ideas that have been powerful in the twentieth century, the continuing vitality of which are, on a global scale, explicitly in question in many milieus of everyday life. For us, the end of this century is far from the Eurocentric phenomenon it was at the end of the last century, distinctively periodized as "fin-de-siècle," and fraught with connotations of exhaustion as well as new possibilities emerging. But it does make problematic once again the notion of modernity, or the modern, in the diverse forms that it now takes. The reportage format of this series emphasizes a direct exposure to the quality of other "voices," other variously situated descriptions by social actors of their interests and predicaments which, we believe, will alter in often striking ways the manner in which contemporary society and culture have been otherwise assimilated in the theories, concepts, and analytic frames of more conventional academic writing.

While this series is meant to appeal to a wide readership, it is especially directed to that vibrant arena of interdisciplinary ferment in Anglo-American academia presently known as cultural studies, but which has been forming in the humanities and some of the social sciences throughout the 1980s. This effort should exemplify ways that the tradition of anthropological inquiry might effectively establish an identity and function in this arena. Anthropology is empirical, ethnographic at its core, yet deeply implicated in the same sources of theory and philosophy that inform the more textually oriented traditions of the humanities which compose the predominant influence in structuring inquiry within contemporary cultural studies. Indeed, from the perspective of the institutional politics of disciplines, some would argue that the main dynamic in the development of cultural studies has been the attempt of literary studies to expand and transform itself into a more engaged, socially conscious activity.

Our intent is to produce a series of volumes that speak to the most important issues raised in academia about processes of change in the contemporary world, especially as they emerge toward the end of the century, but with an emphasis on articulating the point of view, voice, and positioning of relevant social actors through imaginative constructions of interviews and conversations.

The core tension in cultural studies has thus been between text-based practices of analysis, theorizing, and framing questions and a desire to know the contemporary world, with its immense changes and diversity, in a more unmediated way. This tension is to some degree resolved by the slow, trickle-down influence that cultural studies theory, concepts, and issues have had on the way that intensive research on contemporary matters is conducted, but the curiosity, social and cultural imagination, and desire for immediate relevance to what is happening now within cultural studies far exceed the capacity of ongoing research about the contemporary to inform it sufficiently, to meet its desire to "world" itself (a term associated with Edward Said). The gap is filled in the meantime by the general way that scholars come to know their worlds—through journalism and the news media—and by certain celebrity intellectuals and scholars among themselves who come to stand for and interpret social and political situations in the world that are otherwise quite foreign to Anglo-American cultural studies. With its attempt to have scholars of society and culture suspend momentarily their usual styles of research for experimentation with reportage, this series is meant to provide another appealing and, we hope, more provocatively informing medium to address this felt parochialism within a cultural studies short on access to the diverse situations of its own contemporary global concerns and commitments.

We take this "worlding" desire within cultural studies to be a documentary impulse that has arisen before among academics and intellectuals at times of their hyperawareness of great changes at work in the world. There was, for instance, great interest in the description and discovery of new social and cultural forms and the decline of old ones during the last fin-de-siècle. Later, during the 1920s and 1930s, there was an intense interest among intellectuals and academics in documenting changes in culture and society that were not in a reflective, theoretical way easily understood.

Then as now, the desire to know by documentation or description stands, in itself, for a kind of social activism and is one form that the expression of longing for political relevance and commitment takes for intellectuals and academics when other means of participation may be blocked or nonexistent. This may not be true of other parts of the world. From this year's Annual, for example, the extent to which academics elsewhere—in Europe, East and West, in Russia, in South Africa—are directly involved in the great transformations taking place is remarkable. The implications of this for globally minded U.S. academics are one of the key underlying issues of the first Annual.

The series will repeatedly link American intellectuals and academics to their counterparts elsewhere. Through these channels of basic connection, it will then document the immense differences that exist between their conditions and those of their counterparts. This will perhaps suggest new ways to reconfigure and think about academic work in the United States, starting with the arena of cultural studies, which seems to be encouraging such rethinking anyway.

What really differentiates the present documentary impulse from similar past trends with which it can be identified is that there was once more authority and faith in forms of documentary realism. Photography, film, documentary novels, ethnography, travel accounts, introspective autobiography—these were powerful means of providing that direct access to contemporary changes. To some extent they still are, but the cultural studies movement and its intellectual underpinnings have been built on a pervasive critique and deep suspicion of all forms of representation such that the capacity of any kind of realist description to deliver an effect of "knowing the world" has been undermined. Thus, stark, simple portraits of others elsewhere would not adequately serve this series nor its main intended readership. Still, while we do not indulge the dismissal of realist description to the point of paralysis, we are aware (in every piece) that the "voice" exposed in interviews is no more authentic than the photograph or authoritative documentary narration, and that conversations presented in print are no less constructed.

Nonetheless, aside from the obvious general appeal for a diverse readership of the interview form as a journalistic means of providing a sense of very human, direct access to particular experiences and points of view, we think that such a mode of reportage also will address the documentary impulse of cultural studies with its hypercriticism of representation.

First, the interview form, as experimented with in this series, allows, even demands, reflexive framing which at least exposes to the reader the biases of construction rather than hides them, or else preempts a lot of the critique of representation in cultural studies by incorporating it in the reportage itself.

Second, quite aside from the critique of all forms of representation, we have noted how appealing and refreshing interviews seem to our colleagues as another, albeit occasional, genre of academic communication. The literary review conversation is personalizing. It offers otherwise formally presented ideas in the frame of life experience, and to retrieve the same ideas from an interview, the reader as a third party must get engaged, eavesdrop on the exchange, enjoy its ambiguous, life-situated expression of ideas otherwise presented in theoretical or analytic discourse. We thus recognize the success of the reportage/interview form in delivering an "as if" effect ("as if" one is getting access to real personal experience) even to otherwise suspicious colleagues who have learned that everything is a text and is constructed. It is the demonstrated effectiveness of the interview form in satisfying the documentary impulse that has led us to adopt it as the signature format for this series.

Third, and relatedly, what the interview/conversation does present in a less mediated way than most academic writing is others' discourses (edited and arranged, certainly), unassimilated to given concepts, theories, and analytic frames. This is probably the key expression that the documentary impulse takes this time around. In cultural studies research (and particularly for a much longer time in anthropology) there is a deep sense that our own specialized discourses, concepts, and theories colonize those of others and really block access to other experiences. While there are many defenses for preserving the space of rational, detached, reflective reason, these do not speak to the desire nonetheless to have more direct access to others' situated frameworks and discourses.

Ethnography, of course, has been endlessly concerned with such problems of cultural hermeneutics and translation. However modest and flawed our experiment with it may be, our choice here to adopt the interview format is an attempt to address the worlding impulse. This might be understood as the desire to have a kind of access to others' discourses into which the latter are not too quickly assimilated or fixed by familiar concepts.

One other major difference concerning the present trend of documentary impulse to which the series is responding is the widespread sense among cultural studies intellectuals of intense globalism or connectedness which shapes their desire to know other places and other experiences of the contemporary. The issue thus raised for us is not so much to whom this series is to be directed, but whom is it primarily to be about. Of course, in a world of global cosmopolitanism, it might be supposed, perhaps too idealistically, that this distinction between intended readers and selected subjects could not help but be repeatedly blurred.

Our idea is not to present systematic assessments of the current forces of change in the world, but to let expressions of these emerge from conversations with persons interestingly situated in different societies, institutions, and arenas of transcultural and transnational activity. Famous writers and academics generally, who repeatedly or perhaps too prominently have stood for complex local and transcultural processes, are to be avoided as subjects, as are subjects who overly exoticize difference (for example, cult leaders who have no linkages with pervasive institutions of modernity shared with readers). Most subjects will probably be previously unknown (at least to a U.S. readership), but are locally powerful, or empowered, persons who have been importantly involved in the institutions or processes of change in their societies. Their various involvements will constitute the particular socially contextualized "angle" of vision within the conversation. The conversations should be revealing along several dimensions—the sharedness, as well as lack thereof, between the discourses of those interviewed and their interviewees, mainly U.S. academics involved in cultural studies. Among subjects, there should be for readers considerable, revelatory surprise connections of situations and conditions linking, say, the most liberal of persons with the most oppressive of regimes or scientists with literary pursuits; or showing how genres of popular culture become quickly politicized in reshaping national symbols, and how quickly, diversely, and pervasively environmentalism becomes adopted as the most political of causes in different places; or revealing the unprecedented activist roles of academics in the reconstitution of civil societies in the wake of rapid political change. The conversations should in diverse and unpredictable ways bear out the intimate relation between the global and the local, so often paired in contemporary cultural studies discourse. They might also show the relative power or weakness of political upheaval in affecting fundamental cultural changes at the end of this century.

The very large fin-de-siècle issue that this series is trying to address, through selected topics and from such a multitude of sites and situations of personal testimony, is the increasingly salient debate on the viability and relevance of the nation-state (especially in the West) in the wake of recent upheavals and in face of processes and activities that are increasingly organized and operated independently of the control and planning of states. Through the various topical foci of the Annuals we will thus have recurrent interest in the simultaneous exhaustion and emergence of the form of civil society in various places, on the one hand, and, on the other, in processes, institutions, and social movements that are trying to construct new frameworks, concepts, and spaces of operation partly or wholly free of state/civil society notions of citizenship, rights, and so on.

As noted, our aim is not to provide another large perspective on these very large matters in our own voices, but to reflect them topically through very particularly situated voices and perspectives. Also, as noted, we want to evoke a combined sense of familiarity and strangeness in U.S.-university educated readers by selecting subjects that share something of a frame of reference and experience with them, but then differ in often radical and startling ways from them by cultural background and situated fin-de-siècle predicament. It is this kind of ambivalent relationship of those interviewed to the interviewer and the eavesdropping reader that we hope will most effectively satisfy the intense fin-de-siècle desire to know the world more directly.

While the role of anthropology has been emphasized in the creation of this project, it would be a mistake to simply identify it with what a particular discipline has to offer a perhaps overly theorized and textualized cultural studies desiring a more direct connection to events. Rather, as the decade and the series unfold, we hope to extend the range of intellectual and personal backgrounds in our contributors (not all of the first Annual's contributors are trained in anthropology; at least two have backgrounds in comparative literature). This diversification of participation will itself be an emergent feature of the series, a characteristic shared with its end of the century milieu.

However, the Rice University anthropology department and Center for Cultural Studies will act as a kind of institutional anchor for the series, which seems fitting since the critique of ethnography and the rethinking of its uses in relation to cultural studies were pioneered here during the 1980s.[2] Each spring a planning session will convene at Rice with local participants and two or three invited consultants (the guests were anthropologists Vincent Crapanzano and Stefania Pandolfo and historian of science Mario Biagioli). During the course of the next year, participants either conduct interviews or work with material they might already have. In May of each following year, a collective editorial meeting is held at Rice at which the participants review each piece and recommend final revisions.

Participants are charged with contributing something more than a simple journalistic interview and that should maybe even aspire to the French literary form of the engaged conversation, the *entretien,* like the famous ones with Lévi-Strauss or as in the series of discussions between Raymond Williams and the editors of the *New Left Review* (1981). What we have in mind is a cross between what is normally done with well-known literary, political, or academic figures in literary reviews and those magic moments during the course of anthropological fieldwork of unplanned rich and sustained conversation with a local that seems to exemplify and articulate everything that one has been trying to understand. Another variant is the profile (as in the well-known *New Yorker* genre) in which dialogue and quotation are embedded in biographical portraiture that in turn evokes the conditions of a whole society, profession, or locale.

Within the bounds of the conversation form, participants have maximum flexibility to develop their own ideas for their pieces. Some contributors might work strictly from transcripts; others might construct composites; the pieces might take the form of monologue, dialogue, or trialogue (a participant might, for example, be led to a subject through an intermediary who participates in the conversation). Even the results of conversations that were not as rich as hoped can be interesting (see, for example, the piece by Julie Taylor in the first Annual). The first Annual's pieces exemplify such a range of experiences in working with the interview/conversation form.

Finally, our bet or stake in undertaking this series is that the cultural studies arena is, and will continue increasingly to be, the particular expression of at least American academia's position and concern in *this* fin-de-siècle, and that the series will offer one modest, experimental response to the desire among cultural studies scholars to know more directly the diverse contemporary worlds of which they are a part and which they continually attempt to make their difficult-to-apprehend objects of research and reflection.

Fin-de-Siècle as Fantasy Echo

Fin-de-siècle is bound to become a titling cliché, if it hasn't already, employed by ever more works of social commentary as this decade unfolds. Quite aside from the literal end-of-the-century time frame in which we are situated, the undeniable sense of watershed and dramatic change in contemporary social, political, and technological conditions makes parallel reference to the classic periodization of the nineteenth-century European fin-de-siècle nearly irresistible. Then as now, fin-de-siècle was marked by a hyperawareness of both exhaustion and emergence in social trends. We too were certainly beguiled with this reference in the early informal discussions that led to this series, and in planning the first volume as well, even though there was much concern that we might be misunderstood (as being too pessimistic, pretentious, or perhaps Francophilic?) if we actually used the historic reference to title this series. Nonetheless, at the risk of participating in what will certainly become the cliched overuse of this allusion to the last century's end, we continue to think of it as an appropriate period marker in conceptualizing this series for at least two reasons: one in conformity with the usual use of the term, the other in ironic and, for *this* fin-de-siècle necessary contestation of it.

First, our interest in this series is in those contemporary events and processes which cannot be theorized or analyzed with confidence or satisfaction by any one or combination of major perspectives bequeathed to us by the nineteenth century. Like the interviewees in this volume, we are somewhat at a loss to apprehend the great changes around us with given categories. This hypersensitivity to emergent phenomena amid exhausted (at least in their received traditions of development) frameworks of common understanding is what most cogently ties us to the last fin-de-siècle in intellectual atmosphere. Our predicament is to give ourselves some historical sense of the present moment in which our interest is in emergent trends, but for which the past itself is an unreliable guide. This is what employing the fin-de-siècle parallel reference appropriately does for us, since the sensibility of great changes afoot through exhaustion/emergence is defining of fin-de-siècle, then and now.

Second, however, we do not want the parallel with the last fin-de-siècle, a wholly Eurocentric reference, to be taken too seriously or literally. Even though recent events in Europe, especially Eastern Europe, and the former Soviet Union do seem to be moving the focus of dramatic change globally back toward the West, at least for the first part of the decade, the European context of fin-de-siècle is inappropriate and parochial for the contemplation of the same periodization this time around. Not only is fin-de-siècle played out on a global scale of cultural interreference, but it is debatable that the West itself can or should be understood as focally European. Thus, we must be suspicious of the term for its colonizing potential, and should even be playful and parodic about our use of it.

In this regard, a story from Michael M. J. Fischer and Stella Grigorian, this Annual's contributors who conducted interviews in Armenia, is apt. The fin-de-siècle reference was repeatedly mentioned by the interviewers in introducing the project. Though clearly in the midst of momentous changes, the Armenians did not identify particularly with the fin-de-siècle periodization, although they certainly understood the term as a distinct period of European history. But with repeating, *fin-de-siècle* was increasingly slurred in pronunciation and became heard as "fantasy echo." This shift was a matter of amusement among the interviewers and for us when they reported it on their return. But we came to think: yes, of course, that's what *fin-de-siècle* really means for us in this project. It is our own special fantasy or fiction, echoing a past history of change well known to us in our own intellectual tradition, but not necessarily the framework by which all people who become the subject of interviews during the course of this project apprehend or periodize their own times. It is definitely *our* historically echoed fantasy of the emergent present, and the question of who else actually shares this periodization and its parallel with Europe's past is a very open matter. Certainly, fin-de-siècle this time around requires a more diverse, global imagination than the historian's designation for the end of last century within European civilization. In any case, if its use were not so chimerical, we might think of this project in terms of "fantasy echo" instead of "fin-de-siècle."

This Year's Annual

At the end of our collective editorial meeting in May 1992, I asked the contributors to this volume to jot down what they thought was the thematic salience of the papers. I quote verbatim two of the responses, which could easily serve as introductory statements for the first Annual.

Doug Holmes:

> What is this text about? The last decade of the twentieth century is marked by the end of great historical allegories and the creation of ambiguous possibilities. The text contains interviews with individuals who are struggling to reinvent the past and reconfigure the present.

These struggles are provoking "new" cultural architectures mediated through ethnicity, language, art, religion, politics, science, and shamanism. An arresting sense of dislocation and anticipation resonate through diverse testimonies drawn from Siberia, South Africa, Argentina, Hungary, France, Poland, and others. The conversations delineate the unsettling dilemmas and unprecedented challenges facing end of the century anthropology and cultural studies.

Kathryn Milun:

The papers on Eastern Europe articulate the struggles now facing the citizens of that region to formulate categories, concepts, institutions, in short, new representational forms in which their repressed histories, their various identities—ethnic, national, class, personal—can be thought. Clearly, emerging from the period of late paternalism we see that forty to seventy years of Marxist-Leninist state power have produced an incestuous confusion of categories: as these interviews ask people of the area to speak about who they are now, we are reminded of Jack Nicholson's interrogation of incest victim Faye Dunaway in Polanski's film *Chinatown:* Who is this child she's been hiding? "My daughter," she says. "No, my sister. No, my daughter . . ." The interviewees in these papers echo this disorder: without the veneer of internationalism, what does it mean to be Polish and a Jew, Romanian and a Gypsy, a dissident and a member of Parliament (or a dissident who is apolitical), a socialist and a capitalist, a feminist, a writer, a citizen of a democracy?

The interviews with the politician/scholar of the far Right in Western Europe and with those in the Argentine military remind us that the threat of totalitarian solutions continues to haunt both fledgling and apparently stable democracies. In fact, as Holston's discussion of the Los Angeles riots/insurrection and the exhaustion of liberal ideas of the city makes clear, here at the turn of the twentieth century, we are ill-equipped to deal with the configuration of class issues in the multiethnic public sphere which carries both the legacy of colonialism and the hope of democracy.

Uncertainties about social and cultural categories of identity and the struggle to find a new vocabulary or allegory for describing ongoing change in civil society in the wake of dramatic events or political change resonate through virtually all of the diversely situated testimonies of this volume. For example, the combination of the difficulty of finding terms to express ethnicity or social location, as well as on-the-spot efforts to invent conscious programs for mapping fragmented landscapes and placing oneself within it that Kathryn Milun found as characteristics of discourse in her discussion of Sam Beck's interlocutor, Nicolae Gheorghe, is also generally to be found, with very different inflections, in the discourse of the Russian writers in their conversations with Bruce Grant, in that of the Armenian officials in their conversations with Fischer and Grigorian, in that of Maria Stratigaki in conversation with Eleni Papagaroufali and Nia Georges, in that of Jonathan Clegg, Hein Willemse, Bongani Mthethwa, and Barbara Masakela in conversation with David Coplan, and in that of Kathryn Milun's own Hungarian interlocutors.

Some of the subjects of these interviews worried about the fictionalizing quality of their accounts which referred to often harsh and unsettling realities that they were experiencing; others did not. The Argentines, in the wake of the Dirty War and unending economic crises, seemed particularly hesitant to tell their stories out of a deep concern for the necessarily partial and fragmented way in which their accounts would be received. Julie Taylor finally had to be satisfied with an unreflective but vivid testimony by a dissident military officer. In a sense, her own narrative voice commenting on Major Mittelbach's predicament is ambivalently that of an Argentine, given Taylor's long association and personal identification with life in Argentina. In contrast, the South Africans who spoke to David Coplan were only too willing to weave narratives and create texts in the telling, and he saw his task in creating his own text as one of breaking the rhythm of those that were being created by his interlocutors.

What is striking about the South African figures, as pointed out by Taylor in her discussion of Coplan's paper, is the implied polyglot model of culture operating in which the point of conversation or rendering accounts is not necessarily to make conditions transparent or to speak a simple truth clear to any listener. Rather, it is assumed that discussions, testimonies, stories, and the like will at least in part remain stubbornly opaque, and that the point is to establish rapport and connections with interlocutors on the basis of necessarily opaque discourses. Truth-telling versus fiction is not an option in South Africa where there can be no nonracially based discourse—it is impossible to escape such terms.

In the pieces from Russia and Eastern Europe (particularly in the papers by Grant, Fischer and Grigorian, Milun, and Beck) there remain in a period of transitions toward different constitutions of civil society various traces of cryptic or Aesopian discourse—for example, "*You* said that, *I* didn't."— registering the conditions of life under the repressive regimes of the old communist orders. Indeed, one of the valuable contributions of this collection is the comparative range of similarities and differences it offers readers in features of discourse which serve as subtle, and not so subtle, microlevel registers of changes in societies that at least on the macrolevel have made obvious and dramatic breaks with the past. Some aspects of all of these interviews must remain enigmatic to general readers given the specific conditions of the interviews and the particularity of individual situations that they aim for. Yet each, through the quality of voice, a turn of phrase, or a peculiar usage of an otherwise familiar term, provides an access requiring active interpretive work from the reader into the specific terms of ambiguous processes by which identities, social categories, and institutions are actually becoming transformed in civil society after the newsworthy event has itself occurred—the old order has fallen, the disaster has occurred and so on.

While one key advantage of employing the interview/conversation format has been to block the easy or precipitous assimilation of others' discourses to our own frames of analysis, the editorial discussions of this year's contributions demonstrated how rather neutral-seeming terms of analysis resonate unintentionally with the same terms in the subjects' discourse, sometimes with undesirable consequences. For example, Marjorie Balzer and others with experience in Eastern Europe and the former Soviet Union noted that Fischer and Grigorian's use of the "stage" framework in discussing revolution in Armenia cannot help but evoke the pervasiveness of the same framework characteristic of social thought in these regions, there tinged with the dogmatism of communist doctrine and historical thought. Yet Fischer and Grigorian also assimilate, for their own analytic purposes intentionally and in a very interesting way, the original use of the notion of carnivalization by one of their subjects, an official of the Armenian government who is also an anthropologist. Similarly, David Coplan pointed out that the term *multicultural,* a complex political code word of ambiguous meaning in the contemporary United States, is in South Africa synonymous with apartheid. Thus, one kind of repeated therapeutic shock of recognition delivered within this year's contributions is a sensitivity about our apparently global concerns and general conceptual tools which in comparative frames become special usages, suddenly put into association with other meanings.

Another kind of shock effect delivered repeatedly by the papers is unexpected and often ironic associations of phenomena, characteristics, and labels that disrupt habitual alignments of categories—good/bad, left/right, civilian/military, ethnicity/nationalism. In Argentina, for example, Major Mittelbach is an ambivalently sympathetic character; the torturers return as politicians running strongly in democratic elections; free market economic policies and the "dirty war" against subversion are intimately related. In Siberia, shamanism is returning in a politicized form in which this religious status is being bureaucratically produced; further, Balzer's interlocutors, in their concerns with ethnicity and nationalism, give a different value-weighting to ethnicity (conventionally positive) and nationalism (conventionally negative) than their usual associations in Western discussions of these phenomena. Fischer's discussions with Leszek Koczanowicz pose the puzzle of why the now absent Jew, among other absent figures, is still so necessary for the constitution of Polish national identity. Douglas Holmes's interview with Bruno Gollnisch demonstrates how much better the Right understands the Left than the latter does itself, and on the broad canvas of the new, supposedly united Europe, the Right has constructed a powerful and seductive discourse of primordial divisiveness.

The point here, then, is that much of the embedded discourse about recent changes among social actors occurs open-endedly and in response to shifting power dynamics. While dealing recognizably with concepts in which we have a shared interest—ethnicity, race, nation, class, culture, democracy, citizenship, rights—our usual construction of these concepts for analytic discourse or easy reference miss entirely their actual nuances and variations of meaning in social settings. The reportage form employed in these papers thus makes accessible sets of relationships and connections that our conceptual apparatus otherwise cannot.

Indeed, Paul Rabinow insisted that the concern with identity itself that runs rather seamlessly through many of these papers emanates from a particular intellectual culture—that of American (perhaps, Anglo-American) cultural studies. Recently returned from France, Rabinow claimed that there was as much interest there as here in fin-de-siècle contemporary changes and emergent formations, but the identity question or focus was completely absent. In a volume which purports to represent voices from elsewhere, with a sensitivity to their local constitution, it is certainly incumbent upon us to point out the powerful screen of our particular interest in identity formation through which these voices are being constructed by us.

Taylor's response to Rabinow's point is that the papers are not primarily about identity concerns as usually discussed in American cultural studies. Very little power or agency is in the hands of most of the subjects of these interviews of the sort that would enable them to shape or form new identities for themselves. They are in the swirl of recent events, and questions about who they are are matters less of personal identity process than specifically situated and experienced commentaries and observations on rapid changes in the social orders of which they are a part. Impressive about many of the interviews is how much "world" consciousness there is in commentaries on very local predicaments; many of the interview subjects think about their current daily lives in comparison with the specific situations of life elsewhere (this is especially the case of Eastern Europeans thinking about their own conditions in intense association with what has happened elsewhere in the region).

From Taylor's specific perspective on Argentina, from which she in turn commented on the situations of Beck's Gypsy nationalist and Coplan's polyglot, race-minded South Africans, what is at stake is the effect of state power, and often sheer violence, in silencing and excluding entire peoples from public discourse. For her, the papers are most powerful when they reveal on the occasions of the interviews themselves on-the-spot openings to power dynamics, partially released repressions, and uncertain emergences from silences and silencing. The papers are most exciting when they show where new possibilities for voice arise in response to a combination of old patterns of repression, or what is left of them, and new power maneuvers for different kinds of social positions. Identity creation, here, is somewhat epiphenomenal, and certainly not the perhaps sentimentalized and ennobling process that Rabinow seems to attribute as a special interest of American cultural studies. Thus, for Taylor, our interest in what might be termed identity processes arises from real local concerns and conditions, particularly in places like Eastern Europe and Argentina, and cannot be seen mainly as the particular intellectual slant of the interviewers.

If there was one recurrent concern that persisted through the discussions of these papers during our collective editorial meeting, it was the question of framing. Not framing in the sense of systematic, expert background or overview, since this sort of authoritative, capsule narrative is not what this series is attempting. Indeed, it is self-consciously an alternative to this kind of writing. A number of the papers do creatively embed this sort of framing which positions the voices intelligibly in relation to objective social conditions within the editing of interviews (for example, the cross-referencing in Grant's interviews, the careful weaving of other voices around the core Clegg interview in Coplan's paper, the Ford Report inserts in Holmes's paper). But our intention has been to leave puzzles as puzzles and to expect readers imaginatively to help in framing (we hope that engagement with the interviews and portraits will easily get them involved).

Rather, framing as an issue for us had more to do with a sort of reflexive clarity in presenting dialogues and exchanges as published interviews. This issue arose in particular when the material being presented had a disturbing ethical import. The most striking instance was developed by Jim Holston in his critique of the manner in which Doug Holmes presented his interview with Bruno Gollnisch, a member of the European parliament and an associate of Jean-Marie Le Pen. Holmes's own interview style is rather flat and minimal (intentionally so), thus highlighting Gollnisch's comments, which many of us found articulate, seductive, even sympathetic, but whose positions on race and nationality we found objectionable. Of course, this sort of reaction is the point and power of Holmes's presentation of the material. Further, he uses the inserts of the Ford Report as a contextualizing device which effectively juxtaposes the simplifications in "social analysis" commentary to the disturbing complexities of well-articulated right-wing positions. Holmes's point is that the left-right traditional frame of political discourse in the new Europe is evolving into really different kinds of moral allegories that conventional social science or theory, as yet, fails to grasp.

The strongest concern in our meeting, articulated particularly by James Holston's discussion of Holmes's contribution, was about the danger of letting Gollnisch's commentary stand unanswered or unengaged by his interviewer, however effective this strategy of presentation might otherwise be, since at least some readers might actually be seduced by the intelligence, sophistication, and sympathetic self-positioning of his commentary. The same complaint was raised about portions of Grant's interviews (for example, self-serving claims that the Russians have never oppressed anyone), but in his case the staged cross-referencing of the interviews is itself a reflexive technique of presentation which should reinforce suspiciousness of readers about taking any of the statements at face value.

This first Annual's contributions, then, are not simply about personal experiences, but rather about how these can be read as registers of still emergent transformations of civil societies following dramatic change in political order. In the eerie aftermaths of liberation or disaster, struggles for new forms of public life under the banner of establishing democracy, market economies, individual rights, and the participation of previously repressed ethnic and racial groups are clearly what is happening and what media, scholars, and others perceive through the established categories available for talking about society and culture. This volume hopes to have exposed the very rupture of those same categories in the discourses among social actors in such societies. Old tormentors arise in new guises, common words acquire different meanings, it becomes difficult to place politicians on the left-right spectrum, and so forth. In the absence of reliable categories, then, the voices, edited, exposed, and created in this volume, provide another perhaps more ambiguous but also direct access to contemporary fin-de-siècle traumas. The range of cases allow for a variety of anchors from which to establish comparisons on many different levels. There is no doubt that readers will see and add their own contexts of significance across these papers, and the possibility of and invitation to such engagement are what we intend.

Indeed, the specific thematic concern of this year's Annual—the emergent reshaping of civil societies in the wake of the exhaustion or extinction of longstanding political orders and governing ideas about the relationship between nations and states—might serve as a general, recurrent theme for the series as a whole. There is virtually no part of the globe that is not going through some version of the transformations reflected from different angles in this volume. The reorientations of other individuals in other places will continue to be important for us to document. Thus, papers like these will reappear occasionally in succeeding volumes, each with a distinctive thematic concentration of its own.

Late Editions, Volume 2

Following the collective editorial meeting for volume 1 on 9 May 1992, a second meeting was held among a group associated with this project at Rice to consider a thematic focus for volume 2. (Beside local participants, the invited guests were anthropologists Don Brenneis, Ivan Karp, Corinne Kratz, and Fred Myers.) We decided to commission a set of interviews, conversations, and portraits concerning the kinds of social and cultural imaginations at work in various practices of contemporary science. We are particularly interested in scientists operating in transcultural spheres of endeavor, those working on "millennial" big science projects such as the human genome project and the supercollider in Texas, and those working between the university and the corporation with an interest in technological applications in contexts such as the military, medicine, and environmentalism. Our emphasis will be on diverse kinds of cultural continua and connections in scientific practice, probed through conversations and interviews: the "humanities" background and imaginations of particular scientists, the institutional atmospheres in which they work, their politics and formative generational experience (for example, in relation to the emblematic decade of the 1960s); the sense of the sociological landscape in which they work; the relevance of multicultural, social class, and gender sensitivities in and outside work.

A useful preview of the second Annual is an extract of the conversation between anthropologist Paul Rabinow and geneticist Tom White, who are involved in a pioneering collaboration in the ethnographic study of a realm of scientific practice, in this case biotechnology. Their conversation, prepared along with this year's contributions in anticipation of the thematic focus for the second Annual, addresses by means characteristic of the signature format of this series most of the above issues. It is the specific and diverse cultural references of contemporary scientific practices, the most "millennial" and universalist of this fin-de-siècle's emergent developments, that we most want to explore. The extract from Rabinow and White's conversation is a preview and starting point for this effort in volume 2.

Notes

1. The title selected for volume 1 is a variant of the one suggested by David Coplan, "Perilous States: Conversations on Culture, Race, and Nation."

2. See for example Clifford and Marcus 1986, Marcus and Fischer 1986, Tyler 1987, Traweek 1989, Fischer and Abedi 1990.

3. Two participants who were active in the preparation of the first Annual but whose contributions do not appear here were James Holston and Kim Laughlin. Holston was a participant in our May collective editorial meeting, while Laughlin, whose paper was circulated, was in India at the time of the meeting. Holston's paper, which was not completed in time to be included in this volume, offered a vivid access to contemporary Los Angeles tacking between the recent widespread violence there and the dashed utopian hopes for urban planning among local architects, community activists, and policymakers. His paper will be included in volume 2. Laughlin's paper

focussed on the politics of environmental activism at Bhopal, India, the site of the Union Carbide chemical plant disaster. We decided also that a revised version of her contribution would fit more appropriately in next year's volume, on the scientific imaginary.

References

Clifford, James, and George E. Marcus, eds. 1986. *Writing Culture: The Politics and Poetics of Ethnography.* Berkeley: University of California Press.

Fischer, Michael M. J., and Mehdi Abedi. 1990. *Debating Muslims: Cultural Dialogues in Postmodernity and Tradition.* Madison: University of Wisconsin Press.

Lévi-Strauss, Claude. 1969 [1961]. *Conversations with Claude Lévi-Strauss.* Ed. Georges Charbonnier. London: Jonathan Cape.

———. 1991 [1988]. *Conversations with Claude Lévi-Strauss.* Ed. Didier Eribon. Chicago: University of Chicago Press.

Marcus, George E., and Michael M. J. Fischer. 1986. *Anthropology as Cultural Critique: An Experimental Moment in the Human Sciences.* Chicago: University of Chicago Press.

Traweek, Sharon. 1989. *Beamtimes and Lifetimes.* Cambridge, Mass.: Harvard University Press.

Tyler, Stephen. 1987. *The Unspeakable: Discourse, Dialogue, and Rhetoric in the Postmodern World.* Madison: University of Wisconsin Press.

Williams, Raymond. 1981. *Politics and Letters: Interviews with the* New Left Review. London: Verso.

2

DIRGES FOR SOVIETS PASSED

In the last autumn of the USSR, the fall of 1991, six years of social upheaval had reached a point of professed exhaustion. The failed coup or putsch of the preceding August had turned legislative favor for the first time decisively and dramatically in the direction of reformists, and across the country people were confronted even more profoundly with uncertainty in all arenas. Against this backdrop, an acrimonious schism in the notorious Union of Writers of the USSR galvanized the Russian intelligentsia. As leading bards brought into the service of the state ideology, members of the elite union had been the main architects of Soviet culture since their profession had been collectivized under Stalin in 1934. They had long held claim to an almost priestly status in the USSR, and it was consistent with this directive role that the sundering of the union—a split between an old guard eager to preserve the existing hierarchy of power and a new establishment seeking to reduce the union's coercive influence—was widely held to be a metaphor for the crumbling Soviet state.

What I present here are a series of six conversations with Russian writers, editors, and literary critics. From their various positions in the union melee, they speak not only to the extraordinary degree of social engineering that went into the production of Soviet culture, but they offer us a sense of the complex spectrum of political agendas that compete today in the wake of the Soviet Union's demise. Their reflections document a specific historic moment for Russian society, but they also evince a sense of the chaos produced when the collective past changes almost more rapidly than the present itself.

In 1986, less turbulent times, the Union of Writers of the USSR counted almost ten thousand members in its ranks. In keeping with the hegemony of the Russian voice throughout the Soviet system, five thousand of those members were from the Russian republic and two thousand were from Moscow alone. The union's wealth and influence were legion. It administered all the major literary journals and periodicals around the country, countless printing presses, its own massive housing fund, resorts, guest homes, and access to

goods in otherwise chronic short supply. To be inducted into the union was a
coveted privilege, determined in principle by the quality and quantity of a
writer's publications, but more often achieved through private connections or
blat. Hence, as one of its members notes here below, "It's unlikely that there
has ever been another writer's union so filled with businessmen, bureaucrats,
carpenters and psychics." Although the task of the union was to organize the
Soviet enlightenment and exercise ideological homogeneity, it has never been
an entirely homogenous body.

I sought out each of the figures here for their reputations as politically
engaged social critics. Few are of national prominence, but each are well
known within their respective Moscow and Petersburg circles. Indeed, knowing that the conversations would be used in a montage of perspectives, many
referenced to the others' work a number of times over.[1] The conversations
were held separately over the course of November 1991. In each instance, the
questions were largely the same: What had brought about the split in the
writers' union? To what extent did this reflect the broader politics of Soviet
culture? Is it possible to renovate a disgraced past without jettisoning it altogether? At a time when madmen were becoming ministers and the august were
being revealed as grotesque, words themselves were losing currency and vec-
tors of meaning were reversed routinely. Characteristic here are stunning
reversals in the ideas of nationalism, pluralism, dissidence, patriotism, Marxism, and bolshevism. Context becomes critically important in determining
whether these are invoked favorably, dispassionately, or as defamations of the
most incendiary order. If the reader notes that the speakers contradict each
other and themselves in a number of places, then they will come closer to the
urgency and ambivalence that reigned in Russia then as it does now.

An unexpected turn in the cultural and political debates since this schism
took place has been the reanimation of what has long been a much-contested
opposition in Russian culture between Slavic and Western camps. In the nineteenth century, the debate was personified by writers such as Dostoyevsky and
Tolstoy who played upon a geographic and historic setting that pitched Russia
between two polar constructs: an Asia portrayed as mystical, meditative, and
crude, and a West portrayed as cosmopolitan and ruthlessly self-serving. In
more recent years it has been characterized by the difference between Solzhenitsyn and Sakharov. Since the fall of the empire, the contrast has become a
favored tool for Russian nationalists of every stripe. Here the debate is over
more than just an aesthetic of authenticity; it lies at the heart of a score of
political battles in Russia today over what direction to take in a country in
need of reinventing itself.

Each of the writers here speaks to a profound sense of tragedy. But the
slippage between what invokes their regret—a tragedy that the Soviet Union
endured for so long, or a tragedy that it came to an end—points to the con-

tinuing contestation over political and ideological hegemony. These are very Soviet dirges which break away from the conventional sense of the tragic. Rather than meeting misfortune by turning inward as the early Greeks would have, they provoke and challenge; they demand an audience. Rather than dwelling on heroes of mythic, romantic proportions, these professions of lament give us protagonists from a very real world, morally compromised by their pasts and haunted by uncertainty. They also offer us insight into what are arguably the most compelling voices in the current reformulation of the Russian identity, not the voices of the reformists or the communists, but those of the vast majority of Russians who find themselves in between—the people who have almost managed to reconstruct themselves with the changing times, but who are profoundly ill at ease with the implications of the reforms that they hesitantly had acknowledged as necessary.

From the ruins of the present, the interviews speak to a radical reevaluation of the past, leading in turn to new definitions of self based on assertions of blamelessness or complicity. In the course of the discussions, all insist that the old guard is still in power, but who the old guard is depends on who you are talking to.

Galina Andreevna Belaia, professor and literary critic, became well known in Moscow literary circles in the 1960s and 1970s for lecturing to overflow audiences on the works of forbidden writers. For many years she worked at the prestigious Gorky Institute of World Literature in Moscow, and has recently left to organize the new Russian University for the Humanities. We met in her apartment in Moscow off *Bezbozhnyi Pereulok* [Godless lane].

GRANT: I heard of you initially through your defense of Pasternak at the Institute of World Literature, particularly against Dmitri Urnov, who runs the journal *Voprosy literatury* [Problems of literature].

BELAIA: Urnov is in America now, giving lectures or something. On the first day of the putsch he gave an interview on American television where he welcomed the coup.

GRANT: Strangely enough.

BELAIA: There was nothing strange about it to us. The man is a fascist.

GRANT: I met him last year and he remained in my memory as one of those people who managed to reconstruct themselves more swiftly than others. He described himself repeatedly as a dissident . . .

BELAIA: Urnov?

GRANT: He was quite insistent about it.

BELAIA: Urnov? That doesn't have the slightest bearing on reality. On the contrary, he was always clearly in the furthest of right-wing camps along with Kozhinov, Palievksii, the *Pamiat'* people,[2] the Slavophiles. The man has the mentality of a jockey, someone who beats the horse harder and harder in order to get what he wants. He is highly educated, a specialist in foreign literature, and yet he made his career on the party, on the cultivation of "party-mindedness" [*partiinost'*] in literature. And I might add quite a considerable career. His entire work has been devoted to party-mindedness, party-mindedness. Now, thank God, the party has been banned—what prostitution it was. The party was his whip and he got quite far with it. Recently he struck again when he decided to write a preface to a book we were preparing, a collection of articles by the exiled writer Andrei Siniavskii. The preface was vile, raising questions about whether Siniavskii really went to the labor camps or not—he didn't believe that Siniavskii could manage to write about Pushkin while in prison; then he maligned Siniavskii for having rejected Pasternak—that's a joke since Urnov himself can't stand Pasternak. It was just ghastly. He's a horrible person, and today he stands at the head of *Veprosy literatury* because his group has yet to truly fall from power.

GRANT: What does that say about what is going on in the country as a whole? Everywhere you have battles going on between liberals and conservatives, reformists and the old guard, but the conservatives use *perestroika* labels, the liberals turn out to be equally interested in the spoils of power. Most of the time, the result is bedlam.

BELAIA: The Bedlam in Russia today is ironic, since throughout the Soviet period there was a very romantic view of our culture, the idea that we shared a common worldview, common values and ideals. And yet clearly this is far from the truth.

As soon as Gorbachev came to power in 1985, everyone began to say that *perestroika* was a revolution. But revolution is not on people's minds. If you look at what dominates culture, society, and politics today, it is an agonizing dirge, the death throes [*agoniia*] of Soviet civilization. Today, in the wake of the August putsch, there is the smallest, most emergent of hopes that the totalitarian infrastructure will disintegrate as well. Until August, that structure was virtually unshaken. There had been only cosmetic alterations, the lightest of whitewashings. And in all likelihood, that is all that Gorbachev wanted, it just got out from under his thumb. It seems clear that he has difficulty even comprehending the changes. What has struck people in the most fundamental of ways however is the virtual explosion of information, the shattering of the truth that they once knew, the tragic feeling that for seventy years, so many people were blind to what was going on about them, and that so many people perished. Among those lost are not only the people who were liquidated or who died from hunger, but the people who are seventy years old today who realize that their entire lives have been built on lost ideals. We all feel that we are lost, that whole generations have been misspent. I consider myself to be somewhat optimistic, but you can't help but be

mournful for how things might have been. Hence the feeling of failure, collapse. This is the dying stage of Soviet civilization, one of the most terrible
civilizations of the twentieth century.

Nonetheless, the period of *agoniia,* collapse, failure—it still follows certain patterns. If we start by looking at the face of things, what is being published today? We begin with works by emigré writers of the twenties and
thirties. This is an enormous achievement for us—they are in great fashion
now. People publish them regardless of the quality, people praise them regardless of the level of their work. Another layer is the return of the religio-
philosophical idea of the start of the twentieth century. There has also been
a considerable splash made by Anatolii Rybakov's *Children of the Arbat,*
Grossman's *Life and Fate,* works of that type that we call repression literature. In turn we have the strange works of Rasputin, Belov, and the *dere-*
venshchiki ["village prose writers"] who made their names in opposition to
the government in the 1960s and 1970s and who are far more reactionary
today than Gorbachev. Further still we see the works of the real stone age
Soviet Stalinists like Prokhanov with his book about Afghanistan where he
glorifies our intervention there. We toss in Bulgakov, Mandelshtam, and a
handful of other authors that people had little chance to read for decades. All
of this is found in the same soup, as it were, at first glance. And much of it
hinges on the classic division in Russian culture between the intelligentsia
and the peasantry.

For example, what we see throughout the 1860s is the emergence of the
proletariat, and it is important to understand how the proletariat came to be.
The proletariat arose largely from the outcasts of the peasant culture. The
peasantry was cautious in its relations with outsiders, if not suspicious. They
perceived a strong sense of social injustice and were developing the roots of
class aggression. Yet after the emancipation of the serfs, there arose this
middle group, the proletariat, emigrants from the peasant world, as it were,
who found themselves between the two worlds. Among the educated class
they were nobodies. And when Marxism was introduced to this middle
group, to the proletariat, it was truly a tragedy. It appealed to the lowest
instincts: class revenge, class hatred, brutal redistribution, robbery of the
robbers, expropriation of the expropriators—it was a monstrous program.

The point is that what began in the 1860s as the seeds of the revolutionary
mentality continues to dominate in our society to this very day. This is a
mentality that recognizes the use of violence, that denies the existence of the
individual, that still can not understand the people. I always tell people that
the revolutionary mentality in Russia is not a revolutionary ideology—it is
much greater. It is an existential system; it taps the ontological essence of
man. To look at other ways of life—the only path is the victory of communism. To look at other persons—there is nothing easier than killing someone

off. With respect to love—betrayal is fine if it is in defense of the revolution. To kill your husband, to kill your lover—these were acceptable themes in Soviet literature when it took place in the name of revolution.

People were killed, and people were shot, and yet there appears to have been general acceptance of the revolution in 1917. How? You yourself know how many people show up at pro-Stalin demonstrations today. And it's not that they are simply villains—these are real people who genuinely feel their path to be the true one.

After 1917, the revolutionary faction found itself with full rein, and it was from there that socialist realism was implemented in art and literature. Indeed, they managed to build up quite a solid system of poetics by the end of the decade. The genre of the socialist, ideological novel was canonized and the parameters were very clear: there was only one type of hero—the choice representative of the working class, a communist in the avant-garde of the revolution; there was only one fabula and one social conflict—the class struggle; and only one structure which reigned over the author's point of view—where the hero was simply a marionette in the service of the prescribed plot. As a matter of fact, you find this approach even in Solzhenitsyn's *The Red Wheel,* which is also a very ideological novel. This entire artistic mentality was formed with the revolution in 1917.

Therefore, when the *derevenshchiki* appeared in the 1960s, it was like a strange reanimation of the old peasant culture. All of those writers, Belov and Rasputin and Astafev, they all came from the countryside, and in a sense they were an organic link with peasant culture. But, they were not of 1917, but of the 1960s, and by the 1960s there was virtually no peasantry remaining. Peasant culture as it once was had become a caricature. There were still some folk aspects intact, but the Russian Orthodox essence had been extinguished; the peasant ethic had been replaced by a communist one. This is the contradiction at the heart of their work. The romantic peasant ideology cannot be reanimated.

After years of living with fictions, the result is that people are completely unable to deal with real life as it stands before them now. You may recall how Sakharov spoke out at the Congress of People's Deputies in 1989 against the Afghan war, when he said that the war was to the detriment of the nation rather than to its honor. They practically burned him at the stake.

GRANT: His critics made an enormous impression on me. Especially the woman with the mouth full of metal teeth who demanded to know who it was that had given him the right to disagree.

BELAIA: I remember her. She was haunting. It is a complete inability to confront the truth. It is an entire moral phase, the ability to distinguish right from wrong, that has been distorted.

Today that culture is absolutely impotent. They have no concrete ideas.

Look at young people; the Soviet culture was a figment of mass imagination but for them it is already forgotten. And the route through old Russia is also empty; there are no more grandmothers to remind us of what it was like. The educated culture is also in a strange position because, while it tries to move ahead, the revolutionary culture, the one that reigned for seventy years, is still very stubborn. The force of inertia is considerable.

GRANT: You read often about the Union of Writers, but what about the Institute of Literature? Are they experiencing the same kind of schism?

BELAIA: Unfortunately not. At the Institute of Literature there is no schism, unfortunately. Kozhinov's ideology places politics above all else, and politics has been the sole factor in hiring researchers there over the last few years. We had a conference a while back and I couldn't understand what this fellow was doing up at the lectern. He made quite a lot of grammatical errors and appeared to know nothing about literature. I leaned over and asked someone, "Who is this person? It's as if he never finished grade school!" And they said, "You're right. He didn't. He got a law degree instead." "So what is he doing here?" I asked. "He's in the Soviet section and he's writing something about how the Jews killed Esenin." Imagine! Then later I had to preside over a doctoral defense in our section. The fellow was the editor of the journal *Kuban'*. The man surveyed almost all of Soviet literature using the criteria "talented" and "of the people" [*narodnyi*]. He went through the list: "talented and of the people," "talented but not of the people," and "not talented." I asked him why he didn't have the category "of the people but not talented" and he didn't seem to understand at all!

GRANT: I was talking with a friend from East Germany a few years ago, prior to German reunification. Along with most of his friends, he recognized the need for reunification, but he resented the attitude of West Germans who dismissed everything in the east as boring, stupid, and ugly . . .

BELAIA: I was in East Germany, twice, and it *was* boring, stupid, and ugly.

GRANT: Alright. What I was working up to, at any rate, is, what is lost through *perestroika?* Soviet culture was built over seventy years. It was the invention of the new world, and millions of people aspired to its formation. What becomes of this now?

BELAIA: I don't know. I can't help but think that anything to come of this tumult has got to be better than what we have now. Of course, one can say that living a myth at least gives someone peace of mind, but I lived our myth for almost all of my life and it was a terrible life. I'm even an optimistic sort, but there was unthinkable ideological pressure, unthinkable pressure from the party, unthinkable pressure from my director. It was constant fear. Constant fear. It was fear as an existential condition.

So how can I tell you that there is anything to lose through *perestroika?*

Perestroika has brought me nothing but relief. Whatever good there was in the old system was built on the worst of the human condition. I even come from a rare family, where none of our relatives had been taken away. In almost every family you can find a father or a grandfather who was taken away, but we managed to avoid it. So, on the contrary, it brings me only joy to witness the fall of the empire. I tell my students, who are routinely exhausted and hopeless, "Look around you. Write about what you see. You are witnesses to unspeakably important events."

Vadim Valerianovich Kozhinov is an editor and literary critic. In November of 1991, he set aside his post at the Institute of World Literature in Moscow to assume the head of the conservative literary journal, *Nash sovremennik* [Our contemporary].

GRANT: Why don't we start with a short biography.

KOZHINOV: Let's see, I was born in Moscow in 1930. I graduated from university in 1954. I started to be published in 1950, that is, under Stalin. But, such has been my life that I have never supported the Soviet government. I could show you now every single one of my articles that I have published since 1950—I've always felt that it is somehow unacceptable for a writer to cite politicians, Stalin, or Malenkov, or worse, Brezhnev—I never was involved in that sort of matter and never used those kinds of words like *party, socialism, kolkhoz*. I didn't use them, not because I held them to be so negative, but because given our circumstances up until recently, it was never really possible to say what you really thought about those kinds of things.

GRANT: What would you say have been the main consequences of *perestroika* in the writer's world in Moscow over the last five years?

KOZHINOV: Right now I am concerned about the hegemony of the so-called market. Here, strangely enough, everyone has decided that culture must exist under market conditions. Therefore all the publishing houses are on the verge of a complete crash. Editors are able to accept only those books that might bring in a profit. As far as I understand in the United States, only 10 percent of books published bring in any kind of profit. Only 10 percent. Bestsellers, detective novels. Tell me, at the end of your life, is this the kind of literature that you want to reflect back on?

GRANT: What would you want to see happen in order to spare Russian writers from this kind of crash?

KOZHINOV: I think that the position is completely tragic. You've heard no doubt of our proposed economic program, "500 Days," put together by so-called radical economists Shatalin, Yavlinskii, and so on. If you look at the document closely, you can find a small section, "The Nonmarket Sector."

There they mention things like fundamental science, the larger part of the health system and education, culture and art, preserving the environment, and so on, none of which could survive under purely market conditions. And yet it is as if no one has bothered to listen to them. On the one hand, writers have begun to understand that they can't survive in the market system; on the other, the government recognizes that it has no money to support them. Obviously, the future can only be difficult.

GRANT: What has the recent schism in the Union of Writers been about? Is it something entirely internal or do you think that it reflects a broader situation in the country?

KOZHINOV: No matter how people relate to writers, one has to admit that writers in our country are among those who best understand what is taking place. So how has the schism come about? On the one side, you have a group of writers who have come from the heart of Russia, and many of whom who continue to live there, such as Vasilii Belov, who lives in Vologda, Rasputin lives in Irkutsk. These include many of our village prose writers who made their names in the 1960s, writers who truly live among the people, not like in Moscow, which is not quite Russia—it is really something different. And even the remaining people from this group who now live in Moscow, most of them at least spent their childhoods somewhere in the provinces. In a sense, these are people who know the real way of life in the country much better than most. I think that they understand a lot of things correctly.

Alongside them is a second group that by and large has grown up and lived in either Leningrad or Moscow. They tend to be divorced from the pace of life here and orient themselves more to the West. They get fellowships to go to the West and live off of Western funds more often than their own. The best word for them is *yes-men:* they say everything that the West wants to hear. They know how people in the West view Russia and agree with the Western viewpoint. Naturally, this brings some joy to Western observers. "Look, these people think just like us." What we are looking at is not a correct perception of the country but a will to please others. There are rather a lot of this kind of people—in favor of the free press, in favor of erotica, nihilism, and cynicism. So it is within this kind of framework that the schism took place.

What is interesting is that people have started to revolt against this western orientation. Bear in mind all the writers who emigrated to America in the 1960s. At first they were received with great ceremony, but after a short while it became clear that they were really of no interest to anyone, with very few exceptions. The rest are not needed there; they normally live just to send something back here to be published. Any why are they not needed? Because all they do is repeat what is already said in the West.

GRANT: I wonder how effective dichotomies like East and West or traditional and modern are right now when there are hundreds of competing interests everywhere, endlessly different kinds of nationalism at work.

KOZHINOV: You know, there is the false impression in the West, mostly brought about by emigrés, that in the USSR there is some kind of dominating Russian nationalism. It's far from the truth. I have had occasion a number of times to discuss this with people from the West, who ask me . . .

GRANT: I wasn't actually referring to Russian nationalism . . .

KOZHINOV: Yes, but they ask me, "Why do you talk so much about Russia?" It's as if to ask, How is it that the French, the Germans, the English don't talk about nationalism as much as you do? The difference in Russia is that no one here is confident about their sense of national self-worth. A German, a Japanese person, a Chinese person, they are completely convinced of their national self-worth. Moreover, they are often convinced that they are the most important peoples in the world. In Russia, we have nothing of the sort. Here everyone is not only doubtful that he has a right to reign over other nations, but that he even has a right to exist on this earth. In Russia we have always had a considerable inferiority complex. At least until now, after all these decades of national conflicts, take note that Russians haven't done anything. So far. So far. And I hope that nothing will come about in the next few years. There is virtually no example from history where Russians have oppressed another people. Now, you will say, "What are you saying? What about the state?" but that's another matter. To subordinate peoples in the formation of the state, that is one thing. But to say that Russians, as people, as a nation [*natsiia*], ever oppressed anyone, that just never happened. Never over the course of all history.

There is a lot of talk these days about Jewish pogroms. In Russia there was never one Jewish pogrom. Take Russia in and of itself and not the Ukraine, not Moldova, and not, incidentally, the Baltic states where they set upon Jews even before the arrival of the Germans in 1942. In Russia you just won't find that kind of example. I had one friend, one can call him perhaps a victim of the putsch, an active Zionist, Mikhail Agorskii. He and I were quite good friends, and one day I asked him, "Mikhail, you've studied this in depth . . . Can you name even one Jewish pogrom in Russia?" He answered, "Allegedly there was one, in the 1980s, when the workers at a factory beat up their supervisor who was Jewish." So I said to him, "Maybe they beat him not because he was a Jew but because he was the supervisor." The point is that never in a single Russian city was there ever a Jewish pogrom.

GRANT: But how is it possible over all those years to separate the state from the people?

KOZHINOV: I can tell you precisely. It was not a *russkaia* [Russian] empire; it was called a *rossiskaia* [Russianist] empire. It was not a Russian one. Nor was it ever a purely national empire. And I can add quite a surprising fact: by 1830, the nobility, the Russian Orthodox nobility, that is, Russians, Ukrainians, and White Russians, also Georgians and Armenians, the Russian Orthodox nobility composed only 45 percent of the nobility in general. 55 percent of the nobility was not Russian Orthodox. This was in part because of the Polish nobility, the Baltic nobility, and the Muslim nobility. And one can bring up hundreds of examples of how the very highest posts in the Russian state were occupied by non-Russians. The prime minister under Aleksandr II was an Armenian. Or Stolypin, Stolypin himself was more or less the state at one time, but his main deputy was a Jew, the head of the Ministry of Internal Affairs. Those kinds of examples are legion. It would never be appropriate to say that the Russian empire was a Russian Orthodox one.

GRANT: What of the rise of nationalism today throughout the USSR?

KOZHINOV: I should emphasize that of all the peoples acting today on the territory of the USSR, Russians are the least nationalist of all. Of course, you can say that there are groups like *Pamiat'*, although as far as I am concerned, *Pamiat'* is a completely mythological phenomenon. I don't see any *Pamiat'* anywhere. I live here and all I see are people like Vasil'ev . . . I don't even remember the rest of their names. They are all usually shouting about something. They spend most of their time giving interviews in the West; that's their main hobby. Occasionally you see some young people dressed in black suits, they show them on television. Personally, I've never had cause to run into them. Sometimes you hear about a meeting where someone brings a flag, but I think of that in the same way that I see young people interested in rock music. It's not at all serious, it is a phenomenon largely invented by the mass media. There are those people of course, but they don't represent the people in any way.

Perestroika is complicated because the very leadership itself is contradictory. They have made a complete about-face, but they understand nothing and are doing nothing. That's because they have been educated for forty years or more in this school of dogmatic Marxism and can't think any other way. Who could expect otherwise?

GRANT: But do you think that there is anyone in the country who hasn't been touched by that dogma in some way? Is there anyone else left?

KOZHINOV: Of course, there were people who were dissidents, people who presented themselves in opposition to Soviet power. I include myself among them, I have always been a dissident and never supported the Soviet regime. They tried three times to get me into the Party and I risked losing my job by refusing. Three times. I was lucky that nothing bad ever came of my refusals, although there was a period of two or three years when people would not publish me at all. When it was prohibited to have my name in print.

People like that are numerous, but try and name one important dissident in the government today. You won't find one. Instead you'll find these orators who get up and curse the past. This is a rather simple game, regretting the past, but what do they have to offer in terms of concrete political programs? I personally don't find it interesting to judge the past, especially when everyone just uses it to their own advantage.

Natalia Borisovna Ivanova, a literary critic distinguished for her work on the Russian writers Iurii Trifonov, Boris Pasternak, and Andrei Platonov, has been among the most active of recent critics of the Soviet literary establishment. She is deputy editor of the literary journal *Znamia* [The Banner].

GRANT: How would you define "secretarial literature," the subject of so much of your recent work?

IVANOVA: Secretarial literature is the literature of the *nomenklatura*. Americans don't generally know what the Soviet *nomenklatura* means in real life, but for us it is everywhere, certainly in literature. The Union of Writers, which was founded in 1934 at Stalin's initiative, marked the collectivization of writers, the same kind of collectivization that created *kolkhozy*, collective farms. The union is based on a hierarchical structure, like a pyramid, with the Union Secretariat resting at the top. It's a fascinating organization, all very carefully gradated. There is the secretariat of the umbrella union, the Union of Writers of the USSR, and then several subordinate secretariats, such as the secretariat for each republic. A little lower come the secretariats for Moscow and Leningrad, followed by the provincial capitals, and then further still come a panoply of commissions, such as the Commission on Youth, the Commission on Veterans' Literature, the Commission on Interrepublic Relations—there are millions of them.

Every person belonging to one of these secretariats or commissions had a specified access to privileges. The secretariats worked on the principle of cross-pollination. The Secretaries by definition were given the editorships of various journals or publishing houses, practically for life, and their main goal was to publish either themselves or the work of other editors of similar journals. It was an entirely artificial system based on unlimited resources for maintaining homogeneity in what was published. They were given enormous printings. Each author/Secretary had an entire regiment of critics that were assigned to his work exclusively—an essentially servile criticism, or reptilian criticism, as we used to call it. If you rose to the post of Secretary, someone automatically published a book about you, and usually more than just one. Markov for example, Georgii Markov, who was a Secretary in the

Union of Writers under Brezhnev, was the subject of *dozens* of monographs. He was the one who awarded Brezhnev the gold medal, the Lenin Prize . . . *for Literature!* Brezhnev—one of our most brilliant writers. Amazing. You know, at the time, my reaction was repulsion. I wanted to show this for the farce that it truly was. Now, it's more like curiosity. I realize that at the heart of our totalitarian system there were really the most extraordinary things.

GRANT: You use the past tense, but given the recent schism in the Union of Writers, it's unlikely that the totalitarian idea is over.

IVANOVA: Of course not, my goodness, it's all around us. But this is a convulsion of the old guard, this is their dirge. For me that world doesn't exist any longer, it has already passed. The schism is more about a power struggle between the old *nomenklatura* and the new establishment, the new establishment being formed from the intermediary elite, people like Voznesenskii and Yevtushenko, let's say, Yevtushenko being the Secretary of the new, alternative writer's union that is battling with the old one. And me—I too was elected to the new union, so I am a Secretary now too! I am Secretary of the Moscow division. But the difference is in our objectives—ours is to disperse the old secretariat and create the kind of writers' union that exists elsewhere around the world. A writer's union should provide some kind of solidarity, some kind of support to writers in general. The problem with the old writer's union is that it was entirely in the service of the state. The new union must be devoid of money, entirely devoid of privileges. Naturally, there is a battle going on. There is an enormous resistance to parting with power. But for me this is the last battle, it has already taken on a historical character.

GRANT: How does that stand up to the kind of statistics you see in the paper every day, wildly varying statistics about how 45 percent of the population supported the August putsch, or 60 percent or 30 percent?

IVANOVA: Or more. That's the force of our collective consciousness. The statue of Dzerzhinskii might have been taken down from in front of the KGB building, but our consciousness, or our subconscious, is still in the throes of the totalitarian system. If anything, most people feel wounded. We were raised with a different ideology than what we have today. It's understandable, it's natural, but it's still a process, an evangelization, a reformation, whatever you want to call it. It's difficult and protracted. You can't say that starting tomorrow the Communist Party is over, that communism will be dead. The communist idea of equality, in particular, is a profound one for the Russian mentality. The society is changing. It is dramatically different than what it was like a year ago, and what it was like the year before that. But the process is painful. It's difficult to reconcile yourself to freedom when you haven't known it for so long. Even birds sometimes want to go back to their cage when their whole life has been spent there. Let alone people,

people today who can't even find bread. So they reinvent the myth of social protection under socialism—all they know is that their lives have gotten worse. Notwithstanding all the people who were killed, all the people who sat in camps, all the people who were political prisoners, all the revelations of the last few years, all the documents, all the facts, all the new publications—they haven't really influenced people that strongly. You might know, for example, that Solzhenitsyn's rating this year is half of what it was last year, his place on the sales lists.

GRANT: What do you think is the reason for it?

IVANOVA: It's surprising that it didn't produce more of a shock, but who knows? In the first place, there was a flood of his work put out. But maybe more importantly, people just can't take it anymore, they don't want to hear anything more. Most people have stopped reading. I can see that just by readers' reactions.

GRANT: One of the things that stands out to me in your work, particularly in your political essays, is the idea of a moral imperative, an appeal to honor. The problem, I suppose, is how to talk about honor with all the stories everywhere about Soviet soldiers who killed other Soviet soldiers in Afghanistan, about officials renowned for their integrity who turned out to be grotesque figures. Is it really possible . . .

IVANOVA: To resurrect literature given all that has gone on?

GRANT: Is it possible to appeal to morality in a society that might not believe that there is such a thing anymore?

IVANOVA: Readership is down everywhere, in every field, for every publication. And you can see this brought about by the disappointment people feel, by the destruction of the country. It's an extremely profound trial, and this is not even the first time that we've had to go through it. You have to realize that in only one century we have lost our homeland twice. In 1917, we lost the old Russia. Today we are losing our Soviet homeland. There is nothing simple about it. You know that old legend, I forget the name of it, about the woman whose father and mother were killed when she was a girl? Her captors sold her into slavery and married her off to one of her parents' murderers, to whom she eventually bore two children. Then, twenty years later, her younger brother arrives to save her. She tells him, "Enough. I've lived through losing my family once already." This is pretty much the same thing we are going through now. The fall of the empire is something we worked toward for years—liberals and democrats—but now that it is happening I don't feel joy, I feel a sense of tragedy. It may be right, it may be what we wanted, but it is still a profound tragedy. People are suffering in the most extraordinary way.

GRANT: Are there any positive social values that may be lost through *perestroika?*

IVANOVA: It depends what you mean by positive. That is what I had in mind when I talked about our having lost our homeland for the second time in one century. Remember that the Soviet person in this grandiose system felt himself to be special. He knew that while the rest of the world was in flames, the Soviet Union bloomed; he knew that while the West was riddled by racism, unemployment, and poverty, the Soviet Union strove further and further upward. There was a profound superiority complex. Now, as that mythology crumbles before his very eyes, this fellow plunges from superiority to inferiority, and his consciousness is in shards. No one can survive that steep a drop without trauma. Soviet cinema for them, for example, was like a fairy tale, not only something to stroke their consciousness, but of course, something to mold it. So naturally, the unmasking of the Soviet cultural myth is like an attack on their personal standing, on their personal experience, on their personal experience of the past.

A few weeks back I was walking below ground to the subway and saw a man playing music. Most often the musicians play modern songs, but this man was playing old Soviet ones, and I stopped to look. I wanted to see: Who was standing there, who was giving him money? And this man was surrounded by elderly women who were listening to these songs with delight, because remember, for these people the totalitarian period wasn't just the repelling, terrible Soviet system, if that. It was their youth. Their *youth,* and furthermore it was their sense of power, their sense of well-being, the feeling of moving ahead under a common cause. It was a highly defined cultural model, fascist of course, but it existed. People today, people that grew up in a collectivist environment, many of whom never really learned to think for themselves—they are lost when they see that there is no more truth, a Soviet truth, at least as it once existed . . . They are lost when they see that there are in fact hundreds of different points of view that all contradict each other. Meanwhile from the West we are being inundated with the castoffs of their cultural production, of the lowest, most extraordinary sort. The first time I went to Paris, I rushed to see films by Bergman and Forman. It was wonderful. Here, we haven't quite made it to Bergman and Forman . . .

GRANT: It's mostly pornography.

IVANOVOVA: Pornography, and the very lowest kind of mass culture. Soviet mass culture is basically being replaced by Western mass culture. Where does that get anyone? The average Soviet person—what have you—anyone can see that there is nothing to gain from that and much to lose.

GRANT: Given your travels abroad, were you struck at all by the perception of *perestroika* in the West?

IVANOVA: I was surprised, of course. The euphoria in the West has surprised many of us. Just the idea that things here aren't so simple, that Gorbachev leaves much to be desired, that he has excellent translators when he travels but that many people perceive him here quite disparagingly—these are things that most people I met couldn't understand. But this is not so new: the West didn't understand us in the twenties, they didn't understand in the thirties; they didn't listen to the first wave of emigrants, and they didn't listen to the second wave of emigrants. No one really expects anything else. With *perestroika,* the West bought into their own mythology: "Communism has finally fallen, now Russia will be a democracy and we will all live happily ever after." When the West realizes that the fall of the empire threatens them in the most immediate way, whether through atomic terrorism or the Balkanization of the world, then of course things might be otherwise.

> The idea of someone like Urnov or Kozhinov calling themselves dissidents is a new trend. I remember when we were all at the Institute of Literature and they gathered us in the main hall in order to condemn Pasternak. First they brought Siniavskii up on stage and requested that he say what he thought. Everyone knew that Siniavskii had published an article about Pasternak and that Pasternak had liked it very much. Siniavskii has quite a large beard and often mumbled so he kind of hid his mouth and garbled his words. The director said, "Comrade Siniavskii, we can't understand you." Siniavskii shrugged his shoulders and left the stage. Then they called up Kozhinov. Everyone knew that he loved Pasternak's poetry. And he got up and said that Pasternak had no talent, that he had never liked him. He made a compromise, we all know compromise, but to call him a dissident? No. You could never call him a dissident.
>
> —Galina Belaia

> Russia is truly a carnivalesque country. A carnival where people are constantly changing places, being turned upside down. Take note that in the West, literature of the absurd is very popular, yet we've hardly even heard of it. Why? Because our life is already so absurd that no one needs to read about it. In the West life is so orderly by comparison that absurdity appears as a release of sorts. For us it is quite the contrary.
>
> —Vadim Kozhinov

Aleksandr Andreevich Prokhanov, novelist and critic, was "patriotism coordinator" of the spring 1991 conservative manifesto, "A Word to the People," which warned of imminent state collapse and the need for an iron hand to reassert order.[3] He is currently editor of the newspaper *Den'* [Day], formerly listed as "The Newspaper of the Union of Writers of the USSR," and now listed as "The Newspaper of the Spiritual Opposition." It is difficult here to convey his brilliant command of Russian at its most florid. We met in the offices of *Den'*.

GRANT: Alright. Let's start with a little about yourself.

PROKHANOV: Fifty-three years old. Until recently a writer, belletrist, the author of twenty-five or so books, novels. I never served in an army. I never entered the Party. Rather apolitical. What I like in life most of all is new experience, space, new environments. I was a sort of modern folklore writer. At one time I was especially interested in technocracy, I wrote technographic novels where I described new achievements in technology and science. Then I became fascinated by the military technosphere. I studied the entire military-industrial complex of the USSR. I travelled among all the military allies of the USSR at one time or another, from Nicaragua to Kampuchea. Gradually I became involved in cultural politics and eventually I became the chief editor of our newspaper, *Den'*. That's it.

GRANT: Judging by what was written in the manifesto in which you took part last spring, "A Word to the People," would you say that the situation in the country has changed significantly since then?

PROKHANOV: Yes, indeed. "A Word to the People" was written at a moment when the state should have collapsed, when the cracks in the system that we observed should have led directly to civil war. After six years of Gorbachev, when things had come to a point where it was impossible to remain quiet, when the state was repressing integrity, honor, and its own functioning, when the country stood on the verge of collapse and catastrophe, when all the enormously terrifying consequences of this *perestroika* cabal had become clear, we chose to say no in the face of collapse. Our efforts, evidently, were not successful. And consequently, we find ourselves today in the eye of catastrophe, in the eye of the catastrophe, the point of no return. And because we can now no longer look to the statists of the old system who are almost no longer about, nor to the social modernists, such as Yeltsin, the country is in the depths of utter disaster and despair. The likely result of this catastrophe is chaos, slaughter, civil war, and the likely exchange of nuclear assaults between Russia and the Ukraine. So, the prognosis that I offered two years ago through my writings in the press, the algorithm of catastrophe and so on, this is precisely what has come to pass.

GRANT: When I read "A Word to the People" some time ago, I had the impression that it was not only a word to the people but a word to the world, since there are so often misunderstandings in how the West interprets developments in the Soviet Union. If you had to settle on one of the main differences between popular Western opinion on the events of the last few months and your own, what would it be?

PROKHANOV: It's hard to say. I mean, the West is overjoyed and rightfully so. Our empire, our superpower was a very powerful competitor, in the geopolitical, in the political sense—it was an enemy. This enemy now appears to be destroyed, destroyed over the shortest period of time, and what's more, free of charge, without a single shot being fired. And this victory, I expect, can only provoke in Americans pride and satisfaction, because that is precisely what it has been, a victory. They should be happy over what has gone on here. However, in the first place it is a satisfaction born entirely from nationalist egocentrism. It can in no way be joy felt for Russia or for Russian people, because what is going on here is horrible, truly horrible. And of course it is satisfaction over the geopolitical consequences of our catastrophe, consequences which will detonate throughout American politics, which are already being detonated and felt—the rise of American globalism and the fall of Euroasian influence.

Can you tell me, does our chaos fit in to the popular idea of the new world order, to new world harmony? We are in complete chaotic pandemonium and there is no going back. What's more, this chaos has spread to Eastern Europe, has destroyed what were carefully implemented economic ties . . . in a word, Russian chaos. In response to the American variety, we respond with chaos. Whereas before we might have answered with submarines, SS20s and the like, today we answer with chaos. It is completely asymmetrical, a completely asymmetrical response. Something further to confound American rationalism, American logic, and the Rand Corporation—complete chaos. Now we are witnessing the start of the second civil war in Russia over the course of this century. One began the century and now another ends it.

GRANT: Within the next few years?

PROKHANOV: Absolutely, a civil war, the very contradiction that has been created as the direct result of this catastrophic *perestroika*. It can not be put off. This contradiction is so deeply rooted and so fundamental that the government, the powers that be are unable even to react to it. It is an ethnic contradiction, nationalist energy, a complex of the most powerful of national contradictions found in the ruins of the former Soviet Union just as well in the heart of Russia. These are fundamental, enormous contradictions, not tempered in any way by culture or civilization, by power or by ideology. They have been torn from the surface and hurtled into confrontation. In the first place. In the second place you have the social contradiction. The people have been robbed. A people which over three and four generations has been raised on Soviet principles of social justice, that was nourished on precise if dogmatic concepts of equality and fairness. These are dogmas which were transgressed often enough, but they nonetheless constituted an ideal. Part of this ideal was realized. But over the course of the last two years this ideal has been completely destroyed. The people has been completely robbed, *robbed*. And of the prosperity that has been torn from the breast of the people, what remains is in the hands of a narrow, bourgeois cabal. Between this suddenly flourishing social injustice, and the deception and pillaging of some two hundred million people, whether through the KGB or the army or some new guard, it doesn't matter, there will be an explosion. A massive explosion. This national, social contradiction makes the question of this explosion absolutely inevitable. Civil war. That's what I anticipate. What will come after the civil war, that's hard to say.

GRANT: Given the mood of the country since the putsch in August, do you see any kind of way out? What would you want to see happen?

PROKHANOV: Way out? What way out? I just told you—it's as if you find yourself in the middle of an avalanche on a mountain slope. The first wall of snow overcomes you, then the second, then the third. There is no way out. Of course there will be efforts to turn things around, there will be revolts and counterrevolts, there may be attempts to establish dictatorship, there will be lies, mass exodus, hunger, and poverty. What else can I say? It's like a volcano, a volcano, and how on earth do you stop it? You can't. A year ago we might have turned things around, but now it's impossible. To find something positive in the political crisis today is impossible. Events will develop simply catastrophically.

Yesterday all of Moscow was without bread. Not a loaf. In two weeks I imagine the last rotor will stop turning, stop producing electricity. The state is destroyed, virtually destroyed. And not only the state—the economy is destroyed, the supply system as well. We are after all a centralized state, we have a centralized economy, and if Moscow is destroyed, then there are thousands of ramifications across the country. The whole periphery can only die off, and it is dying off. What are you supposed to do? You can't put the center back together again. I think that even if the putsch had been successful, nothing would have come of it. They were already too late. The economic apocalypse is upon us. That's my point of view.

GRANT: What are the social values that you are most concerned about losing as a result? What is lost through *perestroika* from the point of Soviet culture?

PROKHANOV: Everything is lost. Everything. Everything that is going on in our culture today, this disintegration, is loathsome. It's vile. America has flooded us with her spiritual and intellectual detritus. Everything that you see around you on the sidewalks, even in the so-called cultural establishment, it is yesterday's castoffs from the United States. Even Africa pays no attention. That's what things have come to. The talk of a cultural renaissance is utterly misguided.

During the period of stagnation, from Khrushchev onward, we developed an enormous number of positive values. Through a quiet, gradual process, it is as if the culture acquired energy. I mean, I don't even want to talk about it.

Culture develops when it has a great task before it. An important task. Religious culture was built on the idea of paradise, for example. Russian culture, after it was robbed and destroyed by the revolution in 1917, began anew with a slow, gradual process of accumulation and evolution. If our democrats and liberals today think they aren't worth a dime, then they're right. But if they have a high opinion of themselves, and indeed most do, then that is the result of their upbringing in *Soviet* culture. Who was it that created them? Who was it that enabled the flourishing of native cultures in Uzbekistan, in Tadzhikistan? Where do today's politicians, those vultures, think they came from? They were raised on Soviet ideas, Soviet programs, they lived in a country with one of the greatest corpus of engineers in the world, a country that was able to develop the best arms in the world. We were able to transform a virtually empty, dead, and soulless country into a thriving intellectual environment, a center of first-class science—what else, avant-garde technology—it is all culture. Our rural writers, for example, embody culture of the highest value. A beautiful culture. A beautiful culture. It is another matter that our culture was never exposed to the world market. After all, it was controlled for so many years by the communists that the result was utter confusion, when first-class works were sold off for kopecks and fourth-class novels were awarded the Lenin Prize. The result was confusion. So the West may have the impression that our culture was worthless, but I assure you otherwise. It was an impressive, intense, flourishing culture.

Today, after the last six years, this culture is virtually destroyed. Completely destroyed. What they have done with our culture over the last six years is one hundred times worse than what the Bolsheviks managed. We are now in the middle of cultural disintegration, cultural disintegration in all spheres. This is a culture not about to be reviewed. Our culture has been killed off by poverty: it was heavily subsidized by the socialist government. Our culture was killed off by an absolutely counternational elite that prefers a meaningless generic culture to its own. That is to say, they prefer Western culture, and Western culture of the lowest sort. And of course, of course the culture was also killed off by an absence of strategic objectives. Today's artists, for example, have lost a feel for the future. This is what has destroyed our culture.

GRANT: How do you regard the recent schism in the Union of Writers?

PROKHANOV: The schism was nothing new. It has always existed. The antagonism has just been manifested in a more ruthless form. If one were to put it crudely, to put it crudely, our culture has always been divided around two hearths—Westerners and Slavophiles. The Slavophiles orient themselves around the Russian national idea, a Russian Slavic idea which stands in opposition to its Western counterpart. The Westerners, one might say, are more in favor of a universal process than the development of their own culture, and certainly there are impressive examples produced in the West, but they somehow never find root here. It is a polemic that has its roots in the nineteenth century if not earlier, a polemic which never abated, not even during Stalin, hidden perhaps, modified in some ways, but which was always with us. And so, it has come about that our schism takes place under this flag.

The schism consists, on the one side, of a group of Russian writers, Russian artists who are interested in developing the Russian idea, philosophically and artistically, who on the basis of their experience and worldview are very closely tied to Russia. This is the mysterious but tenacious love of the Russian for his country, something very difficult for the West to understand. It is a love both mystic and at times tragic, a mood which is strengthened considerably under adversity. During periods of misfortune and hunger, it becomes a passionate, almost religious, idea. On the other side are the Westerners, most of whom swept up by *perestroika,* interested in politics, in being seen standing alongside Gorbachev, in being oriented to the West, in the renewal of a shamelessly ruined state. It is mainly a liberal group; there are a number of Jews in it, and the Jewish factor is quite strong there. One could even say that the conflict between Slavophiles and Westerners is a conflict between Russians and Jews, although in literal terms of course there are all different kinds of people under each banner. In any event, the schism came about through differences in worldview and politics.

The group that I belong to considers and has always considered that the dissolution of communism is not acceptable at such a high price—the utter annihilation of the state in its entirety. It is not acceptable at such an enormous, terrible price. There are those who think that communism needed to be destroyed at any price, and they are the ones responsible for the situation today. You have a considerable buildup of personal offenses, jealousies, and the like, that finally came to a head. That's what happened.

GRANT: Given what you've said about Russian culture under adversity, could anything positive come of the current crisis, a redefinition of Russian identity?

PROKHANOV: A resurrection? How? Russia is after all an empire. The Georgians have left with everyone else; all that remains are a few Tatars and Bashkirs. Things are collapsing here and things are collapsing in Georgia. The fall of the empire for Russia is catastrophic. Bondarev thinks that we should let Siberia go now too. It's all nonsense, delirium.

GRANT: How do you regard the behavior of the various republics over the last few years? There are those who say that their quick departure is an inevitable reaction after so many years of Soviet power, while others would call it betrayal.

PROKHANOV: The Ukraine has left Russia, it now appears, whereas when they joined, it was voluntarily and forever. And in one hundred years when

the great reunified Germany will be occupying the Ukrainian heartland,
they'll ask to come back. What has taken place is a crime against the Russian people. For better or for worse, it is all absurd, it is all political games,
games on the part of the current generation of nationalist leaders. If a ther-
monuclear war between Russia and the Ukraine starts tomorrow, and both
our peoples go up in smoke, it will be the Ukraine's reward for their aban-
donment of Russia. That's it. I repeat again, what has taken place is a catastrophe. It cannot be judged as good or bad, correct or incorrect—it is a
catastrophe. The very ground below us is in upheaval, and the current generation of political leaders has decided that it should be so. Fine, so tomorrow Chernobyl will blow up, and there will be another inferno. Chernobyl
blows up, and half of Belorussia is in cinders. Who will save Belorussia?
Germany? America? Are they going to come back to Russia once again? I
don't even want to judge the situation, it's not even a question for analysis.
It's an act of swinery that a great state has fallen. It is the result of treachery,
of considerable, careful, malevolent work. We will form an empire again,
we will form an empire again, but what is it going to cost?

GRANT: What do you see as the main tasks of your newspaper now, the
defense of Russian culture of Soviet culture or . . .

PROKHANOV: Soviet, German, American culture—it doesn't matter. There
is a state in ruins. There are a thousand different ideological splinters, splinters of the most distorted and perverted natures. Our newspaper is interested
in the creation of a new ideology, a post-*perestroika* ideology. It is a neo-
conservative newspaper, closest of all to the New Right in Europe. We want
to organize a juxtaposition between the totalitarian, destructive nihilism of
today and, on the other hand, for Russians, a Russian fundamentalism. The
polyethnic, Euroasian society which we want to create depends on an ideology which will permit, on a new level, on a Marxist level, the reconciliation of the national and cultural interests of all peoples. We want to create an
elite, an elite.

GRANT: Isn't there a contradiction between the monocultural, often racist
interests of the European New Right, people like Le Pen, and your multinational state?

PROKHANOV: That's just a political strategy, the political, pragmatic part.
That's the Old Right, as it were. We are interested in the New Right, people
like de Benoist. The rightist parties in France, Belgium, Spain, and so on,
they are relatively close to each other in their ideas of a pro-European,
flourishing framework. It is essentially an anti-American culture, a culture
which resists the imposition of a universal quasi-American standard, a metaphysical culture which has its roots in mysticism and the cosmos, in cultural
archetypes. After all, every culture has its own archetypes. People today
might not agree on the economy and politics, race and ethnos, but they un-

derstand the absolutes that elevate them, their beliefs, their mystical experience. In this sense Russian fundamentalism and Islamic fundamentalism find a common voice in our newspaper. Many of my friends are from Islamic fundamentalist circles. So I repeat, one of main goals is to create an ideology, a new multitiered ideology, an ideology that will promote the complex interaction between individual, social, intellectual, and national development. The ideology would not preclude contradictory positions but would facilitate the formation of hierarchies of knowledge. This is what we're involved in.

GRANT: Where will the line be between ideological fundamentalism and economic fundamentalism . . .

PROKHANOV: We're still in the process of formulating our strategies. Most importantly, we have our goals, our tasks, and the rest will come in its own time. There are achievements and disappointments along the way, naturally, but so far that kind of boundary has not been defined.

GRANT: The only contradiction I see is the economic dimension. On the one hand, you are not proposing a return to the past, but it doesn't seem clear how you want the new society to be economically defined, either with a free market of socialist character or . . .

PROKHANOV: Do you really understand what the market system is? Do you really understand? What is it?

GRANT: I suppose that the least it means is that people can buy and sell as they like, when they like, and to whom they like.

PROKHANOV: Tell me, a project like Los Alamos, the creation of the atom bomb in America, is that a market project?

GRANT: Sure it is. Maybe in public it comes across as a government project and might therefore be thought of as part of the nonmarket sector, but there are dozens of huge firms that make profits from projects like that—of course it's a market project.

PROKHANOV: My God, what kind of profits are there from the atom bomb? Explain this.

GRANT: People make a lot of money off projects like that. It may not be ethical, but that's usually how it works.

PROKHANOV: The bomb is paid for by the federal budget. For the federal budget it means *razorenie* [havoc]. The government assigns a few trillion dollars to the bomb, then finds a few companies to carry out parts of the research, but you can't call that a market. It's more like its own ministry, as we say, it's own superstate. Be it a multinational corporation or a small private company, they all belong to this superstate that directs all the critical social potential. That's how you made the atom bomb and that's how we made the atom bomb. It's been years now since you're have any real kind of market system.

GRANT: But you know perfectly well what I mean by market in the broader context—there's a big difference between the economic systems in the USSR and Europe.

PROKHANOV: Not at all. What the hell does anyone mean by "market"? What does the market matter when the future of humanity is bound by the same earth, the regulation of common problems. Now we have holes in the ozone layer. What kind of firm is going to want to fix that? Who is going to tell people to cut down on their use of freon? Who is going to have to make modifications to the transport industry? That is the specific domain of state regulation. A typically socialist means. Any future economy, including yours, will depend on the ability of the state to control itself, to control itself, and to direct its own development. The question is how to direct development. I ask you, when mankind has invented already a thousand different ways to direct itself, why the market? To let the floodgates down, with the market mechanism virtually uncontrolled, and then stop it up at a moment's notice, well, I can't stand by quietly.

> The battle between the forces of memory and the forces of forgetting goes on still. It just takes different forms.[4]
>
> —Natalia Ivanova

Iurii Poliakov, poet, novelist, and critic, age thirty-seven, is the youngest of the six writers here. He began his career specializing in military poetry, or "poetry from the front." Since 1985 he has become one of the most popular authors in Russia, particularly among youth, with stories ranging from depressing portraits of army life to dry parodies of Soviet bureaucratese to the official aversion to erotica. He fashions himself as a chronicler of Soviet culture, particularly during the Brezhnev period. We met in the House of Literati in Moscow.

GRANT: Let's start with something about yourself.

POLIAKOV: I was born in 1954 in Moscow and, I think in contrast to most Russian writers, who are either from the Muscovite intelligentsia or from deep within the provinces, I was raised in a working-class family. I attended a pedagogical institute and wrote my thesis on poetry of the Great Patriotic War [World War II], poetry from the front. I joined the Union of Writers in 1981 as a poet and enjoyed a certain amount of success; I received a few prizes and so on. But I slowly became more interested in prose, and my first book was published at the onset of *perestroika*.

GRANT: You've indicated an opposition in Russian literary circles between the intelligentsia and the working class, or between the country and the city. What about the popular image of the Slavophiles and the Westerners? The *derevenshchiki* versus the Westerners. Is it a realistic assessment? Is it useful?

POLIAKOV: It's an inevitable contrast, and I think that you can find analogies in almost any culture. One side is more inclined to cosmopolitan influences, while another claims the cloak of authenticity through stricter nationalist sentiments. This rivalry in Russia goes back to the nineteenth century, but in the nineteenth century it was never as mean spirited and politicized as it is today. Back then the warring parties were inclined to finish up their debates by sharing a bottle of vodka; now, they are more likely to smash the bottle over each other's heads. But this is not that strange when you appreciate the crisis we're in; it brings out all kinds of extremes. I look upon it as an inevitable contrast and even a fruitful contrast, so long as one moderates the aggression inherent in the difference. Today there is an enormous amount of aggression, and next to no moderation.

GRANT: You have the reputation of being a "Soviet" writer specializing in Soviet topics—the Party, the Young Communist Youth League, the army, and so on. What made you want to write about that?

POLIAKOV: One of the peculiarities of our social consciousness, of the communist ideology, was the creation of "Soviet" literature. Stalin created the Union of Writers in 1934 by rounding up writers from a number of different organizations—why, of course, because it was much easier to control them if they were all under one roof. Stalin understood well that Russians had a particular relationship with literature, a powerful relationship and one which could easily serve political ends. Both Franco and Hitler were interested in the question of political culture, but hardly to the same extent as in Russia, where literature has always held the seeds of political power. There is the famous maxim at the end of the nineteenth century that Russia had two czars—Nikolai Aleksandrovich [the monarch] and Lev Nikolaevich [Tolstoy].

The Soviets understood this and imparted to literature its due importance. They collectivized culture, in effect. Peasants were the subjects of the major collectivization, but the creative intelligentsia were the subjects of the minor collectivization. For example, people roundly look with irritation today at the issue of socialist realism. But socialist realism was an intriguing phenomenon, not only as a form of pseudoromanticism in the twentieth century, but as a political apparatus. If romanticism was almost always considered to be an individual experience, here we have an entire aesthetic devoted to the inculcation of popular political ideas into the collective consciousness, in effect, a state romanticism.

One of the most important instruments of this state romanticism was the mythologization of civic consciousness. In place of reality the myth ruled. That which the state feared the most was precisely what became mythologized: the question of power, the army, and especially youth. If they were intent on creating the "New Soviet Man," then obviously the new generation was expected to reflect the new system. Everything that was mythologized bore its own importance.

The problem is that real literature can't develop within the framework of false, idealized romanticism. Or at least, literature developed, there were talented writers, but people accomplished this largely by getting around the taboo subjects. One could lose one's head for demystification. The result is a literature where truth can be found only in the pauses between myths.

When I began to write I was sufficiently naive that I wanted to write about precisely that which was taboo, for example, the army. To write about it at that time meant that either you avoided the truth (and there is an entire genre of such military literature) or you ventured into the realm of the symbolic. If you discussed the topic with enough metaphors and allegories you could cloak your real intentions. When I began, I really didn't have any special plan. I just wanted to write something, anything, and so I wrote about what I knew, from when I served in the army. The easiest thing to draw attention to was the stark contrast between the actual experience and that which I had read about and heard about since I had been a small child.

Like most Soviets, I was connected with the *Komsomol* [Communist Youth League] when I was younger. Almost everyone went through the *Komsomol,* and, in fact, it's ridiculous when you have one of the new democratic leaders like Afanas'ev sheepishly admitting that he worked as the deputy chairman of the Lenin Pioneer Scouts. We all know that! The *Komsomol* is mainly a matter of power. It's an astonishing organization when you consider how little people believed in it yet how forcefully they pretended otherwise. You have entire generations of schoolchildren who don't believe in anything, and teachers who don't believe in anything. But the teachers have to give the impression that they believe in something, and the students have to give the impression that they believe the teacher. It's staggering. How are those relations established? That's what I write about.

GRANT: You have a fairly critical approach to your subjects and yet the groups you criticize—the army, the *Komsomol,* the Party—are among your most enthusiastic readers.

POLIAKOV: I'm not very comfortable with the Manichean visions of society that divides any group into conservative and nonconservative. It gets absurd. Not all dissidents are heroes. Take Gamsakhurdia for example, a dissident in power if you like.[5] By the same token, not all conservatives are dim-witted patriots; many are quite progressive and thoughtful. The fact that my work has a few admirers in the army (although I suspect there are more opponents than supporters) or a few readers in the *Komsomol* just goes to show that there have always been some normal people in these organizations that understood that the state had given them the wrong task. In the totalitarian state the individual doesn't choose these things. If someone has any inclination for military life, it's not as if one can join any number of foreign legions. Welcome to the Red Army. If someone has a talent for social activism, where else can they go but the *Komsomol?* To automatically label these people as conservatives is too simple and often inaccurate.

Unfortunately there are a number of our current leaders who popularize these kinds of conservative-liberal oppositions. This brought us once already to civil war in the 1920s when they decided that the entire gentry was conservative. I am categorically against that kind of thinking. In my work, I would much rather try to explain the mindset of a Party worker than that of a dissident. The dissident one can understand. But who can imagine what goes through the mind of the Party worker?

GRANT: How do you look upon someone like that woman who got up and harangued Sakharov after he condemned the Afghan war at the Congress of People's Deputies in 1989? What can you say to them?

POLIAKOV: That's when art becomes a mechanism of consolation, just as in the United States when people look back on the Vietnam War now through book after book, through film after film. Every new work does its part in helping people to understand what took place. That's really the only way. Sakharov was a brilliant man and an accomplished social activist. He was able to distinguish right from wrong. But how can you lay blame on that woman who had probably spent the last ten years in some regional Party office listening to reports about our soldiers being killed in the name of the Afghan people? It would be more interesting to look at the journalists who produced all those lies, the same journalists who have become such ardent democratic supporters since the putsch. There are correspondents who built their entire careers on Afghan reports who will tell you that they didn't have a thing to do with it. And in a sense, they are also right. For all intents and purposes it was their only means of existence. Someone tells them that they are going to report on the war in Afghanistan and that was it. It was not as if there were competing news agencies that people could switch to.

The whole situation is enormously complicated. However, the idea of individual fault in a totalitarian system where no practicable political freedom existed is a great topic. It's one of the things that interests me most of all. The story *Apofogei* is mainly devoted to that. How guilty is someone who didn't have a choice? If someone has a choice, then that's another matter. You have to think, what is fault or guilt all about? It means that you willfully commit an immoral act? Can you involuntarily commit an immoral act? When immorality becomes the status quo, is it still immoral? These questions touch all of us, and we won't be rid of them for decades.

So, while my colleagues are all rushing to write about *perestroika,* I'm more interested in trying to analyze the period of stagnation. There is nothing along the lines of a serious literary work to remind us of this time in our past.

GRANT: The past is having a hard time these days.

POLIAKOV: I don't think it's clear why, for the sake of *perestroika,* for the sake of a new outlook on everything, why it's necessary to relegate an entire epoch to complete oblivion. Regardless of what may have been bad and what may have been good. On the one hand, we return to names that were forgotten, that people were forced to forget, and yet at the same time, we create an insecurity complex of grand scale, we tell everyone that their entire lives up to this moment have been an idiotic waste. How, then, are we any different from the Bolsheviks? Anyone who went through school after 1917 was taught that everyone who lived in the time of the czars was either a cretinous autocrat or a starving worker. So I'm disturbed by this kind of repetition. Besides, people forget that if things were so beastly and inhumane over all these years, then where did they come from? How did they come to be so civilized in their ways?

It's absurd to start pointing fingers. I wrote a review once of Brezhnev's *Malaia Zemlia* when I was in the army; it was perfectly natural. Someone called me in one day, they said, "Private Poliakov, you have a literary background. Write a review of Brezhnev's book for the army paper." There was nothing to it. I sat down and wrote. I didn't give it the slightest thought. It was like drinking a cup of coffee. It wasn't as if I was part of the resistance; I never did anything so noble. The difference is that I will always remember all of my compromises. When I see people tossing about accusations, that X is a scoundrel or that Z is an anachronism, I remember my compromises.

Not long ago we had another Congress of People's Deputies. Iurii Kariakin got up to speak. I admire him quite a lot. He got and started to speak to Gidaspov, the former leader of the Leningrad Party organization, the last first secretary of the Leningrad Regional Council. He had worked as a chemistry professor during the stagnation period. Kariakin pointed his finger menacingly at Gidaspov and said, "You, Gidaspov, do you believe in God?" Gidaspov turned red and didn't know what to say and Kariakin lept on him, "Ahh, exactly." And everyone started to applaud, satisfied with themselves! Look, I'm sorry, but like everyone else I know that Kariakin used to work at the Institute for the World Workers' Movement. "And you, do you believe in God?" People have divorced themselves from their own pasts with such alacrity that it is hard to have confidence in them.

It's as if someone has the given right to call other people to account. But when your conscience is burdened by a mountain of your own compromises, there is no room for appointing yourself as judge. I can't tell you how much it bothers me. More and more of our current political leaders remind me of

chameleons who have just turned from red to green. They've managed to
just turn green except for a little red at the end of their tails, but they're
already accusing those who haven't managed to change color as fast. They
shout, "How dare you be red! I'm green!" It's funny, but it's also sad.

So, it's everyone to his own conscience. I know that the stagnation period
was an important part of my life. I compromised myself for it. I was part of
this system, with all its faults and double standards. That's what makes me
want to write about it, to dig into it. And, I suppose, there is part of me
that always wants to vindicate my generation, not in a political sense but in
a moral sense, to show that it could have turned out a lot worse given the
circumstances. Maybe we weren't dissidents, maybe we weren't heroes,
but there was enough spiritual resistance to hold on to real human values.

GRANT: You are probably one of the few Russian writers who don't have
to worry about the imminent advance of supply and demand in publishing.
Does it disturb you that capitalism is going to sink almost the entire Soviet
writer's community as we know it?

POLIAKOV: It's hard to say because the community itself is so artificial.
There were so many illegitimate privileges attached to being a writer for the
state that the ranks were unusually swelled. The Union of Writers has always
had a lot of accidental writers in it, people who were attracted by all of the
perks that it offered. If Brodskii had been a member of the Union of Writers,
no one would have ever accused him of not doing enough work, because no
one in the writer's union ever did much of anything. No one would have
noticed him. Today most people still don't write, but that's because they can
finally get on with what they may be better qualified for. We're still called
the Union of Writers, but it's unlikely that there has ever been another writer's union so filled with businessmen, bureaucrats, carpenters, and psychics—you name it. There also is the strange question of the state completely
supporting writers. On the one hand I find it rather reassuring, but when you
meet writers from the West and you wonder what would happen to them if
they handed in only a few pages of poetry once very five years, without having worked anywhere, without having taught—you realize how unusual it
was. Finally, the system has encouraged a complete disregard for the reader.
Half of the successful writers you meet here couldn't care less whether anyone reads them or not.

    Literature's priestly role was a necessity of the historical zigzag
that unfolded over a number of decades. Today the place of the "sacred cows" is being refashioned by real writers, while those who
continue to insist on their sacrality are being crowded to the periphery of the literary process. They don't entirely understand it or perceive it, but the transformation of this role has already taken place.[6]
                                             —Natalia Ivanova

Culture is a temple, not a firing range.[7]

—Aleksandr Prokhanov

Poel's Meierovich Karp, critic and translator, is one of the founders of *Vsemirnoe Slovo,* a new journal modelled after the French journal, *Lettres internationales.* We talked in the study of his apartment in St. Petersburg.

GRANT: Why don't we start with a little bit about yourself?

KARP: What can I say? I'm an old guy. I'm sixty-six years old. I started to be published in 1953. You can probably understand why—that's the year that Stalin died. I was almost twenty-eight and I hadn't been able to publish anything for some time. The fact that I am Jewish, that I wasn't a member of the Youth League, among other things, made it complicated. But in one way or another I started to be published in 1953. Then in the years following the death of Stalin, in the 1960s, there was a large wave of activity known as *shestidesiatnichestvo* [the coming of age for a generation of liberals]. This included a large number of my peers. Half of my generation became would-be reformers in the 1960s, while many of the rest became highly placed Party functionaries that remain in place today. I studied, for example, with Svetlana Stalin, while she was still using her original surname.

I never belonged to the *shestidesiatniki* because they were people who believed that things could be put right with simple, honorable reforms, to cast out the corrupt communists and replace them with honorable communists. One could still find upright communists in those days, but they were awfully few. In my parents' generation there were far more, but it is not as if much good ever came of honorable communism in any event.

It was a strange time. If before we were always supposed to say that everything was good, in the 1960s we were supposed to say that everything will be good. I had different feelings, that it wasn't all real. But what was real? Things had gotten better after the death of Stalin, in certain respects. And in any event I was interested in lots of different things. Essentially I worked on translations and wrote on ballet theory more or less until the arrival of Gorbachev.

When Gorbachev first appeared, you could see that his era represented something substantively different from the period after the death of Stalin, the Khrushchev thaw, although Gorbachev himself is the typical kind of person that you would have found back in that time, a real *shestidesiatnik,* and for that matter, a tragic figure who never seemed to understand entirely what he was getting the country into.

GRANT: Would you say that the current situation in the Union of Writers reflects the position of the country as a whole?

KARP: In a broad sense, yes. Like the rest of the country, writers have had to question their very existence, their way of working. There was always a Union of Writers, a highly structured organization, which worked in tandem with a number of state publishing houses. Some houses belonged to the union, but none were independent of the control of the central government. This is important because we have never really had a writer's market in the traditional sense. You write a book, people buy it or they don't, and if they do buy it, you get paid according to its popularity—we have never had that. The author receives an honorarium for his work regardless of whether the state publishes it. If they do, it is not his business. They then can choose who they would like to support and who they don't. To promote the conservative Bondarev, they give him an enormous printing, and they leave out everyone else. The state has always had the upper hand in literary life.

As far as the writer's union goes, it was a very contradictory organization initially under Stalin. It was a very ambiguous organization. If someone does nothing but curse it or praise it, then you spit in their eye, because on the one hand, it was and is a very cruel institution, built on forcing people to sign documents, denunciations about dissident colleagues, obliging them to work on projects they didn't like, or what have you. There was a real atmosphere of persecution and it was terrible. On the other hand, in the instances where they didn't bear down on people, at those times when they didn't make demands, the union could be a fine place, and even rise to your defense. The union was no more democratic than any other organ, but its leaders were far from all monsters. Aleksandr Fadeev led it for a long time. Of course he had a hand in a number of terrible acts, you won't get away from that. But at least you can say that he was a sincere communist. He had been a partisan at age sixteen and went on from there. When there wasn't any direct pressure from above, he honored the idea that literature was something to be promoted, and when possible he tried to help people along or to get them out of tough places. It was such a complicated organization.

Now the writer's union has crumbled. The government, as we have noted, has moved on to other means of pressuring literature, and in conjunction with this, the schism took place. On the one hand, there are people who want the preservation of the old system, both in literary life and in life in general. These are people mainly connected with the original Union of Writers of the Russian Republic: Bondarev, Prokhanov, and others. It is not just that they largely supported the putsch, or took part in "A Word to the People." They represent very powerful, reactionary forces that resist the changes altogether. If the changes go through, there is the question of whether they will even still be writers.

GRANT: So now there is a new union . . .

KARP: A new union! It's a group of people who would like things to be otherwise, to be a little better, but they are still after the same kind of system.

The mission of the old union all these years has been so absurd. You know, religion has never been very influential in the country until just a few years ago, and in the place of the priest we had writers—local, accessible priests of ideology who were supposed to propagate the word of the state. It was in this respect that the state supported writers. But a writer is something different altogether, he has a different place in society. You can't determine in advance what he will say. If everyone already knows what they are going to say, what are they good for? The best writer is someone who opens up a world for us that, on the contrary, we didn't know was there, someone who shows us things that we haven't noticed, that we haven't felt. Someone like Lev Tolstoy. He opened up a new world. Tell me, honestly, what kind of state or union can foretell what will be revealed by some strange, nonsensical writer with a difficult character and a lust for greatness, and with an enormous potential for religious influence? Yet he turns out to be a brilliant writer. No one could foresee that. That was Lev Tolstoy.

GRANT: With regard to the rhetoric of the old guard, do you see any sense in their insistence that they are on the side of Russian patriotism, the Russian idea, that they return to the conflict between Slavophiles and Westerners?

KARP: I think that it's just to attract attention. What was the Slavophile/Westerner debate about anyway? You know it wasn't that different from similar debates in Germany. It's well known that the famous Slavophiles were epigones of German romanticism, Schelling and so on. It was really a question of the fullness of bourgeois development. That is really the key. Westerners wanted a faster pace of development. The Slavophiles, well, the Slavophiles weren't against it, they also stood for the emancipation of the serfs; they just wanted a smoother, milder transition. There's a lot of that in Tolstoy. But when you look at people like Bondarev, Rasputin, you have to understand that these people support the most reactionary elements in our society, the preservation of this system. They aren't interested in changing anything, either with ease or with difficulty. They work in tandem with military generals. What kind of parallel could there be with Slavophiles?

Proponents of the Russian idea pay lip service to Russia but their real goals are imperial in nature. Look at the Kuril Islands. You couldn't imagine anything less Russian—Shikotan, Kunashir. But for them it's Russia, because Russia for them is not a place where Russians have lived since the beginning of time, Russia for them is the places that Russia has conquered. For them, Uzbekistan is Russia. Warsaw is Russia. Budapest is Russia, and so on.

The *derevenshchiki* are fond of thinking of themselves as Slavophiles, but who were they anyway? The village theme, the idea of the ravaging of the countryside wasn't invented by them. A number of people precede them. I don't want to say that these are bad writers. Belov's *A Matter of Habit* is a good story. It is part of a literature of suffering. If you read *A Matter of Habit* you feel for the hero, and you see that the peasant in Russia lives terribly. It's true. And the fact that these writers told the truth is very good. But it's not the whole truth. If you want to tell the story of the Russian peasant, you have to ask *why* he lives terribly. The peasant lives terribly because he was robbed. He was denied the right to earn a living off the land. For years Russia had a revolutionary agrarian movement whose sole purpose was the liberation of the peasantry. There was even a prerevolutionary group, Land and Will. What made them want to try to kill the czar, one of the most liberal, prudent czars that Russia had ever had, Aleksandr Nikolayevich? He liberated the peasants, but he didn't give them land, and will without land led to the peasants' ruin. The same has been the case with Stalinist collectivization.

GRANT: So the twentieth century repeats much of the nineteenth?

KARP: Of course. A great crisis hung over the end of the nineteenth century as well. But Russia has always suffered from two main kinds of problems, agrarian and nationalist. England, and moreover France, were much clearer on the latter point. The colonies were overseas. India was a separate country. For us, who knows where our colonies are? Englishmen were conscious of the fact that it was an empire, that England and India were two different countries. But tell me, can the average Russian tell the difference between Novgorod and the Kuril Islands? Not likely. The agrarian problem has not changed that much either, ironically. In principle it changed with the October revolution, but not for long. Before you knew it, collectivization created another kind of serfdom, perhaps an even worse one than before, not better. In that transition we lost an enormous number of people, talented, resourceful, good people. It's staggering.

GRANT: We were speaking earlier of the idea of surrealism, which people often invoke to explain the popularity of Soviet culture. What about today? People know that the very state has disintegrated to the point of disappearance, chaos engulfs everything, yet most people still go about their business, it almost seems to be normal on the surface.

KARP: The impression of normality is just inertia. I can't assure you that even in two months we will still have that veneer. There are parts of the country right now where people are completely up in arms, where huge crowds gather in the main squares and just stand there, staring. Demonstrations go on for two and three weeks. People are not going about their business. The tension is enormous.

When people walk around today, all these smart alecks say, "Look, communism is dead, it was all all rubbish, it was all evil people who deceived us." Well, that's just not true. That's just not the case. All Marxism did was fail to manifest itself to the full. All it manifested was its partiality, the par-

tial truth that it only could manifest. People who believed the whole package
now walk around crying fraud. They set off on a bridge that never reached
the other side! It was just never built to get to the other side. Of course they
ended up in the river. That's the way it was.

GRANT: There is an enormous urge people have to throw everything out
the window in order to start anew.

KARP: Right, but bear in mind that no one is throwing anything out
the window. All they are doing is renaming everything. If you look at the
question of Leningrad or St. Petersburg, of course I am for the reinstatement
of the name Petersburg. I don't think that one should be able to rename cities
that played an important role in the history of man. You can't rename Rome
or Moscow or Kiev. It's absurd. For the same reason Petersburg should have
stayed intact. It was a profound mistake, and I am for correcting it. But you
can't conclude that just because we are changing the name, anything else
will change. The tragedy is that Bolshevist ideology hasn't gone away, it has
just been renamed. It has stayed in place exactly the same as before. Instead
of saying that they will shoot you in the name of the World Worker's Movement, if you can imagine that, now they say they will get you in the name of
the prosperity of the Russian people, or the prosperity of the Russian Orthodox Church. It is almost down to that. If you are willing to coerce people
into following your reform program, or your church, what is the difference
what you call yourself?

People talk about a democratization of popular consciousness, but where
are the democrats? There are rather a lot of reactionaries about. There is a
certain stratum of reasonable conservatives, people like Gorbachev. There is
a certain stratum of liberals, but an absolutely negligible number of democrats. No democrats! There is no one willing to listen to their opponents.
There is no one interested in representing their constituencies. People even
call Mikhail Sergeevich a democrat. What kind of a democrat is that? He's a
smart person, that's all. He was against a multiparty system for years, against
private property, and most importantly of all, against the self-determination
of nations. Look at how many decades this has gone on. How many years,
and for what?

Notes

1. The original transcripts are up to three times as long as those presented here. In
the editing, the original sequencing of the remarks was preserved. The interviews were
conducted in Russian and all translations are my own. All comments are direct quo-
tations unless otherwise indicated.

2. A radical Russian nationalist group known for its anti-Semitic activism. The
founding of the group at the outset of *perestroika* was one of the more controversial
results of Gorbachev's campaign for openness.

3. "Slovo k narodu" [A word to the people], *Sovetskaia Rossiia, Moskovskaia Pravda,* 23 July 1991.

4. *Osvobozhdenie ot strakha* [Release from fear] (Moscow: Pravda, 1989), 5.

5. In November 1991, fighting was continuing in Georgia between forces supporting the elected president, Zviad Gamsakhurdia, and those opposing his dictatorial and repressive measures. He fled Georgia in January 1992.

6. "*Gibel' Bogov: a slome literaturnoi epokhi*" [Death of the gods: On the collapse of a literary epoch].

7. *Literaturnaia Rossiia,* 22 January 1988.

RETURNING TO EASTERN EUROPE

I first went to Hungary on a student scholarship in 1979. A wannabe Marxist, I had just started straining my uncritical faculties on György Lukács's *History and Class Consciousness*. It was time, I thought, to live in a country of "real existing socialism."[1] How long did it take before I began to doubt the state of my theoretical fathers? Sitting on wads of raw cotton in rubber lined panties a few days each month did get me to wondering about the five-year plan. But this emblematic frustration of East European and Soviet feminists did not completely diminish the products of central planning in my eyes.[2] After living among the glut of consumer products in America, I remember the relief of going to the store for rice thirteen years ago in Budapest and finding there one shelf of brown paper bags with the word *Riz* on them. Now, going to that same store in the spring of 1992, I find I can choose between Uncle Ben's and a few others. Soon, I'm afraid the choice will veer towards the meaningless as it often does in the United States where we know that the proliferation of brands does not necessarily mean better quality.

Clearly a form of capitalism is returning to Eastern Europe. A billboard campaign I saw in Budapest this spring had pictured on one half of the poster three catalogs from a Swedish furniture store and on the other half three shiny red volumes of Marx's *Capital*. The caption read: "Which one makes your life nicer?" Despite the push for more consumer goods, there is a certain irony in the ad. Not many people today in Hungary can afford these Scandinavian furnishings. With an active work force of approximately five million (the country's total population is close to ten million), there are around half a million unemployed people in Hungary today. Since the collapse of communism, the number of jobless Hungarians has doubled every six months.[3] The number of those unemployed beyond the eighteen-month limit for benefits has now reached seven thousand and is expected to climb to eighty-four thousand by the end of the year (*Budapest Week*, 27 Feb.–4 Mar. 1992, 4). With no social safety net to catch them anymore, many in Hungary are wondering about the price of a "nice" life.

Socialist rhetoric, however, can no longer be called on as a critical force in Hungary. A reference to Marxism in the public sphere these days probably means that somebody is trying to sell you something. In Budapest there is a new bar and pizza parlor called *Marxim* where you can order a "Lenin"- or "Stalin"-style pizza while gazing up at photos depicting the faces and events of Marxism in Hungary. To me this is still not as surprising as the fact that there are now pizzerias and all sorts of fast food (American) and ethnically inspired restaurants in the capital city. Ten years ago, eating out meant choosing between Hungarian and Magyar cuisine.[4] This time I tried the first vegetarian restaurant in the city. The food was excellent and affordable and if not for the strobe lights and pounding music it would have been a very enjoyable place. Apparently the owner couldn't entice enough customers with a healthy menu the first time around and was thus forced to reopen the restaurant as a disco. A vegetarian disco. People come up with strange combinations in this heyday of capitalism.

I came back to Eastern Europe in the spring of 1992 to interview a number of Hungarians—some of whom I had known as a student over a decade ago—who were engaged in new ventures of one sort or another. Three of these interviews are presented here in great length. (Given the international sphere which their work straddles, these Hungarians are used to using English as a lingua franca. Thus the following interviews were conducted in English.) The first is with Attila Grandpierre, who has been playing with his increasingly well-known band, *Vágtázó Hallotkémek* [Galloping Coroners], since 1976. Grandpierre has formulated a theory and practice called shamanpunk which is a very interesting reuse of Hungarian history, one which safeguards a utopian possibility in the midst of Hungary's more regressive nationalism. An astrophysicist by training, Grandpierre works at a scientific research center in Budapest. Lajos Boglar, the second interviewee, is an anthropologist who has just launched the first Department of Cultural Anthropology in Hungary. No longer under state constraints to keep the study of Hungarian culture within the realm of folklore, his students are now focussing on contemporary issues like nationalism and the cultural transformations brought on by capitalism. The third interview is with filmmaker Gyula Gazdag, who speaks about his most recent documentary film, in which two former communists and two former dissidents talk about the changes in their lives now that the ideology which once fed their antagonism has dissolved. Complex moral issues arise with the collapse of state communism and Gazdag's approach attempts to show that they cannot be understood in black-and-white terms. In all three interviews I am interested in how the speakers' experience of the current social upheaval is registered in their own practices. I will often intervene to give more background information or to draw from my own experience.

It is eight o'clock at night in the last days of February and I can feel the damp vestiges of the old Austro-Hungarian Empire as I enter the courtyard of this nineteenth-century apartment building in the center of Budapest. On the third floor I ring the doorbell of apartment number four and am surprised when an elderly gentleman comes to the door. I explain that I am looking for rock musician Attila Grandpierre. He nods and wearily gestures to the apartment above his. Once I'm in Grandpierre's flat, sitting in the shadows of tall stereo speakers, guitars, and keyboards, I understand that the man downstairs has heard his share of a music beyond his generation.

Attila and I talk in a large room filled with electronic equipment. Stacks of books and journals loom around us. Seated at his desk with a book on Einstein's theory of relativity and its cosmological implications open before him, Grandpierre looks like an improbable astrophysicist. His face is at once boyish and calmly intense, his frame slight. He must be around my age, in his midthirties. I know that the musical group he formed with four friends—two of whom are also physicists—has been around since the mid-seventies. They have just released their third album (all were produced in what was then West Germany) and when they play now in Budapest their audience numbers between two and three thousand. In the context of the transformational possibilities culture can provide to people in need of rethinking their relation to the social world, Grandpierre offers a way of recycling "Hungarianness" that is not caught up in the region's various nationalisms. He and his musical project are indeed shaped by contemporary Hungarian history—the oppressive life under the communist state, a legacy of historical and cultural influences that distinguish Eastern from Western Europe, and a wonderfully diverse and expansive notion of what it means to be an intellectual.

GRANDPIERRE: I chose to do astrophysics because in this field you have an outer constraint. You work with your mind and your spirit, but your spirit has to work with a finite existence. My studies in astrophysics are also related to my search to answer some alternative questions. To be able to live in my real possibilities. To live a life that I can really enjoy. So this is very good to work with my fantasies, my imagination. This also takes me to the most ultimate questions about how the universe was formed and what the ultimate roots of existence are. What is nothingness and what is somethingness and what is life and why we are here. Now I'm writing a lot of things about the common points between music, philosophy, and science. In reality these are of course not divided. So this is what I'm trying to do.

MILUN: You learn from your experiences in all these domains.

GRANDPIERRE: Yes. When I was seventeen or eighteen, my life sort of burst out of me. I wrote fantastical things about the limits of imagination, and so on. And then, because of the society I lived in, I was involved in a fight against everything. It seemed as if I had to fight against not only this society but also against humanity, against myself, against organic life. The only thing I could bring myself not to hate at that time was inorganic existence.

I think of all the death imagery surrounding heavy metal music and aspects of punk culture, a fascination with the morbid that seems to appeal strongly to adolescent males in the West. As if the only thing left to attract you when you hate the life around you is death. But Grandpierre's music is really about overcoming the attraction to death. The band's name, *Vágtázó Hallotkémek*, (Galloping Coroners) suggests that their task is to deal with society's dead. The title of their first album. "Teach Death a Lesson," addresses something in their audience that is larger than death, something that is greater than the pessimism in which so much of the alternative (male) music scene is mired. Grandpierre situated the gloom of the alternative music in Hungary for me and explained how the Galloping Coroners offered something different.

GRANDPIERRE: The normal thing in Hungary [from the late seventies to the mid-eighties] was to be depressive. Everyone knew that the situation was shit and it was enough simply to say that things were shitty. As if everyone felt that since they didn't have to be happy about the situation they would therefore be depressed and frustrated and that's all. This was the norm.

MILUN: This was the general feeling in society and it was reflected in the depressed modes of rock music?

GRANDPIERRE: Not so much in rock music but in alternative music. In rock music the depression was not so general simply because rock music itself was so blind.

Grandpierre has written elsewhere on the somnambulent character of commercial rock music. Although back in 1982 the Galloping Coroners described their music as shamanpunk, Grandpierre is careful to distinguish their project from that of his punk contemporaries.

GRANDPIERRE: We never were a real punk band. We never thought so. We had some kind of prestige because we appeared in a film once. At the time we thought that if we tried too hard to distinguish ourselves verbally from the punk, then the punk scene would be even more suppressed officially. So that's how the punks came to be good friends of ours. . . . Back in the late seventies-early eighties I had the impression that our audience was mainly university and high school students, punks and intellectuals. After 1987 something happened. Suddenly our audience grew exponentially. We gave a concert and two thousand five hundred people came. At this concert the audience started to act very differently. Everybody was dancing pogo and free ecstasy. Apparently they found a way to express themselves, a way to handle what they were experiencing.

MILUN: Up until then the audience wasn't moving?

GRANDPIERRE: Until then the general reaction to our music in Hungary is that people were very shocked. They had no idea what to do. This was characteristic. We were doing something that was totally instinctive; even we had never experienced this before. So it was totally new, shocking and dangerous. Something you can't foresee. When we first began playing, many people just came to see what was happening. I remember once in 1983 we gave a concert in Budapest and there were about two thousand people in the audience. People were either standing very still on chairs or they were dancing Hungarian folkdances—like a kind of protest since in the newspapers they always reported that the audience was very aggressive. But in fact that was not the case at all. They never described what was really happening at our concerts.

It makes alot of sense for Hungarian youths to break into folkdance, as Grandpierre says, as a means of protest. Like American youths attracted to native American and other alternative cultures in the sixties and seventies— that is, seeking a cultural form which while being outside of the mainstream nevertheless remained phantasmically rooted to their sense of where they were from—young Hungarians in search of such forms began claiming certain traditions which the state had previously usurped as "official culture." Indeed, after Stalin's death, communist ideology in Eastern Europe had sanctioned their own versions of ethnic "folk" culture, producing simulations of ethnicity which sought to appease and control the nationalist tendencies which have long played beneath the surface of the peoples of this region. Thus in the seventies the Dance House Movement—clubs where the Magyar equivalent of the hippie was learning Hungarian folk dance—offered a countercultural practice. I remember attending a few of these folkdance classes with my avant-garde Hungarian-Canadian friend, Oliver, in 1979. He was a student in Toronto and had received, like me, a scholarship to study in Budapest that year. Oliver spoke fluent Hungarian and introduced me to most of the "alternative" Budapest I got to know that year. Here I want to distinguish *alternative* culture from both *official* culture—what is ideologically sanctioned by the state—and the cultural life linked to the so-called *second economy*— practices which were illegal but tolerated (not necessarily controlled) by the state because they provided a sort of safety valve, releasing the tension produced by the impossible constraints of the official system. Cultural practices within the sphere of the second society, then, did nothing to threaten the state. Unlike alternative cultural practices, which sought to offer an alternative vision of society, those associated with a second society provided a way for people to live unofficially within the official realm of power. This distinction is an important one, one which Grandpierre himself alludes to when he distinguishes shamanpunk's message from the negativity of the punk bands, noting that "they"—the state, the government, the police—have always found the Galloping Coroners more threatening than the punks.

GRANDPIERRE: In the early eighties the alternative scene was really powerful. Intellectuals regularly hung out in these kind of places. It was considered a good thing to do. It was a place to meet with other intellectuals but it was also a form of protest. Many but not all of the events going on there were political. Our music, however, was considered much more dangerous because we didn't only say that the situation we were living in was a bad one so lets kick them out, we offered people a way to reach fantastical lives.

MILUN: When you say "them," whom are you referring to?

GRANDPIERRE: "They" is always the Party. [We laugh.] "We" and "they." So, the officals said that we were more dangerous than the other alternative bands because we are not giving only a single reaction but rather we are offering the audience a new way that can lead to certain solutions which have such a fantastical influence that many people really catch it. So they, the Party people, said that this was even more dangerous than the punks, whom they also didn't like.

MILUN: Where did you hear that kind of thing said?

GRANDPIERRE: After we had been invited to play someplace, the organizers would go to the officials, to the police, to ask for permission and they would tell them these things.[5] They would also tell them that this was being told to them in confidence, not to tell anyone else. They were obviously trying to influence the organizers to change their minds about having us play there. And now, even though the situation has changed in many respects, we have found that while we may be living with a different kind of freedom today, our music and our attitude has always offered a different experience of how to liberate our deepest self. And so for us the audience hasn't changed because many people are still very interested in what we are doing. So it is the same audience but also a new audience because it is growing bigger and bigger here.

MILUN: Why do you think that there is still a need for what you do even though there is no longer the same kind of censorship?

GRANDPIERRE: Because now it is clear that you cannot have a good band only if you have good political—of course I mean radical—texts. That's clear. But this was never our characteristic.

MILUN: Why was that never your characteristic? Did you see your shamanistic stuff as having political relevance?

GRANDPIERRE: Yes, of course. But we never had the impression that we had to do something political on the surface because we had political roots.

MILUN: Let's go back to your roots. You've described your music to me as "a trip from one mind state to another . . . some noises, some written pitches . . . not sequentially composed but rather simultaneously conceived . . . an outburst of life instinct"—this is in fact the title of your second album, *Jump Out the World Instinct*—"magical, ethnographical music . . . something that transcends music." Where did you get the idea of shamanpunk?

GRANDPIERRE: At some point, in the early eighties, we started to hear from our audience that what we were doing was not rock music but rather shamanistic music. So the idea of shamanistic music came from the audience, not from us. You see it was something that developed instinctively. Not from books but from the audience.

Grandpierre knows that I've read his theoretical article on shamanpunk. I told him how much I liked the way he went to ethnographic texts on the ancient Hungarian shamans, reclaiming them from the realm of academic knowledge and offering an interpretation that aimed at the experience of self empowerment. In his article, Grandpierre linked this empowerment to a sense of sovereignty. Now I tell him that his description of the link between ecstasy and sovereignty reminds me of the work of the French anthropologist Georges Bataille.[6] The idea of shamanpunk, seen in the context of official Hungarian society where the folk tradition had been politicized by the state, actually meant the creation of a form of political power. How, I wanted to know, did the audience's reaction feed back into what he was doing with his music?

GRANDPIERRE: I thought it was very interesting that what we were doing on the stage turned out to remind people rhythmically of some shamanistic texts. So I began looking into different kinds of shamanistic music, a music I found to be full of some sort of ecstasy. The whole shamanistic inquiry was interesting to me as a human being, not only as a member of the band. But it also had some concrete influence. Something that made the band's aim stronger.

MILUN: You mean, as a concept shamanism made the band stronger?

GRANDPIERRE: No. It helped us be who we are and to keep on doing what we were doing before. It showed us that we had not simply been doing something rootless and abnormal. We were engaged in something that had at one time been real and should once again become real.

MILUN: You were happy to discover that you were part of a tradition.

GRANDPIERRE: As I see it we have two roots, one in the very distant past and one in the very distant future.

MILUN: Why a *distant* future?

GRANDPIERRE: Because we are looking for something that is not completely present in society.[7] Something that can't be reached easily because it's just on the surface. We're not trying to do something which makes us closer to what people are doing in the present society. What we really want to do is what we have to do in the widest sense: to reach those territories in ourselves which are the most difficult to know. In this sense, we consider what people are doing in the present society to be very different. What we are about may someday approach what is offered by the society around us and it's possible that in the past, what we are into now was in fact much closer to mainstream society. . . . What you were saying about power. People used to listen to tapes of our music recorded from the concerts.[8] Then we started to hear that people began feeling somehow inspired to do something because of this, that it somehow gave them so much power. It wasn't that they necessarily wanted to act but that they felt compelled to do so because of the music. When they came to the concerts, they apparently also felt compelled to move [their bodies]. We would hear that these people would then decide to bring their quietest friends to the next concert to see what would happen to them. You see, they were impressed by the fact that what they never thought could happen to them—finding themselves moving in this way—nevertheless did. So they wanted to see if their friends would have this experience too. And with these friends they'd wait about twenty minutes, nothing would happen, and then suddenly these more timid friends of theirs would start to move in this way too.

At this point in our conversation I'm thinking of sending Attila a book by Michael Taussig, *Shamanism, Colonialism, and the Wildman.* For Taussig, as for Grandpierre, the experience of shamanistic power is found to be something of an antidote to an oppressive regime which weighs on its subjects both mentally and physically, culturally and politically, and of course economically.

But I'm suspicious of how this power operates from a tape player. From a concert where one is surrounded by two thousand peers, yes. But once it is mechanically reproduced, how does it maintain its "aura"? The Galloping Coroners are about to release their third album. How does the distance produced in recording affect the ecstatic empowerment he is talking about?

MILUN: What you do in your performances is so alive and connected to something which is unforeseeable, and yet with mechanical reproduction, just playing the album a second or third time, the music becomes so predictable, doesn't it?

GRANDPIERRE: We try to create something you can listen to ten times and still not foresee at all. Some parts are really hard to foresee. I can show you some things you could listen to twenty times and nobody knows how we did it. When we were mixing it in the studio, even the mixer said, "Incredible, how did you do it? It's not possible." And we did it in a way that even we couldn't repeat. We turned out all the lights and started something. It sounded something like the sounds in a jungle. [He plays this piece for me later: jungle sounds which imperceptibly turn into the sounds of a large modern city.] Of course, sometimes we rehearse. In fact, we've always had two attitudes: on the one hand, we strive to keep our music totally spontaneous, and on the other hand, when we feel that we have discovered some really high point, we try to keep some of that. Even in our stage performances, sometimes when things are not going well and we need to bring things to a certain point, we'll use these forms until we're brought things there and then we'll go off. This actually helps us maintain our freedom better.

MILUN: So mechanical reproduction doesn't affect your music?

GRANDPIERRE: Yes it does, but we try to work with the deep level of our music—I wrote an essay, in German, on this topic. We feel that if in your personal attitude you have an experience of a new kind of world, then your attitude, your experience, can be preserved even mechanically. This is not something you can hear consciously because it belongs to a special dimension which is hidden from the conscious mind. The conscious mind cannot distinguish every fine detail. So there is a special range which is only experienced by the unconscious mind. This is the musical deep voice. And if you really experience some new world experience, it really can be built into the musical deep voice. But it remains true that even if it is built into the musical deep voice, then a mechanical reproduction is very different from a live experience. The reproduction has some kind of aura, it has some ability to catch people and to involve them in this new world, but it is still very different from being present. So there are people who hear our music for the first time from the albums, have their favorite pieces, and so on, and yet when they come to hear us in concert they are shocked. They never thought there could be such a big difference.

I tell Grandpierre that his notion of the musical deep world reminds me of Proust's idea of involuntary memory, a mnemonic form which we access involuntarily (since such access is generally denied to consciousness) when, for example, sounds or smells suddenly recall some event or scene from our past. Proust's novel *A Remembrance of Things Past* tried precisely to track involuntary memory. It uncovered an emotional world operating below the surface, so to speak, of the waning world of aristocratic privilege in fin-de-siècle Paris. Shamanpunk, it seems, also seeks to reveal a historical current of Hungarianness lying below the surface of mainstream Magyar culture. I asked Grandpierre what his experience as a Hungarian has to do with his musical project.

GRANDPIERRE: When I start to holler, or scream, or even to play the guitar—because I cannot play the guitar—then it works in the following way: I move the strings and hear something totally new and unexpected. Then the second or third pitch sounds interesting to me, so I try to follow it but I cannot repeat it. So then it seems to me that these pitches I'm following sound a little bit Eastern. And because I am Hungarian—even though, as you can tell from the name, I'm descended from an old French family—I believe I was really recognizing an ancient Hungarian music.

MILUN: Had you ever heard such music before?

GRANDPIERRE: No. But I had the impression that it was a little bit Eastern. And everybody told me that it sounded like an ancient Hungarian melody.

MILUN: Didn't you hear old Hungarian folk music in school?

GRANDPIERRE: Of course, just as everybody here does. You know Hungarian folk music is characterized by its descending pentatonic scale. So maybe this has had some unconscious influence. And then one of my very first musical experiences was at a New Year's Eve party. There was a guy there who wanted to be a guitarist like Jimi Hendrix. He had played for seven years so he was really an expert. He had very good technique. So I took the guitar and started to strum one and the same string without working the frets. Then I turned the guitar over and started beating on the back—it was a very ecstatic rhythm. It had a strong drive. For me it was ecstatic. The rhythm was compelling in the way that a child's nursery rhyme is. It seemed to have some ethnographical or national character and at that time I was very much against all national things.

MILUN: Why?

GRANDPIERRE: Because this is what I got from this country: a hatred for everything that stood for the nation.

MILUN: How did you get that?

GRANDPIERRE: From the schools, from the radio and television, from other people watching television, reading the newspapers. Our country, we were led to believe, wasn't fully developed, and this was linked to a very negative side of our history. We learned that Hungarian people are one of the worst people in the world, everybody was a fascist at heart, and so on and so on.

MILUN: Are you talking about the government or the people?

GRANDPIERRE: The people were very influenced by this in the sixties and the seventies. Even me. Because all my friends, and at this time the most important thing for me was my friends, since my friends had this attitude and because I had never known any different or special experience, I shared this attitude without knowing what I was doing . . . So when I had this experience with the guitar on New Year's Eve, I was suddenly no longer satisfied. At first I thought that maybe there was something deeply wrong with me, a problem in my deep world. My mind seemed to be saying that I was doing something it didn't like. And then after three or four years my mind slowly began to change. It occurred to me that maybe my mind is the thing that is off track and my subconscious mind is what is interesting, as if my mind were the dead one and my subconscious mind the living one. Perhaps then it was wrong for me to tell my inner self that it was the wrong one. This all came up when I went to a movie and saw a certain newsreel; you know, it was common in Hungary at that time to have the news before the movie started. The newsreel showed a Mongolian girl who was coming to Hungary to learn some kind of industrial work, to do textiles, I think. And then the report went on to explain how much better the socialist system was than the capitalist system. This was the usual shit they fed us. So during this shit they were playing some traditional Mongolian music in the background. I was shocked because the music was so clean and so full of emotion that it was like some kind of fantastic dream about the possibility of a totally different kind of life. I suddenly felt as if I were on another planet. And I imagined this girl standing on top of a hill at home trying to express what she feels unconsciously in herself but then having to give all that up. It was like a shock for me. And so I started to make recordings of Mongolian folk music. And then even started to listen to Hungarian folk music, realizing nevertheless that for most people this stuff is just the usual shit, that it doesn't have any value. And then I figured, maybe there is some really good Hungarian folk music which is not known because they don't want it to be known.

MILUN: Who is "they"?

GRANDPIERRE: The government. The Party. And then I went to the documents of the Hungarian State National Orchestra [literally, the State Folk Ensemble]. Even the name is funny: state, nation. I recorded some stuff and even felt that maybe this track could be really good as long as *they* are not playing it. In other words, originally it may have been very good. I called an expert in old Hungarian folk music—this was in in 1985—and I asked him whether he knew of any really ancient Hungarian folk music. He told me that it was impossible to say definitively because the first written material is only from the 1500s. It could probably have been much older. But I found one of these old written melodies and suddenly realized it had the same rhythm that I had played on the guitar thirteen years before. It was then that I thought that maybe I should be investigating this. When we played rhythm with the band, people started to say that it was quite shamanistic. I had no idea what shamanistic was, so I asked an ethnographer friend of ours. I showed him this music and he said that it was indeed shamanistic and then he in turn played me some shamanistic music. Thus I saw that it was characteristically very similar. [Grandpierre chants the rhythm.] So the basic thing is the same in all of them. So I had started with folk music and then afterward it became shamanistic music. It's really a strange process how we reached this.

MILUN: You talk about something that's greater than you, that's moving through you, perhaps subconsciously held, and you also talk about a great antagonism you have against a particular form of authority, the state. I wonder if there's any reason in your mind between the two. Also, why should such music develop here in Hungary? Why are you a vehicle for it? Why should it be so popular here?

GRANDPIERRE: I think that the traditions of Hungary were forbidden for a very long time, close to a thousand years. I read in books that the real Hungarian folk music has been underground since the twelfth century. [We laugh.]

MILUN: It traces the dissident movement in a very different way.

GRANDPIERRE: Maybe if there is a long dissident tradition, it can survive even a thousand years. Perhaps many people are vehicles for it without ever reaching the ability to actualize it. I think that some kind of critical experience is necessary to not suppress this attitude. But if you don't get enough positive encouragement for it, then it can remain underground in you.

MILUN: When you say that some critical activity is necessary to activate it, you mean an ability to criticize what is around you?

GRANDPIERRE: That too, but I'm thinking about the way the atomic bomb needs a critical mass. Likewise you have to have normally two or three impressions which are strong enough to reveal that there is a totally new world you have always wanted without knowing that this is what you want. If you have two or three deep enough experiences, then you can start to live with your real aims.

MILUN: Your musical project has a hopeful tone. When you look around you now and consider the changes Hungary has undergone in the last two years, do you feel hopeful?

GRANDPIERRE: Yes, we have some hopes. But these hopes are mainly that more and more people are reached and more and more people can have liberating experiences, liberating personal experiences. What we see, however, is that the audience doesn't change with the political changes. But the press has changed for us. Under the old regime, at least one critic would grudgingly make some mention of our band. When our first album came out in 1989, ten critics responded in the Hungarian press. Now that our second album is out, the official press writes nothing. So we are not in the press, we're not on the radio, we're not on the TV.

MILUN: But before the changes, before 1989, you were?

GRANDPIERRE: Yes, sometimes.

MILUN: Why was that?

GRANDPIERRE: I'm not sure, I can only guess. First of all, despite the

changes, those who write for the press today are the same as those who
wrote during the communist era. In the last years before the political
changes, these journalists had to do some interesting things just to show that
they are not the old fuckers everybody knows they are. So they wanted to
prove in their deepest hearts that they were good, honest guys. "We know
what the people like," and so on. So they tried to cover even our stuff. Now
they don't have to do this because they consider themselves to be good
democratic journalists, both in the papers and on TV. But everybody knows
that these are the same guys as before. For example, a group from Austria
wanted to produce a joint TV program with Hungary and they were insisting
that our band be included in the groups chosen. But the Hungarian TV said
no and scuttled their project. So this was two years ago, after the changes.
Our band has been filmed by at least twenty Western TV productions over
the years, but the Hungarian TV has never bothered with us. Oh yes, they
made one short piece about a club called the Black Hole—this is the chief
underground music and life joint in Budapest and we happened to be playing
there when they made the program. The point of the program was simply to
say that the Black Hole is the worst place in Hungary: parents, don't let your
kids go there. This was the one-minute message Hungarian TV ever broadcast about us.

MILUN: What kind of radical change would have to happen in your opinion for this situation to be different?

GRANDPIERRE: The press, the radio and TV, should not be run by the old
communist people who do the same old things. There is one radio program,
for example, called "Only for Young People." It's been running for perhaps
thirty years now with the same guy. I remember twenty years ago this guy
said that the Rolling Stones would never be played on his program.

MILUN: You don't seem to see much change going on out there.

GRANDPIERRE: Nothing. These people in charge of many domains like the
radio and TV were selected under the old system because of their cultural
ideology, and these people are still there. These are people who have no new
ideas, they don't really even want to work, they simply want to keep getting
their paychecks. So all these people with no real ideas or abilities depend on
each other for the system to continue. But now there will be a new media law.

MILUN: What do you hope to see from the new media law?

GRANDPIERRE: I hope it will force them to state what the most basic tasks
of the television and radio are. And then if people do not do these things, it
will be possible to have them kicked out. Kicked out if they are not representing the real world to the people—by "real" I mean not only the lying
and cheating that is going on, but some kind of culture, some kind of interesting things. The people in this country need to get some information about
how to live another future. Not the future that the Party had in mind. In that

era, as everybody knows, the idea was only to push the people more deeply down. To stop them from doing anything outside of a prescribed "norm."

MILUN: Watching TV now, do you notice any difference?

GRANDPIERRE: Not really. Somehow it's really the same idea behind it all. They made some kind of surface changes so they can look like the West. . . . But this society can't really offer most kids what they feel they need.

MILUN: What should the society offer?

GRANDPIERRE: Life that is full of fun, full of scandals, full of extraordinary experiences, full of personal connections, excitement, and so on. . . . But you see, the whole educational system and the politics surrounding the media, press, and so on, need to undergo radical change. I think that business, commercial things, should make up a small part of what our daily lives are about. If they have to exist, OK, exist. But from the business, maybe half of the profits should be given to cultural things. And half of that money allocated to cultural things should go to children and young people. But as it is now with commercial/industrial concerns, the problem is not only that they make so much money, but that their minds are so narrow that they don't know how to use this money. Their lives are so narrow and thus the whole society ends up being covered with shit. So really, our social life has to change so that it is not simply driven by a desire for money.

This is the first time I've been back in Eotvos Lorent University (ELTE) since 1981. I enter the side door and, just as before, I go past the *portás* [concierge] and nod my greetings. Suddenly I am reminded of something a friend told me last night. "Of course," she said, "we all now know that concierges everywhere in this country were working as informants for the Party. But does that mean that we should now fire them and have thousands more out of work?" These little receptionlike areas at the entryways of most public buildings (including most apartment houses) would seem strange to an American, but they are ubiquitous in European architecture. In Central Europe they have a strong precedent as part of the surveillance apparatus under Metternich's control of the Austro-Hungarian Empire. So, until Hungary is able to afford the hidden camera system that blends so well into the entryways of Western institutions, I guess the *portás* system will remain intact.

Professor Lajos Boglar's office is on the sixth floor. He greets me at the door. A large man, perhaps in his late fifties, his white hair set off by his black sweater and pants. This kindly face reveals what one of his students tells me later: that he has been a fatherly figure to many students in this new program.

"The Department of Cultural Anthropology is new," he tells me. "It's the first of its kind [in Hungary]." With the aim of introducing an American type of cultural anthropology to Eastern Europe, the Soros Foundation is funding the department completely for its first three years. This is the second year. Before launching this department, Boglar taught ethnology at Eotvos Lorent University. Since 1975 when he first came to ELTE, ethnology was a part of folklore studies. The new cultural anthropology program has thus met with a lot of institutional resistance. But, as Boglar proudly tells me, "in one year I have thirty-five faculty teaching for me and eighty students majoring in the field." He winks triumphantly.

Boglar identifies himself as a Brazilian Hungarian. He was born in Brazil to Hungarian diplomats who were recalled to Budapest during the Second World War, when he was fourteen years old. He still has family in São Paulo, returns often for extended periods, and remains strongly identified with the place. Although much of his fieldwork was in South America among tropical forest Indians, his attention is now turned to things Hungarian and he describes for me the sorts of projects his students are for the first time free to study. "Some students are studying acculturation in those regions where heavy industry has collapsed and the people have decided to work as peasants." Industrialization during the Stalinist period targeted rural towns. Thus the movement of deindustrialization in Eastern Europe will most likely leave jobless factory workers reinventing rural life.

BOGLAR: And then there are all the new ceremonies this society is engaged in as a way of rewriting their past. Reburial, for example. We have a lot of students studying recent Hungarian reburial ceremonies.

MILUN: Reburial? That's an important issue in the United States right now for native Americans. For American Indians it is a postcolonial gesture to demand the return of their dead ancestors from museums and give them a proper burial. How does this work in Hungary?

BOGLAR: Here it is a function of the change of regimes: you have to resurrect your heroes who were vilified during various periods. But its much more complicated than that and actually goes back about one thousand years for us. In Hungarian history revolutionary leaders who were shot down by an oppressor were generally dug up and reburied with the appropriate fanfare as soon as political circumstances changed.

I recall listening in 1990 to the live broadcasts on National Public Radio in the United States of the reburial ceremony of Imre Nagy, leader of the 1956 uprising who was later executed by the Communist Party after Soviet tanks were brought in to put down the revolt. It was enormously moving to hear the names of those who had died fighting in the streets in 1956 read aloud to what must have been thousands of Hungarians gathered at Heroes' Square in the center of Budapest. This was the new noncommunist government's first public ceremony. Two years previously, Hungarians had called for the reburial of Nagy, but the communist government gave them an extravaganza reburial of Béla Bartók instead.[9] "When we reburied Imre Nagy, we also dug up the graves of around eight other what the communists used to call counter-revolutionaries. And imagine, in one coffin there was no body so this became the monument to the Unknown Revolutionary. One of the ministers executed along with Nagy [and then reburied in this ceremony] is named Losonczy. His daughter is an anthropologist working in Paris who is now doing a study of reburial in Hungary. She's interested in the anthropology of patriotism and has decided to study this aspect of Hungarian culture. You see, it represents a very, very deep psychological problem. And it's not simply a political thing; to understand it you'd have to study the history of suicide in this country and the connection of death generally."

Indeed, since World War II, Hungary has had the highest per capita rate of suicide in the world. Boglar goes on to tell me about his work in a Hungarian village he's been going to since 1966.

BOGLAR: I know everyone there. It's a small northern village of around 175 people. . . . The women there are very strong, they organize all the ceremonies. They all speak Hungarian and Slovakian. They change readily from one language to another, and that's very important. For me, tolerance begins with language. If you have at least two languages then you have to understand at least two cultures. But I've watched this culture slowly change over the last twenty-five years.

MILUN: The enormous changes going on in Budapest these last two years, how are they registered in this village? Are they of any consequence to the villagers?

BOGLAR: This village is just over an hour from Budapest. But everything that happens there is slow. For example, during the last elections eighty percent of the villagers voted to keep the old communist party in power! Eighty percent! They had no idea what had been happening here in Budapest. But you have to understand that in a village of 175 people there are only around eight families. Everybody is related to everybody else in some way or another. . . . But one interesting thing is that people in such small villages who were members of the Party are now looking for something else. . . . Now they're more interested in alternative medicine or science fiction than politics. They're reading these other things now. Of course, eighty percent of what people read now is pornography,[10] but you have this other side that is reading alternative medicine . . .

MILUN: "New Age," we call it.

BOGLAR: Yes, "New Age." I would say they are trying to find a new ideology. One day we'll have to study it. You know, when I visit now they always say to me, "You are an anthropologist, you have to explain to us how these [New Age] things work." For example, a woman [in this village] who two years ago was secretary to the Communist Party leader and would usually want to talk with me about political problems now wants to talk about shamanism. But this is outside of Budapest. In Budapest you have many different kinds of religious groups surfacing. . . . There are psychologists studying this too, now. You can see the same things on the streets of Budapest that you see in Munich. But I don't know how deep these things are.

This trip I also noted such new phenomena appearing on the streets of Budapest. A group of Hari Krishnas, for example, with drums and bells, dancing and singing on the sidewalk. In 1979 I remember hearing of how a group of Hari Krishna had tried to sneak into Hungary from the Austrian border and were expelled. I see posters for yoga lessons up in the city center now, a new tactic to cope with modernity. With all these changes going on, I tell Professor Boglar, it seems like a good time to open a department of cultural anthropology.

BOGLAR: I think this is perhaps the last chance to introduce cultural anthropology here in Hungary.

MILUN: Why the last chance?

BOGLAR: Because today intolerance, ethnic intolerance, is really unbelievable. They actually hate foreigners here, it's all coming out. This is what's surfacing in the midst of all this social change. Imagine! You have one hundred and fifty thousand people out of work and they say that there are one hundred and seventy thousand or more immigrants pouring into the country now. These people are coming from the East, from Romania, from the southern areas of the former Soviet Union. All in the last two years. The country is completely open. Every day you hear about incidents with Romanians, Arabs, and so on. You know, as far as crime goes, Budapest now resembles Chicago in 1926. But you'll only hear Hungarians complain if the crime is committed by a Gypsy or an Arab. When whites commit crimes here, the attitude is that it's normal. How can I explain it? Here, if a black man kills somebody, then you'll hear it implied that all black men are killers, they'll soon be killing everybody. But if a Hungarian kills somebody, then forget it! Perhaps he had his reasons, he needs a house, he's got a family to feed, he needs money. But the black man here, he's an immigrant! This is the basic problem. And this is all new, it's a development of the last two years.

MILUN: What about the old socialist rhetoric of internationalism?

BOGLAR: Indeed there was an attempt to universalize culture. The ideological explanation was that there was something called the "soviet" man. All these people in sixteen republics and hundreds of ethnic groups which have very little to do with each other. The main idea was that the inner organization of the country would be socialist, but its outer form would be nationalist. That was the dream of the Soviets. Azerbaijan or Uzbekistan could exist as such but their government, their infrastructure, had to be socialist. Two years ago everything exploded and you can see what's happening. And it's the same thing here. Before you could hear people say, "Yes, we have some problems with the Jews and the Gypsies, but its not that important." Today, however, everything is open and that means every day you have to hate somebody. In my opinion, part of the society is simply sick. And, believe me, among intellectuals you'll find the same sickness. You can't explain it by saying that it is just the simple reaction of the people. Among my friends I see the same sort of reactions.

MILUN: It's as if people are desperately looking for someone on whom to place responsibility. When the enemy was the state, there was no material being or individual to hate.

BOGLAR: Well, you'll see the real problem if you study Hungarian history. We have no traditions of democracy in this country. It's impossible to find a democratic period, it's always been feudal. Before the Second World War, during the Stalinist period, and today, you can see the same sort of feudal dynamic at work. You know, I'm not referring to big landowners here; feudalism is a form of mentality. It assumes that there will be a head or chief and an organizational structure which is always centralized. . . . [For example], I was at the house of a filmmaker here who for years has had an open house every first Saturday where writers, politicians, and other people gather and talk. Last month I was talking with a group of friends there and it turned into a complete disaster. One friend belongs to one political party, another belongs to a different party, and neither of them will talk with communists. So that's one sort of attack. Another, a very famous historian, said, "We have to close the borders and clean up the country." And these are old friends of mine, you know. I think this is a kind of epidemic. People will tell you that they are happy with the new government and the way it is proceeding and that the only problems are with the Gypsies, the Jews, and the Arabs. This is a great and very deeply intellectual problem of Hungarian society.

Back in 1980 some Hungarian friends told me to see a film called *The Cobblestone Trinket,* by Gyula Gazdag.[11] Although Gazdag made the film in 1972, it was shelved almost immediately only to appear spontaneously in backwater movie theaters every few years. *The Cobblestone Trinket* is a political allegory about a summer camp where boys from city high schools would go to help out on neighboring cooperative farms. When it turns out that the farmers don't need the boys' labor one year, the camp turns into an existential vacuum where activities like the daily raising of the flag and the little competitive games the organizers invent to kill time become a means of commenting on the bankruptcy of state ideology. The film's title refers to the spongy cobblestone trinket dangling from the rearview mirror of a young French-Hungarian man driving through the area. He stops and listens to the boys' complaints and then encourages them to follow the example of the 1968 student revolt in Paris—that is, to intensify the conflict and seek shelter from the inevitable clash behind cobblestone barricades, a technique Parisian youths picked up from the experience of the French communards back in 1870. Gazdag's film responded to the regionally specific question of how, after the experience of Hungary in 1956 and Prague in 1968, East Europeans should react to state oppression. The West European and North American student protest movements of the late sixties made this a topic of much debate. While still addressing the despair of Hungarian youths, *The Cobblestone Trinket* successfully demythologized the French commodification and export of revolutionary politics, like "mai '68," by having the Hungarian youths reject the advice of the young Frenchman (the unhappy campers recall that since 1956 the streets of Budapest have been tarred over precisely to prevent such an act.)

Given his critical and comparative perspective on Hungarian culture, I thought Gazdag would be an interesting commentator on the recent changes in his country. After teaching film courses in the United States, since the fall of Communist Party rule, Gazdag has been the chair of the Department of Film and Television at the main theater and film school in Budapest. I spoke to him in his flat which he shares with his wife, who is an art historian, and their two children.

MILUN: Tell me something about your latest documentary film. I know it was recently shown on Hungarian television.

GAZDAG: This was a French production, shown on French television in November [1991] and then on Hungarian television this January [1992]. The French commissioned me to make a documentary of what happened in Hungary between 1956 and 1989. Instead of using archival footage, I made four different portraits of very common people whose lives were marked by this history. One of them, a worker who was involved in the Hungarian uprising in 1956, was "executed" by Hungarian soldiers but somehow survived this execution, unbeknownst to his executioners. He told the story of how he was executed and how in 1960, when he went back to his village where the execution had taken place and ran into one of the soldiers who had executed him, the soldier denounced him to the Communist Party. And so this fellow who had previously escaped had to go to jail because of his life in the "counterrevolution." When I met him for the film, he had not seen the soldier who had denounced him since 1960. But during the shooting of the film he met him again. He knew that this person lived in the same village and so we went there with the camera looking for him. We found him in a small coffee shop and the two of them discussed the matter on film.

Then the second person was the widow of an officer, a former communist secretary who had committed suicide in 1989. After the death of her husband, this woman became a private entrepreneur, so it was a very complex situation. She was in the process of getting her own business started while we were shooting the film. She told the story of her husband, of how he committed suicide, how he became a Party secretary, their common story from the very beginning.

MILUN: Sounds like she was maybe liberated by his death.

GAZDAG: Maybe she was, but she was not aware of it. The third person was a former agent of the secret police. He was a child of a farm family and told us how he became a member of the secret police. After he quit the police he went back to his parents' farm. So when we went to shoot him, he was feeding the animals and doing all those jobs which had to be done around the farm. But we found archival film of a video which was shot in 1988 during a demonstration—of course, shot by underground videomakers. And you could see him in this footage acting as a member of the secret police. In the footage you can see him try to stop the video camera from recording.

MILUN: Did this guy talk to you openly about his work in secret police?

GAZDAG: Absolutely.

MILUN: Why do you suppose he felt he could talk so openly to you?

GAZDAG: Because when he quit his job he felt somehow cheated by the organization he had worked for. So he told his story. The fourth person was a mechanical engineer, a computer programmer who had been working for the national library for ten years. He was a student leader in 1956 and he told his own story as well. For me these four stories also meant taking an account of what was happening in my own previous life, and also what the spiritual situation was in Hungary when I came back this time. These stories raised the unresolved problems of our society. Suddenly you could see surfacing the confusion that had created this mess in which it was impossible to know who was right and who was wrong. These four people were selected so that two of them were from one political side and the others from the opposite political side, in terms of the politics between 1956 and 1989. For example, the woman was an old Communist Youth Secretary, so she was on the side of power. And so was the former member of the secret police, whereas the other two had both fought against this regime in 1956. But after watching the film, you don't feel that these two were right and the other two were not. Rather you feel the complexity of history. I didn't want to judge any of these people. I just wanted to tell their stories.

Gazdag's position here is indicative of a major difference in the way Hungary and Czechoslovakia are attempting to resolve the problem of what to do with former members of the secret police and other powerful figures of the communist period. In October 1991, Czechoslovakia passed what is known as the lustration law. The word *lustration* is derived from Latin and literally means "sacrificial purification." The law is directed against former secret police agents and their collaborators as well as against former "middle management" communists and members of various voluntary groups run by the Party. It also targets members of committees who were used to exclude individuals from jobs and universities after the communists clamped down on independent activity in 1948 and 1968. The law bars such people from holding high-level administrative jobs in the government, military, state radio and television, news agencies, and state-owned enterprises like foreign trade companies, railways, and banks.

Hungary has opted for a different solution. It also had a similar bill, part of the "Justice Plan" platform of the conservative Hungarian Democratic Forum, the largest party in the present ruling coalition. But this bill was recently (February 1992) declared unconstitutional by Hungary's Constitutional Court. and thus there will apparently be no prosecution of old-regime officials in Hungary. While lustration-type laws may violate the European Convention on Human Rights, it remains questionable whether West European human rights standards should apply to cases of Eastern Europe. The fact that former communists remain in positions of public power generates a good deal of moral debate.

Throughout the former empire, East European citizens are confronting this secretive past on a very personal level. I recall reading exerpts from the *Stasi* [secret police] files now accessible to citizens of the former East Germany and wondering whether there might be a file on me.[12] What about that odd East German dental student I met in Budapest in 1980 who spoke perfect English and drove a red sports car (an improbable life-style for any East German in those days)? He suddenly appeared before I was to return to the United States for a month, took me to parties where people offered me marijuana[13] (neither before nor after did I see any in Budapest), wrote pathetic love letters, and even called me a few times back home in the States!

The spectrum of informant activity is quite enormous. Through my scholarship in 1979 I had a room in a flat which was owned (illegally) by a woman who had apparently cut a deal with the guy running foreign student housing. I was there the day they came to install the bugging devices. The next year I moved into a flat with a woman who became a good friend. She was a single mother of two and we worked out an arrangement whereby I would teach her and the children English. Although there was already a perfectly good telephone in this flat, a new phone was installed in my bedroom a few days after

I arrived. (It is important to note that some Hungarians wait decades for even one phone in their flat.) When I go to visit her now, the second phone is no longer there. Contradictory as this may seem, this woman remains a friend. We have never talked about the surveillance she most probably set me and my Hungarian friends up for (I also used the room to tutor other Hungarians in English). Thinking back, perhaps I helped her get some extra money from the state even as she helped me by giving me a room when I had no income to pay for it. There is a certain morality specific to these times, and my impression is that many who lived under the secretive gaze of the state are now left with a troubling sense of what was right and what was wrong.[14]

It took me a good while to come to terms with this surveillance in my personal life. This makes me wonder how people in Eastern Europe will suddenly deal with a system of betrayal whose invisible status has suddenly worn out. In his documentary film, Gazdag is addressing a problem which will be debated for a good long while in both the public and private spheres—in both spheres precisely because such surveillance by the state undermines any attempt to separate the two.

MILUN: Tell me about your department at the theater and film school.

GAZDAG: I'm the head of this department and working now on some fundamental changes. First of all, we have to change the curriculum. Before, the school would train filmmakers only for the Hungarian film industry. And now, since the Hungarian film industry is shrinking and also because all of Europe is becoming a common place, united, I think we have to become more international. I'd like to see Hungarian students prepared for an international market. That way they wouldn't be in trouble working in another country.

MILUN: What does it mean to give an international focus to instruction in film production?

GAZDAG: Well, first of all it means that the students must be exposed to not only Hungarian culture but also to European and international culture. Therefore it will be necessary to invent different courses which are not related to film at all. For example, we are working on a new course which will be called "The History of Storytelling." Many different types of storytelling—from the ancient Greeks to the legends and myths of the American Indians or the South Pacific islanders—will be taught but from the point of view of why a story was told in this particular way and not in another way. We'll look at why a particular historical period created the stories the way it did. I think it's important to include all the possibilities of telling a story because my feeling is that nowadays in films the stories are quite similar to each other.

MILUN: And what is the dominant story form today?

GAZDAG: Today it's the Hollywood three-act structure. For European film-makers there should be a way to find the story form most appropriate to what they intend to tell. So these are the things I would like to do. But on the other hand, since the school's government support is also shrinking, we have to make some money. So part of the school will have to take jobs, filmmaking jobs, which can then be used as examinations or as practice forms for the students. I don't think there's a model for that in the United States. For instance, it's very difficult to teach live broadcasting for television. Since we don't have the equipment for this, some instructors came up with the idea of filming live theatrical productions from the Hungarian stage. There is even someone who is interested in selling videotapes of these theater performances to the Hungarian community in the United States. He would pay all the costs of the broadcasting, the students would direct it and do the lighting and everything else that was necessary. The school would make some money, the students would make some money and they would be able to run something which they otherwise would not be able to do. It could work. In order to do this sort of thing we will need to have people in our film school whose job is to deal with the market. This means a complete reorganization of the school.

MILUN: You're a perfect subject for questions about changes in Hungary because you were living in the States between 1988 and 1991 and experienced the changes so drastically when you returned.

GAZDAG: Yes, I'd been living mostly in Los Angeles, teaching at the film school. I used to subscribe to some Hungarian newspapers and I started watching things change, especially through the ad sections. Suddenly there would appear ads from people wanting to swap apartments from Vienna to Budapest. [The two cities are only three hours apart by car, but for decades Vienna remained the prohibited West.] There were ads in English even soliciting English speakers to work in foreign films. It was absolutely unbelievable and quite obvious that things were changing. The other major thing was that when I returned to Hungary in April of 1991, I suddenly felt that I didn't know the value of money. I couldn't use my evaluation system from before because on the basis of that everything seemed to be so expensive that it would have been impossible to cope. I had no idea, for example, when I was paying for something in a shop, whether it was expensive or cheap. Gradually I got a sense of what values were again. I got my salary and I started to be able to feel the relations. It was also very difficult to cope with the idea of being able to listen to certain things on television. It was just incredible. I mean, you can read that there is no more communism and that there's a different political system. But to see this on television, it was just unbelievable. Not as dramatic an experience as with the money, but still. And I could see that there were a lot more cab companies around town.

In many ways the city had become a lot more colorful. Maybe too colorful. Even before I left I had this feeling that the city was changing. For example, in a tobacco shop you would start to find not only cigarettes but also deodorant sprays. It's so strange. Now, of course, you can go into a tobacco store or even to a bookstore and you can buy whatever you can imagine. I mean, it's like a 7–11.

State-run stores and even the few private ones were well regulated under the old regime. This meant that a flower shop or a shoe store did not have the right to sell things outside that category. There was an expected uniformity to everything. Clearly the legacy of central planning was that everything should be *visibly* in its place. When I first arrived in Budapest in 1979, that was the first thing I saw: an eerie homogeneity—to the untrained eye, that is. For a long time I thought it was due to the fact that the same company [the state] made all the shop signs. Gradually I saw that it was because all the objects were not only stylistically similar but rigorously compartmentalized. This sort of visual control extended to the street life as well. I remember one incident when a young Western street musician tried to set open his guitar case and sing in the main walking street of Budapest in 1981. The police were there in minutes, and though Hungarians on the street protested, the police apologetically replied that such singing in public was illegal without a permit. Thus any spontaneous street life was effectively squelched. "But now it has gone to the opposite extreme," Gazdag said. "It's really become like an Adriatic port where the ships arrive and immediately all the smugglers get out and sell their goods. Yes, since I've been back, I've constantly had the feeling that I live in Dickensian times. Now we have the same extremes as in his times and in his novels. When I was a child I loved Dickens because it was romantic. But it doesn't seem romantic to me now.

Notes

1. This is Rudolf Bahro's phrase to distinguish between utopian theories of socialism from the actual forms socialism had taken in the world.

2. I recall reading somewhere that the Croatian journalist Slavenka Drakulic lecturing in the United States from her book *How We Survived Socialism and Even Laughed,* would generally begin her talk by holding up a sanitary napkin and remarking on the fact that no five-year plan ever produced this useful item.

3. Two or three years ago, more than half of the relatively few people without work were unskilled laborers. The explanation for unemployment at the time accounted for these figures by saying that they were sacrificed to "modernization" which rendered cheap manual labor unnecessary per se. Now that more than half of the unemployed are university and high school graduates this argument appears irrelevant. In Budapest, home to two-and-a-half million Hungarians, the jobless rate is only 2.6 percent, but

in the countryside the average is 25 percent, with villages where nearly 100 percent of the population is unemployed. (*Budapest Week,* 6–12 Feb. 1992, 5).

4. "Magyar" is what Hungarians call themselves. In fact, most countries to the east of Hungary also use some form of the word *Magyar.* Those peoples to the west of present day Hungary, probably due to their encounters with the ancient Huns, refer to Hungarians, as "Ungarnish," "Hongrois," "Ungherese," and so on.

5. Bands always needed official permits to play in communist Hungary. Obviously this was one way of controlling the underground scene.

6. In *L'erotisme,* Bataille's concern with the experience of ecstasy and its connection to self-empowerment has some striking similarities to Grandpierre's project. For Bataille, ecstasy is generally the experience of transgressing a cultural taboo, an experience of a self which has pushed beyond its socially sanctioned limits. As Bataille describes it, human beings experiment with the experience of death—an experience of radical discontinuity with the living, social world—in their erotic play. In fact we invent this form of play, Bataille argues, precisely in order to have a form of self-knowledge which is outside the scope offered by language-mediated knowledge. In doing so, we are seeking to know something about powerful inarticulable experiences, the most looming of which is death. The name of Grandpierre's band, the Galloping Coroners, certainly suggests a group that deals with death. But the bands focus on music which leads to an experience of ecstasy demonstrates that their more general concern is with the outer limits of human experience, especially when the scope of experience can be so thoroughly limited by state ideologies. Such ecstatic experience, Grandpierre argues in his theoretical work, is thus a self-empowering move which he links to a new understanding of sovereignty. (The English translation of Bataille's work *L'erotisme* makes the connection between ecstasy and death more explicit: *Death and Sensuality: A Study of Erotism and the Taboo.*) Further comparisons could be drawn between Grandpierre's project and the work of certain post-structuralist theorists who seek to salvage the domain of unspeakable experience from the tyranny of a society which privileges both language and reason. See Agamben 1989.

7. In his book on the political economy of music, Jacques Attali describes music's function as a "herald," for change, he writes, "is inscribed in noise faster than it transforms society." Music does not just reflect society, according to Attali, it also "foreshadows new social movements in a prophetic and annunciatory way" (i). In listening to a "musical deep voice," Grandpierre works with a similar acoustic temporality.

8. Even though it had no possibility of being recorded and distributed officially, music that was not sanctioned by the state had other means of circulating in communist Hungary. One of the most important ways is described by Grandpierre here: "illegal" concerts would be taped by someone and then cassettes would begin making their rounds and proliferating. This is the musical equivalent of samizdat publishing.

9. Béla Bartók, Hungary's prized composer, died in 1945 in New York where he fled in 1940 from fascist Hungary. See Susan Gal's excellent piece on the symbolic function of this event.

10. This is no exaggeration. I was unpleasantly shocked going back this time to see pornographic magazines everywhere on the streets. Strip joints advertised everywhere, things one would never have seen two years before.

11. The Hungarian title, *Sipolo Macskako,* was originally translated as *The Whistling Cobblestone.* As will be clear in what follows, a better translation would have been *The Cobblestone Trinket.*

12. See Kinzer's article, in which he interviews former East German citizens who have been reading their files and discovering that friends and spouses were in fact spying on them.

13. I politely passed on the joints offered me and a few months later heard a story about a Westerner who had been taken to a similar party and was photographed smoking hashish. These photos were later presented to her by the Hungarian police and she was given the option of doing a little informing or facing court proceedings. She informed.

14. It is important to note that an American student in Eastern Europe during this period was most probably being tracked not only by the KGB. In my case, the CIA also took advantage of my naiveté. For example, in my second month of study in Hungary I received a request from the head of the office of foreign students at the University of Minnesota—the office that administered my scholarship—to make contact with a certain person from the Office of Cultural Affairs at the U.S. Embassy in Budapest. I was actually told that the scholarship would be discontinued unless I spoke to this man. He turned out to be working for the CIA and wanted to help me earn a little extra money that year. Although I did not know it at the time, scholarships like mine to Eastern Europe came from the State Department. There was only one stipulation attached: after returning from study abroad, scholarship recipients were asked to write a report of what they did, where they studied, and so on. It is well known that this was one way the U.S. gathered the intelligence that helped engineer the coup in Chile in 1973; they sent a flood of American students there on one-year scholarships. These reports helped the intelligence agency get an "internal" map of the country, a reading on the political sensibility of university professors and departments, and so on.

References
Agamben, Giorgio. 1989. *Enfance et histoire: Dépérissement de l'expérience et origine del'histoire.* Trans. Yves Hersant, Paris: Éditions Payot.

Attali, Jacques. 1985. *Noise: The Political Economy of Music.* Trans. Brian Massumi. Minneapolis: University of Minnesota Press.

Bahro, Rudolf. 1978. *The Alternative in Eastern Europe.* Trans. David Fernbach, London: NLB.

Bataille, Georges. 1958. *L'érotisme.* Paris: Éditions de Minuit; [Trans. 1962 under the title *Death and Sensuality: A Study of Eroticism and the Taboo.* (no translator given) New York, Walker & Co.]

Benjamin, Walter. 1986. *Illuminations.* Trans. Harry Zohn. New York: Schocken Books.

Budapest Week. 6–12 Feb. 1992, p. 5.

Budapest Week. 4 Mar.–27 Feb. 1992, p. 4.

Gal, Susan. 1991. "Bartók's Funeral: Representations of Europe in Hungarian Political Rhetoric." *American Ethnologist* 18: 440–59.

Grandpierre, Attila. 1984. "A Punk rock összefümégel a sámán-zenével mint népzenével: a müvézet magikus eröinek hatásmechanizmusa" (Punk rock's connection to shamanistic music as a folk music; the mechanical force of art's magical powers). *Uj Világ*. Budapest: Eötvös Lorent University.

Hankiss, Elemer. 1988. "The Second Society: Is There an Alternative Social Model Emerging in Contemporary Hungary?" *Social Research* 55.

Kinzer, Stephen. 1992. "East Germans Face Their Accusers." *New York Times Magazine*. 13 Apr., pp. 24–52.

Laber, Jeri. 1992. "Witch Hunt in Prague." *New York Review of Books*. 23 Apr.

Lukács, György. 1971. *History and Class Consciousness: Studies in Marxist Dialectics*. Trans. Rodney Livingstone. Cambridge, Mass.: MIT Press.

Marx, Karl. 1977. *Capital*. Vol 1. Trans. Ben Fowkes. New York: Vintage Books.

Milun, Kathryn. 1992. "Hungarian Rock Music and Nationalism: A Shaman's Headdress for the New Hungarian Flag." *Surfaces*. Montreal: Presse de l'Université de Montréal.

Taussig, Michael 1987. *Shamanism, Colonialism, and the Wildman: A Study in Terror and Healing*. Chicago: University of Chicago Press.

SIX TO EIGHT CHARACTERS IN SEARCH OF ARMENIAN CIVIL SOCIETY AMIDST THE CARNIVALIZATION OF HISTORY

1. Note: Leninakan and Yerevan, December 1991

Instead of an audacious, romantic nation, we must become a cold, realistic and pragmatic nation whose each step must be circumspect, based on concrete and faultless calculation . . . We must create direct connections with our neighbors such as Iran and Turkey . . . It is in this region that we must survive . . . the Middle East, the Caucasus, the Black Sea basin, the southern regions of Russia and Ukraine will be our larger economic and political region. This will be our economic and political geopolitics.

—President Levon Ter-Petrossian

Revolutionary processes are always buffeted by both internal and external dynamics. While the democratic movement is the focus of these interviews, the specter of war with Azerbaijan over Nagorno-Karabakh hovers constantly. A major population exchange on the order of three hundred thousand people from each side had already occurred between Azerbaijan and Armenia with all the attendant physical, emotional, economic, political, psychological and symbolic-ideological traumas of killings and atrocities. December 1991 was still a moment of hope: Azerbaijan had cut off gas supplies to Armenia, and the economy was grinding to a halt, but the government of Armenia was determined to break the mold of past demonization of "the Turks" and to find accommodations with its neighbors, including, if possible, with the still-unstable government of Azerbaijan. By summer 1992 when Azerbaijan had retaken a number of villages in Nagorno-Karabakh, there was increasing pressure upon the government of President Levon Ter-Petrossian to declare Nagorno-Karabakh's independence and to ignore the danger that such a declaration might draw Turkey into the conflict against Armenia. Ter-Petrossian resisted. It is such resistance, and the search for negotiating partners, that this paper honors.

The sensitivity of Armenian-Turkic relations is such that some readers have complained that we have not given sufficient attention to the Azerbaijani side. But this paper is not an account of Armenian-Turkic conflicts; it is an account of the internal transformations of Armenia, based entirely upon interviews with Armenian leaders of the transition at several levels of society. We have very strong feelings of regard for both Turkic speakers and Armenians, and the nasty fighting between them is a matter for great sorrow and one for negotiation, not for the idle taking of sides.

We interviewed six leaders, three former communists and three intellectuals from the leadership of the independent democratic movement. They are six of our "characters"; we, of course, are two more; anthropologist Levon Abrahamian, through his writings, provides a ninth voice in the following text; and anthropologist Haroutian Maroutian, who helped us with one of the interviews, provided access to the visual materials used by, and now documents of, the democratic movement. We attempt to weave a braided structure in the following essay: introduction, three interviews, a second analytic section, three more interviews, and an analytic recap. The three analytic commentaries focus respectively on the historical trajectory, revolutionary processes, and local-global positioning.

The Intellectuals
    Levon Ter-Petrossian, the president, orientalist
    Hambartsoom Galstian the mayor of Yerevan, anthropologist
    Rouben Shugarian, foreign affairs aide to the president, art historian
The Former Communists
    Karlen Hambartsumian, the mayor or Work Committee head of Leninakan
    Hanoush Hacopian, member of Parliament and former *Komosomol* head
    Rouben Durian, vice minister of construction, civil engineer

2. Ritual Prologue: A Break in the Carnivalization of History?

the tight-rope walker/dancer [*Seiltänzer*] had begun his work. . . .
Just as he was in the middle of his course, the little door opened
again and a brightly dressed fellow like a buffoon sprang out and
followed the former with rapid steps. "Forward, lame-foot, he cried
in a terrible voice, forward sluggard, creeper, pallid-face! . . . The
market square and the people were like the sea when a storm comes
in: all flew apart and over one one another.
                    —Friedrich Nietzsche, *Also Sprach Zarathustra*

It is as though we are looking at a kaleidoscope, composed of fragments of historical revolutions . . . themselves composed of pages ripped at random from the various pages of a history textbook.
                    —Levon A. Abrahamian

One hesitates to see Mikhail Gorbachev and Boris Yeltsin as Nietzsche's two tightrope dancers, Yeltsin vaulting over Gorbachev, causing the latter to lose his balance and plunge to his (political) demise. Zarathustra comforts the dying man, assuring him that there is no hell to fear in an afterlife, and more importantly that the lack of an afterlife does not mean that his life was a meaningless animal existence, like that of a Russian dancing bear ("not much more than an animal which has been taught to dance by blows and starvation").[1] Zarathustra honors him for daring to dedicate his calling/occupation [*Beruf*] to danger, for being willing to perish in its demands.

But a comment by Armenian anthropologist Levon Abrahamian both brings Nietzsche's scene into ethnographic focus and reminds us of the preliminary analytic power that a ritual analysis may deliver for thinking through the ambivalent turmoil of the "Last Days of the Soviet Union" (Karl Krauss, like Nietzsche, can help us appreciate the intertextuality of the two fin-de-siècles of the nineteenth and twentieth centuries).[2] Abrahamian meditates on the dualisms—carnivalesque inversions, symbolic ambivalences or bringing of contradiction into the open, and competition between repetitive versus restructuring outcomes—encoded in the ritual structures employed by societies in times of crisis. He illustrates with both his brilliant Bakhtinian caricatures of the Soviet past and his analyses of the theatricalization of the demonstrations in Theater Square[3] in Yerevan during the 1988 nine-month (February to November) gestation, or first phase, of the present revolutionary process. To set the stage, like Nietzsche, he reminds us of the tightrope walkers who used to be public entertainers:

> In Armenia today, it may be discerned in performances of the last traditional tightrope walkers, when the Father, or rope-walking hero, takes his place above, on the rope, while at the bottom, often on the shadow of the rope, the Son or helper-fool, a shadow of a hero, ineptly imitates him. Interestingly, the foolish helper often reverses top and bottom, literally standing on his head. It is also noteworthy that in life he is generally a former rope-walker, not uncommonly the father of the young hero enthroned above. [Abrahamian 1990b:62]

Hero-Jester (the same reversible structure is used in rodeos, that ritual of transformation from the skills of craftsmen-cowboys and matadors facing death to industrialized ranching and show business, where hero is amateur and clown is professional) is also the pair in the carnival rites of dethronement analyzed by Mikhail Bakhtin for Europe and by Max Gluckman and Victor Turner for Africa.

Abrahamian wants us to pay attention to the fact that in such rites there are often competing scripts, that the outcome is not certain: in the traditional rites, the king-hero is debased temporarily in a rite that vents built-up antagonisms and theatricalizes the categories and divisions of society, but then rein-

Ter-Petrosian addresses the crowd with his back to the last Communist leadership.

SEIZURE OF

stalls the king and the social structure of authority. However, rites can get out of hand, they can become "happenings," they can in the play of the liminal or carnival period of the rite restructure the elements of society so that what comes out of the rite is something new, not the old structure. These latter are what often come to be called revolutions, which in turn have been analyzed both for their symbolic structures which, although drawing from the past, mobilize people in very new ways, and for their underlying social structural processes that can explain the shifts in social power that make the outcomes novel.

Abrahamian's own quip should be read as one on the ways in which revolutions are immersed in history, drawing lessons, "borrowing disguises and languages," adapting tactics and avoiding mistakes from predecessors, but also set within "world-historical time" so that no contemporary revolution could be just a replay of a past revolution.[4] Karl Marx noted that nineteenth-century revolutions were quite different structurally from eighteenth-century bourgeois revolutions, although they borrowed slogans from the latter (as well as from classical times); he and Engels eventually described the failed 1848 revolution in Paris as a death knell of the revolutionary tactics of preindustrial working classes (a point more recently amplified by William Sewell). The so-

Last Communist leadership on dais.

SYMBOLIC POWER
Lenin Square, 7 November 1988

Crowd turns its back on the last Communist leadership.

called peasant or Maoist revolutions of the midtwentieth century (China, Vietnam, Naxilites in India) take on a different form, one quite different from the self-styled "dictatorship of the proletariat" or Bolshevik revolution of the USSR, although they claimed to draw upon the same Marxist inspiration. At the end of the twentieth century, beginning in the penultimate decade with the Islamic revolution of Iran (which continues to reverberate through countries with majority Muslim populations),[5] and definitively in the final decade with the collapse of the Soviet Empire, a new form of revolution is emerging, one that draws upon so-called social movements built around successive moments of ecological, democratic, and economic focus, albeit still bedevilled and leveraged with violent nationalist fantasies.[6]

Armenia provides a particularly vivid example of the stages of this emergent form, an emergence that anthropologist Abrahamian, who is also a political cartoonist, beautifully caricatures in one of the images he contributed to the Theater Square posters and visual tools of the Armenian struggle.[7] The scene is of a woman barber (Russia), who cannot fly, clipping the wings of a little bird whose feathers are the tricolors of Armenia, so that it cannot join the free-flying birds of the Baltic republics and Eastern Europe.

All of the republics of the former Soviet Union have clipped wings, as is noted repeatedly in the interviews below, above all because of the imperial divide-and-rule way the Soviet Empire "integrated" the economies of the republics with suppliers in far distant places, but also because of the divide-and-rule politics of the Soviet Empire which devastatingly exacerbated instead of calming the conflicts between Armenia and Azerbaijan when the autonomous oblast of Nagorno-Karabakh tested the constitution of the USSR under *perestroika* by voting to secede from Azerbaijan and join Armenia. This was the first major democratic test of *perestroika*. Unlike Lithuania, which tested the Soviet Empire by declaring secession from the empire (invoking their illegal incorporation into the Soviet Union in the first place), Armenians in Karabakh and in Armenia (who also were incorporated into the Russian and Soviet empires by force) opted to press within the Soviet constitutional structure for redress, reminding the Soviet center as well of promises in the 1920s by both Stalin and the Baku Soviet that Karabakh would be placed under Armenian jurisdiction; President Ter-Petrossian, two days after the referendum on independence, and one day after the Armenian Parliament's unanimous vote to declare sovereignty outside the Soviet Union, even signed an accord with Azerbaijan agreeing to negotiate in preference to fighting.[8] (Soviet clumsiness in regard to this issue has now been repeated in Checheno-Ingushetia and Tataristan, and threatens other areas as well.) The Soviets backed up the blockage of natural gas and food supplies through Azerbaijan to Armenia through much of 1991, stood by as Azerbaijan continued to shell Stepanakert, the capital of Karabakh, and did little to prevent the stirring-up

Dessin de Lévon Abrahamian.

Soviet barber clips the wings of the newly independent republics; still, they fly away. Cartoon by Levon Abrahamian.

of nationalist antagonisms that led to massacres of Armenians at Sumgait and Baku, and then to major population transfers between Armenia and Azerbaijan (some two to three hundred thousand refugees coming to Armenia from their homes in Azerbaijan); three years ago a half million Armenians lived in Azerbaijan and almost as many Azarbaijanis lived in Armenia, today there are virtually no Azerbaijanis in Armenia and only one hundred thousand Armenians remain (in the autonomous oblast of Karabakh) in Azerbaijan.[9]

Armenia privatized agriculture immediately with a resultant immediate improvement in harvests, and moved relatively easily toward a new democracy, but it remains clipped-winged by the economic blocks to industrial privatization and reorganization of governmental spending, among which are the lack of fuel to run any industry at the moment, and the closure of the two major revenue-producing industries for reasons of ecological safety: the huge synthetic rubber chemical plant at Nayirit (the only such plant in the former USSR, and one of twelve such plants globally); and the Medzamor nuclear power plant which used to sell energy for hard currency to Turkey, but which is of the same dangerous design as the Chernobyl plant.[10]

Interlude: Abrahamian on Three Eras of Carnivalization of Russian and Soviet History

Archaic forms of carnival. In the old days, Russian czars Ivan the Terrible and Peter the Great practiced comic "rituals of reversal" both to assert their political functions and because they enjoyed the masquerade: "Having passed through purgative rituals, having purified himself through laughter (it's not accidental that laughter is an essential part of any carnival performance), the Czar-Father emerges even more powerful and wise, and the society in his custody becomes even more tenacious."

Soviet forms of carnival. If Stalin engaged in such play, it was only among his entourage. The carnivalization of history began in earnest only with the death of the Father (Stalin) and the advent of his jester Son-Fool (Khrushchev):

Khrushchev:

> It is said that, during the the nightly gatherings at [Stalin's] dacha at Kuntsevo, Khrushchev would dance the *hopak* [a peasant dance]. It is possible that Khrushchev at this time was acting the fool to win the trust of the Father, but . . . he maintained this remarkable quality during the entire epoch of the Son, when there was no longer any point in dissembling . . . [Even his appearance fit the role:] he was over sixty, yet he seemed very strong, agile, and jolly to the point of mischief. His broad face with two warts and enormous bald skull, large snub nose, and protruding ears might easily have belonged to a peasant from a central Russian village. This impression . . . was strengthened by a solid corpulent body and long arms which were almost constantly gesticulating . . . [His behavior fit, too:] he changed the places of the low and the high: he slammed his shoe (a low object) on the rostrum of the world's supreme forum (the topmost object); he conferred the supreme title of Hero on "low" people; he himself climbed on top of the mausoleum and thus made himself stand above the Father; moreover, he toppled the Father from his ritual pharaoh-style visible immortality down into the invisible moral grave. Let us also note the vulgar and mysterious "give them their gruel" uttered from high podiums, and Khrushchev's thoughtless policy of growing corn everywhere, . . . his campaign to chemicalize [*khimizatsiia*] the country mocking Lenin's campaign of electrification, not forgetting that *khimichit* has an additional meaning, *mudrit* [making too complex].

According to the logic of the carnival, the Jester-Czar must be replaced with the Father-Czar. So the Brezhnev epoch came . . .

However, the Son was succeeded not by a True Father, but by a substitute . . . a False Czar, an Impostor. For the first time, perhaps, the False Father was a real cartoon image of the Father. Whereas the Father wrote volumes, the False Father authored only three booklets (in fact, he didn't write even those). Whereas the former fought for and won the Big Land, the latter fought only for a Little Land [Afghanistan]. The former had a foreign accent, and the latter had a speech defect. The famous mustache of the Father had a cartoonlike analogue in the False Father: the equally famous eyebrows. A joke demonstrates the relationship: at a meeting in the intimate circles of the Politburo, Brezhnev takes off his eyebrows, attaches them beneath his nose and begins speaking with a Georgian accent. Even the Impostor's birthday was a bit earlier (19 December) than the birthday of the Father (21 December).

After a False Father there must always be a Real Father. Perhaps, this Father was Andropov (let's remind ourselves about his first mass-scale minirepressions against the violators of work discipline). However his rule was too short to be given the status of a historical epoch. His rule didn't give rise to anecdotes or result in a mythology . . . The next ruler, Chernenko, left even less of a trace in history.

Perestroika Carnival: Gorbachev

Now we are living through the *perestroika* epoch, the nature of which will be reflected in a mythological image of its leader . . . and we are witnessing the setting-in of a pattern where, as was the case in ancient times, the ruler combines in his person both the Father and the Son, the Czar and Jester . . . On the one hand, [Gorbachev] is simple and common, easily mixes with the people. Besides, he has a certain carnivallike zest which makes him akin to Khrushchev, though not as colorful . . . On the other hand . . . combined with an apparent sign: a birthmark on the forehead, resembling a heavenly sign marking the future king, an attribute of the Junior Son in fairy tales. A certain duality manifests itself in the circumstance that the birthmark gets carefully painted over on official photographs but is a special feature on cartoons.

Many people saw a real threat of the return of the Father in the recent rushed election of Gorbachev as the country's president . . . Many signs of a reckless Son-Merrymaker [on the other hand] can be seen in the structure of Gorbachev's policy of democratization and *glasnost* which generally carries many signs of a carnival and a strikingly similar in pattern to archaic festivals. Even the words making up the . . . triad—*glasnost*, democratization, *perestroika*—form the familiar pattern of transition from chaos into cosmos. The root of the Russian word *glasnost*—*glas* [voice]—implies a message aimed at the avid listener, rather than some impartial freedom of speech. Significantly, the Armenian equivalent of the notion of *glasnost* is a derivative of the word meaning "city square," which is exactly where people came out to celebrate the feast of glasnost, just as they used to hold a carnival back in the middle ages . . . The slogan promoting "acceleration" was a logical continuation of the festival of the Stakhanovite movement . . . However, this slogan was quickly committed to oblivion following the explosion at the ill-starred Chernobyl power station which had been built with "acceleration."

After some frantic search in the realm of mythology, a holiday was announced which symbolized a ritual chaos from which cosmos was supposed to miraculously appear. The holiday was called in all spheres, including the economy. But a holiday in the economy means the destruction of the latter.

Gorbachev arrived in Leninakan devastated by an earthquake and announced that the city would be rebuilt within two years. It reminds one of a fairy tale where the Junior Son undertakes to build a city overnight, hoping to be aided by some miraculous agents . . . Architects were immediately found who ruined centuries old ploughland to build new prefab blocks of flats. [Abrahamian 1990a, 1990c]

Despite the relatively desperate objective plight of the country: the clipped-wing little birds are still delighted to fly away. (Another of the cartoons from Theater Square shows a former prisoner running away from his cage, but his body has been cut into disconnected pieces by running through the bars of the cage in the process of escape. See also the black humor of Mayor Galstian in the interview below.[11])

The stages of revolution that brought about the final demise of the Soviet Union are worth interrogating in order to get a sense of the emergent new forms of revolution (see section 4).

3. Personnel from the Old Regime

A. *Guess Who, You Know Who—Harnush Hacopian*[12]

One of eight women in the 260-member Armenian parliament,[13] Hacopian received us in the refectory underneath the parliament, a good place to meet and watch other members of Parliament. (For instance, the minister of trade stopped by our table to joke, "Excuse me, she is my lover: according to *Vozni* ["Porcupine," a satirical journal], we've been seen dancing together." They briefly discuss the fact that he is still a member of Parliament and must step down from it and from chairing the important Finance Committee. A little later the chair of the Social Welfare Committee, an economist, stopped by and we briefly interviewed him about the role of economists in the new government and the availability of trustworthy statistics: those from the 1920s

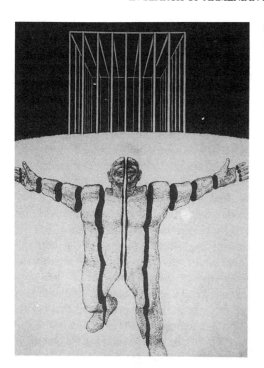

Cut apart in the process of escaping the Soviet cage.

were fairly good quality, the later ones were more corrupt, but those who sift through them can recognize the patterns and degree of biases.) Overhead the loudspeakers let us keep track of proceedings on the floor, and Hacopian would pause from time to time in our conversation to pay attention to the names being proposed as deputy speaker, and to comment on why each was proposed with the sureness of a practiced pol. She freely discussed the transformation of the political system and how she, as a very visible communist leader, has survived as well as her liabilities; for instance, she lost out to a noncommunist for the chair of the Social Welfare Committee: "In the election for committee chair, I came in second to him because the communist members were afraid to stand up for themselves and he was from the *Harasha* (All-Armenia Movement)." When we showed her picture to Russian emigré friends in the United States several reacted strongly as if they could read in her face the evils of the past and they dismissed a government that could still retain such figures. But as she points out, not only was the Party, after all, an ordinary route of being active in society under the communist state, but her own family has had a checkered career often running afoul of the Party, mirroring the uncertainties of individuals, families, and nationalities under the shifting demands of the Soviet regime. She is used to being challenged: in

1988 she visited Houston as part of a delegation of cosmonauts to the Johnson Space Center, and was whisked away by local young Armenians and subjected to hours of intense grilling. She studied mathematics in school and taught computer programming at the university for nine years, by which time she was already important in the *Komsomol* organization.

HACOPIAN: There are no real parties functioning yet. Fifty-one percent of eligible voters must vote for an election to be deemed valid. This is a passive rule, and it would be better just to have those who are politically active voting, so this rule was removed for the presidential election. In that election, 78 percent of eligible voters participated.

FISCHER/GRIGORIAN: What constituency do you represent?

HACOPIAN: Kamo, near Lake Sevan: five villages with a population of eleven thousand. Seven thousand five hundred voted, 6,800 for me. I had two opponents, one a judge-lawyer and one a factory director. I was born in Kamo, and as head of *Komsomol* was well known throughout the republic. I had been in the political arena for ten years, as an old senator in the previous parliament, elected in 1985. (There are about seventy people from the old parliament left in the new one. One of these is also a woman; she was head of the Party.) So I did not need to introduce myself in the election.

FISCHER/GRIGORIAN: Wasn't your past role in the Communist Party and *Komsomol* a reason for people to have voted against you?

HACOPIAN: In May 1990 when I was reelected, the communist leadership was still in place. Levon Ter-Petrossian had campaigned already for a year against that leadership. And during 1989–90 I had begun to recognize that *Komsomol* could no longer hold a monopoly on youth organizations, that it would be dissolved and many organizations would emerge. In August 1990 there was already campaigning against Leninism, against communism, and against *Komsomol* as the sole youth organization. The struggle against us was tremendous. *Harasha* supported the lawyer in the election campaign against me. But the issues of Karabakh, of the earthquake, and of the process of democratization were major activities for the young communists. These three things were the reason that they couldn't strike home against *Komsomol*, because we were doing concrete work. We mobilized to send people to the earthquake region. I could spend hours telling you about these activities. At the All-Union Congress of *Komsomol*, I gave a speech on Karabakh in the Politiburo of *Komsomol*. The Azerbaijani delegate kept disrupting me. His disruptions and my answers were carried in the newspapers. This had a major impact in Armenia, so I never had any doubts about my election chances.

I only went to Kamo two or three times before the election. Now, as a deputy and by law, I go one to two times a month to meet with constituents.

I announce in the papers when I will be there and available to meet with people, the days and times I will visit each village. It's usually three days each time, and usually on the weekends (because people have to work during the week). I'm on the health and social welfare committee in Parliament which keeps me very busy: the constituents are very tense and their nerves are wound up because of the energy crisis and the inflation of prices.

We discussed the reorganization of the political system at the city level and its relation to the state. Hacopian pointed to four issues. First, the old Soviet system claimed to have separation of legislative and administrative bodies, but in practice these were merged in the municipal or regional *Gortskom* [workers' director or mayor]. At the state level this separation has already been effected: Ter-Petrossian is president, Babken Ararktsian is head of Parliament. But cities like Yerevan and Leninakan still have single executive officers who also perform legislative functions. Second, there should be, in a small republic like Armenia, only one legislative body. Third, the *Gortskom* is still elected by the soviet, and should be elected through direct elections. A rationalized version of the present system would properly be something like the prefectural system of France, where the president picks representatives in different regions. Hacopian thinks this the best system, but the present parliament would block it, if only because thirty *Gortskom* leaders are in the parliament. Fourth, parties need to develop. She disagreed with the *Gortskom* of Leninakan, who had suggested to us that a mayoral system might emerge with the privatization of industry and the development of independent interest groups that a mayor would adjudicate among. Hacopian believes that change will come rather from rearrangement of political power, that economic pressures have a secondary force since all enterprises must conform to the laws of the state, for example, in regard to taxes as an instrument of shaping the political economy.

The eight member Social Welfare Committee, on which she serves, has been looking especially at French and American laws on mother and child protection, maternity leave, pensions, unemployment compensation, and so on. Under the Soviet system, there was said to be no unemployment, so no welfare funds existed. In this and other areas, the new laws are much more liberal than under the Soviet system.

FISCHER/GRIGORIAN: How are committee assignments made?

HACOPIAN: Parliament decides what committees to establish, and how many . . . There are sixteen committees. One can serve on only one committee. It is a permanent position; one gets paid one's salary through being on a committee. One hundred fifteen deputies are members. There are also special ad hoc committees. Some deputies also work as mayors and so are not on committees.

FISCHER/GRIGORIAN: Can you explain the dispute over the election-appointment Ararktsian as Speaker of Parliament.

HACOPIAN: When Ter-Petrossian became president, Ararktsian was his deputy speaker. Ter-Petrossian told Parliament—after they could not agree on his successor—that he thought Ararktsian should succeed. The opposition said it was not right for the president to tell Parliament what to do, but I think he has a perfect right to say what he wants. In any case, yesterday Parliament voted 136 votes to confirm Ararktsian as speaker.

FISCHER/GRIGORIAN: Is there a feminist movement?

HACOPIAN: No, not in the Western sense. There's a women's advisory council, left over from the communist days. It was established by Gorbachev for Raisa. It had branches in factories and work places; before there was only an All-Union association.

FISCHER/GRIGORIAN: What are the two or three most important enterprises that generate revenue for the state?

HACOPIAN: Nayirit, of course—the mistake was to close it—and Alaverdi (chemical plants). It should be made more ecologically sound, not closed. Then second, the atomic power plant which was stupidly closed. If we hadn't closed the plant we wouldn't be in this energy crisis. Third, the hydroelectric plant that produces generators and is the largest employer with ten thousand workers. The director was the first secretary of the Communist Party, and a smart man. Nayarit was a monopoly and sold in dollars. Before it can be fully on-line again it should be made ecologically safe, but it should be opened.

FISCHER/GRIGORIAN: Did the atomic power plant sell energy to Turkey?

HACOPIAN: Yes, to both Turkey and Azerbaijan. Shutting it did not make it any less dangerous if, say, there is an earthquake. The uranium is still there. I agree with the president's policies. On 20 October 1990 at the All-Union Congress, the name of *Komsomol* was changed and it was the end of *Komsomol*. But before that, in August, I had already been elected M.P. I am in complete agreement with the leadership, with the President Ter Petrossian's politics. In February the process for independence was first set up and I was one of the main proindependence debaters. In August, Levon [Ter-Petrossian] was in Moscow and said, "The Center has died," and I agreed. To save the economy, the new agreement is the best thing; look at Georgia! One of the main complaints of the opposition in Georgia is that Gamsakhurdia is not signing the Alma Alta agreement. We may be politically independent, but our economies are integrated, there are friendships and cultural ties; one cannot just erase three hundred years.

FISCHER/GRIGORIAN: Is there fear that experienced personnel will be lost in the reaction against the communists?

HACOPIAN: In the beginning the fear was great. Unfortunately, there were communist leaders who were bad, and this reflected on others who were also ousted. But others are recognized as experienced and good people. Khosrow Harootunian, who was just nominated upstairs as Deputy Speaker, was a member of the Communist Party, as was Vice President Gagi Harootunian, who was head of the economic division in the Party. As we go on, attitudes are changing: what is cared for is education and experience. Personally, before, people looked at me as an enemy, but now we're relatives. I try to do what will be good. I will follow whoever is right: I'm not a Party member now, I'm resting from all that. I was devoted; I loved and believed in what I was doing. I was so devoted that my eyes were closed in a way. I could not see certain things, if millions were stolen.

FISCHER/GRIGORIAN: Do you now believe the accusations?

HACOPIAN: Some of them, yes. I could not have known certain of the things. Some I wasn't in a position to know, and many were done secretly. But another ideology has not yet been born better than communism. I mean the values of equality, brotherhood, justice. No other, better ideology exists. As a young person, I believed and devoted myself. It is different from the corruption and misuse of the ideology. Communism didn't survive; it was built wrong economically.

FISCHER/GRIGORIAN: Could it be done otherwise, to achieve the goals of the ideology?

HACOPIAN: Only if there is a strong economy, a good standard of living. Only after these are secured can people pay attention to the humanitarian and benevolent goals.

FISCHER/GRIGORIAN: Are you from an old communist family?

HACOPIAN: My father was a philosopher, my mother director of a school. Both were in the Party. My brother was a top-level person in industry and became a regional director of the Party. One sister is a historian and is not a communist. Another sister is an engineer and is a communist. Remember, there was only one Party and all those who were active were in it. If you were normal, worked well, and were not in the Communist Party, it was strange. In my fourth year at university I was elected into the Party, and I became head of *Komsomol*. Through those means, I was active and could do something. It was the only mechanism to do active work; there was not a multiparty structure.

FISCHER/GRIGORIAN: How about at the time of the revolution?

HACOPIAN: In the 1920s my grandfather was accused of being Dashnak [a party outlawed by the Communists] simply because he was from the area of Nazdeh (the famous guerrilla). For years, they oppressed my father for being the son of a Dashnaki; now they are pressing us because we were communist. Ter-Petrossian doesn't look at party affiliation. I worked with him, he knows me, he's for those who are just.

B. Caught in Between: Vice Minister of Construction Durian

Durian was in Iran in 1982–83 as part of a Soviet construction team building a power plant in Esfahan. His eyes lift up with animated memories. The team comprised some three hundred Soviets, thirty of whom were Armenians. The job was done like international development projects everywhere, including the aid to Armenia after the earthquake from it's fraternal Soviet republics: it was cheaper and easier to bring in everything from the Soviet Union except sand; and the team members developed condescending attitudes about the locals. The other Soviets were not allowed to mix with the local population because there were so many Afghan refugees in the city, and there was fear that they would attempt to kidnap or kill Soviets. Each evening after work, the Soviets were allowed to go to the shops along the street for fifteen minutes, but then they had to go in. The Armenians, however, looked like Iranians and so were free to go where they liked. There were several Armenian construction firms in Esfahan, and Durian socialized with their owners. It was the time of the Iran-Iraq War. Esfahan was being bombed by Soviet-built Iraqi MIGs. Iran was firing back with Soviet-built missiles. "We sold to both sides, and there I was caught in the middle." The contract required the Soviets to hire five Iranians for each Soviet: it was a time of high unemployment in Iran. "Armenians and Iranians are brothers: same blood. They've been Muslims only for thirteen centuries, and we've been Christian for only seventeen centuries. Before that we were all the same. One day the minister of energy paid a visit to our office. He did not realize I spoke Persian, and he commented to one of the other Iranians, 'That fellow looks just like us.' So I said in Persian, 'Maybe it's you who looks like us: I'm Armenian.'" Durian concluded that Armenia should forge strong ties with Iran. His sentiments are seconded in the interviews with Galstian and Ter-Petrossian below.

C. "The Adjustor"—Mayor of Leninakan, Karlen Hambartsumian[14]

Karlen is one of those Soviet names composed of *Karl* (Marx) plus *Len*(in). Other such names include *Melsik* (the acronym of *Marx, Engels, Lenin,* and *Stalin*), *Lendrosh* (*Lenin* plus *darosh,* "flag"; originally Lentrosh for Lenin, Trotsky, and Shaumain, the leader of Baku), and the feminine *Ninel* (Lenin spelled backwards). We met Hambartsumian in his office in the temporary city hall, a building composed of metal boxes [*domiks*] brought in after the earthquake as temporary buildings, stacked in a two-story row, and referred to locally as "the labyrinth." There was, of course, no heat, and we all sat in our overcoats watching the steam of our words and breathing.

FISCHER/GRIGORIAN: Tell us about the economy here now after the political changes. For instance, the big textile mill of Leninakan under the Soviet economic system was supplied with its cotton from Kazakhstan. The earthquake destroyed the mill, and it is being rebuilt. But is it being rebuilt differently, and will its supply and marketing be different?

HAMBARTSUMIAN: The old ties have been cut. In the old system, the ties with Kazakhstan were arranged through special funds, and allocation was done centrally. Now all such relations must be based on mutual agreement. They send cotton, we send manufactured goods like irons for pressing clothes. They've been raising the price of their cotton, so we have had to raise prices too. Such ties are not at the beginning stages. Negotiations will not be at the plant level, but at the national level, through the national Armenian government.

FISCHER/GRIGORIAN: Tell us if there has been a change in the personnel running the city. Are they, as in Yerevan, intellectuals, members of the Karabakh or All-Armenia Movement?

HAMBARTSUMIAN: They are mainly young; a few older ones are left. No, it's not like the government in Yerevan. One vice mayor was in the All-Armenia Movement, but otherwise not. The people in city government here were in positions of power in the local region.

FISCHER/GRIGORIAN: Tell us about your own background.

HAMBARTSUMIAN: I was the head of a factory. It was the compressor factory; it collapsed in the earthquake. I also have been vice mayor for the last eight years. I have been elected twice since the quake. The first time it was more by appointment, but the second time I was elected.

FISCHER/GRIGORIAN: Were there opponents in the elections, platforms?

HAMBARTSUMIAN: Yes, there were eight opponents. Sure, there were platforms, but we are not really that far to have real platforms. It is mainly he who is best known who gets elected. We still need to develop democratic understanding among the people. Actually, my title is not *mayor;* technically I am the head of the Committee for Work. Moscow has a mayor. I was selected by deputies (or city councillors) over three days: on the first day I got sixty-one votes, and then on the third day I got eighty-one deputies' votes. I need seventy-five. There are 150 deputies or city councillors. The system in the past was like this, too. Our self-criticism is that the old system is still in place. The problem is the same with the head of Parliament. [The reference is to the deadlock over the election of the head of Parliament when Ter-Petrossian was elected president and vacated the parliamentary speakership. After a period of deadlock, Ter-Petrossian, arguing that the struggle was delaying important government business, after some time appointed a new speaker, the man who had been his deputy speaker. There was much criticism of this, some members of Parliament saying that there was no need for such an authoritarian measure: so what if there was no speaker for a while.]

FISCHER/GRIGORIAN: Is there talk about home rule? True local government?

HAMBARTSUMIAN: Parliament would have to give us home rule. Maybe it would come after economic reorganization gets a little further along. So far privatization has occurred only in land. It must happen next in industry. At that point, we'll be forced to have a mayor. All industry at the moment is still state owned; and all decisions are made in Yerevan. In the villages, soviets have disappeared: they serve no purpose any more, and this will happen in town as well, and then there will be a mayor. My main job is to coordinate state agencies. But once industries are private, there will be a need to manage competing interests.

FISCHER/GRIGORIAN: What are the main industries in Leninakan?

HUMBARTSUMIAN: There are thirty-seven factories. Two are completely shut down—the compressor factory and a refrigerator factory—because they are in a part of town with a seismic rating beyond our construction code capacities. The other factories are working at about twenty-five percent capacity, a few have been relocated. [Buildings were supposed to be able to withstand eight on the Bal scale. The compressor factory was built in an area rated ten, one point above standard building techniques. The textile mill, which was in an area rated nine, was almost completely destroyed by the quake.]

FISCHER/GRIGORIAN: Did the Russian military base here help the economy, and what will be the effects as the Russian troops are withdrawn?

HUMBARTSUMIAN: No, the military did not contribute to the local economy: it was a closed enclave. It provided no jobs, put no money into the local economy. It was like a small city within the city. It had its own stores.

FISCHER/GRIGORIAN: Why then was Leninakan reputed to be better off than Yerevan? [People from Yerevan would come to Leninakan to shop for things like sausages which were in plentiful supply. Leninakan had a meat-processing plant.]

HAMBARTSUMIAN: Leninakan was not better off, I don't think. Maybe if there was more in the bazaar it was because Leninakan is closer to the agricultural areas of Georgia and Azerbaijan. But basically there were the same goods as in the stores in Yerevan.

FISCHER/GRIGORIAN: What about the role of repatriates in Leninakan?

HUMBARTSUMIAN: Beginning in 1946–47, they were a positive influence because of their educational and technical level. We were not allowed to develop the individual. They brought with them crafts and artistic talents which they pursued mainly in their homes. The present situation would be even bleaker without them. [Because of their connections to the Armenian diaspora?] No. [Because they were businessmen?] No, but they provided roots to the idea of the possibility that one can be a businessman.

FISCHER/GRIGORIAN: What about the recent refugees from Azerbaijan? Are any of them intellectuals or white collar workers?

HAMBARTSUMIAN: There were some three thousand of them; a thousand before the quake. The central government allocated a thousand to us. After the quake, the number rose to 3300. They do construction work, a few are in industry. None of them are white collar or intellectual.

I see from your questions that we could go on for a long time on these topics, but the minister is coming to discuss preparations for the New Year, to try to see that everyone has something on their table. The New Year planning will be difficult. [*One of the vice mayors enters and is introduced.*] See, all my assistants are in their early thirties, all but one come from a communist past. We think we do a better job because of this experience. Sure, favor taking existed in the past, and still does. [As we shake hands and open the door to leave, we see a crowd of people are outside waiting to get in. There are five vice mayors, whose responsibilities are divided like ministries: one is in charge of stores, another education and medicine, another housing. One was a child of repatriates from western Armenia, whose parents were exiled to Siberia in the 1940s.]

4. Political Sociology Intermission: Intellectuals and the Second Pivot

The "stages" of revolution that brought about the demise of the Soviet Union are worth interrogating in order to get a sense of the emergent new forms of revolution. As in classical revolutions, what has been called a second pivot is required as both a catalyst of ideas for change and as a place from which new leadership can emerge.[15] The second pivot is a major group within the *ancien régime,* or parallel to the state structure, that can break away from the old structure, deny it legitimacy, and provide new ideas. Some commentators expected such a second pivot in the Soviet Union to develop from technocrats and perhaps military officers,[16] but in the actual event, it came rather from scientists (like Andrei Sakharov) and scholars (orientalist Ter-Petrossian, musicologist Landsbergis in Lithuania, and somewhat less happily, literary scholar Zviad Gamsakhurdia in Georgia). In Armenia, the eleven-member steering committee of the All-Armenia Movement was composed of seven Ph.D. candidates, a writer, a journalist, and two teachers (see the interview below with one of these, Galstian, now mayor of Yerevan). Geoffrey Hosking, in a lucid article on the structure of the revolution of 1988–89, points out that Gorbachev's political reform of 1988 created this second pivot as a politically potent force by allowing groups of citizens to nominate candidates

for election, and by 1989 these had developed into several political movements. Hosking traces the roots of the second pivot to the "informals"
[*neformaly*] of the 1980s, various protest groups using publicity-seeking
tactics of picket lines, placards, circulating petitions, getting onto *glasnost*-
liberalized television, and rock concerts. Among these rock bands, of course,
is Stas Namin (Anastas Mikoyan, Jr., the grandson of the Soviet negotiator
in the Kennedy years and chairman of the Supreme Soviet until removed
by Brezhnev; also grand nephew of Artyoum Mikoyan, the designer of the
MIG jet fighter; also grandson of Gregory Haroutunian, the Armenian politician who raised the issue of Karabakh with Stalin and was an opponent of
Khrushchev's agrarian policies). Stas Namin has been a countercultural figure
for the last twenty years: under *glasnost* he collaborated with Frank Zappa
and Keith Richards and in 1990 organized the "Landing in the *Glasnost*
Nest" rock festival with Motley Crüe, the Scorpions, and Ozzie Osborne, in
Moscow's Lenin Stadium; released an LP, "Rock Aid Armenia," with Deep
Purple, Genesis, Rush, and Black Sabbath; and created a Children of Ar-
menia Fund.

More important as sources of ideas were the various study circles [*kruzhki*]
formed in many cities by younger scholars in their late twenties to early for-
ties. Tucked away in various academic institutes they investigated such topics
as market economics, constitutional politics, and folklore ethnography as
ways of remobilizing people. Hosking singles out the group that proved to be
critical to Yeltsin's career in Moscow: the *Klub Perestroika* formed in 1987
from a seminar at the Institute of Mathematical Economics in Moscow. This
group discussed new laws on economic enterprises, formed task forces to
advise workers how to make use of their rights under new enterprise laws, to
advise citizens whose civil rights were being threatened, and a key task force
called Memorial to get public support for a memorial to Stalin's victims.
Many of Yeltsin's advisors came from this group. Interestingly, Gorbachev
was part of an earlier generation *kruzhi* of this sort deep within the bowels of
the Communist Party in the 1970s, which tried to model the effects that various political reforms might have; a number of this group came to despairing
conclusions, but Gorabachev went ahead with the ideas developed there.[17]

After 1988 these study circles and informals were able to form into popular
fronts around issues of ecology and ethnicity or nationalism, and gradually
more and more people from the Party and state apparatus transferred allegiance to them. Armenia again is a leading example. The disaster at Chernobyl in 1986 had brought the ecology issue into the open: pollution of the air
and water, the series of ten or more major nuclear power accidents, the ecological devastation of the gigantic irrigation projects—all these began to draw
crowds willing to protest. In Armenia, the Greens Union, led by Hakob San-
asarian, led major demonstrations in October 1987, and then almost weekly
demonstrations through the summer of 1989 that came to include the ecology

demands, the unification of Karabakh with Armenia, and democracy demands; in December 1989 demonstrators blocked rail deliveries of supplies
to the huge Nayirit chemical plant in Yerevan. Eventually the ecology movement forced the shutting not only of this plant but of parts of several other
chemical plants, and of the Medzamor nuclear power plant.

The Nayirit plant is a huge complex, originally built under Stalin in 1933
and updated with a new third production line in 1986. It is one of twelve
plants worldwide, and the only plant in the Soviet Union, which produced
chloroprene (also known as neoprene), a synthetic rubber used in high-tensile
latexes. It employed over four thousand workers. The new production line
used a DuPont and British Petroleum technology package, installed by a Japanese contractor (Kobe Steel), modified to save costs, which meant that when
DuPont did a study of the plant in late 1989, they found that it would require
one hundred million dollars to bring the line up to world safety standards. It
is estimated that at full capacity the Nayarit plant emits six hundred tons of
solid waste per year, thirty-two tons of toxic liquid waste that is dumped into
the Hrazten River, and an enormous amount of gases into the air, consisting
of chloroprene, butadiene, and hydrocarbons. The epidemiological results are
a miscarriage rate of 3.5 percent higher in the surrounding southern district
of the city than in the rest of the city, a stillborn rate of 7.4 percent higher,
and a pneumonia rate four times as high. After the plant was closed, the air
quality in Yerevan improved dramatically, but in 1991 the new Parliament
voted to reopen the plant out of desperation for state revenues. Similarly, there
is now pressure to reopen the Medzamor nuclear reactor, located only some
twenty-four kilometers from Yerevan, which used to sell energy to Turkey for
hard currency.[18]

The ecology movements constituted the second of a four-stage sequence
that Hosking sketches as being common to many of the independence and
democracy movements in the Soviet Empire. The first stage he identifies as
being around causes like historical preservation (for example, defense of a
seventeenth-century merchant's house in Moscow against urban redevelop-
ment; of Hotel Angleterre in Leningrad). The tactics were picket lines, petitions, placards, and importantly, appearances on TV under the more relaxed
conditions of *glasnost*. The groups, however, were still symbolically marked
as marginal: pacifists, hippies, students, rock bands. The second stage was
the ecology movement against nuclear power plants, noxious factory fumes,
and large irrigation projects. After Chernobyl, adulterated foods, poisoned
air, and contaminated drinking water were issues that brought sizeable numbers of people out in public demonstrations. The third stage was the movement of the *kruzhki* into these campaigns. The fourth stage was then the
formation of popular fronts which allowed apparatchiks to begin transferring
their allegiances.

As Hosking points out, grievances of all sorts could be presented in the

TREMBLING OF THE EARTH,

7 December 1988

initial stages of these popular fronts as ethnic issues against Russian oppression, and all sorts of issues of misrule could thus accumulate into a large agenda. In Armenia the 1988 earthquake was seen as a form of Russian genocide since the apartment buildings which collapsed were shoddily built (while older buildings survived); similarly, Ukrainians called Chernobyl a continuation of Russian policies of genocide against them (a continuation of Stalin's purges and elimination of kulaks). Indeed the nuclear and chemical industries were charged as genocidal tactics of the Russian Empire, siting a disproportionate number of toxic and accident-prone industries outside of Russian territory.

Nineteen hundred eighty-eight was the year of the formation of popular fronts: in Estonia, Latvia, Lithuanian, Armenia, Georgia, Azerbaijan, and Moldavia; and somewhat more slowly in Belorussia, Ukraine, and the central Asian republics. Demands included local control over economic affairs, environmental protection, teaching of local histories, cultures, and languages, and explicit recognition of the victims of Stalin. In the elections in 1988 and 1989, these oppositional fronts moved into power. (Russia itself is a different case since it could not have a popular front against an ethnically defined Russian oppression, but Hosking points out that the Memorial movement functioned somewhat similarly, and it was in the demonstrations of this movement that Boris Yeltsin's popular base first emerged.[19]

Armenia provides an interesting example of the shift from ethnic or nationalist framings of these movements into democratic movements (which we might designate the fifth stage). The problem of Karabakh helped bring a second wave of people into the streets of Yerevan, adding onto the ecology movements and accumulating into a broad nationalist agenda. But the evolution of the Karabakh movement and that of Armenia proper, while remaining intertwined, also began to diverge: for many Karabakh was and remains a nationalist issue, although for the All-Armenia Movement stress was laid on its status as a democratic issue of self-determination and right to equitable resources for development; but Armenia itself, under the All-Armenia Movement (which evolved from the Karabakh Committee—the name change is significant) rapidly moved into a democracy movement, in which the basic issues were ones of restructuring the economy and the political system. (This transition to democratic processes has been much less smooth, for instance, in the cases of both Georgia and Azerbaijan. In Georgia, Gamsakhurdia, an increasingly authoritarian nationalist president, was forced from office by an armed rebellion by his prime minister and members of his national guard in early 1992;[20] and in Azerbaijan, a weak authoritarian, former communist president, Ayaz Mutalibov, could not survive the nationalist passions over Karabakh being manipulated by various factions and was forced out of office in March of the same year.)

It is important to note that the philosophy of the All-Armenia Movement, especially under Levon Ter-Petrossian, deliberately refuses to elevate to symbolic centrality the nationalist symbolism that has fueled much of the diaspora nationalism of the past seventy years.[21] There is a stress that one should not elevate a paranoia about pan-Turanist threats and therefore the need for big-power protection against neighbors, but that instead Armenia must construct normal relations with its neighboring states (Ter-Petrossian is interviewed below). This means a refusal to fetishize the old demands of an international recognition of the genocide by the Ottomans and young Turks, or the old demands for territory now in eastern Turkey, but that instead Armenia must forge a pragmatic foreign policy.[22] Domestically, the shift to the fifth phase involves a struggle between democrats and former Communist Party apparatchiks who either wanted to use nationalist power to stave off the *perestroika* initiatives from Moscow or who simply wanted to survive politically. In Armenia this struggle is relatively benign (see interviews below); in other republics it is a much more strenuous struggle.

Three elements of the revolutions of 1989 have been indicated so far. First, there was a sequencing of stages that begin with what are often called new social movements, movements that begin with seemingly apolitical issues of everyday life, like ecology, but which rapidly involve decision-making issues which lead to broad political change. These sequences seem to be different than the classic models of previous bourgeois, artisanal, proletarian, or peasant revolutions in that they do not begin with political demands, they are not organized around cadres or cell structures, they do not rely on armed uprisings, and they do not invoke an ideology of the vanguard of the intellectuals. Second, intellectuals did play a critical role as a leading edge of the second pivot, but not in quite the form of "vanguards." Vanguards traditionally involved codified ideologies and analyses and hierarchies of negotiation between groups conceived of as classes with easily identified interests.

Third, the media of communication, both the new electronic media and older print and theatrical forms, play a different role. Most dramatic are the new electronic media: the influence of the rock bands worked indirectly to prepare a mind-set among the young that was less willing to kowtow to authority; the fax machines and Radio Echo from inside the Russian Parliament building that were crucial in blocking the right-wing coup attempt of August 1991 in Moscow worked directly. In Germany, the role of the intellectuals and the print and radio media converged in a moment of drama in November 1989 when the Writers Association called an open-air dialogue on media freedom and some five hundred thousand people showed up at Alexander Square, supporting the Leipzig radio reporters who had braved official censure to cover protests against Gorbachev's visit the preceding 9 October. This led to a period of democratic reform of the newspapers: editors and apparatchiks were driven out, new editors were elected by working journalists, assignments were worked out collectively, and letters sections were expanded for citizen participation, and when the government responded by cutting money and supplies of paper, journalists worked out joint-venture agreements with West German publishers to get newsprint and supplies. These reforms were subsequently encoded in a new media law. Ironically, this heady democracy died through the unification with West Germany. Under West German law, co-management rights of workers are exempted in the case of "ideology businesses" like the press; the Treuhand agency that is privatizing East Germany has delivered the newspapers into the ownership of West German media giants and parties now dominate the media (see Boyle 1992:133–39).

If the electronic media are the most novel, and if the print and radio media the most institutional, still perhaps the most dramatic forms of the new revolutions are the theatrical street demonstrations. Increasingly in modern times, street demonstrations are not intended to be practical means of force: insofar as they evoke the street barricades of the 1830s or 1848, they do so as moral symbols. During the December 1991 fighting in Tbilisi, a common fear mentioned to us on the streets over and over was that this might turn into a Beirut, that using weapons indicated it was a fight between elites, a terrible development away from what had begun as a democratic movement.[23] Levon Abramian again provides a guide to the theatricalized nature of street demonstrations in the nine-month gestation of what began as the Karabakh Committee and evolved into the All-Armenia Movement, from February to November 1988. The 19 February demonstration in Theater Square, Yerevan, called to support the Armenians in Karabakh, was already led by intellectuals of the second pivot, unlike the leaders in Karabakh itself who were local nationalists but still the old communist leadership. On 22 February, a half million people demanded the Central Committee of the Communist Party call for a meeting the Supreme Soviet. People streamed into the capital from the countryside and were met by ritual chants of "welcome guests" as the crowds swelled to a million. On 7 November, a full-scale second pivot revolution began.

Abramian notes that even the words *glasnost* and *perestroika,* and their Armenian equivalents, *hrapara-kaynutyun* and *versakarucum,* already evoked a town-square, dialogic, staging. Theater Square is actually more round than square (2), like in the Armenian imagination the all-important temples of Zvartnots and Gagikashen that were once symbols of the great Armenian empire (Zvartnots is memorialized today as well as the name of the airport of Yerevan.) Glasnost involves the root *glas,* "voice," while *hrapara-kaynutyun* means a town square, and *hraparak* means democratization. Both the prefixes in Russian, *"pere",* and Armenian, *vera,* mean *re*structuring, *re*turn, *re*storation. The strikes were verbal strikes: the word *strike* was chanted; the form of the chant was dialogic, question-answer ("Karabakh is whose?" "Ours").[24] Trumpets began and ended the meetings/performances (and the trumpet became a visual icon on posters) using as the anthem a movie song, "Why Is the River Gurgling?" (a song about a man caught on the wrong side of the river, the Turkish side). Around the square, old opera and theater play-bill posters were used to inscribe farcical reports of what was going on in the square and in the negotiations with the communists: humor calls attention to the instability of the rules. Hunger strikes were enacted as if at medieval fairgrounds: the hunger strikers wore orange shirts and sat or lay in covered booths; people brought flowers as if to saints or stars on a stage; people observed taboos on smoking and eating in the square in solidarity with the hunger strikers, and many also ate frugally at home; there were evening ceremonies of leaving the strike with torches. Abramian uses a September demonstration as a prime example. When a picket line was set up in the path of armored personnel carriers, the unarmed people sat in the street with their backs to the tanks. Only three youths (continually rotated) stood facing the tanks, the one in the center holding aloft the tricolor banner (of Armenia, of democratic traditions since the eighteenth-century bourgeois revolutions), the other two with their fists raised. (In the early demonstrations people used a two-finger victory gesture. Later this turned into the fist of unity and resistance.) In front of them they laid out the works of Lenin so that should the tanks move forward they would first have to crush those sacred books. Behind them stood a line of people holding hands around the square.

Theatricalization, of course, occurred on both sides, and a key turning point in the symbolic struggle took place on 7 November 1988. The Communist Party leadership was on the dais of the square beneath the statue of Lenin: tapes were playing martial music, cheers and shouts of bravo. But the crowd was not shouting. It marched up to the dais, with Levon Ter-Petrossian in the front row. Amidst the noise of the tape, he began gesturing and talking to the communist leaders: "This is an insult to the Armenian people . . ." The first secretary, in one of those moments of history-defining miscalculations, ordered the tape turned off so he could hear and even passed down a microphone to Ter-Petrossian, who then turned his back on the communists and began addressing the crowd. The crowd hushed. It was a turning point.

Symbolic contestation operates not only theatrically but also visually, and in Theater Square a poster exhibition was mounted in June 1988, and it remained up into July, until a military curfew was imposed. An analysis of this exhibit has been done by Stephanie Platz and a renewed exhibit has now been mounted by Haroot Harootunian at the Sardarabad Museum.[25] Platz, a linguist and anthropologist, notes that the posters deploy the two languages, Russian and Armenian, quite differently: all Russian texts are primarily satirical and use indirection, while Armenian language texts "speak directly and overtly evoke an Armenian solidarity." Thus, Russian texts rely on wordplay, hyperbole, analogy, recontextualization, oxymorons, and ellipsis, for example, "*perestroika* through fascism," or a poster mocking the Aeroflot ads by

Poster caption: "Perestroika Rubix Cube." "Beginning": two figures break out and sweep out the refuse of the past. "Process": colorful hopes of *glasnost*. "End": the two figures are in reversed cages.

POSTER DISPLAY, THEATER SQUARE,
June–July 1988

Fish poster caption: "What rots from the head, yet gets cleaned out at the arse?" (Communism). Cow poster caption: "A red cow cannot change its hide."

showing a map illustrating flights from Moscow to all the non-Russian republics' capitals with the caption "Aeroflot: Fast! Cheap! Reliable!"—for example, invoking not only the notorious unreliability of Aeroflot but more pointedly the Soviet military's ability to occupy non-Russian republics quickly by air. Or a collage done from cutting out newspaper headings: in Armenian the poster says, "Our movement is irreversible"; in Russian, the newspaper *Izvestia* [knowledge] is pasted up without its first letter and with an added prefix *be,* yielding *Bezvestia* [without knowledge]; the official Moscow TV news program "Vremya" is modified to read "Bremya" [burden], *Pravda* [truth] becomes *Krivda* [crooked], and the newspaper *Trud* [labor] becomes *Trup* [corpse].

Equally importantly, Platz notes the way evil is represented in a palimpsest fusion of three oppressors of Armenians: the Soviets, nineteenth-century Turks, and contemporary Azerbaijanis. *Genocide* furthermore becomes an integrative symbol of "root paradigm" that assimilates a variety of kinds of suffering: there was not only the physical genocide at the end of the Ottoman empire ("Turks"), and the killings in Sumgait and Baku in 1988 by Azerbaijanis (also "Turks") of Armenians which sparked intensified fighting over Karabakh, but also: (1) the Azerbaijanization of Nakhichevan is called a "white genocide," that is, one that operates by erasure of evidence of Armenian residence; (2) the air pollution of Yerevan is called "ecological genocide"; (4) the assimilationist policies of Azerbaijan were called "cultural genocide." This is troublesome insofar as all pragmatic people in this part of the world recognize that Armenians must find ways of living peacefully with their surrounding Turkish-speaking and Muslim neighbors.

But note that the posters and banners also indicate how there can be movement in the mobilization of symbols: especially the notion that fighting and negotiation can overcome perennial mourning and disempowerment. Although the rhetoric of paranoia about pan-Turanism and equation of evils with imagery of nineteenth-century Turks with sabers, turbans, and turned-up shoes can become frozen, it is important to note that the identification of a series of evils over time tends to shift blame to political systems that lack accountability rather than to fix blame on historical events, persons, or places. Certainly the leadership of the present Armenian government under President Ter-Petrossian—sometimes in sharp contrast to the older rhetoric of diaspora Armenians in the West—has emphasized pragmatic negotiation of conflicts and has refused to indulge in demonizing others or idealizing the self.

5. Intellectual-Activists

A. *Anthropologist in the Mayor's Office: Hambartsoom Galstian*

Galstian is an anthropologist who wrote a Ph.D. thesis on Russian and Armenian bilingualism. A member of the eleven-person All-Armenia Movement

steering committee along with Levon Ter-Petrossian, he is famous for, among
other things, being the first to announce that the First Secretary of the Communist Party of Armenia was a political corpse: still occupying a title and
office, but politically dead.

FISCHER/GRIGORIAN: Tell us about the strategies of the Karabakh
Committee.

GALSTIAN: It had a modest beginning; it attempted to organize a mass of
people. It tried to guard against overextending itself. It tried to focus efforts
on Sumgait, and to protect against a Sumgait happening here. Only later did
there develop ideas about strategy, and did it develop into a movement and a
party. Only on 29 May did a party or a political organization emerge. There
were eleven members who divided into two sections: one section was led by
Manuelian and was more nationalist; the other was led by Ashot Manucher-
ian and was more focused on democratic issues. The Manuelian section
comprised three people—Vazgen Manukian, David Vartanian, and Babkin
Ararktsian—who had worked together since the 1960s on nationalist issues,
cultural issues, historical legitimacy, genocide, Armenian issues. The Manucharian section comprised also three friends who had been together for
twenty years and worked on direction, on issues of and just elections in
Komsomol and on issues of democracy. I think it was the balance between
these two issues that brought success. There were five others.

FISCHER/GRIGORIAN: In those early days, did you have contacts with
movements elsewhere, for example, in the Baltics, Lithuania?

GALSTIAN: Yes, by the second half of 1988, contacts started with the pre-
Baltics, with Russia, and with what became later the popular front in Azerbaijan. In the summer of 1988 we had a number of meetings.

FISCHER/GRIGORIAN: Was there ever a thought that there could be a popular front that united all these movements?

GALSTIAN: From the beginning it was clear that a single democratic movement couldn't work across the Soviet Union. There were major differences
among the groups. [There was an attempt more recently in May 1991 in a
meeting in Kishinev, Moldavia, to create an Assembly of Popular Fronts and
Movements for Republics, the so-called Kishinev Forum, composed of the
Baltics, Georgia, Moldavia, and Armenia.]

FISHER/GRIGORIAN: What was the background of the leadership? Were
most academics? Outside the Party?

GALSTIAN: Seven were Ph.D. candidates, one was a writer, one was a
journalist, two were teachers. None had held leadership roles in the Party
except Ashot Manucharian who was for two months head of *Komsomol,* and
then was thrown out. Two had been in the Communist Party; one of these
was thrown out, and the other left.

FISCHER/GRIGORIAN: What about the leadership in the city government?

GALSTIAN: I look for three qualities: that people be professional, sincere, and strong. I don't care what political point of view they have. I don't see my role as a political position—it is an economic issue. Even regarding Armenian politics on the national level, on the governmental level there are no political biases. Two of my seven vice mayors have Communist Party pasts. Different department heads come from the Communist Party leadership. What counts is professionalism. We lack people who do it *chinovnik* [understanding and accepting hierarchy].

FISCHER/GRIGORIAN: What is the main economic problem now?

GALSTIAN: I don't know if it's the weather or my mood, but things cannot get any worse than they are now. We have only a two-day supply of fuel left to burn. I just was with the president discussing this. If Azerbaijan doesn't turn on the gas, and it is clear they won't, there will be a catastrophe here. The railroads are closed, there is no heating fuel, energy is at the point of finishing. If there's natural gas, everyone turns on hot plates, wires overload, everything goes bust, breaks. Foodstuffs are getting less and less. All industrial production has stopped for the last ten days. There are no salaries. There is no money in the republic. Even if Azerbaijan opened the railroads, we have no money to buy gas and food. Ten days ago I was the only one saying serious steps needed to be taken against Azerbaijan. Today the whole government is saying this. Everything possible needs to be done, even declaring war. We will meet about this again in two days. [Typical Armenian black humor; how would one fight a war without fuel?]

FISCHER/GRIGORIAN: Is the president in contact with the president of Azerbaijan?

GALSTIAN: Yes, I think he is in occasional contact. But that does not mean anything. Azerbaijan has two weapons against which we have no defense: the gas line and the railroad. We have nothing to block these weapons. We must figure out something else. As time goes by, we're struggling with time. Azerbaijan won't just open the gas line. And even if they did, they would only find an excuse to close it again four days later. It's funny to put hope in humanitarian reason. Between these two republics, what is working is the idea of war.

FISCHER/GRIGORIAN: What about Russia?

GALSTIAN: Russia has enough problems of her own.

FISCHER/GRIGORIAN: What about the U.N.?

GALSTIAN: [*Shrugs dismissively.*] Russia cannot do anything. It is the same state that Russia was: collapsing from within. I have been to Russia a lot recently. In the outer regions they want to break away from the center and form a miniature confederation within Russia. In the Far East and Siberia, the Communist Party is still in the leadership positions. Yeltsin is trying to change things but it is very difficult. I fear that this winter, or next winter, we will see starvation in Russia, and an uprising of the starving Russian.

FISCHER/GRIGORIAN: What about Iran?

GALSTIAN: I was recently in Iran. In seventy years, this was the first official delegation from Armenia. It is an interesting country, but we have to be careful about relations between us. It is the only theocratic country that works by *sharica*. I could talk for hours about Iran. Today's fundamentalists can only last another six or seven years. Even they are conscious of this. Today interesting things are going on there. I talked to the head of the Mostasafan Foundation, who was formerly the head of the Revolutionary Guards. Even such people who were radical realize that being so closed-off is detrimental, and want to begin relations with Christian Armenia. Even the shouting of the slogan, "Death to America" has become routine, and is done without any real feeling. They used to have three "Death to" slogans—to America, to the Soviet Union, and to Israel—now that the Soviet Union has dropped away, they are left with only two. I was staying at the Hilton, now called Azadi, and the slogan "Death to America" is written across the front, but even those who work there say things were good during the American period. In order for there to be progress, Iran will have to take steps with Russia and America. The top leaders are realistic. When we met with them and with Ayatollah Malakuti, their style in talking was such that one felt phrases like "in the name of the Islamic revolution" and so on were just paying lip service, diplomatic phrases, without much meaning. [The phone rings, and he takes a call from the president. In a second he has phones to both ears. Haroot Harootunian takes the opportunity to point out that Iran cannot send or sell gas directly to Armenia, even if it wanted, because no pipeline comes directly across the Armenia-Iran border, and it would take two years to build a bridge for a pipeline.] Azerbaijan is dealing primarily with Turkey, and Iran is upset about this. To develop a balance in the region, Iran will perhaps have to look to Armenia. Iran would find it more profitable to look to Armenia because Christian Armenia has no demands on Iran. Within Iran there are eighteen to twenty million Turkish speakers: Iran is upset by [former Soviet] Azerbaijan's slogan, "One people, one state" [i.e., including Iranian Azerbaijan].

FISCHER/GRIGORIAN: Has your anthropological training helped in dealing with these issues?

GALSTIAN: [*Raises eyebrows and smiles at fellow anthropologist Maroutian.*] It helped in Iran maybe. I don't know if it helps here. Before I went to Iran, Haroutian gave me a book on the etiquette of Middle Eastern peoples. Whoever was with me did not catch on to the style of saying a lot without meaning much. [*Laughs and imitates:*] "From the south of the Arax to the north of the Arax River, the Armenian people are rising . . . Khomeini is the guiding sun of the revolution . . ." If they like this style of speech, well, why not cater to their style? Iran is a rich country. They have the essentials to become the second most important partner for Armenia in the region after Russia. It seems their economy has a good future.

FISCHER/GRIGORIAN: What about Turkey? Could it serve as a stabilizing force in the region? It wouldn't want war in its backyard.

GALSTIAN: Turkey is complex, and I am not so familiar with the Turkish issues right now. But Turkey is not interested in war on its borders, no. Ayatollah Malakuti, the leader of the Iranian Azeris and Khomeini's representative to the Azeris told me [*laughs*]: you got rid of one *shaitan*, don't fall in to the hands of another *shaitan.* Thinking about everything, even given this dismal situation, Armenia is in a better situation than the other republics, except the Baltics, because we've taken major political steps, we've given land to the peasants—this year we've gotten four to five times more harvest than in the past—we've started privatizing production [industry], there's no internal conflict and we have an elected government. Compare in Georgia, where there is civil war, and there may be the same in Azerbaijan soon. Don't worry about it, it's been a hard day, and I enjoy talking about it.

FISCHER/GRIGORIAN: If we can be of any help from the outside . . .

MAROUTIAN: They live in Houston, Texas. Have them send oil.

GALSTIAN: Yes, send oil. [*Laughs.*] Houston is a sister city to Baku. Yerevan's sister city is Cambridge, Massachusetts. How did this happen? Yerevan, a city with one and a half million people; Cambridge has only one hundred thousand. I guess we were persuaded because it is a good city, a university town, book stores. I was in Cambridge: oh, to be young and to study at Harvard. Now it is possible to send students there; when we were young, Moscow was where we could go. I did graduate work in Moscow at the Institute of Ethnography. The structure of education and scientific research must change. These institutions did not feel like real places of research, they were more places of prestige—correct me if I'm wrong, Harout. Since salaries were low, the people who worked there had other means (with some exceptions, like your friends, Harout): they were children or wives of highly placed people. True researchers were squeezed out: they couldn't support a family in such a place. With a few exceptions, people in these institutes, even in the political sphere during the movement, were not able to properly decide what was happening: they were conservative; they were stuck in the middle.

FISCHER/GRIGORIAN: How can that structure be changed?

GALSTIAN: The challenge of national issues will lead to a burst of professionalism.

FISCHER/GRIGORIAN: How?

GALSTIAN: New people, new ways of thinking, free people—if you do not feel free, you cannot be professional, strong.

FISCHER/GRIGORIAN: But if children now go to school only on and off? In Leninakan the schools have been closed for a month.

GALSTIAN: You are taking an extreme situation. It's an extreme situation that is causing what you describe. You are conflating spiritual freedom and the realities. We will have a generation without fear. We are now at point zero; before we were below zero. This year it is cold; but it won't always be like this. Don't worry: we've lived through a lot. We've lived through the Soviet period.

MAROUTIAN: Would you call this a bourgeois revolution?

GALSTIAN: Leave aside such Marxist words, let's stick to the word *democratic*. . . . The important thing is, we've worked to privatize land and industry, and we're trying to set up a society in which the rights of peopleare respected. Human rights—in New York, they like to talk about human rights.

GRIGORIAN: [*chiding*]: What? You're doing what you learned in Iran?

GALSTIAN: OK, OK. The situation is that the garbage of society is also rising: crime, legal nihilism, corruption. In the past there was fear of authority, but no respect for authority. We took away the fear, but there is not yet the respect. To bring respect, we need to pass proper laws, and then have a strong government which can defend the laws. It is now no longer the communist economy, but the laws remain the old communist ones. So many take advantage, and the line between can and cannot remains blurry, a situation pregnant with danger.

B. Art Historian as Spokesperson: Rouben Shugarian

We walked across the street from the Academy of Sciences to the Parliamentary Office Building. Security was minimal. No one was at the gatehouse. We walked up the stairs. Inside the main door two uniformed guards had little slips of paper with the names of people to be expected. We walked up to the third floor where Ashot Andinian, the head of the media office, was standing outside his office waiting for us. He welcomed us into his office to await a signal from the president. His office was the warmest in the building, he said, because at night the guards use it and have hot plates going. Rouben Shugarian, the Assistant to the President for Foreign Affairs, came in and sat and chatted while we waited. He had some interesting observations to make about the transitional nature of the present government, and the role of the diaspora. He had been with the president's office only two months. Earlier he was with the Foreign Affairs Committee of Parliament, and before that he had been a spokesperson for the All-Armenia Movement.

In an article summing up the first year of the Ter-Petrossian government, he listed five areas of success: (1) avoiding of civil war by managing to persuade the Armenian National Army to give up its arms; (2) economic reorganization in two sectors: land privatization within the first few months of the new government and movement towards privatization of small- and medium-sized state enterprises; (3) introduction of the beginnings of a multiparty system of government: seven parties have been registered, and fifteen more are beginning the process of registration; (4) peaceful separation from the Soviet Union by working within constitutional frameworks, by complying, for instance, with the demand by Moscow that a referendum on independence be put off for a six-month deliberation period between it and the earlier resolution for independence, and by issuing a declaration *on* independence rather than *of* independence; (5) in foreign affairs, Ter-Petrossian was the first to meet with Yeltsin after Yeltsin was elected president, and travelled as well to Georgia, France, and Italy. Most importantly, Ter-Petrossian signed an accord with Azerbaijan brokered by Russia and Kazakhstan in an attempt to negotiate a peaceful solution to the Nagorno-Karabakh struggles, including a willingness to yield claims to soveignty if Azerbaijan would grant greater home rule. This willingness to pursue a pragmatic nonconfrontational course cost the government the services of its first prime minister.

Rouben laughed when asked about his training and if he had a particular specialty background in foreign affairs. He is a Ph.D. in art history.

SHUGARIAN: None of us are professionals . . . We are transitional people. In five years the government must be staffed with professionals . . . We have help from abroad: you know, of course, about Rafi Hovanessian [the thirty-two-year-old Minister of Foreign Affairs, a California lawyer, and son of the head of the Middle East Center at U.C.L.A.]. Then as head of the European Department, we now have Christopher Gastapian from France, an expert in international relations. Soon the head of the North American Department will be Mathew Dermanuelian (former director of the Project Hope earthquake relief project). [A key drafter of the new Armenian constitution was also an American, Vartkes Yeghiayan, of Glendale, California. He sought advice from another American, Bernard Siegan of the University of San Diego, who drew up the new Bulgarian constitution.]

FISCHER/GRIGORIAN: Yes, but these are only a few individuals. How can you get people like Rafi to leave very well-paid jobs to come work for 450 rubles a month?

SHUGARIAN: [*smiling*]: Whenever you say such things, I remember the example of Israel.

FISCHER/GRIGORIAN: Are you only looking to the West for help? What about the diaspora in Beirut, Iran, India? Are you asking them to come back too?

SHUGARIAN: Well, sure. I guess first we look to the West for technical assistance, to the civilized world and then to Oriental countries.

FISCHER/GRIGORIAN: [*laughing*]: "Civilized"!? [*Shugarian laughs in acknowledgment.*] "Developing"?

SHUGARIAN: Armenia is not resource poor. We have resources. We are not yearning for help. What we need are partnerships. We have had official visits from Iran and Turkey. As for the Confederation of Slavonic States, we have expressed interest in joining, but a number of issues need clarification. For instance, customs and hard currency policies need to be coordinated, but the question is how? Also, Yeltsin's counsellor, Galina Staravoytova, has observed that if all the republics end up wanting to join the confederation, the Ukraine has indicated it may withdraw, feeling that would be too many. Things have been very tense the last few days regarding Azerbaijan. [There has been more bombing of Stepanakert by the Azerbaijanis. This morning, Azerbaijanis were taken off a train and taken hostage, and five Armenian train engineers were then seized by the Azerbaijanis. Later in the day, the television reported that Armenians had seized a number of Azerbaijani special forces.] President Ter-Petrossian warns of instability: everytime he stabilizes things, something else occurs. He has imposed a curfew on the border area of Meghri and Navajehan [where the latest incidents have occurred].

FISCHER/GRIGORIAN: Is the president in contact with his counterpart in Azerbaijan?

SHUGARIAN: Yes, he has had phone conversations with the president of Azerbaijan, but the internal politics of Azerbaijan are not stable, and it is not clear that President Mutalibov will be able to survive. Both he and the opposition are stirring up nationalism in an effort to gain control. The same is true in Georgia: Gamsakhurdia is unstable. Georgia is trying to be the most independent country in the world. It has declared that it will take a quarter of all goods shipped through its territory . . . Azerbaijan has cut natural gas supplies, and is demanding dollars for any such supplies, although it is not their gas but only being transshipped through their territory. [We were called into the president's office. Rouben came along as a translator for the president, who speaks French but not much English.]

C. Orientalist in Charge: President Levon Ter-Petrossian.

Ter-Petrossian is a "repatriate": he came to Armenia from Western Armenia (Syria), when he was a year old in 1946. [*Ter-Petrossian* is the western Armenian linguistic form; *Der*-Petrossian would be the eastern Armenian equivalent]. He graduated from Yerevan State University in 1968, obtained an M.A. from Leningrad in Armenian and Syrian philology, and a Ph.D. in 1987 in philology, also from Leningrad. He is the author of six books and over seventy articles in Armenian, Russian, and French. Married to a Russian Jewish woman, he was not part of the first Karabakh Committee, but was a key member of the second one, which became the All-Armenia Movement. A thin, chain-smoking intellectual in those days, he became a hero in the 7 November 1988 demonstrations in Theater Square (see p. 30 above).

Immediately after the 1988 earthquake, Ter-Petrossian and the other leaders of the All-Armenia Movement were imprisoned. Released on 31 May 1989, he was elected to the Supreme Soviet of Armenia in August, and in February 1990 became a member of its presidium. Reelected to the Armenian Parliament on 20 May, he was elected president on 4 August by the Armenian supreme soviet, defeating Communist Party chief Vladimir Movsisyan on the fourth ballot.

The interview began with some general observations about the two key problems of shifting from a totalitarian state to a European-style community of independent states, and from a command economy to a self-regulating market system. Armenia was in the forefront of supporting a new economic and political alliance, but firm in rejecting Yeltsin's first idea of a core of Slavic and central Asian states with a secondary peripheral tier of states like Armenia. As to the role of the Armenian diaspora in helping with these transitions, the president noted three components: (1) in terms of investment, the diaspora behaves like investors anywhere, and will not help much until conditions for the penetration of capital are met—political stability, economic reforms, and guarantees; (2) there is an emotional reaction in the diaspora to the changes in Armenia, but aside from some help with earthquake reconstruction and other specific projects, it is only an emotional reaction; (3) expertise from diaspora is welcome—for example, Rafi Hovanessian and the about-to-be-named Minister of Energy, Sebough Tashjian (fifty-six years old, born in Jerusalem, and the manager of cost engineering at Southern California Edison)—as is help in shaping international public opinion especially in France and the United States, where there are strong Armenian communities. As to the extraordinary role of intellectuals from the academy in the new government, the president noted two different issues: first, the new political and economic system has no specialists corresponding to the new demands, a problem common to all the successor states of the Soviet Union; and second, there is no reserve pool of leaders with experience and ideas because there were no political parties. The Communist Party was closely interconnected with the administrative system, and so was distorted. Gradually, as a multiparty system develops, government officials will come from new parties. In the meantime, everything possible is being done to invite specialists from abroad, to send their own people abroad for training, and to establish new training facilities such as the recently opened American University of Armenia.

Asked about the difficulties of repatriates adjusting to Armenia and why so many do not stay, the president, referring to the hundred thousand Armenians who immigrated to Armenia after World War II, and the more recent three hundred thousand from Azerbaijan, noted that apart from the normal difficulties of adaptation and the pressure that people feel to give political rather than social meaning to their patterns of emigration, there has been discrimination and tension because the repatriates in the past represented private property. They were largely petit bourgeois, tradesmen and craftsmen, who were deprived of the freedom to pursue their previous activities. This has now changed, and emigration from Armenia for *these* reasons will stop, although it will continue because of the harsh conditions for the immediate and indefinite future. Being probed for psychological dimensions of the repatriate condition and asked about his own family, the president claimed never to have felt psychologically different or like an outsider (although born in Aleppo, he came to Armenia as a toddler).

FISCHER/GRIGORIAN: There is another comparative angle regarding both repatriates and the diaspora. Both Israel and Greece are countries with large diasporas and with repatriates who have helped to shape their new economies and political systems. Do these countries provide models of any sort? They both have also experienced difficulties and tensions with their repatriates.

TER-PETROSSIAN: Israel, well the kibbutz was like our kolhoz. The collective farm was started with the so-called kibbutz, the kolkhoz, the state farm . . . Yes, of course, problem arise with repatriates, but I am interested in results, was it gainful for Israel and Greece or not? Can you show me that bringing in repatriates was bad in the long run for either Greece or Israel? I see that in the society both in Israel and in Greece, serious social problems can arise between local people and newcomers, but did the state eventually benefit from it or not? . . . Armenia will have more possibilities of repatriation first of all from Armenians in the Soviet diaspora.

FISCHER/GRIGORIAN: In thinking about Israel as a model, one might not think so much about the kibbutz, but rather that Israel has staked its economic future on being part of the high-tech economy. In order to do that it has needed a fair amount of state intervention in deciding what to subsidize or support, and this is an effective strategy for emphasizing the basic science needed for high technology.

TER-PETROSSIAN: Well, yes, a mixed economy. Here too we will have that.
FISCHER/GRIGORIAN: For instance, the textile mill in Leninakan that is being rebuilt after the earthquake and gets its cotton from Kazakhstan. Is there not a problem of low-technology industry placing Armenia in a potential colonial position in the world economy.

TER-PETROSSIAN: The situation is one of circumstance, not psychology. We are always ready for the new technology, but we need credit and reserves for it; at the moment we have no means.

FISCHER/GRIGORIAN: The other part of the question, say regarding the textile mill, is what role Armenia will play in connecting with the East, and whether Armenia wants to play such a role.

TER-PETROSSIAN: You said rightly that we receive raw material from far republics such as those in central Asia, but this is not a partial thing, this is a common phenomenon. The economy of Armenia has been built so that we were in better relationships with far republics such as Ukraine, central Asia, than with near republics. We have more serious connections with Lithuania and Ukraine than with Georgia and Azerbaijan. This is an extraordinary phenomenon.

SHUGARIAN: It is not a natural phenomenon.

TER-PETROSSIAN: And we have to look forward to bringing these economic connections geographically close to each other. From this point of view, it is quite natural that we must create serious economic connections with our outside neighbors such as Iran and Turkey. And in this direction we took some decisive steps from the first day of the creation of our authority. We do not only look at the East or the West. I would like to say that we must manage to create very close relations in our region first.

FISCHER/GRIGORIAN: Can Iran or Turkey realistically be economic partners for Armenia?

TER-PETROSSIAN: We have just sent a mission to Iran. It is in this region that we must survive. It is not so much a reorientation as it is making denser connections. I am sure that the Middle East, the Caucasus, the Black Sea basin, the southern regions of Russia and Ukraine will be our economic and political regions: this will be our economic and political geopolitics.

6. Recap: Restaging Global-Local Interlocutors: Repatriates, Expatriates, Anthropologists, Therapists, and Musicians/Artists

An important part of the transformation of the Armenian polity is its repositioning in the global community. The interviews above are framed in the prologue and intermission by considerations of the "new revolutionary processes" of the last days of the Soviet Union, which is a kind of "internalist" account of processes contained within national boundaries (of the former USSR of the Armenian nation-state). In the interviews with Vice Minister Durian, Mayor Galstian, and President Ter-Petrossian, these transformations were also framed through a kind of "externalist" account of global processes. All six interviews locate themselves in global-local points of restructuring metonymically sited/sighted among the roles of repatriates, expatriates, anthropologist/ethnographers, therapists, and musicians, filmmakers, and creative writers.

Repatriates

As we have already noted, there have been several major migrations of Armenians to the Republic of Armenia in this century. Three of the most important were the large migrations after the First World War (the village north of Yerevan, Musa Dagh, is named after the Anatolian village made famous by Franz Werfel's novel *The Forty Days of Musa Dagh*), after the Second World War (President Levon Ter-Petrossian is one of these, the minister of culture is another; people were recruited after World War II so that Armenia would not fall beneath the minimum required for an autonomous USSR member republic: some 250,000 people came), and today after the population exchange between Azerabaijan and Armenia, which brought some 300,000 from Azerbaijan. These populations have brought various kinds of skills and sensibilities to the country. Armenia has funded scholarships to bring members of the diaspora to Armenia for training. Rafi Balian, the physiatrist who headed Project Hope's team in Armenia during 1992, now a Canadian but born in Beirut, received his medical degree in Yerevan on such a fellowship. (Due to the civil war in Lebanon, he migrated to Canada instead of returning to Lebanon.) Armenia gave twenty-one such fellowships each year in medicine. As noted above, Armenia has been able to draw on a select few individuals from the diaspora to help with the process of constructing a new polity: the foreign minister, the energy minister, the director of the foreign ministry's North American division, the director of the research department of the parliament, the drafter of the new constitution, a few others from the Armenian community in North America, and a few others from France. A few wealthy Armenians, such as Charles Azanour(ian) in France and Kirk Kevorkian in the United States, have been instrumental in organizing earthquake relief, as has the Armenian community as a collectivity.

Like Greece and Israel, Armenia has a large diaspora. It exists not only in the West but also in the other republics of the former Soviet Union. The latter diaspora is estimated at one-and-a-half million people. An Armenian, Abel Aganbegyan, was the chief economist for Gorbachev. A Cypriot Armenian is currently (1992) the chief U.N. negotiator among the warring factions of Afghanistan. Greece and Israel may provide some models for Armenia, but conceptually it is perhaps more important to recognize that almost all lands of the "Old World" have such diasporas. The influence of repatriates, temporary returnees, remittances, and lobbying efforts is something that is largely known only anecdotally, except in the case of economic calculations of remittances that appear as major items in the economic balance sheets of nations.

Expatriates

The influence of guest workers and international crews of various kinds of expatriates has also become a major component of the economy of most countries, including even such "homogeneous" ones as Japan. In the aftermath of the 7 December 1988 earthquake that completely destroyed the town of Spitak and devasted much of Leninakan, Armenia's second largest city, as well as damaging a third industrial city, Kirokavan, various kinds of expatriate help was dispatched to northern Armenia both from within the Soviet Union and from the West. Compare the observations of Vice Minister for Construction Durian in the interviews with our arrival scene at Yerevan's Zvartnots Airport.

Standing in line on narrow steps guarded still by Russian customs agents, we found ourselves with Yugoslav contractors for a new Red Cross–donated hospital, paid for by the Swiss, and an Austrian employee of an American air-conditioning multinational subcontractor on that project. The project manager, a friendly Yugoslav woman, engaged in the usual expatriate chatter about the inability of the locals to do anything right, to exercise any labor discipline, to get things done on time, and so on, and how things were difficult with the electricity shortages due to the ethnic conflicts over Karabakh. All materials and all personnel were flown in from Europe on the fourteen-month project nearing completion. Asked what part of Yugoslavia she was from and what she thought about the events going on there, Oh, she replied, Yugoslavia was nothing like Armenia, she was from Bosnia-Herzegovina where everything was quiet, where Muslims and Christians lived peacefully side by side, what was going on in Serbia and Croatia was strange beyond belief, such hate, such lack of love, her generation had seen nothing like this, she knew it only from the TV. (So much for the travails of Sarajevo both as the flashpoint of World War I, and in the present, not to mention the devastation of Bosnia-Herzegovina in the coming months.) Standing next to her, another member of her team, was the head of the Vienna office of Tran, the LaCrosse, Wisconsin-based air-conditioning and heating company. Tran's Vienna office has been operating in Eastern Europe for the last decade, and also in Kuwait and Iraq: Tran did the air-conditioning for Saddam Hussein's bunker. The head of the Vienna office, although Viennese, had grown up in South Africa the son of a heating and plumbing engineer and had all the behavioral characteristics of an Anglophone.

We headed for Leninakan, a palimpsest of global-local layerings. Locals joke that the name derives not from *Lenin,* but rather from *len* [big] and *beran* [mouth], and refers to glibness of tongue and quickness of wit that is said to characterize its people. After the collapse of the Soviet Union, the name was changed back to an ancient Armenian name, Gumry or Gumayri. In the nineteenth century this was Alexandropol: Czar Alexander built a girls' school and a school for merchants here. The old buildings of the town have the aura of the old Russian and Victorian worlds. They are known for their black tuff stone, ornate rainspouts, and wrought-iron balustrades. Under the Soviets, Leninakan was an army garrison. Although a quarter the size of Yerevan, it was known as a place of sophistication and good living, with more commodities and food. The buildings that collapsed in the earthquake were mainly those built in the 1960s and 1970s with shoddy Soviet prefab construction. The characteristic prefab concrete wall panels have led to Leninakani black humor: A man to his wife as they lie buried in a collapsed building says, "I'm cold." She replies, "So, pull another panel over you." Or, "You're from Leninakan?" "Sure. What, I should wear a panel as identification?"

After the earthquake, construction teams were sent from Kazakhstan, Lithuania, and elsewhere to help rebuild. Like international construction crews, they brought their own equipment and material. They put up a whole new section of apartment buildings on the outskirts of town. But when political and economic conditions worsened in their home republics, they left, taking their machinery with them and leaving many buildings unfinished. Crews from Lithuania built an entire village or subdivision with pitched rooves looking very northern, very unlike Armenia. The Austrians also built a new village of detached cottages for handicapped victims, with a kindergarten, and streets named Franz Werfel, Mozart, and so on, although the cottages have steps instead of ramps and the doorways don't look big enough for wheelchairs. The French donated a new telephone switchboard, but not the cables to hook it up to outside grids. The Danes built a clinic, the British a school. The telephone example is but one of many examples of well-intentioned donations that were uncoordinated and thus less useful than they should have been. The Red Cross hospital was designed for specialized therapies that are not needed. The Joint Distribution Committee is building a clinic for occupational therapy and Project Hope is training therapists in a struggle to introduce a new field to the health care system against tremendous resistance. Reconstruction, of course, is also being vigorously pursued by local residents; government loans are available to rebuild older sections of town in the traditional style; others are building fancy new housing on the outskirts of town.

Anthropologists (Ethnographers)

The authors, both anthropologists were of course interested in their counterparts, some of whom have played active roles in the democracy movement: Galstian, Abrahamian, and Maroutian are three who are given some prominence in these pages. The Institute of Ethnography provides a paradoxical insight into the structure of probably many former Soviet institutes.

The scene: a freezing December day, academics gallantly welcome a visitor and all sit in overcoats in offices without heat or electricity trying to pretend that all is normal. The "normality" problematized here is a utopian future defined by not being under economic blockade, by having passed through the transition from an archaic academy into a free market of ideas, and by being in constant interaction with colleagues around the world.

Folklorist Sarkis Harootunian is the assistant director of the institute. We asked him how folklore is being analyzed, what theoretical lines of inquiry seem currently most useful. He replied that under the Soviets, folklore had been stifled by theory, and now people just wanted to collect. Folklore collected and organized through Soviet categories now has been devalued as "false folklore"; today, folklorists concentrate on "nonfalse", authentic, "traditional" folklore. The problem with this natural reaction, he went on, is that it leads to a strange lapse: the Soviet period tends to get omitted, but much folklore was produced, including jokes. Under Brezhnev, oddly enough, jokes were freer. For example, a man stands in line muttering, "It's all his fault." He goes to another line this time for bread, and continues to mutter, "It's all his fault." By the time he is in a third line he is getting angrier, and the KGB has been alerted. They hustle him off for interrogation. Who is the referent of *his?* The man looks at them: "Why, Hitler, of course." The KGB interrogators say, "OK, you can go." The man says, "Wait, who did you think I meant?" The KGB interrogators, now embarrassed, say, "No, no, never mind."

We met with Vartanian, the head of the ethnography department of the institute, and as many of the staff as were available, some nine persons, sitting in chairs around the edges of the room. As people introduced themselves and the subjects on which they work, an interesting dualism began to emerge not unlike that which Sarkis Harootunian had alluded to in folklore. While on the one hand anthropologists/ethnographers have been leading figures both as activists in and as analysts of the democracy movement, on the other hand, qua ethnography the grey scholastic categories of descriptivism seemed to form an occupational s/hell. Thus Haroutian Maroutian, the energetic and creative documenter of the democracy movement and curator of the exhibit of posters and banners, described himself as a specialist on house types. His coworker on the exhibit, Svetlana Poghosian, similarly introduced herself as a specialist on costumes (and indeed was responsible for the lovely costumes in the Sardarabad Museum). A third man worked on the demography of Armenian communities in the nineteenth century; a fourth cataloged traditional sports; a fifth worked on traditional crafts. Two women worked on particular ethnic groups: a Russian woman worked on the minority of fifty thousand Russians who once were in Armenia; sadly, she said, there were now only twenty-five thousand left; no one else expressed any sadness. A man, who arrived late, in a jocular yet serious way introduced himself as a specialist on traditional transportation systems and accused Derenik Vardunian, the head of the department, of having condemned him to waste his career on this meaningless subject; it was a dispute conducted with the feel of having been aired often over the years, both friendly and exasperated.

Most interesting was the late Zavan Kharatian, who tragically and suddenly died in the winter of 1992 at the height of his powers and just as his skills could have been put to real use. He was just finishing a series of studies of marriage and life-cycle rituals analyzed in structuralist terms and was about to initiate an interdisciplinary set of studies with psychiatrists and psychologists of the earthquake victims and post-traumatic stress and coping. The difference, he quipped at one point, between Malinowskian anthropology and Soviet ethnography was that Malinowskian students went to learn from other cultures while Soviet anthropologists went to teach other cultures.

More seriously, ethnography in the hands of such creative persons as Abrahamian, Maroutian, Kharatian, and Galstian might be seen as having a double life: a procrustean one of dusty and safe museology and an inquisitive, interactive one with the contemporary issues of Armenian social and cultural development.

Therapists

Like anthropologists/ethnographers, therapists provide a dual access to internal organization and external discourses. Therapists need to work within the local health organizations, yet physical therapy in particular is something new to the Soviet Union, where in the past it has been limited to massage, where the physically disabled have not been encouraged to seek independence, and where they have been shut away in homes or institutions. Here we have a case of the internal-external dialectic of new expertise touched on in the interview with President Ter-Petrossian.

We attended a meeting called by the Joint Distribution Committee (which Grigorian directs) and Project Hope teams with the doctors who head the local hospitals. Most of the latter were women, who arrived in elegant fur coats and hats at the J.D.C. temporary clinic. There was, of course, no heat or electricity (except for two kerosene stoves in two back rooms). So we all sat in a freezing, candle-lit room, while presentations were made by repatriates, expatriates, and locally trained therapists. The latter, primarily young women, carry little authority. They attempted to demonstrate techniques of exercise with a young boy patient. (What might have been more dramatic would be a video demonstration of the changes a patient can undergo over a period of time.) The doctors seemed mostly unmoved. The physical therapy now is not so much for earthquake victims as for the normal problems that any society suffers: muscular dystrophy, cerebral palsy, and so on. And the young therapists carry on with their caseloads as best they can.

Other kinds of therapy might be important as well. One of the translators for the J.D.C. clinic talked about a series of problems since the earthquake, compounded by the economic blockade. Schools are regressing: you cannot have classes when the children have to sit in coats and gloves and daydream only about going home where it might be warmer. Many of the children are traumatized and depressed. There are two clinics where children are encouraged to draw and talk about the earthquake. Some the children say, "Why study? I might be dead tomorrow." The translator, a young woman in her twenties, lost a sibling and in-laws, and says, "As a child, one heard about massacres and war when every family lost someone, but I thought it would never happen to me. People don't talk about their losses. At first, people did not say, Did you lose someone? but, How many did you lose? Now they don't talk about it. Everyone has their own grief." [26]

Musicians/Artists

But if there are serious difficulties, there is also joie-de-vivre expressed in food and in music of all kinds. Saturday mornings there is an open-air arts and crafts market in one of the main parks of Yerevan. An old man sat on a chair on the sidewalk playing a cello.

Loris Chaknavorian, a young conductor, has returned to Armenia for three years to transform the symphony. His concerts pack the hall. When we went, he did not conduct, but his young assistant began the concert by thanking us for coming despite the cold. "We will warm you with music, don't give up." The audience sat in their overcoats, and at intermission the violinists gathered around a small space heater to try to warm their hands.

Christmas Eve we were invited to a wonderful dinner party at the home of Roman Yessaian, an architect and former head of the Design Institute in Yerevan. There we met the newly elected president of the composer's union of Armenia, who regaled us with his music on Roman's piano. Present also was a television journalist. Earlier that evening we had been guests at another, equally wonderful Christmas dinner party given by the physician mentioned above with Project Hope. He invited a twelve-year-old neighbor girl to play: a concert-quality artist, who already had been abroad in several tours, she enthralled us, playing on a valuable old violin owned by the state and lent to her for her use. Also at the table was a young composer, a repatriate from Syria, who had come to Armenia for training.

Music and the arts—as also referred to in allusions to Saroyan, Egoyan, et al. in our subtitles—provide not only utopian and aesthetic escape from the harshness of everyday life, but they also help transform that harshness into vehicles of contemplation, critique, and rededication.

Notes

1. At a Christmas Eve dinner (American, not Armenian Christmas) in Yerevan, 1991, the television was on as we waited for Mikhail Gorbachev to resign and acknowledge the fait accompli of the demise of the USSR. When his image would appear, people would gently gibe us. "There's *your* friend, the one Bush likes so much." We shrugged and smiled and tried to reply, like Zarathustra, that he had served his function, and we honored him for that, but that he had been, like Nietzsche's first tightrope walker, too slow and conservative for the task. He had disappointed Armenians, too, as we well understood, failing to support Nogorno-Karabakh in its constitutional right to secede from Azerbaijan and join Armenia, making wildly unrealistic promises about rebuilding the earthquake-devastated city of Leninakan, and failing to do anything about the natural gas and economic blockade imposed on Armenia by Azerbaijan.

2. Karl Krauss, *Die letzten Tage der Menschheit* (The last days of mankind; 1992). Rather than belabor the parallels between the end of the Austrian Empire and the end of the Soviet Empire, one might consider the ethnographic comic or carnivalesque technique of seeing through words. Erich Heller comments, "the technique of Karl Krauss, if indeed it was technique, was literal quotation. He took the material of experience as it was: the coffee-house conversation of the journalists, the stock exchange rendezvous of the racketeers, the fragments of talk that reached his ear in the streets of Vienna, the judgment of the law courts, the leading articles of the newspapers and the chatter of their readers . . . not by recasting, shaping, modifying his material. No, he quoted verbatim. 'The most improbable deeds which are here reported,' he says in the preface to *The Last Days of Mankind,* 'really happened; I have registered only what was done.'" His cast of characters, not unlike Nietzsche's caricatures, are "troglodytes living in the skyscrapers of history, barbarians having at their disposal all the amenities and high explosives of technical progress, fishmongers acting the role of Napoleon, ammunitions salesmen crossing Rubicons, and hired scribblers tapping out the heroic phrases of the bards" (1975:243–44, 248). Compare Abramian's analysis below of the triad of slogan words in Gorbachev's *glasnost*-democratization-*perestroika.*

3. Also called Opera Square, but as Abramian notes, the name Theater Square came to be used during the demonstrations, appropriate to the turning of the square into a highly theatricalized set.

4. For a lucid exposition of Marx's theories of revolution as they are set within world-historical time, see Elster 1985.

5. For an analysis of both the symbolic, theatrical form and the stages or social processes of the Iranian revolution, see Fischer 1980.

6. The unfortunate name *social movements*—unfortunate because so lacking in descriptive specificity—has come to designate the various political movements orga-

nized with the idea that more important than the political dramas at the governmental level are changes in the fundamental social relations of everyday life. Thus these movements often spend much time trying to institutionalize decentralized modes of decision making, more ecologically sound life-styles, and so on, rather than focusing all their energy on short-term instrumental political battles. The Green Party movements in Europe are often taken as a key example.

7. An exhibit of posters, banners, photos, and cartoons from Theater Square in Yerevan, from the period of mass demonstrations, has been curated by anthropologist Haroot Harootunian, et al., and is currently on display at the National Museum of Armenia at Sardarabad.

8. On 23 September 1991, Ter-Petrossian signed an agreement with President Mutalibov of Azerbaijan, brokered by Russian President Boris Yeltsin and Kazakhistan President Nazarbayev. This agreement called for noninterference in internal affairs of sovereign states, observance of civil rights, return of deportees, and the yielding of Armenia's claims to Karabakh in exchange for greater self-rule by the Armenian majority there.

9. The claims to Karabakh themselves constitute an interesting study in the use of ethnohistory for purposes of legitimization (Platz 1990). *Karabakh* is a Turkish word; the old Armenian name for the area is Artsakh; in Persian the highlands were called *garmsir* while the lowlands were called *sardsir*. It appears that Turkic pastoralists used the lowlands in the winter and the highlands in the summer, while the mountain villages of Armenians were agricultural; that is, there was a sharing of territory by two different ecological regimes and ethnicities. Platz notes that ethnohistorical claims go back much further: Armenians claim Karabakh was part of historic Armenia since the fourth century B.C.; Azerbaijanis claim to be descended from Caucasian Albanians (no longer extant) who after the Muslim invasions of the seventh century C.E. assimilated into other Islamic Caucasian populations. Armenians say that Karbakh has been continuously and predominantly inhabited by Armenians, and that such Albanian population as lived in the area was absorbed into the Armenian population through the Christianization of the fourth to fifth centuries C.E. More relevant recent history includes the massacre of thousands in Shusha (then the capital of Karabakh) by Ottoman troops on their way to Baku in the early decades of the twentieth century; in response to Armenian protests, the Baku Soviet and Stalin announced that Karabakh would be placed under Armenian jurisdiction, but this was never done. Representations were made again to Khrushchev in the 1950s. Apart from ethnic-nationalist claims, the Armenians of Karabakh have felt that their blast has been deliberately underdeveloped by the policies of Azerbaijan. It was the communist leadership of Karbakh that voted for transfer to Armenia in 1988. The Azerbaijani Supreme Soviet denied the legality of the vote. The first secretaries of the Communist Party of both Azerbaijan and Armenia were dismissed as the dispute escalated, but nothing was done to stop the rioting and violence that erupted with the massacre of at least twenty-six Armenians in the industrial town of Sumgait and then continued through the summer of 1988, reaching a peak in the systematic killing of Armenians in Baku.

10. Armenia has approximately 3.7 million people, of which 45 percent live in the cities, 32 percent work in the industrial sector, 13 percent in the agricultural sector. By April 1991 only 120 kolkhozy and soukhozy remained of the thousand such

agrarian units. Eighteen percent of Armenia's economic output comes from mining, with 40 percent of the USSRs molybdenum, and significant amounts of copper, aluminum selenium, tellurium, silver, gold, rock salt, and construction stone (Armenia was the largest supplier of construction stone in the USSR, especially of pink and grey tuff, gypsum, limestone, and bentonite). Armenia's chemical industry produced synthetic rubber, polyvinyl and acetate-cellulose plastics, and acetate fibers, with big plant complexes in Nayarit (Yerevan), Alaverdi, and Kirovan (a seven thousand-ton West German plant installed in 1977). Energy has come from hydroelectric (5 percent), thermal electric (dependent on gas transported through Azerbaijan), and nuclear power plants (Szalkowski 1992.)

11. In December 1991 people were still in good spirits. By March complaining had become a daily hum as electricity dwindled to fifteen minutes at odd times of the day or night, as money began to run out, as food prices shot up, as benzine became hard to find, and as the dangers of expanded war intensified.

12. May William Saroyan forgive the purloining of his title, but perhaps he would agree that his people enact the Human Comedy as vigorously in Armenia as in Armenian California.

13. Two hundred forty have been elected so far; twenty seats remain to be elected from Karabakh. Each thus represents ten to thirteen thousand constituents.

14. This tag, in the lighthearted mood of alluding to the richness of Armenian literary and artistic production, is purloined from the remarkable 1992 film *The Adjuster,* by Atom Egoyan, ostensibly about an insurance adjustor but poetically about the dilemmas of displacement and reconstruction.

15. Crane Brinton's *Anatomy of Revolution* (1938) remains one of the best accounts of the stages of revolution in what he called the four great modern democratic revolutions (the English, the American, the French, and the Russian), to be modified, of course, by the observations of changes in the form of revolutions noted above. Hosking identifies the Long Parliament in the English revolution, the Estates General in the French revolution, and the Duma in the Russian revolution as such second pivots (Hosking 1992).

16. Hosking cites Lithuanian emigré political scientist Alexander Shtromas's *Political Change and Social Development: The Case of the Soviet Union* (Frankfurt: Peter Lang, 1981) as both among the first to apply the idea of a second pivot to Soviet society, and to suggest that it would be found among the military and technocrats.

17. Alexander Zinoviev, a Soviet exile living in Germany after having been stripped of his citizenship and position in the Russian Academy of Sciences, among other things, for his merciless satire of the communist system in the novel *Yawning Heights* (1978), described this group in a lecture and private conversations at Rice University in 1987. He was extremely pessimistic about the sincerity and outcome of Gorbachev's *glasnost,* saying that the *kruzhki* had modelled all the things that Gorbachev was trying and the outcomes in the model were disastrous.

18. These figures are from Berberian 1991.

19. Memorial sponsored a week of conscience in November 1988, erecting a "wall of memory" (à la the Vietnam Veterans Memorial in Washington, D.C., or Yad Vashem in Jerusalem) where thousands of pictures of victims of Stalin and the gulag

were pinned up, where people came to seek relatives and leave notes. A poll asked who should lead the movement, and the only politician to receive votes was Yeltsin. The Memorial group then organized political meetings for him, rescuing him from the political exile to which he had been consigned by his purge from the Central Committee in 1987. In 1990, Yeltsin, with the advice of members of the Memorial group, was able to shift his base to the "Democratic Russia" electoral bloc, invoking Sakharov's proposal for a new Soviet constitution and declaring sovereignty for Russia over against the Soviet federation. Yeltsin was narrowly elected speaker of the Russian parliament, but the following year was able to be popularly elected as president. Hosking points out that "Democratic Russia" functioned well enough against the apparatchiks, but is not a functioning political party with an agenda, and there has been a fissioning into many splinter groups.

20. As in other republics, the leadership came from "second-pivot" intellectuals: Gamsakhurdia was a literary scholar; so were his colleagues, who ousted him. Gamsakhurdia began living full-time in a bunker in the Parliament in September 1991. Full-scale fighting broke out 22 December and on 6 January 1992, Gamsakhurdia fled in a Mercedes, accompanied by sixty armed men, first to Azerbaijan and then to Armenia, before slipping back into Georgia. At least ninety people had been killed in the fighting and 700 wounded. Former Georgian Communist Party boss and former liberal Soviet foreign minister Eduard Shevardnadze was called back in February 1992 to help head the now-irregularly constituted rump government.

21. See Malkasian's review of the edited volume of nine essays by leaders of the All-Armenia Movement, *Armenia at the Crossroads: Democracy and Nationhood in the Post-Soviet Era,* edited by Gerard J. Libaridian. Libaridian is an American-Armenian, a Ph.D. from U.C.L.A., and former head of the Zoryan Institute in Cambridge, Massachusetts, who now directs the Department of Research and Analysis of the Armenian Parliament.

22. Disagreement over such issues caused the resignation of Prime Minister Vazgen Manukian, particularly over the signing of an agreement with Azerbaijan on 23 September 1991 that traded a territorial claim by Armenia for greater self-rule by Karabakh's Armenians. The cease-fire that went with the agreement was violated on the following day, and Azerbaijani President Mutalibov refused to discuss the breach.

23. In Armenia, where developments in Georgia were watched with care, people analyzed the situation structurally, pointing out that Armenia was lucky to have escaped the fate of Georgia. There had been a moment, a number of people said, when a figure quite similar to Gamsakhurdia might have been elected—the nationalist Paruyr Hayrikian—who, however, was exiled from the country to Los Angeles from 1988–90, but then returned to Armenia and is an elected member of Parliament. He garnered 7.6 percent of the vote for president (Ter-Petrossian took 82.3 percent). The structural situation was the appeal of otherwise untested nationalists for a public that wished only to elect someone who had not been a communist.

24. Note also that the acronym of the Karabakh Committee of Russian Intellectuals in Moscow, KRIK, spells the Russian word for "shout." Yelena Bonner, widow of Andrei Sakharov, was a member (she is half Armenian).

25. See also his paper written to accompany his slide documentation, "Armenian

Genocide, Popular Memory, and Changes in Stereotype based on the Karabakh Movement Banners and Posters." Typescript.

26. Over 25,000 died in the earthquake, 30,000 were injured, 500,000 were left homeless.

References

Abra[ha]mian, Levon A. 1990a. "Chaos and Cosmos in the Structure of Mass Popular Demonstrations: The Karabakh Movement in the Eyes of an Ethnographer)." *Soviet Anthropology and Archaeology* 29:70–86.

———. 1990b. "Archaic Ritual and Theater: From the Ceremonial Glade to Theater Square." *Soviet Anthropology and Archaeology* 29:45–69.

———. 1990c. "Perestroika as Carnival." *Twentieth Century and Peace* (June): 45–58.

Bakhtin, M. M. 1965. *Rabelais and His World.* Cambridge, Mass.: MIT Press.

Berberian, Viken. 1991. "The Nayarit Syndrome: Will This Industrial Goliath Save or Suffocate Armenia?" *Armenian International Magazine* 2:24–27.

Boyle, Maryellen. 1992. "The Revolut of the Communist Journalist: East Germany." *Media, Culture and Society* 14:133–39.

Brinton, Crane. 1938. *Anatomy of Revolution.* New York: Vintage.

Elster, Jon. 1985. *Making Sense of Marx.* Cambridge: Cambridge University Press.

Fischer, Michael M. J. 1980. *Iran: From Religious Dispute to Revolution.* Cambridge, Mass.: Harvard University Press.

Gluckman, Max. 1952. *Order and Rebellion in Tribal Africa.* London: Cohen and West.

Harootunian, Haroot. [n.d.] "Armenian Genocide, Popular Memory, and Changes in Stereotype based on the Karabagh Movement Banners and Posters." Typescript.

Heller, Erich. 1975. *The Disinherited Mind.* New York: Harcourt Brace Jovanovich.

Hosking, Geoffrey. 1992. "The Roots of Dissolution." *New York Review of Books,* 16 Jan., pp. 34–38.

Libaridian, Gerard J., ed. 1991. *Armenia at the Crossroads: Democracy and Nationhood in the Post-Soviet Era.* Cambridge, Mass.: Blue Crane Books.

Malkasian, Mark. 1991. Review of Libaridian, ed., *Armenia at the Crossroads: Armenian International Magazine.* 2:31.

Marx, Karl. 1852 [1963]. *The Eighteenth Brumaire of Louis Bonaparte.* New York: International.

Platz, Stephanie. 1990. "The Karabakh Demonstrations: Visual and Verbal Representations of Armenian Identity." M.A. thesis, University of Chicago.

Sewell, William H. 1980. *Work and Revolution in France: The Language of Labor from the Old Regime to 1848.* Cambridge: Cambridge University Press.

Szalkowski, Kelley Ann. 1992. "Armenia's Viability as an Economic Entity." Typescript.

Turner, Victor. 1966. *The Forest of Symbols.* Ithaca, N.Y.: Cornell University Press.

———. 1977. *The Ritual Process.* Ithaca, N.Y. Cornell University Press.

Zinoviev, Alexander. 1978. *Yawning Heights.* New York: Random House.

TWO URBAN SHAMANS:
UNMASKING LEADERSHIP
IN FIN-DE-SOVIET SIBERIA

I was teased recently for having said to some journalist that we are
pregnant with talent. But we *are* pregnant with talent.

—Andrei Savich Borisov, Minister of Culture,
Sakha Republic (1992)

In 1987, a close Sakha friend asked me, "Why do you term what you study
ethnic consciousness? Why not just call a spade a spade and describe our
growing nationalism?" I answered that I was studying both as interrelated
processes. I had made a similar distinction between ethnicity and nationalism
under considerable pressure in 1986 at the start of my fieldwork in Yakutia,
when a highly Russified, Communist Party Yakut (Sakha) bureaucrat questioned my approach to nationalism in a very antagonistic tone. At that time, I
stressed burgeoning ethnic consciousness as nonpolitical, nonthreatening cultural awareness. By the time of fieldwork in 1991 and 1992, however, open
political expressions of nationalism were not only acceptable but fashionable,
simultaneously despite and because of the legacy of Soviet propaganda and
policy.[1] Sakha nationalism then centered on the formation and consolidation
of a new "sovereign" republic, within the federal framework of Russia. In
1992, the Sakha legislature passed a new constitution confirming their identity
as the Sakha Republic. In doing so, they were rejecting even the compromise
"Yakut-Sakha" title they had proclaimed in 1990 by omitting the term *Yakut,*
which Russians and others had called them for centuries.[2]

Two Sakha leaders exemplify contrasts and convergences in rapidly evolving and interacting political and cultural processes. Both are activists, proud
of their Sakha heritage, but leery of being perceived as chauvinist anti-
Russians. One leads the movement that has become the political equivalent of
a Popular Front, called *Sakh Omuk* (The Sakha People). He is Andrei Savich
Borisov, Minister of Culture of the Sakha Republic and an elected deputy to
the All-Union Parliament until it imploded. His politicization began well before the Gorbachev era, incubating when he was a young acting student in

Two Sakha Cultural Leaders

Left: Andrei Savich Borisov, center dancer, Minister of Culture of the Sakha Republic. Photo taken by M. M. Balzer in a forest grove at the top of the Lena River Cliffs, June 1991. Andrei Savich is dancing the Sakha circular line dance *ohuokhai*.

Right: Vladimir Alekseevich Kondakov, president of the Association of Folk Medicine of the Sakha Republic. Photo taken by M. M. Balzer in the small office of the association, in Yakutsk, the republic capital, August 1992. Vladimir Alekseevich is holding a photograph of the shaman Nikon. Nikon was persecuted by the Soviets and died before *perestroika,* although it is said that he predicted it.

Moscow, and emerging when he became the star director of the main republic theater. In 1986, Andrei's sensitivity to his own culture was evident in the confession that he surely would have been a shaman, a medical and spiritual intercessor for his people, if he had lived in another time. I agreed, for shamanism was the most creative, dramatic outlet for leaders and nonconformists in pre-Soviet Sakha life. Andrei has supported the evolution of a new Association of Folk Medicine, led by the second Sakha leader featured here, Vladimir Alekseevich Kondakov.

Vladimir only recently moved to the capital of the republic, Yakutsk, from a remote area of northern Yakutia filled with poverty, hardship, and sickness. As an *oiuun,* a Sakha shaman, he travels widely in order to perform curing séances, and he has recently begun a difficult campaign for the legitimation of shamanism, long discredited by Soviet Russians and many Sakha (Balzer 1990a). His mission—to bring curers together as professionals, pool private and republic resources for revival of faith, and create a school so that shamanism can be passed to future generations without fear—is paradoxical on many levels. Most shamans are loners, competitive with other shamans, and wary of political activity after long years of experiencing persecution. Vladimir's identity as a Sakha shaman is controversial among urban and rural Sakha. Yet many believe not only in his powers to cure individuals, but also in his ability to help rejuvenate the Sakha people themselves. For both Andrei and Vladimir, this is the ultimate goal of their new brands of urban shamanism.

The Minister

> When I was born, my grandfather, the one who had taken me in, fed the fire spirit and at the same time crossed himself and prayed to God. And when I was born, a reindeer was killed. Well, sacrificed. So they fed the fire, sacrificed a reindeer, and prayed to God for me. And so the line of faith, of belief, comes to me from mixed ancestry. This is in general empowering . . . I was even recently baptized . . . and I fed the fire before I travelled to America.
>
> —Andrei (1992)

I first met Andrei Savich Borisov in 1986 at the Sakha language theater, just before a glittering performance of one of his most daring yet politically correct plays. The theater was easily the largest, most impressive building in Yakutsk, with modern sleek white architecture serving as a frame for huge wooden doors carved in swirling ancient Sakha fertility symbol patterns. The play was equally disconcerting, by a well-known Sakha writer Dmitri Konovich Sivtsev (pen name Suoron Ommolon), set in South Africa about black revolution against apartheid. It ended in a burst of rock music and dancing, with a rich white girl brandishing a machine gun after joining the revolution. Ostensibly about a remote Third World rebellion against capitalism and racism, in which issues and people were literally black and white, the play could also be construed metaphorically as depicting the complex relations of Russians with their nonwhite indigenous peoples. At least some of the Sakha audience "read" the play this way, but it was 1986, the tentative dawn of the Gorbachev era, and such analysis of Russian colonialism in Siberia was not stated directly.[3]

I learned later that Andrei and the theater producer had been watching my reactions during the play. They were trying to gauge my comprehension, sincerity, and humanity, to determine whether it was worth talking to me again. Backstage, I arranged an interview with Andrei for several days later. When I arrived, the busy Andrei had someone in his office, so his beautiful young Sakha assistant led me to her office for tea and introductions to other theater personnel. I was welcomed into an intense, loving yet teasing, squabbling family, and indeed I later became close to several people I met that day. In Andrei's office, we both felt awkward as I began with a standard question about how he had gotten into theater. "Let's not do a normal interview," he suggested. "You're not a journalist and I'm not a typical theater director. Let's talk about things that really matter."

He told me he had recently gone back to his rural homeland for a small private ceremony, in which he had put up a *sergé* in a clearing near abandoned old houses, as a gesture of communication with his ancestors and a way of expressing his cultural roots. *Sergé* are tall carved poles, usually with representations of a sacred Sakha traditional symbol at their top, for example, a horse head, a wooden cup (*choron*) for drinking of fermented mare's milk (*kumys*), or an eagle. *Sergé* were originally used as horse-hitching posts, but have come in the past several decades to mark important rituals in Sakha lives, from annual communal festivals (*yhyak*) to weddings and even graduation from high school and college (Balzer 1992:239–40). Andrei explained:

> *Sergé* are important monuments that will last longer than you. They tell much about a person—tall, straight, beautiful, elaborate . . . People will praise how long a *sergé* has stayed upright. It is a very bad sign for a *sergé* to tilt . . . It is leaving a trace of oneself in the outback. It gives a powerful feeling of calm and connection to Sakha ancestors and to Sakha culture. It is a living thing. I am glad I did it.

Andrei, unconventionally, painted his *sergé* white, knowing that "it will change over the years, from white to weathered." Through adaptation of this symbol, Andre was exploring for himself themes that also recur in his work: the creative tension between old and new values and forms. He was seeking to capture the essence of revered tradition without being literal.

Andrei proudly called my attention to another symbol that he had chosen to adorn posters of a theater debut in Moscow. It was a shamanic mask face with three antlers coming out of its crown, taken from the ancient pictographs found on Lena River cliffs (see illustration). For Andrei and many other Sakha, this exciting cliff art, including runic writing, has revealed ancient Turkic roots of their culture, which was also syncretized with more local shamanic traditions (Gogolev 1986; Okladnikov 1970). "The three antler prongs are reminiscent of old shamanic crown headdresses of iron," Andrei, turning ethnographer, reminded the ethnographer. "But I chose to put different colors on them, white, black and red . . . I read somewhere that in ancient

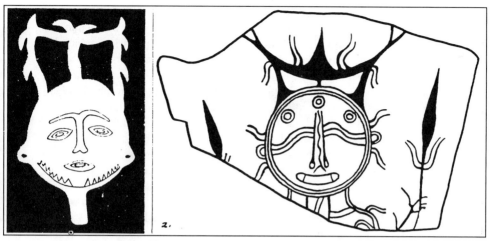

The Art of Linking the Past to the Present

Left: The mask face, from a petroglyph, that has become a Yakut Drama Theatre logo. The image was reproduced by theatre artist Gennady Sotnikov, working closely with Andrei Savich Borisov. Note the ambiguous gender of the face, and the crown of antlers or possibly plant stalks protruding from the head, marking the figure as a likely shaman.

Right: A petroglyph from the South Siberia site of Chernovaya VIII, kurgan 4, identified by archeologist Anatoly Martynov as dating to the Okunevo Enolithic. He labels it a "fertility diety" and links its masklike face to an ancient fertility cult that also featured shamanic and solar iconography. From Martynov (1991), p. 267, fig. 139, by permission of the University of Illinois Press.

Asian theatrical arts these colors stood for the three major emotions of the stage—laughter, tears, and love." The three prongs can also be seen as "tragedy, comedy, and satire," but, Andrei grinned, with wry dig at the Soviet establishment, "we really do not have true satire here." Adding further subtlety to his symbol, Andrei called my attention to the "ambiguous" gender of the face: "The face is male, rimmed with a tiny beard, but it is also very soft and feminine."

Andrei's own mustached face is white, kind, and gentle, not as round or dark as that of some Sakha, with almond-shaped but not heavily lidded eyes, framed by long, dark, extravagantly thick curly hair. Given his over six-foot height, he might pass for a European, yet he also looks Sakha. His discussion of gender ambiguity was the first of many times when I found Andrei's thinking or choice of emphasis dovetailed with popular foci in Western anthropology. Clearly I was running a risk of attributing to him concepts that stem from my own philosophical roots, but I used his constant indications of sensitivity and intelligence to explain how kernels of his ideas fit with Western ones. His thirst for cross-cultural comparisons and new slants on old ideas was great.

Thus I described the fascination of anthropologists of Melanesia with hermaphroditic symbolism (MacCormack and Strathern 1980), and I outlined Victor Turner's (1982) ideas of multivocal symbols in the African context. I was rewarded with a further discourse on the multiple meanings of the mask, which is an *emiget* in Sakha, a spirit holder-protector. For Andrei, the mask image he chose embodies the spirit of *kumys,* and of celebration, festival, creativity, beauty, improvisation—and, "above all, Sakha identity."

At various times we discussed the dangers of traditional symbols and ideas becoming banal and superficial, in the theater, and in co-opted versions of Sovietized, Russified Sakha life. To tear the mask off this and still maintain his high standing in the cultural establishment was a constant balancing act for Andrei, as for many native intellectuals. In 1986 he saw three diverse routes for his theater, all of which he wanted to pursue: historical-classical, modern, and folkloric-poetic. By *historical* he meant adaptation of Russian and classical European traditions. By *modern* he discussed experimental theater in the spirit of "Brechtian alienation" rather than Stanislavsky's "propagandistic survivalism." By *folkloric* he wanted not cheap, flashy imitations of traditional culture but creative use of a deep-rooted dramatic Sakha oral poetry genre called *olonkho*. To delve further into his passion for *olonkho,* Andrei had initiated a series of contacts and informal evenings with ethnographers of the Academy of Sciences (Institute of Languages, Literature, and History), saying "our theater will reach its potential when it can utilize our cultural well-springs, with advice from specialists in ethnography."

When Andrei's actors were "struggling over something really hard," he would promise them "we will do *olonkho.*" This was a crucial assurance, for actors and audiences alike, since *olonkho* had become a marker of Sakhaness well before the Gorbachev era. The most famous of the *olonkho* was a long epic poem called *Niurgun Bootor,* written by a folklorist-poet-revolutionary named Platon Sleptsov (pen name Oiunsky, from one of the Sakha words for shaman). The traditional poem, featuring a quintessential Sakha hero-warrior, took one animated storyteller weeks of near all-nighters to enact. An *olonkhohut* (almost always male) changed his voice to take on multiple male and female roles, as tiny attentive audiences gathered round the hearths of isolated Sakha farmsteads.[4] *Niurgun Bootor* was staged by the Sakha theater several times in abridged operatic forms, with much local success and Russian suspicion, but never was done justice, in Andrei's eyes. Nor was a modernized semiepic play, based on Oiunsky's poem called "The Red Shaman," worth reviving, since it played on Sakha themes to make heavy-handed revolutionary points. Andrei was searching for a new, less well-known *olonkho* to render into soul-rattling theater. He described why: "*Olonkho* is not a fairytale. It is not even an epos. It is *olonkho.* It is beyond . . . simple depictions of good and evil." Instead, "*olonkho* captures details of the beauty of traditional culture, the way a saddle was decorated, the magic of improvisation." For Andrei, *olonkho* had become a synecdoche for Sakha culture itself, and its flexibility.

> Even my daughter creates new and wonderful phrases in Sakha. It is in her—we have this very strong line of improvisational creativity. Of course young people do not like to memorize whole huge chunks of *olonkho,* but why memorize that way when we have the theater? This does not mean *olonkho* will completely die. The spirit of *olonkho* will come out in new forms. We have been too strong in having *olonkho* survive and come back to let the tradition be lost now. I am an optimist about the power of Sakha culture to endure, but it must be in new forms. Sometimes symbols of the summer festival *yhyak,* of weddings, can be superficial to young people. But then they can deepen with their age, or even with fashion, as more attention is paid to traditions. There is more beneath the surface, of a *sergé,* for instance. It is like the rhythm of life, on and off in time, like in waves, superficial, and then deeper. Now we can look into the past, after our dry spell.

Andrei is still looking for an *olonkho* to satisfy his own and others' spiritual thirst. In 1992 he confidently promised actors that he would go into the woods where horses could come up to the windows of his cabin to write a scenario adapted from *olonkho.* But in 1986 he was coming out of a period of self-doubt and Communist Party reprimand, gingerly emerging as a culture hero amongst the Sakha intelligentsia. Aware of this, he struggled with his own ego. This was all the more tricky for an exceptionally talented Sakha man of thirty-five, since a widely accepted Sakha moral code, alive in the urban as well as village environment, held modesty as a prime value. Andrei's mixed feelings on the subject of fame and ego emerged when he discussed the widespread phenomenon among Sakha writers of taking pen names. One writer had, for instance, taken the name of another *olonkho* hero, Bolot Bootur, and some said the name was too big for his britches. Andrei charitably noted the author may have chosen the name for inspiration, "not just egotism." [5]

It was to protect his career that Andrei tapered off our informal and warm contacts at the theater. I understood, although I was somewhat hurt. My own profile had grown to nearly intolerable size because of the politics surrounding a university student street demonstration in which I had been allegedly involved as an "outside agitator." This was far from the case, but it seemed to serve KGB interests to spread the rumor. I learned informally that some members of the local KGB had even tried to have me sent out of the country, but cooler heads had prevailed, rightly pointing out that I could truly become an angry enemy if sent home on faked charges. The protest itself, focussed narrowly on anger about lack of Russian police response after a drunken brawl in which Sakha students were hurt, was the talk of the town. But I did not learn of Andrei's sympathies for it until years later.⁶ At the time, I was rumored by some to be a spy. Few who knew me believed this, but certain prudent acquaintances broke off contacts entirely. In retrospect, I am grateful for the friends who stood by me. In one amusing incident, a few actors decided to test the spy theory by getting me to translate an English rock ballad about a female spy, carefully judging my reactions to the words. (I burst out laughing, and then got serious, telling them that I was not the spy they were searching for.) Andrei heard about the incident, and about a month later found a way to talk to me on "neutral" turf, far from the capital, at a crowded village festival commemorating Oiunsky. "I understand some people think you are a spy," he began, with amazing directness. "But these people have overworked imaginations and seem to think, the minute they see their first American, that reality conforms to spy novels. Unfortunately, some such people are still in power, despite Gorbachev. We are still waiting for our perestroika."

How had this maverick, attuned to many layers of his culture in relation to the outside world, and emerging as a leader, begun his journey to sophistication? Andrei grew up in a tiny village in northern Yakutia, with only one school and few exceptional teachers, Russian or Sakha. He was inspired by a single, lively, dominant, and domineering Russian teacher, who taught nearly everything. "He dramatized Jack London's story of *The Sea-Wolf* for the class, and this made a big impression. But I only realized later that Jack London was the source of the drama. He had made it his own." Andrei was bright enough, and good enough in Russian, to go on for further schooling outside his village. In the early seventies he studied acting at the Malyi Teatr in Moscow. After a stint of acting back home, and a term in the army, he completed his director's training in Moscow in 1982, at the Lunacharsky State Institute of Theatrical Arts.

Andrei was married in Moscow, to a fellow Sakha artist, the lovely and already renowned actress and singer Stepanida. "Our wedding was held in a Moscow restaurant called Minsk, with both Sakha and Russian friends. A friend sang an *algys* [prayer], and they even strewed green grass on the path leading to the restaurant, for the road to a fresh new life." The pair walked through an arc [*artyga*], "to mark the changed status of our life together." Guests danced both modern dances and the traditional sacred Sakha line dance, *ohuokhai,* during which the leader chants a line of improvisational poetry and the rest of the dancers repeat it, giving the leader a chance to compose the next lines.

By 1986, Andrei had staged some of the most extraordinary plays ever seen in Yakutia, especially one about the traumatic initiatory hunt of a young Amur River native, based on a story of the famed Kirghiz writer Chingis Aitmatov

(1983), who was a strong intellectual influence on Andrei.[7] Aitmatov had said his story could not be turned into an effective play, but after he saw Andrei's prize-winning production in Moscow, they became friends. Semiconsciously expressing an us–them, approach–avoidance attitude toward Russian culture, Andrei explained "any national theater director looks to the work of Aitmatov for inspiration." Another non-Russian whose work Andrei dramatized was the Yukagir writer Semen Kurilov (1983), who wrote the locally acclaimed novel, *Khanido and Khalerkha,* a mournful love story about the demise of his tiny aboriginal hunting people. Andrei also staged Gogol, and was planning a Sakha version of Brecht's *The Good Person of Setzuan.* He asked if I had ever seen a production of this, and when I said I had seen one "in the round," he took in every detail I could dredge up, with fascination.

An emerging self-awareness caused Andrei to answer my most plaintive 1986 question, "Where have all the shamans gone?" with the dry observation, "I am sitting here." In another generation Andrei indeed would have been a shaman, a curer of hearts, minds, and souls (the combination of which Sakha call *kut-siur*), through rivetting séances and interventions with the spirit world. Unlike many Sakha in 1986, he acknowledged shamanic ancestry. Yet, as a director, he channelled his talents into performances of others. His plays became mass séances, and, at their best, they were able to lift the spirits of his predominantly Sakha audiences with a special brand of Sakha identity consciousness raising. He was said to be "not a particularly great actor," by those who had seen him act. He became a charismatic speaker only at the height of working passion.

By the late 1980s, as *perestroika* began to take hold, and the first even remotely democratic elections for an all-union parliament approached, the theater of "real life" captured Andrei's imagination and drew him out of the theater of the stage. He decided, after urging from his audiences and from networks of kin back home, to run for deputy to parliament representing a Viliuisk district. When he campaigned, he recalled in 1991, he was astonished at the rapidity with which people threw themselves into the "democratic process," using already existing networks of friends and relatives. His following was huge, given the frequency his theater had travelled in popular road shows, and given the in-place networks, which he had not organized himself. "People came up to me and gave me signalled handshakes. It was almost like a mafia." He was many things to many people: a newborn politician who had nonetheless been a member of the Communist Party since 1981; a culture hero who was nonetheless not chauvinist or anti-Russian. He was elected by an overwhelming margin, going on to Moscow to become a "liberal" deputy, usually voting with the "interregional group" led by Andrei Sakharov and Boris Yeltsin.[8]

As with many all-union deputies, the 1989 election did not mean that An-

drei was expected to give up his local life. He kept a few major theater projects, working with participants at odd hours, including at night. And he
eventually agreed to take on the daunting role of republic minister of culture,
hoping to "change from within" a stultified system. But perhaps his most
dramatic and uncharted new role was as one of the founders and leaders of a
mass political-cultural movement for the revival of Sakha consciousness,
euphemistically called an "informal group" in fin-de-Soviet parlance. The
group organized as Sakha Omuk (the Sakha People) in 1989–90 and helped
to push through the "Yakut-Sakha Declaration of Sovereignty" in 1990 and
the constitution in 1992. Though it started with a base of Yakutsk intelligentsia responding to the ineffectiveness of a local popular front, its following
quickly spread beyond the city.

Sakha Omuk was not born smoothly, nor has its short life been easy. In
1991, Andrei recalled, it was founded "because the time was right for it . . .
Finally, there was enough energy for a real movement," and enough serious
response to Gorbachev's call for "new ideas." He hastened to add, "It is not
a party . . . perhaps only now are people ready for another party; earlier
people were too afraid." Instead, as the Sakha Omuk Vice President Vladimir
Nikolaev described it, Sakha Omuk was an umbrella movement that grew out
of and encompassed other smaller groups. These included an ecology movement that had been active since late 1986, a group called Sakha Keskile that
focussed on Sakha language rights and the drafting of a new language law for
the republic, a nascent shamanism revival group, an interest group agitating
for stronger "national schools," and several others. Sakha Keskile, led by an
Academy of Sciences linguist, Lazar Afanasev, was the main contender for a
similar umbrella leadership role. A debate ensued at the first public meetings
of the movement as to whether the movement should be called Sakha Keskile,
the name of a famed early group of Sakha nationalists who had been repressed
in the twenties.[9] The name had multiple historical and current nuances, since
keskile glosses as both "future" and "perspective." A Sakha Omuk group
was also active in the 1920s, and it was this simpler name, pushed by Andrei,
that won out. By May 1990, Sakha Omuk was massing support for the
"sovereignty project" in the regions. Members agitated for constituency-
broadening politics that could incorporate Russians who were sympathetic to
ecological concerns, had a stake in the republic's future economy, and were
willing to try to learn the Sakha language within several years.

Andrei's satisfaction at the large turnouts for early meetings was mitigated
by subsequent ebbs of enthusiasm. "I work from inside, and so I can see how
far we are from a real movement. People are still conservative. We seem now
to be used to fighting *against* something, but not fighting *for* something. The
psychology of our people is still too slow." But beyond concern about pushing
people toward diverse reforms, Andrei was also worried in 1991 about some-

thing less tangible. He puzzled over the 1920's history of his people, feeling as if their struggles for a national identity were being repeated in very similar terms and debates. He even knew whose role he had taken, as if he were outside of himself, looking on as he himself was "making history":

> I seem to be [A. I.] Safronov. It is uncanny. Safronov was responsible for the Sakha theater in the 1920s, and went on from there to lead the national movement. We have the same concerns. And yet, when I look back on the debates, I see that people were too insistent in their positions—so black and white [about revolution versus tradition] . . . when both positions are correct . . . Of course from the perspective of the twenties, I should not worry so much about numbers of people at meetings . . . The intelligentsia was very small then. Perhaps only nine people would show up for meetings of clubs like *Tuskul* [Benevolence] and *Aimakh* [Kin]. What really counted were the rural teachers in the intelligentsia.

Andrei, as a member of the cultural, reformist elite, was feeling misunderstood. He wistfully named Sakha historical heroes like Safronov, Oiunsky, and the ethnographer Kulakovsky, saying, "They were all scared in their own way, but there is a sense now of not letting the elite be elite. These people were a natural aristocracy. We wanted sacred enlighteners then, and we needed them. We need them now too, but the Sakha themselves seem to be afraid of this." He added that people were legitimately suspicious of those who want power. "There *is* a power hunger in leaders. I admit I have it too. But that is not why I ran for deputy. There has always been an elite. Even the bogatyrs of epics were special, somewhat separate from their people . . . But now anyone who tries to be a spiritual or political leader is constantly shot down . . . including by the press."

I was able to observe Andrei's new leadership roles and responsibilities in 1991. He was constantly giving awards with speeches, and presiding over prestigious exchanges involving foreigners or representatives of other republics. I asked to attend the next meeting of Sakha Omuk, and several days later was included in an excursion that leaders of the group decided to sponsor for themselves and their families. A business meeting would be part of the trip, I was assured, and indeed at one point after midnight, we had a "business meeting," in the midst of what otherwise was one of the most elaborate, delightful, marathon parties I had ever attended anywhere.

The venue for the excursion was the homeland of Manchari, a nineteenth-century Sakha Robin Hood. Had someone remembered my fascination with Manchari in 1986? Was the historical museum and village where he stayed, hosted by local Sakha Omuk activists, simply a convenient rest spot? Andrei and others explained their people badly needed some relaxation, and that they themselves wanted to do homage to Manchari. The trip entailed about sixteen people meeting at the Yakutsk ferry dock to cross the Lena River, and then taking a small chartered bus several hours further inland. We sang Sakha songs along the way, and casually debated some of the issues that were bothering group members, such as whether Manchari was a (Soviet) hero or a (czarist) criminal and whether some of the sacred Sakha seasonal rituals were being diluted by their performance out of context all year long.

The bus abruptly stopped in a field at the edge of a forest, where we got out to leave offerings at the local sacred tree that had been one of Manchari's refuges. Each village or region has a sacred grove, usually kept secret from outsiders, whose people leave offerings of ribbons, money, or food. Whenever I was taken to one of these places, I was awed, grateful and ready with a purple ribbon to tie on a tree branch. People milled around the tree, a huge, gnarled larch covered with offerings, set inside a wooden-fenced area with a neat gate (to keep out animals and make intruders think twice before violating the spot). Nearly everyone placed ribbons on tree branches. The atmosphere was festive, not hushed. Andrei stood off to the side, singing something to himself, and he then, (playfully?) placed a piece of birch bark upright on the gate. I noticed, picked up a long raven feather, and tucked it near the birch. He took the feather, stuck it in his hat, but then thought better of it and put it back.

We went on to a modest abandoned farmstead, where, according to the mythology, Manchari had spent one winter holed up with a woman he kidnapped, who had then become devoted to him and defended him against czarist Russian police. Our destination for the night was an outdoor historical museum complex, next to a small village by a pond, with fields filled with horses and grazing cattle. The privately run museum, partially funded by donations from Sakha Omuk, had traditional Sakha houses: an oblong, low winter *balagan* with a thatched roof and mud walls; and a tall, spacious summer *urasa,* the Sakha version of a huge tepee. We feasted in the village club house on fish, meat, pastries, and traditional dairy delicacies at a long *U*-shaped banquet table. We toasted (with *kumys,* wine, and liqueur), sang, gave speeches of joy at being together, sang, toasted, and feasted some more. The group, with Andrei presiding but not monopolizing, included some of the musicians, actors, and writers who have been the backbone of the Sakha cultural revival movement, and thus the level of singing and poetry was quite stunning. Guitar and accordion were incorporated into rotating performances, as was the traditional Sakha instrument, the trump or jaw harp. Andrei had me listen closely to one of the songs, written and sung by Anastasia Varlaamova in honor of her brother who had died in Afghanistan, about grass and its rejuvenation each year, the timelessness of the ecological cycle, and about death and reincarnation. Yet the style was still Russian banquet baroque, so I was pleased when we all got up and headed for the more traditional buildings.

It was dusk, and near midnight; we were far enough north for nearly perpetual day at midsummer. Our excursion had acquired the spirit of a midsummer night fest, better than a dream. A fire had been laid in the center of the
urasa. Andrei and several other Sakha Omuk leaders, including our local
host, lit the fire and gave the fire spirit [*uot*] an offering of alcohol, with a
prayer. The rest of us were seated on the comfortable fur-covered benches
built along the rounded wall. Only three people gave speeches during this
more serious part of our evening: Andrei, his vice president Vladimir, and an
elder historian of Sakha culture from the university who had taught many of
the younger people present in the group. The historian, Egor Alekseev, was
deeply disturbed by the lack of reverence most Sakha pay to their own culture
and language. Vladimir was concerned about mobilizing people for specific
tasks, especially regarding upcoming republic legislation and the crafting of
the new republic constitution. Andrei tried to encourage people to bring more
active members into the group, so that ecological, educational, and cultural
programs could be realized on a broad base of mass support. There was some
discussion after the speakers, but people were clearly ready to relax again,
and so a "smoke break" was called.

We poured outside in time to see a sunrise on the heels of a sunset, and
walked across a field to the smaller *balagan,* where we crowded around the
central hearth, and lit another fire. This time, after several other people had
made offerings of alcohol and prayer to the fire, it was my turn. Sprinkling
liqueur, I said a few words of thanks, but Andrei and others would not let me
get away with standard ritual phrases of good wishes. I was asked to comment on Sakha Omuk and the republic's newfound sovereignty, and, to my
own surprise, I found myself mentioning my sorrow at what I had seen of
their infighting. (for example, between the Sakha Keskile and Sakha Omuk
groups), as well as approval for their strong efforts at language and ritual
revival.

We walked back across the fields to the club house, for more drinking,
feasting, and, since the sun was up, for outdoor line dancing, *ohuokhai,* cele-
brating summer, led by a young man with a magnificent undulating voice,
who had recently won the *ohuokhai* poetry championship of Suntar, the most
famed annual *yhyak* festival (Balzer 1992:238; see figure 5-1). Weeks earlier,
at another *yhyak* festival by a lake in the distant Viliuisk region, Andrei had
asked why I thought *ohuokhai* was so magical, sacred, and persistent through
the "ages of Sakha culture." I discussed, like a student searching for the
correct response, the beauty of improvisation within set poetic rules and the
communal solidarity of hours-long, arm-linked dancing. Not until I mentioned my own feelings of near mesmerization in the group experience did his
eyes light up. "Yes, this is it. It provides us with a trance that lets us feel at
one with our surroundings and our people."

The metaphysical core of traditional Sakha philosophy, called folk wisdom by both Sakha and Russian scholars, is the concept of *kut-siur*. Crudely glossed as "soul-reason," it has been resurrected in the new probing of the Sakha intelligentsia into their culture. It came up numerous times during the Sakha Omuk excursion and in my talks with Andrei. Some of the members of Sakha Omuk have created a TV video about the multiple meanings behind *kut-siur*, in part to reeducate the public about the subtleties of shamanism. Kut-siur is also the new name of yet another cultural group. Andrei noted, "We had *kut-siur* as a foundation of our philosophy long before the new group was created. It is our source, our way of trying to reach the *aiyy* [benevolent spirit forces] inside and outside of us." [10] Andrei is trying to capture a creative manifestation of *kut-siur* by producing *olonkho*. "But it is easy for us to get sidetracked. Recreating *olonkho* is not enough. We need to take the essence of *kut-siur* and leap with it into the avant-garde . . . *Kut-siur* is inherent in the nuances of the Sakha language, its many channels, its density. We have an expression that words are more than the person who says them. And that words can come from many winds."

Andrei trusts his intuition to understand *kut-siur*, the essence of Sakhaness. "Sometimes I feel that this comes from here," he smiled, touching the back of his spine. In 1992, when I was reading him excerpts of this text, he elaborated:

> It comes close to the [García] Marquez. Not just because life seems like a montage. But also because there is such a strange feeling of premonition. [Premonition? I asked.] Well, intuition. Yes, that. It is called *kiusym karaha* [literally, hidden eye]. [Like the shamanic third eye?] No, although it is true the shamans dance with metal attributes [symbols representing spirits] on their back, the shamanic eye is more like the eye of reason. And for me, this is the eye of intuition . . . Where is your soul? When a person talks of soul, the sense is that it is in the eyes. But the eyes in front are for one thing, to give direction, and the other, in back, is for something else.

Given Andrei's love of the Sakha language, it is ironic that he was nearly attacked by some "hooligans with very strong national feelings" on a bus one night. They took him for a Russian, or a Europeanized Yakut who did not know the language, and demanded he say something in Sakha. He shamed them rather fast, but was startled by the incident, since most people recognize him. He usually feels safe walking the streets of Yakutsk even late at night, when other people prefer not to be out. He used this story, which occurred in 1989, to make the larger point that, while young extremist chauvinists, including some educated politicians who should know better, do exist, they are a minority, and that "some of the young hooligans do not even speak Sakha themselves that well." Rather, claimed Andrei, with or without Russian propaganda for internationalism, the Sakha have always had an acceptance of other peoples.[11]

In 1991, Andrei worried less than many other Sakha intellectuals about specific losses of traditional culture, but he said, "I live in debt to my ancestors . . . As Socrates said, we must know we do not know. This helps us to know what we know. And much has been lost."[12] By this he meant both what has been lost from the vast body of Sakha folk wisdom and what can be gained from contacts with the wisdom of many other cultures. He seemed to have become more attuned to a sense of fate and reincarnation since 1986, without being trapped into inaction by belief in fate. At an awkward moment waiting for a plane after a mundane transport mix-up, Andrei found me in the midst of a crowd and pointed approvingly to a mutual friend (an American folk musician) who had gone off in a parking lot to play his flute in solitude. Andrei said, "We truly live in the world of the absurd. It is no less incongruous than Marquez's world. Yet sometimes, I have the sense there is some purpose in it all. If we had not been late for our plane, we would not have been here when a Japanese diplomat arrived. She wants to see our festival, and she would have been stranded."

On that festival trip, our mutual sense of the absurd, particularly in the fin-de-Soviet context, allowed us to cathartically joke about what had happened to me, and to our relationship, after the student demonstrations of 1986. I told him that when I write about it, it will be like a Rashomon story, with multiple perspectives on the same incident. Andrei made the mental link to Kirosawa's film *Rashomon:* "Of course . . . No one sees the elections in 1989 the same way . . . We look at Russian imperialism much differently than most Russians do . . . And everyone reinterprets history and *olonkho,* especially after what the Communist Party did to them." In 1992, recalling this conversation, he joked, "Remember we sat on the bleachers and talked? You said there was no one Truth in this view. You acted like you were saying something forbidden, conspiratorial. [Yes, that was because there was a TV cameraman listening nearby (*Laughter*)]. But this is not so new . . . and Truth can exist, in principle, through literature . . . through drama."

In one of our most meaningful 1991 conversations, Andrei returned to *olonkho,* Oiunsky, shamanism, and the theater. Both his interpretation of Oiunsky's *olonkho*-like "The Great Kudansa" and a separate theatrical biography of Oiunsky had closed with audience-shocking decapitations of his heroes.

> The rolling skull is a metaphor of life and death together, and intertwined. Oiunsky himself was a simple revolutionary. He stood on soap boxes in town squares and beat the drums of revolution. But the poetic language he used, and his style, came straight from shamanic tradition, and it was incredibly effective. He thought he could change

the world, but he brought his death on himself . . . and he very nearly killed the source of his own talent, shamanism.

Today Andrei is trying to resuscitate both the language of shamanism and shamanism itself, in part by helping to support a new Association of Folk Medicine, founded by Vladimir Kondakov. As Andrei and Vladimir break through the repression of past generations, brought on by the fevers of both internal and external revolution, they, and I, wonder, Is the killing over? Has the curing of the Sakha *kut-siur* begun?

The Curer

Andrei was elected president of Sakha Omuk after a dramatic speech in which he railed against those he considered too bitter, chauvinist, "deformed," and nationalist:

> There is another very important nuance here. My heart was beating very fast. When I went out onto the podium, I thought I would fall over. [Even you?] The crowd was massive, and in its center sat, I saw, Kondakov. [Ah.] Well, we are relatives. [Oh?] You did not know? I thought you knew. Even very close relatives, very close. And so this uncle was sitting there, and from him, I felt a warmth, a very warm energy. He looked at me—so. And suddenly out from me came a voice, a really strong voice. I spoke so that it was impossible not to listen, with such a voice, and such words, I amazed myself. Everyone looked straight at me . . . [So Kondakov. Did you ever mention this to him?] Yes, he just looked at me and laughed knowingly.

Vladimir Alekseevich Kondakov is a man driven by his curing mission. In 1992, when asked to comment on this moment of connection with Andrei, he paused and them beamed, replying, "Yes, there was something like that. Andrei had something like a heart spasm. He was very tired. And his face was even beginning to turn blue when he got to the podium. I did help him. I sent energy to him. And all of the sudden his very weak voice turned very strong. And he got totally involved in his speech."

Despite being relatives, Vladimir and Andrei see each other rarely, and Vladimir is unused to being included in or courted by the cultural elite. A 1991 Ministry of Culture invitation to join a delegation of scholars to an international conference on shamanism held in July 1991 in Seoul, South Korea, made him hesitant yet intrigued, since the invitation represented a kind of legitimacy that he had wanted and that had been elusive in the recent Soviet past. Sadly, in this case, too, satisfaction was elusive. After agreeing to travel with his drum, perhaps even to give séances in Seoul, he was forced to give up the trip when "higher authorities" in Moscow deemed his visa request too late. The group left without him, thus, so many said, without the one person who truly would have been able to offer international audiences, fascinated by shamanism, a taste of "the real thing."

With shamanism, and indeed with most folk curing anywhere, judging "reality" and "success" is a difficult task. Vladimir hopes his patients will be satisfied and that his general reputation will grow on the basis of cures, not rumor. In 1992, he was pleased to be asked to say the opening prayers (*algys*) for the annual Yakutsk city *yhyak* festival, and he had stepped up the numbers of patients he felt he was helping by conducting a few popular large audience séances, sometimes lasting five hours each, and featuring group hypnosis. But mostly his practice consisted of private therapy sessions, aided by several assistants, one of whom he considers a talented potential shaman. In 1991, the Sakha grapevine, called the "fur book telegraph" in Yakutsk, touted his successes and decried his lack of a visa to Seoul. Vladimir has weathered public and private setbacks by focussing on the Association of Folk Medicine, the fledgling organization he founded in 1990:

> Our association should be a loose organization of true curers. We want to build on diverse traditional methods, and also to be able to create new methods of curing . . . But there are many dangers. We have our own internal conflicts. There is an effort for the association to be taken over by the simple massage artists. Traditional Sakha folk medicine is much more than this. And then there is the alternate danger that the association could be taken over by the adventurists, the con artists. The association has become my struggle."

Vladimir named his organization, which received its government charter 29 April 1990 "from the Presidium of the Supreme Soviet of the Yakut-Sakha Republic," the Association of Folk Medicine in order to diffuse potential lingering public prejudices left over from harsh Soviet and Russian Orthodox propaganda against shamanism. In 1991, he called himself a shaman [*oiuun*], explaining: "First and foremost I am a Sakha *oiuun*. I am also what the Russians call an 'extrasens' [psychic]. I am both. I like to think of the word *extrasens* in its literal Russian meaning: someone who has extra feeling. That is what a true curer has. Sometimes I envy those who do not feel very much."

In 1992, at a public forum, when asked if he is an *oiuun*, Vladimir said, in his low, deep, resonant voice, "It is possible." Knowing the Sakha belief that true shamans do not advertise themselves but rather let others do it for them, he chose to be modest in public. At this same forum, he kicked out of the hall one self-professed *extrasens,* an imposing woman he considers a charlatan, who he later explained had written a book filled with misleading and grisly descriptions of traditional Sakha curing techniques. She also, as I was told by several friends, passes herself off as a Sakha shaman in Moscow, and had nearly paralyzed the spine of an acquaintance with a rough massage, giving all folk healing a bad name. In 1992, Vladimir considered that in all of Yakutia only about five practicing traditional curers were actually true shamans, and two of these he feared were "black" (potentially using malevolent forces). To demonstrate his own credentials, Vladimir waved before the audience jars of kidney stones extracted from patients without intrusive, cutting operations.[13]

Vladimir is trying to establish conditions for curers (shamans and lesser folk healers) that will enable them to easily connect with appropriate patients and cure in an organized and effective manner. He bemoans lack of support in Yakutsk, and concentrates much of his organizing and curing activities on rural areas. He has rented one expensive room in a multistory office building in Yakutsk to see patients and administer the association. He is hoping to impose a new social order on a traditional profession that has been, to outsiders, quite chaotic and competitive, but that has had its own set of traditional rules and hierarchies. He pleads to any who will listen.

> For the growth of folk medicine, we need new and better conditions.
> We must have a traditional atmosphere, including a hearth, and the
> ability to have contact with the earth. We must be on the ground
> floor, if we are going to be in a modern building. It is better for us
> to build new, large stone yurts or *balagan,* as was traditional—even
> in the city. An *extrasens* or *oiuun* on a second floor just does not
> work. A shaman needs access to upper and lower worlds.

Vladimir first agreed to talk to me after mutual Sakha friends called him and explained my interest in his new organization. Our initial meeting was at the home of the Sakha art historian friends with whom I lived, for Vladimir confessed to them over the phone that he did not feel that his ramshackle wooden apartment house on the seedy outskirts of town, with outdoor plumbing in the courtyard, was a place he wanted to show to foreigners. The argument that I already had seen plenty of such places did not dissuade him. When I opened our door to him at the exact appointed hour, I was in the role of cohostess, helping to serve tea and later supper, and Vladimir was in the role of honored guest.[14]

Vladimir in 1991 discussed the basic goals of his association: "to establish, study, and put into practice the best traditions and methods of Sakha curing." To test my previous knowledge, and to guarantee that I understood the wide range of traditional Sakha specialists, he asked if I knew that as many as fourteen different kinds of doctors, or categories of doctoring, had existed in Sakha communities, even before the arrival of the Russians in the seventeenth century. We reviewed these specialists—for instance, the *otohut,* or bonesetter and herbal specialist, from the root *ot,* meaning "grasses"; the *algyshut,* or prayer and incantation specialist, from *algys,* glossed "prayer"; the *kuturukhut,* or shaman's assistant, who literally helped the shaman not to fall into the fire during trance; the *ilbiihut,* or massage ritualist; and the *oho keur-teurkheueuchchu,* or elderly midwife, from the phrase "lifting the child out." Each of these specialists continued practice throughout the Russian period, including secretly in Soviet times, but often in losing competition to Soviet doctors (Balzer 1992:236).

In 1992, Vladimir was also concerned that I, as well as other students of shamanism, understood six main techniques that underpin Sakha curing. The most dramatic is *sullerdeehin,* or "operation without cutting," a nearly lost art, while the more common *bokhsuriuyy* involves sucking poisons of illness, and *ilbii* glosses as "pushing out illness." Other methods, requiring séances, drive out spirits of illness, harmonize the three aspects that make up a human's *kut* [soul], and influence patient psychology (Kondakov 1992:42–47). Vladimir also uses acupuncture, cauterization, bloodletting, and herbal knowledge.

Early in our discussions, Vladimir reminded me that a linguistic gender distinction between male and female shamans is very important in Sakha, so that a man is an *oiuun,* while a woman is an *udagan.* Truly skilled shamans know how to use their gender and that of their patients to counterbalance gendered spirit forces. Thus certain trees, for instance, the birch, are considered female, and are used in the curing of men. *Oiuun* and *udagan* move through different levels of skill over a lifetime, often, but not necessarily, beginning as *kuturukhut,* shamanic helpers. There are various, popularly understood, informal ranks. Thus lesser *oiuun* are likely to practice bloodletting, bonesetting, and predictions of the future. To be an *oiuun,* they should have at least one helping spirit. Middle level *oiuun* have a greater range of skills, and a greater number of helping spirits, acquired through spirit-journey trances to both upper and lower worlds of the complex Sakha cosmology. Great *oiuun,* who were rare even in earlier times, have wide reputations for knowing hundreds of techniques and controlling numerous animal and other helper spirits. The fire spirit is the crucial entrée, during a séance, to the spirit world.

The goal of this rich shamanic "philosophical system" was, and is, to try "to balance forces of the three worlds, and of evil and good." To help people live in proper balance within the middle world (earth), the shaman must travel (potentially) to nine levels each of the upper and lower worlds. The directions, east and west, are also associated with balance between middle world forces of good and evil. Thus, the West is related to relatively evil spirits and dark forces [*abaaghy*] and the East correlates with relatively benign forces [*aiyy*]. "The danger today is that the middle world is destroying itself, and the balances are out of kilter." Shamans can use both the *abaaghy* and *aiyy* for their purposes of balance, for instance, to try to correct local ecological problems, counteract other shamans, save cattle, find lost objects, predict the future, see into the past, or to cure an ill patient.

Vladimir's careful explanations of shamanic specialists, hierarchies, and cosmologies correlated well, although not exactly, to what I had learned from others and had read in works of Sakha ethnographers (Alekseev 1975; Kulakovsky 1979). I was eager to proceed to more controversial questions, such as how he rated female shamanic power in relation to male. Women were more likely to be lesser shamans, in his view, although certain *udagan,* such as the famed Alyhhardaakh, an indirect ancestor, had great powers. "I called the well-known female shaman, Zoia Duranova, to try to help take care of my sick daughter," he noted, with sorrow in his voice that I did not understand until later. On the debate over whether shamans can be divided into "white" (benevolent) and "black" (malevolent) categories, Vladimir answered (in 1991):

> Few shamans are purely white or black, today or in history . . . A purely black shaman is especially rare. Most shamans are mixed in the forces they use and in their purposes. They themselves must feel the balance. If they do evil, they will be punished themselves. An evil shaman will be judged at death. This is not in Christianity. All of nature punishes people who are evil [*Set ete tol bit*]. The Sakha person has always tried hard not to do evil or truck with evil. Sakha are frightened of *set* [retribution]. This was not their Christianity. This was before Christianity.

Vladimir nonetheless considered the white shaman a key to the history of the Sakha people, and a legacy of their roots in Turkic and Mongolic cultures farther south. In this he agreed that he was following the ethnographer N. A. Alekseev, now ironically nicknamed *oiuun* Alekseev, although much of his Soviet-style writing has condemned the shamanism he has researched. One of Alekseev's main points (1975), quite popular with the Sakha elite, is that the Sakha originally had only white shamans, but gained more evil-doing black shamans from neighboring Evenk (Tungus) influences, after Sakha ancestors travelled north. Vladimir's view of black shamans was more complex, and more personal, but he, too, speculated:

> The white shaman was governmental. He was the leader of his tribe. He opened the *yhyak* festival with *algys*. He performed white shamanic rituals in service of the cult of the sky god Ulu Aiyy Toyon, and he was the messenger of this greatest of sky gods [of the ninth sky]. He cured, but this was not the main issue. He advocated when to go to war. He was skilled in diplomacy. He predicted the weather; he knew how to save his tribe in emergencies. He was a main advisor to whomever was the main tribal leader, if he was not this leader himself. The first shaman was probably white. His power was from Ulu Aiyy Toyon. But the black shaman was local. Not because he was evil did he become a black shaman, but perhaps because of

tragedies and suffering in his life that he tried to counteract. Perhaps a white shaman had hurt him, and he turned to darker powers
for help.

This last statement turned out to be revealing, for Vladimir later confessed
that he himself had once used darker forces for revenge. He had done this in
his youth, when he was just testing the limits and confusions of his own
powers. Apparently someone had insulted him quite severely. "I did not want
to hurt him," Vladimir assured me, "just to scare him a bit."

> It was one of my first attempts at a séance, and I was by myself. I
> started near my hearth, dressed in [traditional] clothing and using a
> drum I had made myself. I did not know what would come of it, but
> I started beating on the drum and chanting. Soon two beings, exactly,
> definitely two, appeared on either side of me. I did not know what
> to think. I even asked myself, "Am I normal?" Most shamans are
> perhaps abnormal, so the thinking of many people and some scien-
> tists goes. But this is just an illusion. My mind was sound. My logic
> was intact. Indeed I am always psychologically healthy. More than
> most. So I looked and I saw I was very far from my hearth. It was
> receding and I came into the house of the man who had insulted me.
> He was very frightened. I am not sure what I or the spirits did. The
> next day I came to him in person. He looked at me in horror. I
> laughed and walked out. To this day, when I see him, he turns away.
> We do not greet each other. [*Laughter*].

A close Sakha friend, a musician, ethnomusicologist, and museum director, Aiza Reshetnikova, was with us, and asked incredulously, "You mean
you really do not know what happened? How he was scared?" "No," replied
Vladimir, smiling. "And I never asked or talked about it with him." [15]
That same evening, Vladimir, having heard Aiza had a headache and was
tense from a very traumatic period of nursing her seriously ill mother, offered
to help relieve some of her symptoms. Gently, he asked her to close her eyes,
and he stood over her, counting her into relaxation. He slowly moved his
hands along her head, spine, and legs, and then around the rest of her body,
always keeping them about three inches from actually touching her. He was
doing the basic "bioenergy" movement that has come to be very popular
among Sakha and Russian folk curers and *extrasens*. He took what he described as impurities away from her, repeating this process, as I quietly
counted, nine times (the most sacred number in the Sakha belief system). He
also had her lean way back into his arms twice. With small, and then more
expansive hand motions over her chest, he waved away ill "energy." With
one hand lightly placed over her eyes, he leaned into her neck, sucking at
something, but again not touching her. To bring her out of what was a semi-
hypnotic state, after about fifteen minutes, he began rubbing her sore legs,

and then had her continue this for herself. He counted with her to bring her back to full consciousness.[16]

While Vladimir's soothing use of bioenergy did help Aiza feel temporarily better that evening, something he had said to her earlier disturbed her greatly. She described the agony her mother was going through, after what seemed to us all to be a botched cancer operation and late diagnosis. Vladimir's contempt for the local Soviet-style medical establishment was blatant and understandable. Among many other things, standard procedure in Soviet hospitals is refusal to tell patients they have cancer, although close family are told. In this case, the doctor also had to repeat a procedure that even he admitted to Aiza had been done improperly the first time. "Poisons" had been building in her body, without being properly "drained." On learning the horrendous specifics of the case, Vladimir said to Aiza, "Why didn't you bring her to me in the first place? We cannot do anything now. She has already been cut. They have already botched it. We generally do not take cancer patients who have had operations. Most of these so-called modern operations in Soviet hospitals fail." He added, "When we have a patient with a tumor, depending where the tumor is, of course, and how far along it is, we can often effect a cure, without any kind of cutting. We dissolve the tumor itself. We have our ways. This is the sort of thing 'modern' medicine could study from us." [17]

In 1991, the shaman most famous for miraculous cures, including of cancer, was a twenty-seven-year-old shaman of the Viliuisk region whose reputation had skyrocketed after he helped "dissolve" the tumor of a local Viliuisk clinic doctor, enabling her to avoid an operation. Vladimir was impressed by this young man, whom he described as potentially becoming a "Sakha *oiuun* of greater than middle rank," capable of regaining lost credibility for shamanism. Already, said Vladimir, this young man had surpassed Vladimir himself in skill. He was needed for the association, but was as yet hesitant to join. "He says he has his own territory, and he does not want any conflicts. This is how he has operated form childhood. He does not want anything to do with the city, or the association." I should travel to him, Vladimir urged, and see for myself.[18]

Vladimir, a tall, heavy-set, lightlybearded, imposing man of fifty-one, seemed more comfortable talking about the young Viliuisk shaman's background than his own. They were originally from the same area, and knew or worked with two of the great elder shamans of the Viliuisk villages, in secret. "He worked with Nikon, a very strong curer, by reputation especially a bone-setter. The two greatest *oiuun* of the area, in that generation, were Gerasimov, my teacher, and Nikon. These two were not enemies, although there was a certain competition between them. Sometimes boats, headed for Gerasimov's, stopped at Nikon's, even when their owners had no intention of stopping there." These great mentor-shamans despaired of finding successors in the

Soviet environment, saying, "after us there will not be any true shamans." But first Vladimir and then a few others appeared. Nikon heard of the special powers of the young Viliuisk shaman, and summoned him, first in dreams, then in writing, when the boy was still in school, and Nikon was in failing health. Today the young star shaman still communicates with the dead Nikon, at his grave, as Vladimir and later the young man himself explained.

Vladimir's own story was equally dramatic. "I was born in the taiga, near a big lake. We lived not far from a village, but separate, as the Sakha people used to do. We did not even drink tea, but only *chaga.* Nearby was just one other *balagan,* besides our own solid little house. I had only one older sister. Our family lived very isolated, and I was very separate, alone, as I was growing up." Still in childhood, Vladimir became fascinated by a shaman who lived nearby, "in the next field." "D'anna was a middle-level shaman. He did *ilbii* [ritual massage] and knew his grasses. In the fall, when many were hurt with eye trouble from the dust, he would help them. He also said incantations." Vladimir was encouraged by this neighbor, who said he had extraordinary talent. But he was scared and unsure.

"When I was only four years old, and my elder sister read out loud 'Miuldu Bege the Strong' by Kiuniuk-Urastyrov, I, not knowing how to read, of course, completely reproduced the text, in full verse form. People thought I had learned to read." [19] "I thought at first," said Vladimir in a press interview, "that everyone had such talents, and so it was not really until I was into my thirties that I realized my abilities to hypnotize and to be an 'extrasens.' But even in childhood, I could project and transfer my thoughts onto other people. They did not notice. For instance, I could walk behind a comrade, will him to fall, and have him fall." Vladimir gave up such pranks, but still remembers that in childhood "it seemed as if the trees were breathing, and I could telepathically communicate with them" (Senkina 1991:5).

Vladimir, feeling the pull of the Sakha past in many directions, decided to become a historian. Through history he could at least fulfill at love of "the ancient material and spiritual culture of my own people." He studied history, and became a schoolteacher, which was his official occupation for many years of harsh life in northern Soviet villages. As an adult, however, he was inspired by two great curers, one, the shaman Egor Gerasimovich Gerasimov, and the other, a non-Sakha "doctor-hypnotist."

> In 1968 I found Egor Gerasimov . . . An old woman requested that I find him, sent me to him. He was very glad to see me, to have help. People laughed at this, at his kind of curing. It was forbidden. But still, many came to him. I entered, and many people, about thirty, were already there. His *balagan* was stuffed. Only spines were visible. But I could hear his voice, a low, low bass voice, saying, "Well, it seems a big man has come in." It took me a minute to

realize he was talking about me. The crowd parted and people stared. They waved me to him, and he looked at me with joy in his eyes. "You are not sick," he said. "You will help cure the sick. Tomorrow we will talk."

Vladimir recalled that Gerasimov's homestead was set up to serve many patients. They stayed in a large tent, near his *balagan,* and were served tea at outdoor benches and tables by an elderly woman who helped Gerasimov. "I could not sleep that night. The mosquitoes were bothering me, and much else. I saw the old man in the morning, curing a group of people, one after another. I watched him all day, calling his spirits in front of the fire. He asked me to stay, ten days at first, and later in longer sessions." Vladimir, as had many shamans before him, learned that to cure his own ills, he needed to cure others. "Gerasimov showed me everything . . . He was a natural hypnotist, a natural curer . . . But he too suffered from his own powers. If he had been a scientist, he would have been a great one. He managed to cure even tuberculosis, bone diseases, and other serious illnesses. Venereal diseases, even."

Given the atmosphere of repression surrounding shamanism in the Soviet period, Gerasimov was very careful not to term what he was doing *shamanism,* or to do extravagant tricks, as was done in the old days. "He lit his fire, and he called his spirits. There was nothing complex, with lots of fancy dances. He did not even have a drum—they [Soviet activists] had taken it." Gerasimov was also careful about his relations with his patients, who were mostly old and very ill Sakha. "He figured out what was sick, where the pain was, and he cleared it up. Afterward, he only asked his patients, 'Where are you from? and sometimes he was lay and did not even ask this. But he also told them to call for him, if they really needed him." Gerasimov himself had been seriously ill only three times, each time associated with an increase in his shamanic powers. "By the end of his life, he had become very powerful, and was making very important predictions about the eighties. But he did not live to see this."

> He told me what to do, but to keep it secret. "Do not tell anyone until you are forty years old. Then it is your business. Tell your true patients, but do not tell anyone else. Many will be against you. Some will be jealous. Do not take any money. Many will tell you that I am not a shaman, but this is temporary. Indeed, sometimes my own spirits do leave me. And I feel deserted, but each time I get stronger . . . There will come a better time for shamans, but I am afraid by then there will be few talents left."

Gerasimov taught Vladimir "how to call his [Gerasimov's] spirit, when things get tough" (Kim 1992:2). Vladimir, while working with Gerasimov, followed the advice of his own spirit helpers and made a shamanic cloak, with dangling iron ornaments to signify the spirits, and a drum. He was never satisfied with the drum that he had made, however, and was thus thrilled when another shaman, Maxim, passed on his own drum to Vladimir, "with appropriate *algys*" and spirit transfers. This inheritance of a drum is not traditional, since drums and clothing of dead shamans are usually said to belong with these shamans in the afterlife. Even some Sakha who follow Vladimir's career closely voiced suspicions that Vladimir's acquisition of Maxim's drum was unconventional, and possibly dangerous. But Vladimir is convinced of the legitimacy, indeed blessing, of the transfer. The drum shortage would not be so critical, of course, if shamans had not been persecuted so severely. "In Christian times," said Vladimir in 1991, "shamans were also hounded. Their drums were taken and some were even killed. But it was much worse with Soviet power . . . Shamans were truly punished when their drums were taken. That was like taking the strength of people like Gerasimov and Nikon."

Vladimir's own life has had its share of tragedy, not only from official discouragement of his initially covert curing practice, but also from more personal causes. He is married, with a son, who is "a worker," and a recently deceased daughter. When I met him, he was still grieving for his nineteen-year-old daughter, who died in 1991, after the family had moved to Yakutsk, where she had been a student at Yakutsk University. [She was much more talented and wiser than I. She criticized me, and rightly so. She felt her strength, even when she was very young. She had a great mind, and she always made great grades in math. When she decided to go on to Yakutia State in the Russian division, she got great grades there. She read the classics of Russian, knew the Greek classics, and also the Sakha classics: from the *Iliad* to Ellei."[20] Vladimir called upon the *udagan* Zoia Duranova to cure her, but is sorry that he did not call for the young star shaman of Viliuisk.

Vladimir's daughter had shown some shamanistic tendencies. Thus his sorrow was doubly severe, given how few potentially great shamans are left in the republic. "She died of a liver ailment. And she foresaw this in a dream. In the dream, she said me, her father, 'I am dying of ailments arising from a five-story stone building.'" Vladimir did not explain this, but friends say it may be a reference to the devastating pollution of their home region. (I now wonder if the illness could relate to asbestos or radiation poisoning.) In another dream, Vladimir's deceased daughter said to him, "You yourself know why I died." Vladimir blamed the horrible conditions of their current Yakutsk housing, including traipsing to an outdoor toilet in the winter, for exacerbating her illness. But he avoided any further speculation with me. Others were not so restrained. Some Sakha, including scholars of shamanism, suggested his daughter's well-known death could have been the price Vladimir paid for his shamanic practice. Perhaps he had offended spirits in some way (for instance, with Maxim's drum) or he had misused his own powers, they explained. The death of family members of shamans, one scholar pointed out, was something that occurred rather frequently in traditional lore. "Once one enters the realm of the *abaaghy,* one pays for mistakes with the lives of loved ones," a frightened would-be shaman declared. Belief in the dark side of shamanism is still very much alive.

Vladimir naturally stressed the long-ignored beneficial aspects of shamanism, with me and in press interviews, although he also warned that "shamanism requires great study. To use it one must be very careful" (Senkina 1991:5). Calling shamanism "the experience of many generations," he enumerated some of his successes. One heart patient turned out to be the father of the young star Viliuisk shaman. "I cured his father, and then he believed in his own son." In 1991, with a small "brigade" of folk healers, Vladimir travelled to the Kobiaiask and Ust-Aldan regions. There they cured four people of painful gallstones using a combination of "noncontact massage" and "hypnotism." The group also used "shamanic secrets," including understanding the natural properties of magnetism, to cure nervous illnesses. "A good curer becomes an intermediary between higher powers and people, through understanding of nature . . . Each folk curer must help everyone toward the good and the sacred, and must fight any powers that interfere with this" (Senkina 1991:5).

Vladimir's own connection to nature was affirmed for him unexpectedly in a magic moment during a Namsk region *yhyak,* which he led with opening *algys* and described in 1991:

> I addressed the spirits, by chanting the prayers, without my drum, as a white shaman would. I was connecting with the Earth by pouring *kumys* to her, by a fire. Then I connected with the spirits of the sky, by tossing *kumys* to the Great Upper Sky God. And suddenly rain came, just in the area where we were, gentle and not for long. We brought rain to the village. Nature, all of nature, listened. I saw this. I felt this.

I juxtapose this triumphant symbolic recognition of the spirits through rain, still recalled vividly and with pride in 1992, with Vladimir's earlier cri de coeur, "Sometimes I envy those who do not feel very much." His scope of perception and his goals indeed seem larger than the frameworks of most of us struggling to understand merely small pieces of the middle world. He has compensated for the pain and sacrifices made as a Sakha shaman with a sense of mission and balance with the "universe of nature." His confidence in shamanism has been honed by persecution from those he calls "little people," those, whether Russian or Sakha, with questionable moral qualities, and those who think shamans are crazy. "It is not the spirits who are to be feared," he says, "for they are able to be directed; but rather it is people. People I fear.

People with their greed, and misunderstandings and malevolence." Somewhat defensively, he reminds, "Shamanism is a great philosophy. Shamans are not stupid. They never were."

Conclusions

Who shapes the sacred and its interpretations in the brave new post-Soviet world? Less than ten years ago, the premises behind this question would have been reviled by Soviet scholars and even most Siberians themselves. The revival of shamanism in Siberia was laughed at as an impossible dream by some and as a ridiculous nightmare by others. But strivings for identity through spirituality have recently become crucial in a society starved for the sacred and its reconstruction. In the broadest sense of the term, new concepts of "sacred" are emerging as Siberian leaders redefine who they are and who they want to be. Many, like the "urban shamans" featured here, are deriving spiritual and intellectual sustenance from their past, discussed and debated predominantly but not exclusively in "ethnic" terms.[21] Yet creativity is in their vocabulary and their consciousness. They are not paralyzed by nostalgia, nor are they sticklers for traditional rules. Because of their adventurous flexibility, both these leaders are controversial with their own people. Yet this same flexibility enables them to shape themselves into effective leader-shamans. This unfinished process is fascinating to watch, yet painful for participants. They are in many ways still burdened by the legacy of Soviet and Czarist repressions.

People participate in their own repression with varying degrees of consciousness and collaboration. Andrei the minister had a history of Communist Party membership that Vladimir the curer would not, and could not, share. Andrei, who spread his wings remarkably wide even before the Gorbachev era, would not, and could not, view the Russian cultural heritage he imbibed from early childhood as a liability. Vladimir, too, has a respect for selected aspects of Russian tradition and for specific Russians. Each developed multi-faceted identities and admirations through the prism of growing up "Soviet," with Russian and Russians often a reference for defensive measuring of Sakha culture. An "us-them ethnic boundary" sensibility was subtle in Andrei's life history, and more blatant in Vladimir's (Barth 1969). But for both, ways of coping with and absorbing outsider's values were integrated with other, more Sakha, and thus more seditious, ways of knowing (Humphrey 1983; Vinokurova 1991).

The resulting dilemma was to maintain one's inner integrity while wearing the chafing masks required by various roles of communist society. A release from the inner tyranny of such masks occurred briefly during Tiananmen Square in China (Bao Lord 1991:120), and on a smaller but perhaps more enduring scale, with student demonstrations in 1986 in the Sakha Republic. The protest helped many Sakha toward crystallization of a Sakha identity, less Russian-oriented and less accepting of the word *Yakut*. The once unavoidable hypocrisies of dual messages for dual constituencies (official and personal) have only recently been crushed by people like Vladimir, who has transformed what was ritualized lip service (for example, opening *yhyak* prayers) into a religious experience. He has thus helped return a sense of higher spiritual purpose to those of a wounded and tattered people who care to listen. Many do, and their numbers, hard to estimate, are growing. "Earlier," Vladimir says, referring to prerevolutionary times, "we had order in our lives, moral fortitude. This came from religion. A people with religion does not die" (Aprosimova 1992:5).

Leaders inspire. Yet take-me-to-your-leader ethnographers searching for noncontroversial "representatives" of a given people's elite search futilely. Leadership is constantly, refreshingly opposed, unless it is imposed by force or spiritual terror, thus conforming only to the narrowest, least productive definitions of leadership (Bohannan 1960). Traditional shamans were also controversial. Indeed, labels of *black* and *white* shamans have as much to do with who is doing the designating as with particular rituals or intents attributed to these prominent, now legendary, figures.

Shamanism is an ideal medium for the message of creative anti-Soviet leadership, given both its legacy of being persecuted and its inherent spirituality. Andrei and Vladimir, in their own ways, are using this medium to further the healing of their people. They are more than merely the (official) Minister of Culture and the (unofficial) Minister of Health in a society of victims preoccupied with official face. In 1992 a conference on shamanism was sponsored by the Ministry of Culture (not Health; see illustration). Shamanic training is being institutionalized through the Association of Folk Medicine. As legitimation of shamanism proceeds, Sakha confidence in their ability to revive their own culture increases. Shamanism, like *olonkho,* becomes synecdoche for and symbol of the richness of the Sakha past. It provides a means to attempt at least partial cures of the body politic, and a medium in which to interpret dreams and emotions (Comaroff 1982:49–65; Marcus and Fischer 1986:155).

Can this be translated effectively into today's contexts and terms? The Sakha are in a stronger position than some of the demographically smaller Siberian nationalities because of their relative size (382,000), the relative persistence of their language, and the growing number of talented shamans (though still few) emerging from the underground. Some Sakha are tapping into the creative spirit of shamanism in new ways: from making videos about *kut-siur* to using the *khomus* (jaw harp) for patient therapy in clinics; from broadcasting séances on TV to sponsoring conferences, schools, and associations. Debate has also begun on whether to create a "house of spirits" in

Invitation and identification card for the International Conference on Shamanism, held in Yakutsk, the Sakha Republic, August 1992, organized by Aiza Petrovna Reshetnikova and the Ministry of Culture. Note the multilingual message, in Sakha, English, and Russian. The perpendicular letters on the left spell, in the Sakha language, "the land of the Sakha," and those on the right the Russian word for the region, *Yakutia*. The central design, of a praying shaman superimposed over the back of a nine-pointed shamanic drum, also includes in its iconography the Sakha cosmology of three suns. The logo, inspired by a petroglyph of the Mokhsogolookh-Khaia culture found near Pokrovsk village, was designed by the late Sakha artist Vasilii Sutakov.

Yakutsk to bring shamanism out of the *taiga* into the city. Bounds of séance behavior are being pushed, but not forgotten. Vladimir may syncretize certain of his curing techniques with new-age bioenergy theory coming from Moscow and Kiev, but he, especially after his daughter's death, refuses to do anything that might offend spirits. He would not, for instance, risk evoking his helper spirits in a high-rise apartment merely to demonstrate the beauty of his spirit-calling poetry. But he did praise and recommend the sexy dreamlike shamanic poetry of the Sakha female writer Omsuura. And he did, after banishing the tape recorder, chant some of the lines of *algys* that he used at his Namsk festival. The following fragments give a feel for his sense of responsibility.

> Spirits of our homeland
> Spirits of labor for us . . .
> To you spirits I give prayers
> My tongue speaks for us
> Understand my speech
> The Sakha person
> Strains to ask an important favor
> That the spirits bring good fortune to our people
> Assuage and banish evil spirits and enemies
> From our homeland
> Dispel the darkness
> Dispel all knowledge of terror.

Just saying these words does not abolish evil spirits and enemies, these days openly considered to be Moscow officials, ecological despoilers, and industrial exploiters. But understanding such words in new political contexts has enabled a public mood conducive to change for the first time since the 1920s. For many Sakh, as for other fin-de-Soviet peoples shopping for diverse models in a politically porous world, it is "potentially a highly creative moment, one whose essential relativism forces us to recognize and reconsider the moral basis of our cognitive outlook that is so often masked by taken-for-granted communicative conventions. It is an equally dangerous moment for it can always stimulate backlash" (Crapanzano 1991:438). The internal dissent that I rashly criticized at a late-night Sakha Omuk ritual is part of an emergent brokering of national images (Anderson 1983). Anthropologists and national leaders can all try, without homogenization, to both respect the details of *olonkho* and, as Andrei suggested, "to take the essence of *kut-siur* and leap with it into the avant-garde."

Notes

1. Interviews relevant to this article have taken place in the field in 1986, 1991, and 1992, and in the United States in 1987 and 1992. Funding for fieldwork has been through the International Research and Exchanges Board, to which I am grateful and indebted. In June 1992, the Sakha drama theater participated in a festival in Chicago, where I, with some trepidation, translated excerpts of this article for the Minister of Culture for his reactions. In August 1992, several long sessions with Vladimir Kondakov enabled an update of 1991 discussions. Throughout Soviet history, policies and theories about nationalism fluctuated (Tillett 1969; Kuoljok 1985; Krupnik 1990; Tishkov 1992). But emphasis was on expunging all traces of nationalism for the glory of Soviet "internationalism."

2. There is considerable speculation on how the term *Yakut* originated, and whether it is derogatory. It is probably a Russian corruption of an Evenk word (Kulakovsky 1979:414).

3. Dmitri K. Sivstev, the author of the play and a venerable Sakha elder, continues to view the role of the Russians in Sakha history as predominantly benevolent (interview, July 1991).

4. My first sense of the extensive beauty of *olonkho* came from my Sakha teacher, Klara Belkin, to whom I am very grateful. See also Oiunsky 1975 and Pukhov 1975.

5. The idea of taking pen names became popular in Stalinist times with a generation of writers who wanted some superficial cover and who wished to choose Sakha names to express their Sakha identities. Almost all Sakha last names are Russian, a legacy of Russian empire taxation and missionary record keeping.

6. For political context, see Balzer 1990, 1992, and Vitebsky 1990. The highly publicized demonstrations were among the first of the Gorbachev era, and resulted in the arrest of student leaders. The local Communist Party official Iu. N. Prokop'ev (1986), excoriated the students as ungrateful nationalists.

7. This was the play brought to a Chicago theater festival, where it was well-received. Publicity for the play included Andrei, on National Public Radio, tracing his influences to shamanism, Russian "psychological" theater, and Japanese Kabuki.

8. Andrei in 1992 could not precisely recall when he had dropped his Communist Party membership, saying, "it just became ludicrous and irrelevant."

9. For sources on the history of this 1920s period see the contemporary journal *Sakha Keskile,* and Sakha Omuk's journal, *Ilin.* The leader of the group advocating the name Sakha Keskile, Lazar Afanasev, is critical of Andrei for not being Sakha enough (interviews with Lazar Afanasev, June–July 1991, August 1992).

10. See below for more on *aiyy* and their evil counterparts, *abaaghy.* Ideas of the group *kut-siur* are expressed in Afanas'ev, Romanov, Petrov, and Illarionov (1990).

11. The radicalization of Sakha nationalists stems in part from a fear of Russian nationalism. Andrei's approach fits with his background, exemplified in the expression "ikki atakhmaakh kihi aimakh" [person from clan with two legs]. But historically the Sakha have not been so accepting of others, unless they were willing to assimilate. Russian settlers and various northeastern Siberian peoples were "Yakutized" in the nineteenth century, learning the Yakut language and intermarrying.

12. Socrates said something analogous within Plato's *Dialogues* (1961:22). Andrei adapted the Socrates meaning, which was that in order to know anything we must understand we know nothing. Believing in a hypothetical catalogue of what to know is more positivist than Socrates' original meaning. In 1992, Andrei related Socrates' statement to European philosophy, saying it was preferable to merge East and West: "the Eastern, the Asian, view is that a person can know, discover, everything, inside himself."

13. See also Kondakov 1992a. The public forum was held in conjunction with, but was not part of, a 1992 international conference on shamanism, sponsored by the Ministry of Culture and organized by Aiza Reshetnikova, the director of the Museum of Music and Folklore, and Anatolii Gogolev, a Yakutsk University ethnographer. Vladimir Kondakov, though on the board of the conference, had second thoughts about its role, which he expressed widely (for example, Kim 1992). His main objection was that it stimulated further charlatanism, encouraging a faddish wave of pseudo-curers and gullible but potentially disillusioned patients. A second objection was that the energy stirred by many *extrasens* being in the same place was dangerous, and that without proper ritual handling of spirits, there was potential for accidents and sickness. The tragic robbery and murder of a young artist associated with the conference, prior to its opening, only confirmed this objection (see fig. 5.3).

14. I am grateful to my hosts Vladimir and Zina Ivanov, and to Aiza Reshetnikova, for their interest, support, and friendship.

15. In August 1991, I checked with C. W. Duncan Sings Alone, a friend who is a Cherokee healer, on whether shamanic amnesia was a common occurrence, and he confirmed that he does not always remember his séance spirit journeys (Balzer 1993).

16. A "bioenergy" wave has swept Russia, with many curers, some from Yakutia, training with the Russian spiritualist Juna in Moscow, or with the hypnotist Kandyba in Kiev. I have been the subject of bioenergy techniques, gaining temporary headache relief, but not with Vladimir. The method is based on beliefs in auras and energy fields. There are certain diseases Vladimir feels are not easily cured through shamanic

techniques, among these tuberculosis, eye disorders, malaria, epidemics like small-pox, Spanish flu (Kondakov 1992:44).

17. Aiza, whose own superb music training in Moscow led her to be receptive to "Russian" medicine, was bitterly torn after this encounter. She was inclined to believe that her mother would have benefitted more from traditional practitioners, given the sorry state of Soviet medicine. See Feshbach and Friendly 1992.

18. This Viliuisk region shaman lives with his parents in a small and isolated village, where many villagers think he is "just weird, not a healer," and his own mother is terrified of his fame. I made a personal and professional pilgrimage to this Viliuisk shaman later in 1991, and am honoring his request not to use his name in print. I hope to work with him in the future. He revealed enough telepathic skill to cause me to reevaluate my own assumptions about shamanism in relation to "science." Those who believe in his powers, whether or not they consider themselves his followers, say that he knows whenever his name is said aloud.

19. This is from an interview by Nadezhda Senkina (1991:5), a reporter whose father, Vasilii L. Senkin, has a wide reputation as a folk curer, and who has explored some potential curing skills in herself. I am grateful to them for many conversations and for sending the interview.

20. This comment was a pun on the Greek *Iliad* epic and a Sakha ancestor, Ellei, who is the hero of some Sakha epics, and the founder of the annual *yhyak* festival. See Sakha ethnographer Ksenofontov's 1977 *Elleiada*. See also Ksenofontov's superb 1992 studies of shamanism from the 1920s.

21. This analysis dovetails well with Mihály Hoppál's 1992:197–209) parallel use of the phrase "urban shamans," except that I make less of a rigid distinction between "sacred" and "profane," and thus between "religion" and "belief system." See also Roberte Hamayon's 1990:729–744 theory of shamanism as "managing the unpredictable."

References

Aitmatov, Chingis Torekulovich. 1983. *Pegii pes, begushchii kraem moriia.* In *Izbrannoe.* Frunze: Kirgizistan Press.

Afanas'ev, L., A. Romanov, R. Petrov, N. Petrov, and V. Illarionov. 1990. *Aiyy yorehe* [Teachings of the spirit]. Yakutsk: Sakha Keskile, Kut-Siur.

Alekseev, Nikolai Alekseevich. 1975. *Traditsionnye religioznye verovaniia Iakutov v XIX- nachale XX veke.* Novosibirsk: Nauka.

Anderson, Benedict. 1983. *Imagined Communities: Reflections on the Origin and Spread of Nationalism.* London: Verso.

Aprosimova, Liudmilla. 1992. *Aiahym ortoturgar syld'abyn* [I'm in the middle of the path]. Sakha Sire. 8 Aug. 1992, 5.

Balzer, Marjorie Mandelstam. 1990. "Nationalism in the Soviet Union: One Anthropological View." *Journal of Soviet Nationalities* 1, no. 3:3–22.

———. 1990a. Introduction. In *Shamanism: Soviet Studies of Traditional Religion in Siberia and Central Asia.* Ed. M. M. Balzer. Armonk, N.Y.: M. E. Sharpe.

———. 1992. "Dilemmas of the Spirit: Religion and atheism in the Yakut-Sakha

Republic." In *Religious Policy in the Soviet Union*. Ed. Sabrina Ramet. Cambridge: Cambridge University Press.

———. 1993. "The Poetry of Shamanism." In *Poetry and Prophecy: Cross-cultural Perspectives on Inspiration and Verbal Art*. Ed. John Leavitt. Forthcoming.

Bao Lord, Bette. 1990. *Legacies: A Chinese Mosaic*. New York: Ballantine Books.

Barth, Fredrik. 1969. *Ethnic Groups and Boundaries*. Boston: Little, Brown.

Bohannan, Laura. 1960. *The Frightened Witch*. In *In the Company of Man*. Ed. Joseph B. Casagrande. New York: Harper.

Comaroff, Jean. 1985. *Body of Power, Spirit of Resistance: The Culture and History of a South African People*. Chicago: University of Chicago Press.

Crapanzano, Vincent. 1991. "The Postmodern Crisis: Discourse, Parody, Memory." *Cultural Anthropology* 6(4):431–446.

Feshbach, Murray, and Alfred Friendly, Jr. 1992. *Ecocide in the USSR: Health and Nature Under Siege*. New York: Basic Books.

Gogolev, Anatolii Ignatevich. 1986. *Istoricheskaia etnografiia Iakutov*. Yakutsk: Yakutsk University Press.

Hamayon, Roberte. 1990. *La chasse à L'âme: Esquisse d'une théorie du chamanisme sibérien*. Nanterre: Société d'ethnologie.

Hoppál, Mihály. 1992. "Urgban Shamans, A Cultural Revival in the Postmodern World." In *Studies on Shamanism*, pp. 197–209. Ed. Anna-Leena Siikala and Mihály Hoppál. Helsinki: Finnish Anthropological Society; Budapest: Akademiai Kiado. *Ethnologica Uralica* 2.

Humphrey, Caroline. 1983. Karl Marx Collective: Economy, society and religion in a Siberian collective farm. Cambridge: Cambridge University Press.

Kim, Natalia. 1992. "Ia chubstvyiu vlianianie belykh sil." Interview with Vladimir Alekseevich Kondakov. *Yakutia* (15 Aug. 1992): 1–2.

Kondakov, Vladimir Alekseevich. 1992. *Emteehin Kisteleng neritten* [A few secrets of folk-curing]. Yakutsk: Association of Folk Medicine.

———. 1992a. "Uiruurdaan uola" [Son of Uiruurdaan]. *Sakhaada* (5 Aug. 1992): 9.

Krupnik, Igor. 1990. "Natsional'nyi vopros v SSSR: poiski ob'iasnenii." *Sovetskaia Etnografiia* 4:3–15.

Ksenofontov, Gavril Vasil'evich. 1977. *Elleiada: Materialy po mifologii i legendarnoi istorii Iakutov*. Moscow: Nauka.

Ksenofontov, Gavril Vasil'evich. 1992. *Shamanizm: Izbrannye trudy*. Ed. A. N. Diachkova. Yakutsk: Sever-Iug Firm for the Museum of Music and Folklore of the Peoples of Yakutia.

Kulakovsky, Aleksei Eliseevich. 1979. *Nauchnye Trudy*. Yakutsk: Institute of Languages, Literature, and History.

Kuoljok, Kerstin Eidlitz. 1985. *The Revolution in the North: Soviet Ethnography and Nationality Policy*. Uppsala: Almquist and Wiksell for Acta Universitatis Upsaliensis.

Kurilov, Semen Nikolaevich. 1983. *Khanido i Khalerkha*. Moscow: Sovremennik.

MacCormack, Carol, and Marilyn Strathern. 1980. *Nature, Culture and Gender*. Cambridge: Cambridge University Press.

Marcus, George, and Michael M. J. Fischer. 1986. *Anthropology as Cultural Critique*. Chicago: University of Chicago Press.

Martynov, Anatoly I. 1991. *The Ancient Art of Northern Asia*. Trans. and ed. Demitri B. Shimkin and Edith M. Shimkin. Urbana: University of Illinois Press.

Oiunsky (Sleptsov), Platon Alekseevich. 1975. *Niurgun Bootur Stremitel'nyi. Iakutskii geroicheskii epos olonkho*. Trans. V. Derzhavin. Yakutsk: Yakutsk Press.

Okladnikov, Aleksei Pavlovich. 1970. *Yakutia Before Is Incorporation into the Russian State*. Trans. Stephen P. Dunn and Ethel Dunn. Ed. Henry Michael. Montreal: McGill-Queen's University Press.

Plato. 1961. *Dialogues of Plato*. Trans. Jowett. Ed. J. D. Kaplan. New York: Washington Square Press.

Pukhov, I. V. 1975. *Olonkho—drevnii epos Iakutov*. In *Niurgun Bootur Stremitel'nyi*, pp. 411–30. Trans. V. Derzhavin. Yakutsk: Yakutsk Univ. Press.

Senkina, Nadezhda Vasil'evna. 1991. "V. A. Kondakov: Tselitel'—lish' posrednik mezhdu vyshimi silami i liudmi." *Molodezh Iakutii* (14 Mar. 1991): 5.

Tillett, Lionel. 1969. *The Great Friendship: Soviet Historians on the Non-Russian Nationalities*. Chapel Hill, N.C.: University of North Carolina Press.

Tishkov, Valery Aleksandrovich. 1992. *Sovetskaia etnografiia: Preodolenie krizisa*. Etnograficheskoe Obozrenie 1:5–20.

Turner, Victor, ed. 1982. *Celebration: Studies in Festivity and Ritual*. Washington, D.C.: Smithsonian Institution Press.

Vinokurova, Iuliana A. 1991. "Etnopsikhologicheskie osnovy mezhlichnostnykh natsional'nykh otnoshenii." In *Mezhnatsional'nye otnosheniia v regione (po materialam Iakutskoi ASSR)*. Yakutsk: Institute of Languages, Literature, and History.

Vitebsky, Piers. 1990. "Yakut." In *The Nationalities Question in the Soviet Union*, pp. 304–19. Ed. Graham Smith. London: Longman Press.

6

RACISM AND THE FORMATION
OF A ROMANI ETHNIC LEADER

I met Nicolae Gheorghe in 1979 when I returned to Romania to research the relationship between ethnic group development and occupational specialization in the Brasov district of Transylvania. He and I cooperated in a survey of the region. He was a young research sociologist who was exploring his Romani ethnic identity and ethnic activism.[1] To find any Romanian involved in these activities, much less a Gypsy, surprised me. Marxist-Leninist theorists and Ceauşescuites had eliminated ethnicity as a viable form of political organization. Romanians did not consider Gypsies, known as *ţigani* in Romania, a nationality; rarely were they considered even an ethnic group. This put Nicolae in the precarious position of having to deny his activities in organizing Romanies around their ethnic identity. My work with Nicolae placed both of us in a political grey area at best and a forbidden terrain at worst.

As I got to know him better, I learned that he often had to explain his behavior to the authorities. This made him suspect to anyone who understood the precariousness of what he was doing. He walked a tightrope between the authorities and the people who judged his public and research behavior. At times, this condition curtailed his ability to continue research among the Romani and to advocate their rights. In Romania, it was one thing to advocate the rights of Hungarian, German, and Jewish ethnic minorities (a dangerous and dubious activity as it is); it was yet another matter to advocate the rights of *ţigani*.[2]

Far from making ethnicity extinct, Romanian *socialist nationalism* actively produced ethnic distinctions. Ethnic minority groups either reacted against Romanian presumptions of Romanian hegemony or they struggled to claim cultural characteristics and behaviors that symbolized their differences to make them stand out. In either case, ethnic minorities endured Romanian ethnonational ascendancy and publicly suppressed their cultural, social, economic, and political group identities. In a world of other states, the formation

Nicolae Gheorghe and a Hungarian Roma (seminomadic Kalderari) tin smith. The picture was taken in the summer of 1979. Nicolae is translating and reading from a journal on Romas written mostly by Romas. The Kalderari is looking at a copy of New Testament selections translated into Romani. The discussion took place in Sacele, a town near the city of Brasov in Transylvania.

of the Romanian nation-state created the conditions in which ethnic minorities had to claim their identities or lose them.

Communism in Romania created the context in which hostilities between Hungarians and Romanians persisted (see Beck and McArthur 1981; Verdery 1991). Ethnic Hungarians in Romania and ethnic Romanians remembered the atrocities and competition over Transylvania during World War II. During the war, Hungarians and Romanians evacuated their respective communities as the "enemy" created the conditions of displacement. After the war, many displaced people returned home to communities in which members of enemy ethnic groups were supposed to live side by side. The potential for conflict between Romania and Hungary, over Transylvania, and their respective ethnic populations persist.[3]

The population transfers after the war included the mass depopulation of Romania's Jews.[4] There were nearly 900,000 Jews in Romania before World War II. Between 1950 and 1990, Jews left for Israel in such large numbers that now they amount to less than twenty thousand in Romania. Similarly, Stalinist policy blamed German ethnic minorities, as a class, for the horrors induced by Nazi Germany. Displacement from their homes, the trek to Soviet labor camps, and difficult camp conditions caused much death among Romania's adult German population. The result of post–World War II policy and the 1960s international agreements for family reunification created a massive migration of ethnic Germans from Romania to Germany.[5] During World War II, the Romanies of Romania suffered the same fate as Jews. The Nazis and their sympathizers forced Gypsies into concentration camps. However, first they were allowed to die on their northward trek. Then they were killed because of inhumane conditions of the camps.[6]

Under communism, the Romanies simultaneously experienced improved and worsening conditions. Forced settlement and increased surveillance of them as a social problem exposed them to strenuous assimilation forces.[7] The non-Romani populations understood the privileging of Gypsies in this way as an improvement. Of course, those Gypsies who understood their future in Romania as a process of assimilation took advantage of the preferential treatment they received through the communist government.

The Romani made up a large part of the lower socioeconomic strata in Romania. *Ţigani,* as an "oppressed" class, were privileged in the new worker society. After World War II, the Communist Party recruited them into local cadres of leaders and activists. Given their lumpen class status, they received priority in access to housing, jobs, political positions, and education. This stage of privileging Gypsies, as was the case for some Jews, did not persist and was applied unevenly, resulting in a complex matrix of contradictory experiences by Gypsies under conditions of communism.

Nicolae Gheorghe introduced me to this world of the Romani under Ceausescuite communism and exposed me irrevocably to the complexity of interethnic relations and states. Nicolae's place in society was not a simple one. It was textured by the multiple identities he assumed and that others foisted upon him. He characterized himself as a sociological researcher with aspirations to create a space in which the Roma could practice their ethnicity without harm. Even if he wanted to, he could not escape his heritage. His skin is dark and his facial features easily identify him as a *ţigani*. Through him I met other Romanies. They spoke to me of their life experiences and informed me about what Romanians said about Gypsies and how they behaved toward them. Over the course of a year I also made my observations. I quickly learned that Romanians understood Gypsies as a *social problem*. Enlightened leaders, such as Nicolae Gheorghe, understood Romania as having a problem of *interethnic relations*. I assessed the Romani social condition as one of *racism*.

My professional relationship with Nicolae started with a survey of the Olt-land (*Tara Oltului*). I was studying what he wanted to learn more about. This region is among the most intensely studied in Romania. It has a feudal history of highly concentrated "free" and "ennobled" ethnic Romanians. In the in-terwar period, sociologist Dimitrie Gusti's action-research team carried out extensive work here, resulting in a large body of published material. Other scholars, such as Stefan Meteş (1935), Alexander Barbat (1938), and David Prodan (1970), also carried out notable research here, often including infor-mation on Gypsies. Only Ion Chelchea, a member of Gusti's research team, focussed special attention on *ţigani* 1944.

Romanian claims to this region as an "archaic" ethnic Romanian region (among others) are used to assert rights over Transylvania. This contested region, according to Romanian ethnonationalists, rightfully belongs to Ro-mania. It does not belong to Hungary, the claim goes, because of its longer ethnic Romanian settlement history (see Prodan 1970; Verdery 1991). The habitation of ethnic Romanians in the uplands of the region is central to the argument made by Hungarian ethnonationalists. According to them, Transyl-vania was an "empty land" before the Magyars came to settle it.

In interviewing Gypsies over the expanse of this region, we realized that the diversity of the Roma was even greater than either one of us had sus-pected. Language, occupation, custom, local and regional history, their mi-gration routes and length of settlement, and the nature of their interaction with non-Romanies segmented them. They developed identities that separated one group from the other, often supported by social organizations of exclusion and endogemous marriage patterns. Non-Romani people used the term *ţigani* pejoratively. This was less a term used to identify an ethnic group, although it was similar to it. *Ţigani* is a Romanian term of deculturation and deterri-torialization. Romanians commonly called the *ţigani* "uncultured" or "un-civilized." They were perceived as a migratory population, which despite sometimes centuries of sedentary existence, and therefore had no real home-land or state to speak of. For the most part, the term referred to behavior Romanians found unacceptable, often a condition of *ţigani* poverty.

"Blaming the victim" prevented a more critical analysis of what caused conditions of poverty in the first place.[8] *Ţigani* were perceived as unchanging. Ethnic Romanians often claimed that even when Gypsies received the luxuries of sedentary existence, they destroyed them. They destroyed highly coveted apartments in newly constructed buildings and "built fires in the middle of their living rooms." In the communist period, Romanians explained Gypsy behavior not as an element of their ethnicity, of customs. They explained Gypsy behavior as a genetically induced flaw: "They are unable to live otherwise." Romanians treated the Gypsy problem as a matter of class, but understood it as a matter of race. Non-Romanies did not recognize those *ţigani* who fully assimilated and became successful in the sense of majority society. When ever it was convenient, non-Romanies chose to focus on negative traits that identified inescapable *ţigani* behavior and attitudes.

This is how Nicolae and I came to realize that the term *Gypsy* is an aspect of oppression. It derives from the misconception that Gypsies are descendants of Egyptians. During the thirteenth, fourteenth, and fifteenth centuries, Gypsies appeared in increasing numbers over much of Europe. At first, they were received with the courtesy of a nobility. However, quite rapidly they were marginalized as a suspect group. Rumors spread rapidly that they were criminals, petty thieves, child abductors, and murderers. In Europe, the more common term for Gypsy is a derivative of *ţigani: Zigeuner* (German), or *Cigan* (Slavic). This term has its root in the Greek word *Hatsigganoi*, "the name of a Manichaean sect in the Byzantine Empire with whom the Rom were confused" (Hancock 1991:253). This term, also Gypsy, pejoratively denotes low status, negative behavior, and uncleanliness. The customary use of these terms prevented the idea of Gypsies as acceptable members of society. This is a central feature of oppression with which ethnic minorities have struggled.

Over the course of our work in 1979 and 1980, Nicolae and I came into increasing contact with the authorities, from local police to the secret police. Our interest in *ţigani* and our participation in their activities increased our visibility as outsiders. At time they merely questioned us. The authorities did this in the aggressive manner that people in power can take, knowing that they can cause great harm if they so wanted. Once they brought us to a regional city's police station. They detained and interrogated us separately behind closed doors because we were seen to be talking to *ţigani* at a regional fair.

The Romanies were a taboo subject, even for Romanian researchers. Denying the Roma the dignity of their culture within Romanian history is an important feature of their oppression. As a decultured and deterritorialized people, their access to resources and work places were limited. In writing about African-American consciousness, Bernard Magubane found that "deculturation is almost always a stage preceding and prerequisite to acculturation" (1978:45). Slavery in both instances had a ramifying impact on a people whose self-identity was put into jeopardy.

Even under the best of circumstances, the study of Gypsies takes place at the margins of social scientific and humanities disciplines. Gypsies are an exoticized group whose position in society is one of equivocation and ambiguity. They are viewed as inconsequential. They are not perceived as an indigenous population anywhere and do not belong to any state. Rarely are they seen as people who have legitimate claims in their settlements. They are not perceived as colonizers of any place. By definition, they wander. They are universally understood as victimizers, rarely as victimized. They elicit little sympathy for their condition, one that is perceived as self-made. They are seen as "naturally" having to live in the manner they do. It is their "culture of poverty."

Their origins and well-known patterns of migration are more often viewed as an aspect of their culture and crucial to the group's economy and, therefore, survival. Their place in society is normally not understood as a consequence of economic and political forces that marginalize them. They are perceived as nomads, moving about wherever need takes them, even when they have been sedentary for centuries. They are a population of Europe, but they are not considered European. No country in which they have resided has wished to claim them as citizens. States often seek Gypsy expulsion.[9]

The events of the Romanian revolution and then of the transition, from the end of 1989 until the present, has reinvented the tradition of scapegoating Gypsies. The manipulation by television news created the image of *ţigani* as a people without social conscience and ravenously feeding off the free marketing. The Romas were seen to be disturbing the peace, begging in increasing numbers in city streets, participating in the black market with difficult-to-obtain goods, and apparently making much money.

During the rioting of miners in Bucharest in 1991, among those targeted for violence were *ţigani*. Later that year, several Roma settlements, in many provincial settings, were burned down and the inhabitants were chased away from their homes. Nicolae Gheorghe and his colleagues sought to explain these attacks, prevent them, reduce their intensity, fight for reparations and obtain the rights and resources for resettlement. He was not alone in seeking to limit and eliminate this form of hostile interaction. Several Roma associations and political parties were born in this period. Romas from all walks of life sought to prevent the acceptance of anti-Gypsy violence and prejudice.

Many Gypsies have appropriated the identity given them by majority populations. Yet, even under hegemonic and assimilationist circumstances, their inability to escape a Gypsy identity provokes cyclical occurrences of discrimination, repression, and violence. Gypsies have responded through their mobility and activities at the margins of the economy. In this context, they help reproduce the conditions in which discrimination occurs by fitting the stereotypes, the icons, imagined by the majority.

Over a period of centuries, Gypsies have experienced a transnational existence, not because they wanted to but because they have had to. Their place within "host" societies has been defined by biased preconceptions that

Gypsies are inherently different.[10] They lacked a state that would enable them to center their nationality. They have been perceived as unable or not wishing to stand and fight for the rights of the people with whom they are engaged.[11] This has resulted in efforts to push them out of settlements and further to marginalize them.

Nicolae Gheorghe's initial conversation with me in 1979 (which I reproduce in part below) was also a means of working out his place in society. He sought to discover who he was and what he should be doing as a scholar/ researcher, activist Gypsy, intellectual, and Romanian citizen. Simultaneously, he was working out a plan of action to liberate *tigani* from the yoke of a denied discrimination based on race. This liberation strategy considered the *tigani* and the majority population. Nicolae understood his role as an organizer and, perhaps more importantly, as an educator. He sought to set the context in which groups of people could learn about each other and discover their common humanity.

The text below documents Nicolae's development as a Romanian, a *tigani* intellectual, and one among many international leaders seeking to legitimize the Roma as an ethnic group with the qualities of a nation but that lack a state. From the very beginning, Nicolae sought to globalize *tigani* issues. He sought to show the unity of people, whose diaspora covers much of the planet, and in their unification create an independent source of power. This also was a tactic for gaining access to the international press, which could protect him from the authorities who feared bad press.

In 1979, Nicolae sought to place his search for identity and his need to organize "his people" in the larger political context and the wider ethnic discourse. Nicolae sought to break communist constraints, yet to work within the confines of this system. To compensate for his inability to travel outside Romania, he educated himself about the outside world through discussions with members of the foreign community. His interaction with the international community in the 1970s and 1980s also was a means for protecting himself from the incursions of the Securitate (Communist Romania's much-dreaded and feared secret police) and other authorities. By being "well-connected" in this manner, he could seek support for efforts to rescue him in the eventuality that he would get into difficulties. He also could provide information to the authorities to gain their support and to allow him to carry out his work with less interferance. He created a new vocabulary for himself and those he could influence. He used a liberatory language that enabled the formation of a social movement based on Romani ethnic group identity.

He understood that his place in society was less a matter of ethnicity or even class, but one of race. He came to learn that racism against Gypsies is not merely a Romanian phenomenon, but one that penetrated Euro-American traditions. He sought historical roots, instances in the past, to create a social model based on actually existing social processes. These would give him the insights he needed to understand who the Gypsies in Romania have become and what they might be and do in the future. His emergent vision under Ceausescuite communism was utopian. Looking at his vision now, thirteen years since my first interview with him, I am hard-pressed to describe him as anything less than visionary. His vision has come true.

His search was for a political voice under communism. Here, only one form of formal politics was possible and ethnic politics were understood either as a threat against the state or illegal chauvinism. He sought to create multiple Gypsy voices that could insert themselves into Romanian national politics. With the revolution, he and his colleagues, who have been part of this struggle, have accomplished this for the moment. This has not come easily. It was not without costs and personal sacrifices.

With his discovery of the extraordinary diversity among Gypsies, he struggled to understand the interplay of their different voices and experiences while simultaneously recognizing common interests. His research with them turned into a discourse among Gypsy leaders that empowered and encouraged him as he came to identify himself with them. Yes, he, too, as a *tigani*. He wanted to identify himself in this way as a matter of pride, not as a matter of self-defense and shame.

Nicolae called me on the telephone on 5 December 1991 saying that he was in New York City and that he would like to see me. This year alone, he made fifteen international trips out of Romania, participating in international conferences that included those sponsored by the United Nations, the European Economic Community, and the International Romani Union. He became a member of a wide-ranging international network of Roma leaders. As such, he became responsible for bringing the world's attention to the plight of the Romanies in Romania, although he would vigorously decline taking credit for this. Throughout the year he successfully mobilized international journalists to cover the impact of the revolution on the Gypsies. This has included stories on forced evictions of Gypsies from their villages, the confiscation of their property, and the burning down of their homes. He has drawn attention to West European resistance to admit migrating Gypsies. In December 1991, Human Rights Watch honored him for his work as a human rights monitor in Romania.

He did these things out of a conviction that what he is doing is just and must be done. He has sought to limit his notoriety and feels uncomfortable with his portrayal in this document. He would be the first to say that his activities pale in comparison with the work of others. Some have died, others continue to work, and still others have tired of working in the tension-filled intimacy of participating "within the Roma community."

When I interviewed Nicolae in 1979, he theorized practice. He reflected on the possibilities that he was not honestly approaching the service he was offering his people. These were a people with whom he was only slowly accepting as his as he explored his identity, simultaneously accepting and rejecting *romanipe* (Gypsiness).

BECK: When did you become conscious of yourself as a *ţigani?*

GHEORGHE: Both my parents are *ţigani vatraşi.*[12] My grandfather on my father's side, was a village *fierar,* very dark in color.[13] He was also a peasant, having received land through the agrarian reforms after World War I. His sister married a famous *lautari* from Turnu Magurele. His brother was an itinerant merchant of little things [*marunţişuri*] who travelled to market days all over the country. He lacked an occupation but he liked to read. It is his name I carry.

My father's sister was a washerwoman all her life. So from my father's line one can detect some central *ţigani* characteristics. All my father's family is very dark in color.

Neither my grandmother, nor my grandfather on my mother's side, is visibly *ţigani.* My grandmother and grandfather were more like village peasants. They came to the city from a village nearby to sell milk and other things. They were viewed as *ţigani ţarani* [peasant *ţigani*].

My family enjoyed prestige on the street where we lived. People perceived them as "a different kind of *ţigani.*" My mother taught me to be clean and to be well behaved, not to partake in street life and not to mix yourself with *ţigani.* My mother taught me my entire life, "Don't be a *ţigani.*" My mother socialized me in terms of the Roma—more drastic than those of the Roma. The Romas represent a pure element among Gypsies. They are authentic. *Ţigani* have lost their social structure through assimilation and drastic changes they experienced over time. The Romas have social standards they continue to practice, even in the face of oppression.

When I was three or four years old I lived in the countryside with my grandmother. There I was free. I could play on the street with the other children. I didn't feel that I am a *ţigani.* Segregation was much more powerful there because in the structure of a village, everyone knew who was or wasn't a *ţigani.* It was clear who my family was.[14]

My memory of being a *ţigani* started from age five and six, when I returned to my old community. I remember two or three families of poor Romanians living on my street. We were among the best fed on that street, an important sign of local prestige. My father worked in Bucharest and would send us packages by train filled with food, bread, and other necessities. Every time we went past the Romanians on our way to the city, to the train station, or when we had to walk in front of their house, the children would yell out at us, "*Ga, ga, cioara, țigane!*" [15] At this time I started to feel the feeling of discrimination.

When I started to go to school in 1952, I was about six years old. This is when my embarrassment about being a *țigani* started.

With school something new started in my life. I seemed to have a special ability for reading that my teachers, who liked me very much, recognized. Yet, some of my classmates, at recreation time, or during breaks and play, would call me *țigani*.

I was always a little ugly. I was always a bit thin, stunted in growth. I was very black and a bit yellow and frail. I always looked a bit sick. My lips were always a bit thick, the focus of much name calling. I remember one kid with whom I competed in school. He came from a very good family. He was seven or eight years old, very well dressed, very white, very beautiful, and sometimes a talented student. He taught me my first nickname, "-seven kilograms of lips," or "Yo, little *țigani!*"

After the war, it was forbidden to say *țigani*. Anyone who said *țigani* could be taken to court, given fines, and so on. Even children knew this, so, usually, they wouldn't say it directly or publicly. They were more discrete. They would just make sounds, like "*ga, ga.*" Or they would tell you, "*Cior-ma!*" [You crow!].

Once my family made an excursion to the river, near my city. We met some *țigani* on the public promenade there, who lived at the end of our street. They saw my mother well dressed and said, "Even if she dresses herself in silk, she will always remained a țiganca. Among *țigani,* she inevitably remained a *țiganca.*

My mother used to tell me a story about World War II. On 8 September, in one of those war years, she went to the fair with one of her nieces, who is very dark. It was evident that she is a *țiganca.* An order had come to collect all *țigani.* The police and the gendarmes encircled the fairgrounds sweeping up all the *țigani* to deport them.

Many *țigani* were concentrated then all over the country. The gendarmes cordoned off the fairgrounds with wagons and isolated the *țigani* in one area. They forced my mother and my cousin to stand there for hours. They knew that they all would be sent to the Bug River concentration camps. Fortunately, a Romanian acquaintance recognized her. She went to some people in the city who knew my mother, a niece of my "auntie" Marița, in whose house my mother washed clothes. They came and rescued her and my cousin. If this relationship had not existed, like so many others, they would have been moved from one place to another until they died. Or they would have ended in the camp where their survival chances would have been limited.

When I finished second grade, at age eight, I moved to Bucharest. My father had already worked there for a long time, coming home only now and again, every two or three months. My mother cared for the household and raised us. Bucharest meant something new for me. On the street, ethnic relations were not so intense. I played with Romanian children. I was among the oldest of the children and I became a leader in the group.

When I was in the fifth grade, my mother wanted me to learn a musical instrument. So I stayed in the country for some time with my uncle who played the accordion. When I came home they bought me a very good accordion and told me to practice. I didn't like it because, even if I had a certain talent for it, this was one sign of being a *ţigani.* I hated myself for learning the accordion and that I could not change being a *ţigani.* I thought, "Am I destined to be a *ţigani?"*

When I was in the sixth grade a new kid appeared. He was one year older than me. Each time he would see me, he would yell out at me, "Yo, Gypsy!" He even tried to beat up on me. I fought with him because of the way he behaved. Sam, I can't tell you what I invented in my mind to escape meeting him. Something would profoundly agitate me; something would gnaw on my guts when I would see him. I feared what he would say. I knew which words would come out of his mouth. At any moment he would say, "Yo, *ţigani."*

On my daily trek to school, I had to walk down the street on which he lived. I tried to avoid him by circling around his house. This was a most painful time in my life. This guy haunted me because he could always show my inferiority.

I always took first prize in school, except the fourth grade. My mother and father always pressed me to do well and I always did. I also took first prize in the fifth, sixth, and seventh grades. Do you understand, first prize? The end of school came in the seventh year, when I had to take my exams. I did well.

My mother wanted me to play music. This was during the Soviet period, when we only saw Soviet films. I was an avid reader. I would go to the public library and read in the fantastic Russian war literature. I saw many war films and then somehow I knew, instinctively, that I should join the military.

My mother was practical. She wanted me to go to music school. You could always earn your keep playing music. I refused. Not that I didn't play my accordion. I played for friends. For some children, parents decide this at childhood; not for me. I never played the accordion outside the household.

I remained stubborn about going to the military lyceum. I really wanted to leave home. I wanted to leave my street. This was my opportunity. I went to the military lyceum despite my mother's pain.

They laughed at me from the start. They would say to me, "You African!" After about two months I became the assistant to the platoon commander. This lasted three years. There were many elements that powerfully crystallized within me in this time. I was a fast learner. I was in a hierarchical relationship with my colleagues. I was a very good UTCist [UTC was the Communist Youth League]. I was among the best.

In my adolescence I developed a complex about my physical appearance. I knew I wasn't good-looking. This was a terrible period for me. Some of my colleagues made fun of me behind my back and I became terribly insecure. I became increasingly introverted, unsure, isolated, and unhappy. I always felt as if there was a double "something" in me.

After the military lyceum, I wanted to enter medical school. I got a job at the neurosurgical hospital not far from my home. I studied and prepared myself until I started reading in philosophy and sociology in 1967 and 1968, when sociology was revived in Romania.[16] It was a period in which sociology was dogmatized. It was almost messianic; something that would resolve all problems. It would deliver us. Philosophy would be combined with practice. To my father's pain, I chose to pursue sociology. I took the exam and entered the university.

I became the president of the student association. Most students entered the Party and so did I. I did not develop a *ţigani* identity at the university. On the contrary, I became very Romanian. Remember, it was a particularly intense nationalistic period.[17]

Although occasionally my colleagues in the university hazed me, there were no open anti-*ţigani* attacks on me. I had a Romanian girlfriend. Even here I kept my distance from *ţigani*. I only had contact with my kin. In my family I avoided discussions about *ţigani*. I avoided the subject. Yet, whenever they talked about them, something within me would be roused.

I finished university in 1972. In the fall of 1973 through the spring of 1974 I went through a personal and professional crisis. I felt finished, dismembered. I wanted to go on in the university, but could not. I had applied for my doctorate, but placed second. I moved from the university to the Sociology Center, where I started to work on the problem of systematization.[18] I was unhappy working on this topic and profoundly dissatisfied.

Right after finishing university, I went home for a visit. My mother put on this record. "Troubles, Troubles," a Gypsy song by Rodica Buceanu. This was the first time after many, many years that I heard this song. It stirred something within me. I felt something that was very close, but without connecting it to my *ţigani* identity.

After many, many years I asked myself, "So, what is this part of me, the *ţigani* part? What should I do with this?" At some point, I realized that I was denying myself my identity. This was a period of profound despair.

In the summer of 1974, I had to prepare for an exam in social anthropology to take my doctoral exam. I started to read anthropology. I read Lévi-

Strauss, *The Elementary Structures of Kinship*. I read this *Structural Anthropology* and *The Savage Mind*. *Elementary Structures of Kinship* influenced me greatly. Another important source for me at this time was *One Hundred Years of Solitude,* by Gabriel García Marquez. It was so powerful! One beautiful symbol in the book is a *ţigani,* a very small figure, but with universal wisdom.

In 1973 I visited the Sibiu area [in Transylvania] and went to the village of Dumbraveni where I encountered *corturari* (tent dwellers who then were sedentary).[19] I felt something special among them. It was that feeling I got from listening to Gypsy music and reading Lévi-Strauss. Reading Lévi-Strauss gave me the idea to find something original, something traditional among the *corturari*. So I thought, "Hey, let's do an anthropological study of the *corturari!*" On Saint Nicolaus Day, in December 1974, I went into the field.

As time passed, I identified myself with this group. When I was among them I said, "I am a *ţigani* too." Some believed it, others didn't know what to believe. At the start they were afraid of me. They did not accept me. In 1975, they did. I was absorbed by my role with them as a researcher of *ţigani,* as a knowledgeable person of *ţigani* matters, and in my capacity of translating *ţigani* issues for colleagues at the institute and with officials.

Our self-identification comes from diverse social sources in which we participate. Ethnic groups are one of them. That is the theory. My principal identity, not only officially, but also in relationship to my quality as an intellectual, is my professional role, my position in the organization. Anyhow, I am an intellectual.

For me an ethnic group is more than a reference group. The way I live now manifests my ethnic identity. It is very important to understand my ethnic identity as a spiritual process. I was not socialized as a *ţigani*. Ethnic identity for me is a symbolic issue because I am not part of a concrete group of *ţigani*. It is all ambiguous.

What I would like more than anything else, beyond my need to participate in society, I would like *ţigani* to be acknowledged through some national discussion about them. They should have some role in social life.

I couldn't obtain formal acceptance for my research among the *ţigani*. Yet, as a researcher I could still be with a group of *ţigani* for five years. I had this very intense contact with *ţigani* as a formal person, but unofficially, more like a friend.

I am developing a plan where I can be spiritually involved in my research, not just as an outsider. I want to develop a formal voluntary association in which people can come together because it is in their interest to do so. I could say to them, "Look, I am from this association. I am going to do something for you. Or, what do you need done?"

If *ţigani* could be organized like this, this would means access to publishing and mass media, theater, and so on. They could easily reach people in localities. This is where artistic groups are organized. I don't mean that they would organize formally into political bodies.[20] I am looking for a social field behind such councils, made up of people who would be involved in social actions.

If *ţigani* would organize like this they could represent different groups and so their social actions could be much larger and stronger. Then whoever wants to, can.

In such a situation, I would much prefer to appear with my identity as researcher, which implies some kind of detachment from the issues. As a member of the Sociology Center, I could work as any other researcher on this social problem. I would have much more credibility among people with whom I work. If I were participating as a *ţigani,* then I would be suspected of pursuing personal interests. Someone could say, "Hey, he's trying to be political."

There was an organization of Roma before World War II. It was an organization full of tensions. When you read this paper, you will see that they cursed each other. Some of them slandered others because it was a matter of power. As an intellectual, power tempts but simultaneously repulses me. I know there is something dangerous about it. I do not want to be an intellectual in a position of power because the result is that your relationship to people changes. Politics are something else than science and knowledge. It also is different from social action.

People do not suspect me. I think that what I do is political. The question is, "Do I want it to be this way?" I am looking at this a bit idealistically. I want to be political, but not my personal politics. It should be the politics of the other! My work is based on sacrifice, public service, in the interest of the collectivity. This transcends any personal interests I might have.

These organizations should be tied to the symbols that *ţigani* evoke. The *ţigani,* who is always a fiction, evokes something different in different people. To people, the *ţigani* is something strange, interesting, and even important, something with power. *Ţigani* have a kind of power over those who encounter their myth and believe in it. This inspires them. The organization I have in mind should be created by the *ţigani* and controlled by them. It should not be an organization imaged by non-*ţigani.*

Many *ţigani* are sedentary and have been so for a very long time. These are acculturated *ţigani,* or assimilated at various stages of assimilation. Those who are assimilated most often use the criteria of success and prestige of the larger society around them. Larger society and many *ţigani* groups view people who develop visibly public careers who have large earnings with great appreciation.

Perhaps a lawyer could be a leader. *Corturari* leaders have limited appeal. Perhaps their wealth, knowing that they have gold, would attract adherents. We need a leader who has a successful public image, not necessarily an intellectual. He needs some wealth and the ability to unite people around him. Our gatherings also should be shaped by custom and not the gatherings in which we now participate that take place in halls. We should use rights of passage, rituals, and celebrations to bring people together, where we can talk about politics. Such events should attract *ţigani* as *ţigani*.

BECK: When did you start thinking about *ţigani* symbols in this way?

GHEORGHE: I started to think about this more in political terms this fall, not in policy terms, but in terms of politics. I started to think about politics in terms of values, in terms that are action oriented. I want to see people get together. Initially I sought to understand how *ţigani* think among themselves and how they want to change their condition.

I believe that our Romanian society has the abilities, in its own ideology, to help resolve the problems that *ţigani* face. We need new symbols for the *ţigani* because even from the perspective of the state and the Communist Party it is difficult to discuss this matter. We are unable to talk about anything else except *ţigani,* in the negative sense of the word.

This should be a consecrated discourse. A language should be used that all know and in which all participate. Yet, what images do people have about *ţigani?* What meaning does the word *ţigani* hold in society? How nuanced is this term? When using this word, can we understand the total history of this population?

In this respect the Romanian language is seriously flawed. In Romanian, the word *ţigani* does not have a pleasant meaning. When someone calls you a *ţigani,* it is not understood as a compliment.

Because of my preoccupation with *ţigani,* I have become much more interested in the problems we have in this country. I now have found something for me to do here. The challenges ahead energize me. I am discovering something about myself. If you are a researcher whose profession asks you to be detached and objective, can you feel comfortable? Is it possible not to interest yourself in the effect of your work on the people whom you are researching? Shouldn't we ask ourselves, "Who is this for?"

You asked before if I have a model in mind for myself as I work. A story I read as a child comes to mind. It was about a secret police officer. It is about Comosi Sandor, who went to Tibet. He wanted to rewrite Hungarian history. This was at the end of the eighteenth and the start of the nineteenth century. He was unable to find the origins of the Hungarians, but he became one of the first to develop the basis for Finno-Ugric comparative philology. He studied dialects and compared them to the Hungarian language. He did what I aspire to do, to give people a sense of self-identity. I want to help people develop a sentiment of belonging. The possibility that I could resolve some tensions in people's souls motivates me. This is worth doing for the *ţigani.*

Gypsies have different types of behavior. I realized this from you. You are the one who made me think about this in this manner. Now the idea that I had about diversity has become clearer. There is a difference among the different *ţigani* groups.

These groups should talk among themselves and with the outside society. People should communicate. Without social contact and without interchange among them, it will be impossible to formulate a common identity. *Ţigani* groups do talk to each other, but they have to do it within preexisting structures and forms. They are forced to communicate through established state institutions.

The official figure for the number of *ţigani* in Romania is 240,000. What do they have in common? Do they have as much in common as 1,800,000 Hungarians? These Hungarians do have something in common, but is it as much as 240,000 *ţigani?* When we speak about 240,000 *ţigani,* what are the characteristics they share? Most of them are most likely not working in formal jobs. The majority has a disorganized life-style. It is a mistake to think that these *ţigani,* who are the most visible, represent all the *ţigani.* They stigmatize all the others. *Ţigani* find it difficult to identify themselves as *ţigani,* even among themselves.

Romanian Romas were involved in unifying movements even before World War II. According to Ian Hancock,

> In Romania, Association of Roma was founded in Clabor, in 1926, and between 1930 and 1934 published a journal called *Romani Family.* Another organization, the General Association of Roma, was created by a non-Gypsy called Lasurica. It was avowedly nationalistic in orientation, but survived only through 1933, managing to produce two widely distributed publications during the time, *The Romani Voice* and *The Rom.*
>
> In the same year in Bucharest, in October, the General Association of Gypsies of Romania organized and held an international conference under the title United Gypsies of Europe. Its leader was Gheorghe Nicolescu, an educated Rom whose inclinations were towards integration and education for his people. In the August 1935 issue of *The Romani Voice,* he spoke of the pain of the Romani experience as motivation for change, and of the necessity of alliance with those free of anti-Gypsy prejudice. "As long as we travel the paths of justice, honor and duty, no one and nothing can detract us

from our goal, for we have with us a steadfast and loyal ally—suffering. The way towards emancipation is clear: those who care about us will be cared for in return, and we shall march together forward, ever forward." [1991:258]

The appeal to unity among Romani leaders, among other things, is an effort to thwart the efforts of historical forces to wipe them off the face of the planet. Their history and their ability to organize themselves in relationship to local conditions led Gypsies to territorial dispersion, cultural fragmentation, and marginalization, not territorial concentration and cultural unification. In viewing their physical and cultural survival, the conclusion we come to is that such a system of social organization was adaptive. The leadership that Nicolae Gheorghe represents is pulling Gypsies away from the margins and into the center. The center is the commitment that ethnic groups make to operate within a state system, while gaining the rights to sociocultural independence. Acquiring civil rights should result in the acquisition of state resources and legitimation.

Ethnic group solidarity among Gypsies has been a goal for only a very few and at rare moments in their history. The period during and since the 1989 revolution in Romania is such a moment. Greater disparities between rich and poor, the growth of interethnic intolerance, and the targeting of Romas as the cause of social and economic problems increasingly defined postrevolutionary Romania. Obtaining a legitimate place for Roma, as one ethnic group among others, will limit the systematic violence perpetrated against them because they are "different." The issue of their "race" is the most difficult barrier to acceptance. Their place in society has continued to be at the very bottom of Romania's production and social system.

The Roma Ethnic Federation was initiated in May 1990 as an umbrella association for the different political parties, cultural associations, trade unions, and many other organizations that were established after the revolution. Among these is the Democratic Union of Roma, created in February 1990, which defends the rights of Roma as a distinct minority in multiethnic Romania. The federation is affiliated and works directly with the International Romani Union, a nongovernmental organization of Roma in the world with consultative status at the Economic and Social Council–United Nations Organization since 1979.

Social, cultural, and economic development is no longer a matter that may be understood or acted upon in isolation from global processes and knowledge. Ethnicity and interethnic relations have become a matter of global concern, particularly among those groups with a transnational character. This is increasingly the case among postcolonial societies, but also societies whose underdeveloped regions border or are near regions of development.

Political elites of the post–World War II period most often have been characterized in two ways. There are those national elites who support a tight integration and dependency on metropoles and "First World" knowledge. Then there are those who seek independent, autochtonous development. This bipolarity was framed by cold war language and ideology. Ethnic minorities are taking on new characteristics with the end of the cold war and the alignment of states. Among these is the formation of ethnic political elites who can play both domestic and international roles, not unlike the leaders of nation-states. Nicolae Gheorghe represents one of these new ethnic leaders, whose political role is by definition transnational and innovative.

Acknowledgments

Research was funded by IREX (1979–1980), the MacArthur Foundation award to Cornell University Peace Studies Program (Summer 1991) and the Western Societies Program (Summer 1991). I would like to thank George Marcus for his encouragement to develop my project in this fashion and to the Cultural Studies Group at Rice University for a stimulating seminar.

Notes

1. I use the terms *Gypsy, Roma, Romany* (pl. *Romanies*), and *ţigani*. These terms are used by Romanies interchangeably. The political leaders of the pan-Romani movement prefers *Roma* and *Romani* to *Gypsy* and *ţigani*. I consider *Gypsy* and *ţigani* as terms of prejudice and oppression and Roma and Romani as terms of liberation and unification.

2. Ethnic minorities who are represented by nation-states have much greater access to power than those who are not. This is particularly true if those nation-states are among industrialized powers, such as Germany and the United States. Israel has developed a unique power base for Jews all over the world through its special relationship with the United States and its ability to use the Holocaust in arguments that protect Jewish minorities. The position of the Hungarian state in relationship to Hungarian ethnic minorities in border countries also has some unique features. Hungary successfully mobilized the support of the Soviet Union in disputes that put Hungarian ethnic minorities, especially in Romania, at risk. Moreover, Hungary has been equally successful in acquiring support from European countries and the United States because of lobbying efforts by Hungarian associations in those countries.

3. See Kürti 1989. While I focus on divisions and hostilities among ethnic groups, we must seriously consider the struggle of people to transcend conflicts and seek points of unity. In the heat of conflicting claims, unity in common purpose often is forgotten. It is the tension between the struggle for group identity and common purpose that generates the dynamic of social and cultural change.

4. To speak about Jews in Romania is not to speak about one common, unified, or similar group of people. Their marginalized place in European society as an oppressed population by virtue of their common religion and ethnoracial makeup created the

myth of a unified folk. Romanian Jews were as diverse as their migrations from different parts of Europe and the Near East. Sephardin were among the first settlers. Hungarian and Austrian Ashkenazi came next. Those from Poland came in particularly large numbers at the end of the nineteenth century.

5. The Germans, too, represent a diversity far greater than is normally recognized. In Transylvania, the Saxon Germans, who were invited settlers of a European frontier, came in waves over the course of many centuries. Initial settlement took place in the twelfth century. To this day, Saxon Germans speak dialects that differ widely from village to village. The Swabians settled the Banat region of Romania, Hungary, and Serbia in the nineteenth century. Other German speakers arrived in Romania as specialists and craftspeople.

6. I discuss Gypsy diversity below. I only mention in passing here that unlike Europe's Jewish survivors, who received reparations from former Nazi governments, particularly Germany, Gypsies were classified a social blight rather than an ethnic group with civil rights as any other population governed by states. Social deviants, so the arguments go, do not receive reparations. Were the Romani struggle for reparations to succeed, it would signal the recognition of Gypsies as an ethnic group with rights equal to those of other ethnic groups (see Hancock 1991:5 for a more complete discussion of this issue).

7. Assimilation among Romanies was more likely to take place with those groups who had been settled in the centuries past. Resistance to assimilation took place most severely among the groups that had experienced a migratory life-style, still spoke their own language, did not alter their style of dress to conform to those of the majority population, and had a darker skin color.

8. A polemical but important analysis of Gypsy history and the role of Gypsy slavery in Romania is found in Hancock 1987. Also see Gheorghe 1983 and Beck 1989.

9. As I write, news of anti-Romani persecution reproduces the cycle of discrimination and oppression. On 19 September 1992, the *New York Times*'s front page covered the story entitled "Germany Reaches Deal to Deport Thousands of Gypsies in Romania" (see also Beck 1985).

10. There is real danger in seeking to characterize Gypsies, or any ethnic group, for that matter, as a uniform social unit. As I have indicated above, Gypsies were invented by Europeans. The term is not a native concept. It is a term of oppression. The conceptualization of Gypsies as only migratory creates the illusion that when Gypsies appear in settlements they are not "true" Gypsies, that they do not belong there because they are migratory, or that they will pick up and leave at some future date because "movement" is in their blood." Deterritorialization, deculturation, denationalization, dehumanization, and so on, are the social processes that characterize Gypsies to the point that even when Gypsies assimilate they are unable to escape these identities.

11. This notion is patently false, of course. Gypsies often were inducted into military forces raised by various politicomilitary organizations, from principalities and nation-states to empires.

12. The history of Gypsies in Romania is richly documented as a history of slavery. From the earliest times, in the early part of the fourteenth century, Gypsies were

documented as slaves [*robii*]. Initially, slavery in Romania was most likely based on the capturing of enemy troops as Romanian princes fought vigorously to protect their territories against the incursions of Turko-Tatar military campaigns. While the records of Tatar slaves are limited, that for Gypsy slaves are rich with documents that illuminate the purchase and sale of human commodities.

Slaves in large numbers worked the lands of monasteries and princes. Some slaves became house servants or Romanian princes and eventually worked in the homes of urban merchants, doctors, and lawyers. Some *ţigani* were free to roam the countryside, but had to pay an annual tribute to their masters. Other *ţigani,* perhaps runaways, formed nomadic "free" groups (see Hancock 1987; Gheorghe 1983; Beck 1989).

Popular notions of Gypsies has limited our understanding of Gypsies as anything but the romantic and exoticized image of colorful roaming bands. Gypsies are known only as marginalized and, more often than not, a petty crimial element (thieves and scam artists) in whatever host society they happen to be in at any given moment. This is not at all factual. In Romania, as is true in much of the Balkan peninsula, for example, Gypsies have a long sedentary history. In Romania, *ţigani* were settled from the very beginning of their history as slaves. *Ţigani vatraşi* were village Gypsies. *Vatra* in Romanian refers to "hearth." *Vatra satului* refers to the village hearth or the essence of Romanian community life. *Ţigani vatraşi* refers to sedentary Gypsies.

13. Of all the *ţigani* in Romania, *fierari* (and *lautari*) have been among the more privileged of the Gypsies. Their privileges refer to the heightened tolerance that Romanians displayed toward them. Sedentary *fierari* are viewed by Romanians in an acceptable light in that they are seen more like Romanians, "hard-working" people. In some communities, *fierari* intermarried with the other people settled there.

In Romania, skin color is important when people make associations between an individual's dark skin color and the likeliness of *ţigani* origins. Such speculation is normally associated with behaviors that are viewed as characteristically those of *ţigani,* including occupation. Color is important among Gypsies, too. Lighter skin is viewed as more attractive. This may not always have been so. The negative association with dark skin is a hegemonic device of subordination. Is it possible that the origin of the separation of the dark-skinned from light-skinned people is an element of cultural formation, the emergence of racialism and racism? Did it grow out of the enslavement of "people of color" in the wars of the eastern European corridor that separates Asia from Europe between sedentary and nomadic populations? Martin Bernal, in his provocative *Black Athena,* makes reference precisely to this point.

By the fifteenth century, too, there is no doubt that clear links were seen between dark skin color and evil and inferiority, when the newly arrived Gypsies were feared and hated for both their darkness and their alleged sexual prowess (Bernal 1987:201).

Certainly by the time that Africa was being explored and colonized by European empires, such a distinction was being made in Europe. By the eighteenth century, the primacy of European civilization was established through the acceptance of European romanticism and the inferiority of people of color.

14. Minority groups, particularly those who suffer discrimination, have a much stronger sense of self-identity when living in the context of their own group. It is in life among "others," particularly dominant and hegemonizing people, that self-identity is attacked.

15. *"Ga, ga"* is the Romanian rendering of the sound a crow makes. *Cioara* is the Romanian word for crow. It is also the pejorative tag given *ţigani*. The relationship is one of color. Crows are black and so are *ţigani*. However, crows are also considered a nuisance, very much like *ţigani*. They are always around when you don't need them.

16. Under Marxism-Leninism, sociology returned to the Romanian academy in the 1960s. Miron Constantinescu was instrumental in bringing it back and shaping its instruction and popularity in this initial period.

17. Nicolae could not have foreseen how much more nationalism would get during the Ceausescuite period. The 1980s proved to be even more nationalistic.

18. Systematization was an effort at social engineering. Romania planned to re-organize the entire country based on principles of production. Different types of production zones were outlined, industrial, agricultural, pastoral, and so on. The systematization plan eventually was to eliminate about seven thousand rural communities, consolidating their populations in urban centers (Beck 1991).

19. *Cortuarari* are literally tent dwellers. These are Romanes speakers. Until recently, they did not wear Western-style garb, but instead the men wore adaptations of Romanian pastoralist's clothing. The women wear large and numerous layers of skirts. This group maintains much of their wealth in gold coins and medieval cups, *takhtai*. They are everything that one imagines a "traditional" Gypsy to be.

20. Nicolae is forced to use a language of denial because under conditions of Ceausescuite communism, organizing people along political lines could be severely punished. Reading between the lines is an important skill, acquired under repressive conditions.

References

Barbat, Alexandru. 1938. *Dezvoltarea si Structura Economica a Ţarii Oltului cu un Plan de Organizare.* Cluj: Tipografia Naţionala S.A.

Beck, Sam. 1989. "The Origin of Gypsy Slavery." *Dialectical Anthropology* 14:53–61.

———. 1985. "Romania's Gypsy Problem." *Papers from the Fourth and Fifth Annual Meetings of the Gypsy Lore Society, North American Chapter.* Ed. Joanne Grumet. New York: GLS (NAC) Monograph No. 2, pp. 100–109.

———. 1991. "What Brought Romanians to Revolt." *Critique of Anthropology* 11, no. 1:7–31.

Beck, Sam, and Marilyn McArthur. 1981. "Romania: Ethnicity, Nationalism and Development." *Ethnicity and Nationalism in Southeastern Europe.* Ed. Sam Beck and John W. Cole. Antropologisch-Sociologisch Centrum: Universiteit van Amsterdam.

Bernal, Martin. 1987. *Black Athena: The Afroasiatic Roots of Classical Civilization, Volume 1.* New Brunswick, N.J.: Rutgers University Press.

Chelchea, Ion. 1944. *Ţiganii din Romania: Monografie Etnografica.* Bucureşti: Editura Institutului Central de Statistica.

Gheorghe, Nicolae. 1983. "Origins of Roma Slavery in the Rumanian Principalities." *Roma.* 7, no. 1:12–27.

Hancock, Ian. 1991. "Anti-Gypsyism in the New Europe." Typescript.

———. 1987. *The Pariah Syndrome.* Ann Arbor: Karoma Publishers.

Kürti, Laszlo. 1989. "Transylvania, Land Beyond Reason: Toward an Anthropological Analysis of a Contested Terrain." *Dialectical Anthropology* 14:21–52.

Magubane, Bernard Makhosezwe. 1978. *The Ties That Bind: African-American Consciousness of Africa*. Trenton, N.J.: Africa World Press, Inc.

Meteş, Ştefan. 1935. *Situaţia Economica a Romanilor din Ţara Fagarasului, Vol. I*. Cluj: Ştefan Boier and Act. Stoichita, Arhivelor Statului din Cluj.

Prodan, David. 1970. *Urbariile Ţarii Fagaraşului, 1601–1650, Vol. 1*. Bucureşti: Editura Academiei Republicii Socialiste Romania.

Verdery, Katherine. 1991. *Transylvanian Villagers: Three Centuries of Political Economic, and Ethnic Change*. Berkeley: University of California Press.

WORKING THROUGH THE OTHER: THE JEWISH,
SPANISH, TURKISH, IRANIAN, UKRAINIAN,
LITHUANIAN, AND GERMAN UNCONSCIOUS
OF POLISH CULTURE
OR
ONE HAND CLAPPING: DIALOGUE, SILENCES,
AND THE MOURNING OF POLISH ROMANTICISM

I. Introduction

Anthropological accounts step into an ongoing stream of representations.
Anthropology in the late twentieth century is no longer the "discovery" of
terra nova or undescribed cultures, but rather a method of informed critique,
pursued often by placing into strategic and disjunctive juxtaposition different representations or perspectives so as to throw light upon the social
context of their production and meaning, and to draw out their implications.
Timothy Garton Ash reminds us that

> few peoples in the world have lived so closely together as the Jews
> and the Poles . . . A hundred years ago, on the eve of the great
> emigration to the United States, four-fifths of world Jewry could still
> be found in the area of the old Polish commonwealth . . . As late as
> 1939 the Polish Jewish community was still the largest in Europe,
> comprising some 10 percent of the population of the pre-war Polish
> state; more than three million people. Almost all of them perished in
> the Holocaust. The few who survived and chose to remain in Poland
> played a very significant part in the political and intellectual life of
> the post-war state, for good and ill. But in 1968 an appalling "anti-
> Zionist" campaign orchestrated by powerful factions in the Com-
> munist Party and security services forced most of the remaining
> Polish Jews to leave their jobs and finally the country . . . There has
> also been an extraordinary divorce of Polish and Jewish memory. A
> Polish child growing up in the 1970s learned next to nothing about
> the immense Jewish part in Polish history . . . Certainly he would
> never have met a Jew, until perhaps as a young man he accidentally
> discovered that his best friend was a Jew . . . It would be no more
> than a slight exaggeration to say that most Poles remembered those

Wojciech Prazmowski, "Inside Portrait" (1992). (Lacanian?) mirrored image interpellated in (historical?) layers of broken glass (through a glass darkly?), crumbling fortresses (nostalgias of power), and decaying walls (socialist colonialism). Houston Photofest 1992, poster image.

three million martyred Jews only as martyred Poles, while most Jews remembered those three million martyred Poles only as anti-Semites. It was as if each martyrology felt compelled to exclude the other. This was both tragic and ridiculous. A young Pole, brought up to regard his nation as a righteous and heroic victim of history, was shocked by a Jewish indictment that seemed to declare him more guilty than the Nazis . . . It was above this gloomy landscape of amnesia, prejudice, and lies that Hanna Krall's extraordinary interview with Marek Edelman exploded . . . in 1976 . . . 10,000 copies sold out in just a few days (and another 30,000 in the second printing) . . . A decade later . . . in 1985 [after the showing of Claude Lanzmann's film *Shoah*] you could not open a Polish newspaper without finding yet another article about Polish-Jewish relations. (1986:vii–x)

The story of the Holocaust is no longer a simple story of (re)discovery: a steady stream of newsreel footage, historical archival work, oral histories, survivor's accounts, novels, films, and investigative journalism continues to deepen both knowledge and ethical response to one of the most devastating upheavals in modern times. At issue now are reflections upon the rhetorics of narration and the ethics that ensue.

Hanna Krall's interview with Marek Edelman, the last living survivor of the Warsaw ghetto uprising, is already a piece of Polish new journalism that is very self-conscious about writing against already existing representations and expectations, and across linguistic and cultural associations:

Just before she died, the religious old lady had asked for something to eat. "Doesn't matter," she'd said, "it doesn't have to be kosher, it can even be a *kotlet wieprzowy*. But one has to tell the story in English to one's English cousins, so in English, Grandma was asking not for a *kotlet wieprozowy* but for a pork chop, and at that moment she simply stops being that dying grandmother. It becomes possible to talk without hysteria, calmly, the way one might tell an interesting story at a civilized English dinner. (Krall 1986:12).

The heightened historical sense and ethical responsibility for the ways in which representations are treated has to do not only with the writing style but also with the ethics of daily life: Edelman is a physician involved with a professor of cardiac surgery, and their contemporary interventions in the game of life against death is foregrounded. In attempting untried surgical procedures in cases where the patient is certain to die if the intervention is not attempted, the professor is afraid for all the normal reasons, but also, should he fail, "that his colleagues will say: *he is making experiments on human beings*" (23). Edelman is the one who urges him on. Edelman's ethics are affected as well: he denies the elevation of death in battle, and the demeaning

of death in the gas chambers: "the only undignified death is when one attempts to survive at the expense of someone else" (37); so, too, his theology:

> —People have told me, Marek, that when you're taking care of
> simple and not terribly serious cases, you do it in a way out of sense
> of duty, that you only really light up when the game begins, when
> the race with death begins.
> —That is, after all, my role. God is trying to blow out the candle
> and I'm quickly trying to shield the flame, taking advantage of His
> brief inattention. To keep the flame flickering, even if only for a little
> while longer than He would wish.
>   It is important: He is not terribly just. It can also be very satisfying
> because whenever something does work out, it means you have, after
> all, fooled Him. (85).

II. Anthropologist and Philosopher:
Curiosities about the Other

The heart of dialogue beats with questions.
                                        —Edmond Jabès, *The Book of Dialogue*

Leszek Koczanowicz, a Polish professor of philosophy, an expert on
George Herbert Mead and Ludwig Wittgenstein, came as a visiting scholar to
the Center for Cultural Studies at Rice University during 1992. His project
was on concepts of the self in American pragmatism, and the center was
curious to see if a European philosopher might engage such a subject with
cultural-linguistic tools or historical sensibilities and implicational associations different from Americans. The center has been interested in engaging
the sociological, cultural, and historical approaches of anthropology and the
social sciences with the humanities. We, of course, were also interested in the
contemporary dramatic developments in Eastern Europe, and Koczanowicz
proved to be a gifted expositor of the complexities of recent Polish cultural
history, both nationalist-romantic and Marxist-Soviet colonial. I was also intrigued by the denial/assertion of hybridity in Polish identity, which parallels
conundrums in various nationalisms as well as contemporary American ethnicities. I am interested in these paradoxical structures of emotional investment as part of a larger concern with the reconstruction of pluralist civil
societies after social trauma in the modern world. Leszek, in turn, proved
very interested as a philosopher, not only in the methodological procedures
and theories of meaning in our style of anthropology as cultural critique, but
was also very curious about the current debates about the conditions of postmodernity in which that anthropology has been involved.

One of the most intense debates we had on these last issues was not caught
on tape, but in essence Leszek wanted me to know that he disapproved of

relativism and thought that there was something objective and essential about Polish identity and culture. I tried to point out that this was extremely interesting, given the fact that the conversations we had been capturing on tape all developed in elaborate detail the ways in which Polish culture was constructed out of different intercultural elements, historical and social strata oppositions, and ideological strategies, and that he had repeatedly stressed the centrality of poetry written by intercultural Jewish Poles or Poles thought to have Jewish backgrounds, as well as Lithuanians who write in Polish. His protestation had been occasioned by my essay "Ethnicity and the Postmodern Arts of Memory"; a mutual friend and colleague, the philosopher Mitchell Aboulafia, amused, told me that Leszek had confided, "You know that fellow Fischer is really into this postmodern stuff." But in a later conversation, when I tried to return to this topic, we could not find real terms of debate: Leszek's latest "take" (14 July, 1992) is that "postmodern thinking" reflects well enough the side of human nature that is madness, disorder, and uncertainty, and yes, Polish-Americans are often neither Polish nor American but something in between (referring to the ethnicities in my essay), and even the topics of the present essay lend themselves to postmodern "categories"; but that thought and culture also try to transcend the flux of life—the two sides are complementary, neither can be dismissed—that scientists who stress the objective and transcendent side of knowledge are also partial, and postmodernism reflects the madness of the end of the century. Friedrich Nietzsche, he notes (insofar as Nietzsche is sometimes cited a precursor or early source of inspiration for some postmodernist thinkers), was proud of his Polish heritage and played off his Polish identity as Dionysian versus his German identity as Apollonian. This, for me, is a confused use of the word *postmodern,* conflating all kinds of empirical referents, sociologically unlocated, and not what I recognize in my own fairly restricted use of the term. But, in any case, the terms of opposition that Leszek invokes (flux, madness, and uncertainty versus transcendence) do signal to me something important: the old tropes of romanticism.

Indeed the "intervening term" which we have explored at length is the nature of Polish romantic tropes used as ideologies of nationalism and resistance which are today, Leszek suspects, no longer viable under the dissolving agent of Western popular culture. "Relativism," he had decided correctly, is an archaic debate that is too simplistic to be of much interest, not least because Polish romantic tropes assume intercultural flux and are cultural, often quixotic, constructions to stave off dissolution within this flux. Their layered construction, picking up resonances through shifting historical strata, on the other hand, give them emotional investments that are sometimes "irrational" in the present and that can contribute to unnecessarily nonnegotiable ethnic conflicts such as are erupting across the former Soviet empire. Poland, perhaps, will be saved some of this bloodiness because the horrendous traumas of the recent past have made it a relatively ethnically homogeneous population, and hence it is only the ghosts and remnants of its former Jewish population, and similar Ukrainian, German, and Lithuanian shadows, that remain unnervingly potent.

The primary set of discourses which have opposed nationalist ones, of course, have been those concerned with the "social questions," that is, what go under the various labels of socialist and leftist discourses. In Poland and Eastern Europe, of course, these discourses were usurped by, or made to play cat-and-mouse games with, a totalitarian bureaucratic state whose rationalities have been long parodied in the literatures. The social sciences as well have been subject to these games where social statistics can only give empirical results, but not the "objective scientific" understanding that "correct theory" would provide. The cat-and-mouse games with the totalitarian state for rhetorics and languages in which social analysis might be conducted can, if handled with the appropriate skeptical humor, provide a first mapping of the alternative publics and social segments that evolved over the past seventy years, within as well as among the intellectuals, the Party, the church, the army, the security police, the workers, and the peasants. Leszek's wry account of the three rhetorics the state tried to use to legitimate itself but which undermined one another, as well as the appeals to a gentry-based national identity by an alleged workers' state, provide a certain hard-earned absurdist humor.

Whether, then, this case study in the cultural dynamics of "nationalism" and "cultural resistance" can serve as a useful foil to nationalist illusions elsewhere remains to be seen, but it provides an interesting "family resemblance" to ethnicity in the contemporary United States, both by being different in its social and historical depths, but by being similar in its intercultural internalizations.

There are in the conversations between Leszek and myself three or four strata in the construction of Polish identity: (1) most important is the long career of Polish romanticism, which gained a renewed vigor under the Soviet colonialization of the past seventy years, because the nineteenth-century socialist tradition had been usurped by Soviet Marxism, leaving only the older cultural resources as vehicles of resistance; (2) however, quite interesting in their own right are the subtle maneuvers to preserve a Polish set of Marxist or leftist discourses that were different from Russian Marxism and that could be used to contest or critique the communist state; these borrowed from Western Marxism and from the language of existentialism, but eventually, inevitably, left Marxism behind except in the refined discourses of the university; (3) the Church and its checkered career as symbol of Poland's being part of the West rather than the Orthodox East, as tied to the peasantry (the least socialized agricultural system of the Soviet bloc) and thus ambiguously related to Poland's gentry-based culture of romanticism, is an element only partially explored in our conversations; (4) the transformations of the post-1989 period, in which Poland again sees itself as a Western beacon of change (not sufficiently supported by the West) but in which the old gentry-based culture of romanticism seems to be at the end of its long career under the combined threats of Western popular culture and a changed mode of production in which the market and individual labor are no longer devalued by either gentry or socialist ideology.

The eleven 1½- to 2-hour taped conversations (and over sixty single-spaced pages of transcript) from which the following excerpts are drawn began from two serendipitous stimuli. Already when I first met Leszek with his wife, the filmmaker Maria Zmarz-Koczanowicz, and son Tadeusz, in the car on the way into town from the airport, the subject of Polish-Jewish relations popped up as a theme of great interest to him. This was quite unsolicited since I, like many children of refugees from the Holocaust, would be unlikely to direct attention to such subjects with strangers, and as a host not knowing his guest's politics would not have raised such a potentially fraught topic on a first encounter. My own background is not Polish, it is Viennese, and more distantly through my maternal grandparents Ukrainian (Berdichev) and Czech (Brno). So as an interlocutor for Leszek's concerns with Jewish Poland, I could only play interested listener, interested particularly as most accounts of this topic in America come from either Jewish or Polish emigré sources, or from the oddities of contemporary Polish politics. I was intrigued, if wary, to be cast into what seemed might be the role of a transference figure, but delighted as an anthropologist to be able to talk to such an articulate intellectual from the younger generation of contemporary Poland. I mentioned my recent visit to Armenia and found that Maria had been to Armenia, and that there had been talk of an alliance between Armenian and Polish filmmakers on the grounds of commonality in being countries beleaguered and surrounded by cultural and religious others. (There is an Armenian community in Poland, there since the sixteenth century.) Another theme of the following conversations had been signalled, one again with complications and historical depth.

The second immediate stimulus for these conversations was Jack Kugelmas's essay "Bloody Memories," which happened to be on my desk: since it had to do with Poland, and given the conversation in the car, I thought Leszek might find it interesting. I was curious about what his reactions might be to this very personally written and Jewish-centered point of view. In that essay, Kugelmas argues that in the structure of the tropes used by Poles and Jews to talk about themselves and each other there is an almost irreconcilable conflict: Poles, in order to preserve a sense of continuity of historical tradition and to deal with the traumatic disruptions of World War II, call upon a heroic vision of themselves, a vision constructed in the medieval period in which Jews are the alien other within by which the self is defined. This Polish identity cannot do without the Jew, and yet this view of the Jew insists on a character type that uses its intelligence in nonloyal modes of cunning that are not the proper patriotic or heroic type of the Pole. Inversely, the tropes called upon by Jews also invoke a tropic structure that constructs the Poles as radically alien, or worse, as fellow Poles who betrayed the Jews. Kugelmas uses a vignette of his own encounter with a Pole who had survived World War II and a Jew who has remained in Poland, surviving the war by being taken in by a "righteous gentile" who later became his brother-in-law and who taught him to become a fruit farmer. Kugelmas's vignette is poignant; the three men in their different spaces are eager to interact and exchange accounts with one another, yet each is separated in his own world.

Leszek's reaction was to say that while in many ways Kugelmas had captured something true about the nature of the Polish-Jewish relationships, it was a self-limited view, one that did not explore the larger implications, and that did not probe the difficult dilemmas that face the democratic movement of Poland.

He began by registering several reservations about Kugelmas's conclusions. As a sociological description of the situation, Leszek questioned the value of the impressionistic methods Kugelmas uses to characterize a complex history and contemporary sociology; for example, the trope of cunning which Kugelmas says Poles attribute to Jews as the opposite of Polish nobility is in fact a trope central to the definition of Polish nobility itself (in the shape, for instance, of the concept of "patriotic treason" figured in Konrad Wallenrod, or the double loyalties about which Joseph Conrad wrote, or the figure of the patriot General Bem who converted to Islam and lived in Constantinople); also the "alien within" definitions of Jew and Pole operate as well for other cultural dimensions of Polish identity—Lithuanian, Ukrainian, German, Russian—and they too are sources of conflict-generating stereotypes. So, while much of what Kugelmas describes might be true—Leszek consistently as a matter of ethical honor affirmed the truth value of what Kugelmas describes: he is insistent on not trying to deny the various strands of anti-Semitism, or failures of appropriate behavior on the part of Poles both past and contemporary—and while perhaps much of the nonintellectual population fits into the patterns Kugelmas evokes, Leszek was concerned to point out: (1) the ways in which Polish intellectuals of his generation have tried since the rise of Solidarity to reconstruct Polish understandings of these issues not merely as a "memory project" but as a serious endeavor to reconstruct a progressive democratic politics for Poland; and (2) the civilizational or "philosophical" challenge that the Holocaust constitutes for Poles and for the West beyond its specific historical meanings in the destruction of Jewish and Polish lives. The resistance narratives and nationalist ideologies built around the tropes of Polish nobility, of patriotic treason in defense of Poland, the participation in liberation struggles throughout the nineteenth and twentieth centuries (in which Poland always seemed betrayed by its Western allies), these are Romantic tropes useful even against the Russian-Soviet empire, but which are now spent.

What is most important, perhaps, about "Tools for Reflection," the collage of quotes put into "dialogic play" at the end of this essay is the movement from Leszek's denial of the possibility of real dialogue between Poles and Jews (and my affirmation of the existence of dialogue through history, textuality, and cultural legacy) to his sociological observations on post-Soviet Poles, Russians, and other Eastern Europeans learning the dialogic skills of cross-cultural understanding through the market, through manual labor, through travel, and through the media of popular culture. In our third taped conversation, Leszek noted that the strikes of August 1980 still used the symbols of Polish romanticism—nineteenth-century socialist symbols could not be used because they had been preempted by the communists—but that this "probably was the last time we used these symbols so extensively. For better or worse, Poland is going to be a normal state [upon reflection he modified this a few months later: not a Western-style normal state, maybe more like a South American state of consciousness awash in constant discussion]. It is difficult to predict in which direction our culture will go in its confrontation with Western popular culture."

What made these conversations so engaging was of course the play between the richness of the cultural and historical content and the philosophical/cultural critique registers, which is the essence of both good anthropology and post-Wittgenstein philosophy. As we spoke, more and more issues seemed to uncover themselves, ranging over the nature of Polish romantic imagery; poetry and its intertextual and intercultural polymorphism; the gentry structure of Polish cultural forms in play against cosmopolitan aristocracy, peasants, and shopkeepers; the socialist rhetorics and politics of the communist period, student politics in the 1970s and 1980s, and the checkered careers vis-à-vis the communist state of leading intellectuals; the turns of Marxism and philosophy in Polish universities; post–World War II childhoods in mixed ethnic Polish towns; Polish modernism in drama, painting, and politics; the struggles of the younger intellectuals to think through the meaning of the Holocaust and communism for Poland's future.

What also makes the conversations engaging is their rich play upon the absurdities, reversals, inversions, quixotic posturings, claims of nobility, and failure out of which Poles construct their sense of self and literature. In this there is continuity between the eighteenth and nineteenth century and the communist period. It is not only Alfred Jarry who situates his absurdist play, *Ubu Roi,* "in Poland or Nowhere." The more we worked with these stories of Polish nationalism and of Polish Marxism, the more I sensed they are thoroughly structured by an absurdist black humor. We cannot capture on the page the laughter and chuckles that punctuated Leszek's narrations, but the reader should know they are ever present. The absurdist tradition of black humor is different—or is it?—perhaps more stark and modernist, than Polish Yiddish humor (more familial, the vernacular language of governesses and maids, with all the diminutives that lend themselves to satirizing adult pretentiousness), yet they share a heritage, and part of the humor comes in the constant question of who is Polish, what is Jewish, as if this tale were being written on the surface in Polish but by Jewish or converso poets. (One should remember that while there was separation and difference, as Leszek says in one of the quotes dated 25 February 1992 in the conclusion, there was also considerable learning of one another's languages, Polish maids and governesses serving in Jewish houses, as well as Jews learning the language of the majority as they professionalized). Jewish conversos transformed Christian culture in an earlier period, and it sometimes reads here as if Jews and Jewish converts had a similar impact in Polish culture. In any case, we suggest that one read with an eye toward the humor not only of Leszek's narrative art but of the conundrums, reversals, and inversions of Polish life. (Maria Zmarz-Koczanowicz's films similarly are structured through the use of this sort of humor. Perhaps most striking is her 1989 documentary, "The Revolution of Major or the Elves," on the carnivalesque happenings and satirical campaigns during the 1980s orchestrated by art student Waldemar Friedrich, which upset the communists and Solidarity alike, but which helped transform the atmosphere of Wrocław, and of Poland, not unlike the theatricalization described in the essay on Armenia [chapter 4 in this Annual].)

III. Excerpts

A. Romantic Tropes of Polish Nationalism: Gentry Culture, Joseph Conrad, and Konrad Wallenrod

There are five key romantic tropes that we discussed: (1) stereotyping as a strategy of defining self versus other; (2) quixotic uprisings which cannot succeed militarily but which are intended therefore to shed enough blood so as to drive a symbolically potent and historically effective wedge against the enemy; (3) participation in movements of liberation beyond Poland with the hope that Poland itself will gain in the rewards, and the resulting sense of betrayal when, almost inevitably, these rewards are denied; (4) patriotic treason, in which one joins the other side so as to undermine it; and (5) use of church symbolism (as in the August 1980 demonstrations) because the more secular and socialist nineteenth-century traditions of resistance have been usurped by the communist state in the twentieth century. The Polish romantic notions of "nobility" are literal in being grounded in gentry culture, set in opposition to cosmopolitan aristocracies as well as to peasantries and shop-keepers. This gentry culture prides itself on its individualistic anarchy as coded in the parliamentary rule of equal votes for all whether landed or not, the ability of one member of parliament to veto any action, and in the Thomas à Becket-like figure of St. Stanisław (who was killed for questioning the authority of the king). Gentrification was a relatively open process especially for Jewish converts, and the great literary documents of gentry culture such as Adam Mickiewicz's "Konrad Wallenrod" and "Pan Tadeusz" are often suspected to have been written by persons of Jewish background.

Stereotyping 31 Jan. 1992

The famous statement of Gombrowicz that after the First World War Poles gained passports but lost their souls, not having the adversity of partition (of Poland among Russia, Germany, and Austria) to react against.

KOCZANOWICZ: In our national anthem, there is a line . . . we should convince ourselves that we will live to be the Poles. Because of the threat of being dissolved or absorbed in other nations, the most popular way of describing ourselves is in opposition to other nations . . . we had only twenty years of independence between the first and second [World] Wars, and then . . . we had the same problem, how to preserve our national identity . . . , Poles refer to themselves as a wall of Western culture against Asia, against Eastern culture, against Byzantine culture . . . there is a kind of competition in the Slavic world between Russia and Poland: . . . Poland accepted Roman Catholic religion and Western European civilization; Russia accepted Byzantine civilization. So there is a strong competition, who should lead the Slavic world. Of course, Russia is bigger, but in the seventeenth and eighteenth centuries, we were also . . . you know, but the issue is: I would like to show why in our relations with our neighbors we should refer to them as un-Polish . . . [vis-à-vis Germans] we don't like German *Ordnung,* we are people with imagination, we were more free, not so obsessed with the state, and we are more anarchic; and similarly against Russia: we are more Western.

Jeszcze Polska nie zginela, poki my zyjemy—a curious sentence built of past and present tenses: Poland has not yet perished, as long as we live. *Narod Polski,* the Polish spirit of *tesknota* [nostalgia] and *zal* [bitter sadness] can be heard in the mazurkas and polonaises and that special sound of Chopin.

paraphrased from Douglas Hofstadter, *Metamagical Themas*

FISCHER: You were saying yesterday that relations with Ukrainians are as rigidly stereotyped as with Jews, and that one source of this was the killings that the Ukrainians did . . .

KOCZANOWICZ: No, not only. Oh [*sigh*], this is a difficult task, because I should refer to Polish history: it is impossible to understand without the past. I am not sure you want to listen to a short course in Polish history, but . . . you know, for hundreds of years we were a bistate . . . Lithuania and Poland. There was expansion into Ukraine . . . and there was an attempt made . . . to set up the Ukraine as a third state of the federation, but it failed, blocked by the Polish gentry who had colonized the Ukraine . . . There were a lot of uprisings against the Polish rule of the Ukraine. And of course the Ukraine was a special place: it was like the West for the States. The peasants in Poland escaped to this place and set up their own free communities, and the Polish kingdom, the Polish-Lithuanian kingdom, tried to subordinate these free communities by war and some by treaty . . . After the division of Poland, Ukraine was divided between Austria and Russia . . . In the Austrian part there was a struggle for power between Ukrainians and Poles. There was pressure in the nineteenth century in Eastern Europe to set up states for nationalities, and there was a Ukrainian revival to set up a state, the Lithuanians did the same, and to some extent the White Russians did the same, but the Poles prevailed in the Ukrainian region . . . Poles played an important role in the Austrian Empire. Poles sometimes were prime ministers of the Austrian imperial government. During this period, Ukrainians tried to gain independence and attacked the main Polish city in the region, Lvov; and it is now part of Polish mythology how in 1918 Polish youth defended the city against the Ukrainians. When the Soviet Russians came, Poles supported the Ukrainians, but because of Polish support, probably, the Ukrainians did not rally. Ukrainian leaders asked for Pusudiski's support, but the majority of Ukrainians saw this as betrayal. Pusudiski's idea was for a federation of Poland, Lithuania, and White Russia. The Polish population did not support this because they wanted to be an independent Poland . . . Ukraine took advantage of Hitler and of the Russian invasion of Poland to take some land for the Ukrainian Republic. And when Hitler invaded Russia, Ukrainians helped him.

In this region of mixed populations, there were massive murders of Poles. That is what Poles remember; but Ukrainians remember that we oppressed them. It was a region where the cities were Polish and the villages were Ukrainian, where the gentry was Polish and the peasantry was Ukrainian (and the large Jewish population was caught in between: many being innkeepers accepting the gentry script in which peasants often were paid for alcohol and necessities as in a company town). A similar situation existed in Lithuania. There are famous families who could choose their nationalities.

For instance, the famous poet Czeslaw Milosz: his uncle was a French writer, Oscar Milosz, who chose to be Lithuanian; he was in France and became the Lithuanian ambassador. Or there is the famous Polish general whose brother was the Ukrainian bishop of the Ukrainian Church and an ardent Ukrainian nationalist. For us, the stereotype of the Ukrainian is very vivid. After World War II there was a guerrilla action, and so the Polish government moved the Ukrainian population to other places, and so it was that my home town [Legnica, near the German and Czech borders] came to have so many Ukrainians. This population movement was condemned by the Polish senate some years ago, but the resolution angered those who remember World War II and thought the resolution should also have condemned the Ukrainian murders of Poles.

We are getting far from Polish-Jewish relations, but the point is that they are not so exceptional. To summarize, the Poles describe themselves as unothers. It is the same for others as Kugelmas describes Poles saying about Jews: Jews are smarter, but not so noble as Poles. So, too, Poles say: Germans may be wiser than Poles, but we are more free, have more imagination, are less subordinate. About the Czechs, Poles say that they may be more orderly but have less sense of fantasy than Poles. The Russians are able to beat us and create a superpower but they are subordinate to their state, are less individualistic. You know in Dostoyevsky, Poles are painted as ugly characters probably because he recognized Poles as smugglers of Western culture into Russia.

Gentry Culture

KOCZANOWICZ: It is typical for Poles to describe themselves as noble. There is a historical reason: Poland had the largest gentry population in Europe. In the eighteenth century, 10 percent of the population was gentry. In Spain, by contrast, only one percent was gentry, although Spaniards like to claim they are all hidalgos, gentry. We had ten times as many. And in Poland there was no aristocracy, no official aristocracy: titles like *Graf* or Baron were forbidden. In fact, of course, Poland had one of the largest aristocracies, but ideologically all gentry were equal. Each noble had one vote in electing the king; you know, we had an elected king, elected by the gentry. Even the gentry who had no land, no property at all, had one vote each, and veto power: one vote could prevent an action, which is why, some say, the medieval state became paralyzed and fell. So our culture is a gentry culture. Our intellectuals in the nineteenth century were former gentry, and they adopted gentry habits, including their attitudes and relations to Jews. Jews ran inns, were shopkeepers for the gentry.

There was, of course, a large Jewish population in Poland. And there are many things one could discuss. First of all, perhaps, there is the relation between Jews and Christianity: this is a big and multifaceted topic. On the one hand, Poland has a Catholic culture, but on the other hand, there is also the interesting history that Jews who converted to Roman Catholicism were immediately gentrified in Poland. In the eighteenth century there was a movement among Jews to conversion: two hundred families converted and were gentrified. So, there is probably a lot of Jewish blood in the Polish gentry, more than people like to think. There is a big debate about our most famous poet, Mickiewicz. He remarked that his mother was of Jewish background, but there is no clear evidence about her origin. Probably he believed she was Jewish, but people did not like to accept such conclusions.

There is much anxiety about the purity of Polish culture. Just before I left Poland (a week ago), I read an interview done by Michnik with Konwicki about a third writer, a woman, Dabrowska, the most popular writer between the 1930s and the 1960s. She was not just a poet but a moral authority. You know, writers in Eastern Europe have this role of being more than just writers, being moral authorities, because they preserve our sense of identity. She wrote a famous paper against anti-Semitism before the war, but when her diaries were published, the intellectuals were quite upset to find that she regularly distinguished between pure Poles and Poles with Jewish backgrounds. For instance, she would remark, "I spent last evening with friends, and they were all Jews except for X." In the 1980s, intellectuals were offended by such remarks. Michnik, who is of Jewish background, hypothesized that it was because of her humanism that she was against anti-Semitism, but that at the same time she was afraid for Polish culture, that she feared that the Jewish spirit could change this Polish culture by introducing cosmopolitanism. So on the one hand she refused anti-Semitism, but on the other she wanted Polish culture to preserve its own character.

So there is a debate about the origin of our leading poets, because Jewish culture influenced Polish culture more than people want to acknowledge. For instance, perhaps, think of the concept of Polish messianism, the idea that Poland is one of the chosen nations, an idea which was vivid in the nineteenth century.

FISCHER: But isn't gentry culture itself cosmopolitan? Gentries were built around courts and had relations with courts in other parts of Europe.

KOCZANOWICZ: Yes, but the soil of our culture is in the middle gentry. In the eighteenth century there was a big movement against the French influence in the aristocracy.

FISCHER: So there was a division between the upper gentry and the middle gentry. Do you know the work of Witold Kula, and is that description connected with what you are describing?

KOCZANOWICZ: Kula? You mean the account of medieval Poland?

FISCHER: Well, yes, the interrelation of the feudal system with the local and world markets in the sixteenth to eighteenth centuries. What about the role of the church itself, not just Christianity, but of the Roman Catholic church as an institution and its relation to the Jews?

The Church

KOCZANOWICZ: You know, first, in the sixteenth and seventeenth centuries we had a great Protestant movement, and perhaps Protestants even predominated: in some years the parliament had a Protestant majority. People sometimes forget, and to be sure the stereotype is that Poles are Roman Catholic. But in any case, I'm not so sure about the church's attitude to the Jews; I do not think it was much different from the church elsewhere. There is of course the controversy over Maximillian Kolbe, you know, who is said to have sacrificed himself at Auschwitz for another, but who is said to have been an anti-Semite. And there is the controversy over the convent at Auschwitz, which is perhaps a good thing to discuss, because our church was not fair: it promised to remove the convent but did not do it. But you know, I'm not really that familiar with the church. I was brought up . . . my father was very religious, but I myself am not. I wouldn't describe myself as a Catholic. I used to say I was an atheist, but after philosophy, I have to call myself an agnostic because philosophically one cannot know. But I baptized my son because of cultural reasons, and I would send him to religious classes, because it is necessary cultural background. But I didn't participate, and that has led to problems. You know, Maria and I did not get married in the church, so when we asked the priest to baptize our son, he wanted us to do this first before he baptized the boy, but we refused.

A lot of priests, I think, come from peasant backgrounds, and so they maybe are more prone to be anti-Semitic. But this controversy over the convent is perhaps a good example of misunderstanding. Many Poles would say, What is it you want us to do? The nuns are mourning the Poles who were killed in Auschwitz. OK, the sophisticated explanation that the Jewish religion forbids prayer at a cemetery, they don't know about that. What they . . .

FISCHER: That's not the Jewish objection, I don't think. Jews pray at cemeteries, Jewish prayers. The objection, I think, rather has to do with the placement of Christian symbols—nuns, crosses, a convent in the center of a Jewish graveyard or memorial. I don't think there is objection to Christian prayers, or to the convent if it was moved further away, or to memorializing the Poles who died. Some Jews objected, I think, feeling that the nuns were not acknowledging sufficiently the genocidal specificity directed at the Jews that Auschwitz represents.

KOCZANOWICZ: No? Well, whatever the reason, doesn't matter. The point is, say, about Glemp's sermons. You remember?

FISCHER: Yes.

KOCZANOWICZ: Glemp said things about Jews who control the mass media and finances. What he said was very Polish. Jews, of course, could be very upset. But Poles would think only that people from outside don't understand us, and that if, as the old stereotype had it, Jews were important in the media and finance, they were key people to address so outsiders would understand Poles better. The intentions were good, they were not to offend Jews. Glemp's intent maybe was to open a dialogue. Of course, one should expect more from a cardinal, but the strength of the Catholic church in Poland has always been its closeness to the common people.

Take the recent case of the Greek Orthodox church in Przemysl. It shows the limits of church power. Again, I should refer a bit to Polish history. In the seventeenth century, in the Ukraine, there was a union between the Greek Orthodox and the Roman Catholic churches. It was set up so that there was a Greek Catholic church with a priest who could do marriages and perform the liturgy, but he would be under the pope. The Russians were suspicious of this arrangement, viewing it as a Polish attempt to gain hegemony in Orthodox territory. But the irony is that in fact this church became more and more Ukrainian nationalist. And so the Polish government actually supported the Russian Orthodox church against this nationalist church. Later, when the territory fell under Russian rule, the Greek Catholic church was forbidden; for the Vatican it was like an advance outpost. The Greek Catholic church was suppressed in Poland under the communists, too. Under Gorbachev it was made legal again, and in Przemysl, a city in southeastern Poland, the Roman Catholic church wanted to give back a church to the Greek Catholic church, but the local population prevented it. They went on a kind of demonstration. The bishop came and asked them to give up the church, but they refused. Then the pope was to come, and the demonstrators were asked to disperse so that the pope could come, but they said no.

It is not so simple as the idea that Poles simply obey the Roman Catholic church. You know there are a lot of jokes about people in the highlands. There's the story that a highland father is sending his son to school in the city, and tells him, "You should kiss the hand of the parish priest, but you should think for yourself." And this is a general Polish attitude: respect the church, but think for yourself.

There's another such story, about Glemp. In 1989, during the "one-third free elections," the roundtable discussions, where some parliament seats were reserved for the communist party, but one-third of the seats were to be freely elected, there was the idea among the old regime that the Party might win some of these seats, too. They didn't. The brother of our cardinal Glemp ran in these elections. Now he spells his name slightly differently. The Cardinal is Glemp; the brother is Glemb. In Polish it sounds the same. He did not win the seat, but he got more votes than most of the other candidates, and it is not clear if this is because of the confusion of the two brothers. (One brother to the seminary, the other to the Party.)

What's Polish? Jewish?

KOCZANOWICZ, 31 Jan. 1992. But back to the Polish-Jewish relations. I find talking about this interesting. Perhaps it is a kind of psychoanalysis, exploring the unconscious of Polish culture. You know, a kind of joke. I have a friend who was a theater director as a student, and he was obsessed with the purity of Polish culture. He wanted to stage the work of one of our three great poets: Mickieicz, Krasinski, and Slowacki. He wanted to stage them, but he wasn't sure that Mickiewicz and Slowacki weren't partly Jewish; Krasinski was from a great aristocratic family, so he staged him, and the irony is that of the three he is the least good poet. Krasinski's fame is not in the quality of his poetry, but rather from the fact that he was among the first to predict a workers' revolution. In his satire, the *Nondivine Comedy,* he takes a cue from the Lyons textile workers' revolt, and fantasizes a world-wide workers' revolution led by converted Jews that succeeds except in one place, defended by Polish nobles, who are in the foxholes and trenches of the Holy Trinity.

Our greatest Polish poem, by Adam Mickiewicz, "Pan Tadeusz" (like my son's name), begins with the line, "Lithuania, my homeland," because Mickiewicz comes from this Lithuanian part of Poland. He is our greatest Polish poet, but he never visited Warsaw, the capital, nor Kraków, the cultural center of Poland. He only was in Vilna and Posna. Then there is the famous but mysterious line in the poem foretelling the coming of a Polish hero who would free Poland, "his blood is from foreign heroes, and his name is Forty-Four." Because Mickiewicz has Jewish blood, many interpret the line to refer to Jews (foreign blood) and to the cabala (the forty-four).

There is a permanent tension between the fear of losing national identity, on the one hand, and on the other, the need to be enriched by the outside. It is hard to define Polish culture. What, for instance, goes an old joke, is Polish cuisine: Ukrainian borscht, Lithuanian dumplings, and Jewish fish.

Patriotic Treason: Konrad Wallenrod, Joseph Conrad

KOCZANOWICZ, 4 Feb. 1992. So the first thing is the problem of treason because one of the main points of Kugelmas's paper is that the main feature

of these reverse images is the problem of treason, that Polish people see
themselves as a very noble people who are not able to commit any treason,
and are prone to ascribe to Jews such attitudes . . . I would like to say some
words about this problem of treason in Polish culture because it is very important. The point of departure is another poem by Mickiewicz. I should say
again that the poets of Poland are more than only poets. Like prophets in the
Bible, they are guardians of our self-identity. And especially Mickiewicz is
probably the most important person for our culture. There is a famous poem
of his called "Konrad Wallenrod." Now I would like only to summarize this
poem. In the fifteenth century we waged a great war with—I'm not sure of
the English name of this order—a knight's order in Prussia. But you know
the story, that there were knight's orders in the Holy Land, and one of them
was set up by Germans, and they moved to Europe, and then they moved to
the Baltic Sea to convert Prussia, I mean the Prussian tribes, because you
know the name Prussia is "pagan": there were pagan tribes in this region,
they were conquered, but the name survived. This order was a very interesting society: they set up a relatively big state, and they became a big threat to
Lithuania on the one hand and Poland on the other. We were Christian, but
there was an effort in the Vatican to prove that in fact we were pagan; that,
too, is a big story. But in any case, it was a dangerous threat for Lithuania
and for us. Probably because of this threat, Lithuania agreed to set up a unified state with Poland. In 1410 we won a great battle at Grünwald, where we
stopped this order. Alexander Nevsky won a similar battle defending Russia
against another branch of this order—you probably know the film [by Ser-
gey Eisenstein]. After some years, in the sixteenth century, they decided to
become Protestant; that was the origin of Prussia.

Anyway, this Mickiewicz poem described the story of the head of this
order. This is the story: a Lithuanian fellow decided to enter this knight's
order so that he could betray them, to lead them into a trap. Like in many
nineteenth-century poems, there is a kind of box-in-a-box story. The direct
stimulus which made him think about this task was that he listened to a song
about the Arab-Spaniard war. There is a story, you know, that the Spaniards
won the war, and only one castle remains in the Arab's hands—it is Gre-
nada—and there were only a handful of people in this castle, and they were
led by an Arab knight, al-Manṣūr. He decides to surrender the castle to the
Spaniards, but in fact he is deadly ill due to some infection, and he asked
the Spaniards to exchange kisses with him, and he contaminated them. So
this is a very famous expression in Polish culture, al-Manṣūr's kiss, the kiss
of treason. But, you know, in this Mickiewicz poem, he is a positive hero,
and Konrad Wallenrod, listening to this story, decided to do the same. So on
the one hand, he is a member of this knight's order, he took the oath of this

order. After our discussion I noticed two points. I am not very familiar with Polish literary criticism, but it was striking for me that this concept of positive treason was transferred from the non-Christian world, because the Arab was not Christian, and Konrad Wallenrod was Lithuanian, not Christian, and he had to betray the Christian knights.

And now, why it is important for Polish culture: because on the one hand, as Kugelmas rightly states, we like to see ourselves as noble persons, but on the other, it is very important for our culture, this concept of treason, because, for instance, in the nineteenth century, Polish people served in foreign armies, in the Russian army, in the German army, and so on. And they faced this dilemma because they took the oath to the king of Prussia, and they were officers; and for soldiers, for officers, honor was the important thing. Yet on the other hand, they were the Poles, so if they decided, and a lot of them decided to participate in our uprising, they betrayed the oath to the kings to whom they had sworn allegiance. And this point was very important for the communist era because people in power, it would not be an exaggeration that they presented themselves as if there were a quiet agreement: they hinted that they were a kind of Konrad Wallenrod. In such a situation as we had, they had to collaborate with Russia, but on behalf of the Polish nation. So . . . the concept of treason is very important, and has a special name, *Wallenrodism.*

And, of course, if you remember some Joseph Conrad stories, you probably noticed that he was obsessed with this problem of being loyal to two principles. It is very often in his stories the situation that a

FISCHER: Compare the *Tale of Kieu,* the national epic of Vietnam, borrowed from a Chinese novel, built around the figure of a heroic woman, forced to sell herself to save her family. This figure of split loyalty becomes the figure of national resistance.

KOCZANOWICZ: But different than the *Tale of Kieu,* every Polish child knows the story of the Polish princess Wanda, who killed herself rather than be given as a peacemaking booty to a German invader. So, too, Mickiewicz has a famous line that revenge for the nation is more important than any other, even divinely mandated, ethic.

FISCHER: Well, that's not quite the point. Vietnam has famous women warriors, who fought valiantly on the battlefield and who committed suicide when finally defeated. The point is the figures used in each tradition for situations of complicated loyalties, and use of cunning for ultimate values.

captain, a sailor, is hired by somebody in London, a thousand miles away. His honor is to serve him as well as it is possible. You know, of course,

Conrad was Polish, and you can see now that it was not by chance that the problem of loyalty and treason was the most important problem in his stories. So for the war generation, the generation of the main interlocutor in the Kugelmas paper, Conrad was the most important writer, especially *Lord Jim*, because it was the same problem, the same dilemma for Polish history, what to do, to be noble. There is, moreover, a wonderful contemporary twist to this story: the leading Polish specialist on Conrad is Najder. He lived in Germany, and worked with Radio Free Europe; he was accused of being a spy and sentenced to death in absentia in a trial which was used as a none-too-subtle threat against the intellectuals inside Poland; so then he became head of the Polish Radio Free Europe. After the collapse of communism, he returned to Poland. We then had our period of accusations and counteraccusations of who served with or collaborated with the secret police; Najder was said to have been an agent whose code name was "the [cigarette] lighter," but when this accusation surfaced, it was noted that Najder was not in the country, but in France writing a paper on Conrad (itself an enactment of the Conradian conundrums); he subsequently returned to Poland.

So this is a . . . Some stories are incredible. I would like to tell you one story which was the basis for a very popular novel. It is a story that in 1863–64, we had a big uprising against Russia, and it was a very Polish uprising: no chance. No chance in fact; it was only guerrilla action, winter, no city was occupied by Polish troops, and in fact we acted as terrorists. People don't like now to remember this, but in our museums there are knives which were used by Polish people to stab collaborators. And there was a person who led this uprising in Warsaw, the capital; of course, he led an underground. And, of course, in this movement there were two main wings which fought each other, not with weapons, but . . . and somebody from the rival wing wrote in an Austrian newspaper accusations against him about something or other, and he decided to leave his post in Warsaw to go to Kraków to have a duel with this man, so he left his post for two days to go to have a duel, and he planned to come back, but he didn't because he was killed. So, he was killed not because of the uprising, not by the Russians, so . . . On the one hand, it is very stupid, but on the other, it is very Polish. The last leader in the uprising, his name was Trauguth, was a colonel in the Russian army, so he was a kind of Wallenrod because he had to break his oath to the Russian czar. So this is like a constant in Polish history.

If we are speaking about this uprising, 1863–64, the January Uprising, because it began in January, this time was probably the time of the closest Polish-Jewish relations, because the Jews in Warsaw took part in this uprising. This uprising began in a big street demonstration in Warsaw, a street demonstration. It was like, probably this is a good comparison, like in Iran under the shah, in that one day thousands of people came into the streets, they were attacked by the Cossacks, by the Russians, there were people killed, and after a few days there was a funeral, which was the occasion for the next demonstration, and so on. And during one demonstration—usually the cross was carried in the front line—there is a very famous image in Polish history that the Pole who took this cross was killed, and a Jewish boy picked it up, and he was killed, too. This is a very important image for our history, and there was a very famous poem written by the Polish poet Norwid about this event which describes the Polish-Jewish relations and appreciates Jewish contributions to Polish culture.

After breaking this uprising, the Russians closed schools and universities; they even closed the churches in Warsaw. Thus began a very interesting period, because some years before this region had gained autonomy. The Marquis Aleksander Wielopolski, head of the local government, had gained autonomy for the region. His emphasis was on the economy. His idea was to develop the economy and culture of Poland. He founded a university in Warsaw, and got permission from the Russians for it. He collaborated with the Russians, but stressed development. The idea was not to fight with weapons, but preserve Polish culture through developing it. He was condemned by many Poles. In December 1862, he found himself at a crossroads: he knew about underground preparations for the uprising, and he decided to go with the Russians. Many young people, potential members of the uprising, were rounded up and conscripted into the Russian army. The underground learned about this plan, and so many escaped to the forest, and began the uprising, but with no preparation. The uprising was crushed but Wielopolski was ousted from his post, and moved to Germany, to Dresden; and the autonomy of the region was broken.

In the 1960s there were a lot of Polish plays about this period, about two strategies: whether to collaborate but preserve Polish culture, albeit under the threat of being assimilated into Russian culture; or to fight without a chance, but to shed blood which would have the political effect of dividing us from the Russians, driving a wedge across which there could be no reconciliation. The Russian intellectuals, including those in the democracy movement, all joined in the calls to break the Polish uprising, all except one, Aleksander Herzen. Herzen was the only one who supported us, and for this reason he lost all power in the Russian democracy movement. After this, economic competition became so great that Polish-Jewish relations became worse and worse. The novel that describes this is *Lalka* [The Doll] by Prus.

We had a national hero, General Bem, who led our artillery in the uprising of 1830–31. We had in the nineteenth century two big uprisings against Russia, each thirty years, the one generation was defeated and the next generation began again; and we had a revolution in 1905 and it is a big discussion among our historians if it was really a revolution or if it was the next uprising, but never mind. So we had the uprising in 1830–31 and General Bem headed our artillery, and then he was commander-in-chief of the Hungarian army when Hungary had its great uprising against Austria in 1848, and in fact defeated the Austrians, but the Russians came and suppressed the Hungarians. Bem's adjutant was the great Hungarian poet Poetofy, who was killed in this battle by the Russians. Bem escaped to Turkey and converted to Islam. Why did he convert? Because he believed that with Turkish help he could free Poland. It was a vivid idea, and some Poles decided to settle in Turkey, and a small Polish village in Turkey survives. Its name is Adamopol, named after the first name of the poet Adam Mickiewicz. Mickiewicz himself died in Constantinople because he went to Constantinople to support Turkey in its battle with Russia. So then, this General Bem was, of course, a traitor to Christianity, but he is very much appreciated in Poland because, you know, because he converted, but he converted for Polish nationalism. And, of course, there is a very famous poem by this same poet who wrote about the Polish Jew in the uprising, Norwit, about the funeral of General Bem. But, of course, it is a great contradiction, because we survived because of the Catholic church, and here he is a convert.

[Poland had long relations with the Ottoman world: the Polish king John III Sobieski, called by Leopold for help, stopped the Turks at Vienna in 1683. The gentry dress of Poland is derived from Turkish styles. The Turks never accepted the partition of Poland, and apparently at audiences the Sultan's page would announce the ambassador of Lahistan and then say because of many troubles at home he was not able to come.]

In the seventeenth century we fought three hostile powers—Sweden, Turkey, and Russia—it was a century of almost permanent war. And we defeated them all, but in the process Poland was so weakened that in the next century it could be partitioned. There is a very famous and popular series of books about these seventeenth-century wars, Sienkiewicz (he is also the author of *Quo Vadis?* about Christianity). There is a famous afterword to the series in which Sienkiewicz says his purpose was to support our hearts in the present time, that is, in the nineteenth century—he wrote about the glories of the seventeenth century to keep people's spirits up. Faulkner used Sienkiewicz's line in his Nobel Prize acceptance speech, the line about the purpose of literature being to support our hearts in the present.

In the nineteenth century, our fate was like a pendulum, swinging between the strategy of loyalty to a great power while attempting to develop our culture, and fighting with weapons. This became a dilemma for Polish conservatives: conservatism is supposed to preserve the status quo, but no one wanted that, with the exception of one writer who said we should reject our own language and learn Russian. It was clear in the nineteenth century that the liberation of Poland was connected with revolution across Europe: it was not possible to free Poland without liberating Prussia.

Poland Betrayed

KOCZANOWICZ, 30 Jan. 1992. After 1989, especially in 1990, Poles felt betrayed by the outer world. The common attitude was that we were first, we first opposed the communist government, we suffered under marital law, and so on, and when Solidarity in fact won during the round table discussions, people expected massive support from Western countries. They expected that our economic situation should change in months, a year. And, of course, it didn't happen. So they felt betrayed by Western countries again, as they had felt betrayed in Yalta. This attitude—we are a good people who are betrayed by our neighbors, not our neighbors, in fact, but the Americans, the Brits, the French, and so on—in this frame, reactions to Polish-Jewish relations would be a function of the broader attitude that we are pure people, we are good, but we are constantly accused of doing wrong things. It is, in fact, interesting because probably Jewish-Polish relations are better described than Ukrainian-Polish relations, which I think, are more fixed; also Lithuanian-Polish stereotypes need to be overcome.

20 Feb. 1992

It's all related to the nineteenth-century slogan, "For Our Freedom and Your Freedom"—Poles were always disappointed. Poles became involved in any war or uprising, but it always turned out to be without profit for Poland. This mood was very vivid in the Polish mind. We stopped the Russian army from interfering in Belgium in 1930 because there was an uprising in Poland at the same time. Poles participated in the Paris commune: Jaroslow Dambrowski, Wroblewski; a Pole was even the commander-in-chief of the communards. People felt the situation repeated itself in the recent events: we began the uprising against the USSR, but the West did not care about us. So our relation to the West is a love-hate one. The West is the only source of aid for our resistance to the USSR, but the West betrayed us as it did after World War II. So many Poles are very suspicious . . . that the States are more interested in relations with Russia than with Poland. Poland's treaty with England and France, and again the Yalta arrangements, all worked out against Polish interests. Even progressives in the West put more emphasis on Russia. When I was in Oxford, even a left-wing historian said Russia was invaded from the West three times, it has the right to set up a bastion of defense, and it is just too bad about Poland.

Americanization and the End of Romanticism as Resistance

KOCZANOWICZ, 4 Feb. 1992. Ok, I've told you a lot about Polish history, Polish culture, and such things, but the problem is that—and it is not only my opinion, it is also that of a famous Polish specialist in literary criticism, her name is Janin—nowadays a very important period in Polish culture is ending, the period of romanticism. As I told you about Mickiewicz, Krasinski, and Slowacki—they were romantic poets like Byron in England, Goethe in Germany, and they wrote about the same kinds of things, nationalism, a kind of prophecy, whose specialty was connected with particulars in Polish history. These strikes in 1980, August 1980, were in fact under the influence of this romantic culture. For that reason, the interpretation of these strikes was so difficult for Western intellectuals because a lot of them did not understand how it was possible for the workers to go on strike with church flags, prayers, masses, and such things. In fact, it was the shape of our uprising: the priests, the crosses, public masses, and so on . . . We did adopt some socialist symbols because the socialist movement was very powerful at the end of the nineteenth century, but because of the communists, these symbols were abandoned. People didn't want to use red flags, and so on. And so they used our romantic symbols. But, in fact, probably it was the last time we used these symbols so extensively. For good or bad, Poland is going to be a normal state (14 July 1992: Well, maybe not a normal state. After the last month I no longer think Poland will be a Western-style normal state, maybe more like a South American state of consciousness awash in constant discussion). It is difficult to predict in which direction our culture will go in its confrontation with Western popular culture and so on.

But I would like to talk about something which probably was very important for Polish-Jewish relations and was important for the breaking down of this romantic culture: that in fact after the Second World War, in the seventies and eighties, Poles adopted a lot of features which they before ascribed to Jews. What do I mean? That Poles became probably the most important bargainers in the Eastern bloc. We were relatively free to travel, so people began to do the same things we ascribed to Jewish people: that they took an opportunity to earn money, that they sold anything—including priceless things—for high prices, that they are shameless in bargaining, that money is the most important thing. And a flood of Poles went to Western Europe, to other parts of the world, India—you know that there is a lot of smuggling of Polish guns in India, in Singapore—of course these are big people, but I mean small people. Probably any tourist travel for Polish people was connected with this bargaining. And of course Poles sold small things on the streets of Western countries, especially in West Berlin because we didn't need visas for West Berlin. So in fact we took the place of these small Jewish bargainers. It's like a Jewish anathema: for many years we were proud that we didn't adopt these ways, but like a Jewish anathema, they were killed on our soil, but in fact we adopted some of their features. So I think it was important for our understanding. Maybe Polish people didn't realize it to the end, but it was obvious for some change. This problem of small bargaining in Eastern Europe is very interesting because, in fact, it showed the important role of the free market for the mutual understanding of people. In the last two years we had a flood of Russians who came to do the same thing we did in Western Europe, and it was funny, because in fact people understood them. And it was very common that Polish people who bargained with them used to say that we did the same things a few years ago in Western Europe. So I think it was very important for changing attitudes towards the Russians, because before, Polish people saw them as a nonhuman power. But then they met the Russians, the Ukrainians, talked with them, made some deals with them. It was very important. And I think this common involvement of Poles in bargaining was important for our mentality. And also it was very important that a lot of people went to Western European countries to do physical labor. Physical labor was for many years condemned in Poland because of our gentry background. But then a lot of people, intellectuals, decided, some of them, some of my friends decided to go to Western countries, to Germany, Scandinavia, the United States, to work there with their own hands. And probably this period changed our culture, and of course this romanticism was important when we were suppressed by the Russian power, it was a kind of resistance to the Russians, and now we are independent, and we face other problems, I mentioned, confrontation with Western pop, Western popular culture, and we can lose our national identity not because of power but because of being dissolved in world culture. These romantic symbols were very important weapons in this period of being oppressed by the Russians, but I don't think that they could be so good now in the confrontation with American action film or comics and so on. So our culture is changing. Even our school programs are changing. I had a big course in Polish literature, very detailed, but now this is changed.

B. Poetry

Poets, Leszek stresses, are repositories of moral authority. They are to Poland what prophets are to the biblical tradition. Among the many poets we discussed, three sets are most important: (1) those formulating the romantic tropes of past Polish culture, for example, Adam Mickiewicz; (2) those that articulate the moral struggle to come to terms with the Holocaust; and (3) those that articulate the moral struggle with Stalinism and the communist state.

The Holocaust (KOCZANOWICZ, Feb. 1992)

The Survivor	*Still*

The Survivor

I am twenty-four
led to slaughter
I survived

These labels are empty and
  synonymous:
man and beast
love and hate
friend and foe
light and dark

Man can be killed like the beast
I've seen:
cartloads of hacked-up bodies
who will never be saved.

Concepts are but words . . .

I seek a teacher and master
let him restore to me sight hearing
  and speech
let him once again name things
  and concepts
let him separate light from dark
    —Tadeusz Rozewicz (1947)

Still

In sealed box cars travel
names across the land . . .

The name Nathan strikes fist
  against wall
the name Isaac, demented, sings
the name Sarah calls out for water
for . . .

Don't jump while it's moving.
  Your son will be Lech . . .

Cor-rect, cor-rect clicks the
  wheel . . .
cor-rect, cor-rect, crash of silence
  on silence

    —Wislawa Szymborska

I show you these poems because . . . [while] it is right from the Jewish point of view to see the Second [World] War as a war of the Holocaust . . . I would like to show you that it was a shock for a generation of Poles, and there was not shock only because of the Jewish Holocaust but the shock of any values of Western culture, in fact. So, I can say again that this problem of Jewish-Polish relations, the problem of the Holocaust is for us an issue in a broader context of losing any sense of Western culture, of Western philosophy, Western art, and Western values.

[Leszek had begun by citing Arthur Sandauer, a Polish literary critic of a specific generational political background—a proponent of the avant-garde even after Stalin's death, but in the 1980s increasingly connected to the communist government and alienated from Polish society—who wrote a book about Polish poetry, which he subtitled, "the book I should not have written by myself," because he was a Jew, and a Pole should have written the critique of the use of poetry to remember the Holocaust. Still he draws attention to a number of important poems, including two by Nobel laureate

Czeslaw Milosz. Sandauer is part of a leftist generation that remained true to
its ideals, viewing Stalinism as a mistake; some were suppressed by Stalin
for being avant-garde, only to find in the post-Stalin period when they could
travel to Paris again that geometric abstraction and other avant-garde explo-
rations were no longer fashionable.]

These two poems [by Milosz] are a kind of illustration of the kind of poetry with which I tried to defend the Polish effort to understand Jewish, to
understand the Holocaust, to understand the purpose, real meaning of the
Holocaust for Western culture, for our culture. It is not much, this literature,
not as much as it should have been, but it is enough to justify to some extent
the opinion that Kugelmas was not so right in saying that we didn't make
any effort to understand the fate of the Jewish people.

Czeslaw Milosz's poem "Campo dei Fiori" draws parallels between the
square on which Giordano Bruno was burned and the Warsaw ghetto, speaking of the spring and the time of merrymaking just before Easter. The motif
also occurs in the novel *Holy Week*
by Andrzejeweki, about Polish-
Jewish life during the ghetto uprising,
with the image of a carousel near the
ghetto during the week before Easter
where people came to enjoy themselves, while on the other side of the
wall, Jews were killed by Germans.
And, of course there is this ambiguity in our relation to Jews during the
ghetto uprising. Istvan Deak, in the
New York Review of Books, suggests
that Poles did not help the Germans
kill the Jews, as did Ukrainians and
Lithuanians, but that the Poles
fought the Germans so hard that the Germans did not dare to give them
weapons. The main idea of Deak's argument is that there is no clear connection between resistance to the Germans and the rescue of the Jews, that Jews
had better situations in countries which collaborated with the Germans, such
as Italy and Spain, Romania and Bulgaria, and even Denmark, because he
argues, you remember, that the story about Danish resistance to the Germans is largely fable. The image of the sky carousel is about the ambiguity
of the relation between the fate of Jews and Poles, both under threat by the
Germans. A second poem by Milosz, "A Poor Christian Looks at the
Ghetto," is more complicated . . . but the crucial point is in the last verse,
"I a Jew of the New Testament waiting two thousand years for the second coming of Jesus / What will I tell him, a Jew of the New Testament?"

—Was it possible to see anything
beyond the wall on the Aryan side?
—Oh yes, the wall only reached the
second floor. And already from the
third floor one could see the other
street. We could see the merry-go-
round, people, we could hear music
and we were terribly afraid that this
music would drown us out and that
those people would never notice a
thing . . . the struggle, the dead . . .
that nothing, nothing about us, would
ever make it out. (Krall 1986: 7)

The poem by Tadeusz Rozewicz, "The Survivor," is recognized as typifying the Polish mood after the Second [World] War, as is his "Lament, 5." And Wislawa Szymborska's poem, "Still," is important in this context for the clear recognition that the Holocaust took place on our soil . . . This verse is most important, "Let your son have a Slavic name, for here they count hairs . . ." She writes "for here" . . . and of course the next verse, "Your son will be Lech" . . . a very Polish name, Slavic . . . implying that Jews will have to convert, become Polish . . . And the last verse is also important, because it is a reference to our remembrance of the Holocaust.

There is the tragic case of the poet Tadeusz Borowski, who was sent by the Germans to Auschwitz. He spent three or four years in Auschwitz, and wrote stories about the camps . . . seen through the eyes of a well-adjusted man who has gotten used to the system, and treats it as normal, becoming familiar with the Germans, able sometimes to help others in situations where it would not harm himself. [Many people misunderstood, did not differentiate between the narrative subject and Borowski, but the stories were] good because they were an accusation of the system, of adaptation to the system to survive . . . After the war, Borowski rejected any values of Western civilization, writing of the Greeks that it was just one big concentration camp, and becoming a strong supporter of Stalinist Marxism, and finally in 1953 he committed suicide. It was around the time he was sent as a journalist to cover a show trial of small nomenclatura for forcing peasants to collectivize. Maybe it was a shock for him to realize what was going on. Milosz wrote a poem about him, treating him as typical of Polish intellectuals caught between a nationalistic, conservative church and a totalitarian state, with little chance to find a third way. There is the story about Maria Dabrowska, who tried to keep her distance from the communist government, and did not publish during the Stalinist period, though she did socialize and not refuse to have contacts with government officials. When Stalin died, she was asked to write a short statement, and after some hesitation she did so, saying only that a big man had died, but without appreciation of his deeds. It is said that when her name came up for the Nobel prize, someone used this statement about Stalin as a way to ruin her chances. So it was probably a difficult period for intellectuals.

Coping with a Communist State

KOCZANOWICZ, 4 Feb. 1992 cont. Some tried to not have contacts with the Communists. Zbiginew Herbert is an example: he did not publish during the Stalinist period, and did not compromise with them. I do not like his poems, I will explain, but this is a poem about his relation to the communists, "The Power of Taste": "No our refusal, dissent and obduracy / didn't require great character / we had a pinch of indispensible courage / but basically it was a matter of taste." This poem was put out in the 1980s, and in the volume of interviews I mentioned, *Domestic Shame,* Herbert is the only person not involved in the Stalinist period, and he accuses everyone else of being under the influence of Stalinism. It was both funny and sad, that some people tried to dig into his poems to show that he, in fact, had also supported Stalinism. But I don't like his poems because they are elitist . . . they demand to be a kind of hero in times when ordinary intellectuals worked under tremendous pressure requiring some compromises. (20 Feb. 1992: What upsets me about Herbert's poems is his Greek and Roman references, the false elevation of the analogies at the expense of actual life.)

A poem of his, very important for the war generation, is "The Elegy of Fortinbras": "Now that we're alone we can talk prince man to man / though you lie on the stairs and see no more than a dead ant . . . It is not for us to greet each other or bid farewell we live on archipelagos / and that water these words what can they do what can they do prince." This poem was published probably after Stalin's death, because Herbert began to publish in 1955/56, he was in his late thirties, and you probably notice the two attitudes, heroic versus normal, two different ways of life. This was the problem of this generation, because they were heroes during the war, but life became morally complicated under Stalinism . . . the reason this poem was so important for this generation was because it very clearly presented these two ways . . . as very far from each other: we live on different islands . . . I think only big people could afford to keep their distance, like Dabrowska: she was well known, so she could play a kind of game with the government, but not normal intellectuals . . . The situation became more and more complicated and unclear. Under the pressure of a totalitarian state, the pressure was very bad, but the choices are not so clear as in war. We had fought the Germans: Poles are very proud that we had no collaborators who set up a government like Quisling in Norway. The Germans tried to find such people, but nobody, even among those who had had fascist sympathies before the war, was willing, though it is unclear how hard the Germans tried to actually find such people. People were condemned even for writing in the official [Nazi] newspapers. There is the case of a Polish writer in Vilna so obsessed with Stalin during the war that he decided to write some anti-Stalinist pieces in the official Polish language newspaper, and to this day there is a discussion whether or not he was a German collaborator. Even though the Poles hated the Russians, it was uncommon to support the Germans.

C. Marxist Rhetorical Games and Their Demise

KOCZANOWICZ, 20 Feb. 1992. Even our Communist Party was a little different. The Communist Party was dissolved by Stalin, a lot of people were killed, and many who survived the purge kept their distance from the Stalinists . . . But even our handbooks of Marxism were translations from French and English, not Russian . . . books by Maurice Comforth from England and the Frenchman Garody (who later became Muslim—first a Stalinist, then a revisionist, and then a Muslim). So our Marxism was to some extent different from Russian marxism, and our well-known intellectuals were treated a little better. After 1956 . . . Marxists became more and more revisionist, and used this revisionism to talk about "alienation," that is, whether alienation is possible in a socialist state . . . In the late fifties and early sixties there was much discussion about alienation, Marxism with a human face, the connections of Marxism and existentialism . . . In the late sixties the Communist Party tried to regain control over the intellectuals. In 1966 Leszek Kolakowski was expelled from the Party for saying that nothing was left of the Polish October, and others left too. This spelled the end of any real influence of Marxism in Polish intellectual life. After 1968, discussion turned much more to democracy, organizing the workers, and turned away from "alienation" . . . A sophisticated Marxism survived, of course, in the universities, a Marxism of science, Marxism mixed with hermeneutics, the cultural status of Marxism, and so on, but Marxism was no longer a vital movement in Polish life . . .

25 Feb. 1992. The situation of the Communist Party was somewhat complicated: (1) it was not, as many would now like to say, alienated from society, but on the contrary, particularly in the seventies under Gierek, tried to become a kind of broad umbrella party, and even earlier in 1956 Gomulka tried to co-opt elements of the church (actually the church hierarchy kept its distance except maybe in 1957 when Cardinal Wyszyński supported the holding of an election; but there was a Catholic organization of clubs which lent support, and then there was Pax, a right-wing, Italian-style fascist organization, founded by Boleslaw Piasecki, whose mother—another of those Polish ironies—was Jewish: the church disassociated itself from Pax, and Resetsky attacked Gomulka for not being sufficiently pro-Russian); (2) it was supported by much of the Right because it had fulfilled three basic right-wing goals; (3) the opposition came from two, maybe three, quite different directions: the revisionist Left (stressing the social issue), the nationalist Right (stressing nationalism), and the workers who had a history of organizing and demonstrations that arguably are quite distinct from the agitations of the intellectual Left.

The three right-wing goals that the communist state achieved were: (1) regaining lands in the West from Germany, which had been ruled by Polish counts in the sixteenth and seventeenth centuries, but which long were no longer thought of as Polish except by the extreme Right; before the war, Poles thought of the most Polish cities as being those in the East: Lvov,

Vilna; (2) creating a strong state, especially in defense against Germany, and hence rightists were often in favor of alliance with Russia; (3) a homogeneous population of Poland. Before the war, this last was not possible because of the Jews, Ukrainians, White Russians, and Lithuanians; but after the war, the Jews had been killed, the Ukrainians were largely in the Ukraine's new borders, with only a relatively small group left in Poland, and in fact 90 percent of the population is now Poles. Put in historical terms, it might be called a change from Pyast to Jagelonian politics. Pyasts were the first important dynasty, and were concerned largely with the western borders to Germany; while the Jagelonian dynasty is identified with the eastern issue, fighting Russia and the Ottomans.

It is a seeming paradox that the communists should revive the right-wing Pyast concept of Polish politics, but it is a common issue in Eastern Europe that the communists should pretend to be very nationalistic, an ambiguous stance, since the Party could not be very nationalist given the dependence on the Soviet Union. But in this way, many very right-wing people entered the Communist Party, including Tejkowski, the founder of the most extreme nationalist party in Poland, not taken very seriously. (There is a second, more traditional, nationalist party, led by Giertych, whose father was a prewar nationalist party leader, and who himself was educated at Oxford as a biologist, an expert on trees, and who returned to Poland in the 1960s. In the 1980s he became very active in politics. Besides being a nationalist, he is also a creationist.)

There were members of the Left who remained communist, particularly of the generation of the twenties, who felt that Stalin had been a terrible mistake, but that the basic goals of socialism remained important. But of course one major part of the opposition movement was revisionist Marxists, most importantly Modzelewski and Kuron. They began with some connection to Trotsky. In the early 1960s they wrote a famous open letter to the Party, and were arrested. Kuron in his memoirs writes that they were arrested twice, and each time, Modzelewski was given half a year extra imprisonment because of his Jewish background. If the Left opposition stressed the social issue, there was also opposition from the nationalist Right. A third stream of opposition, emphasized in a recent book published in England, is a kind of underground pure workers movement, unconnected with the left-wing intellectuals. There were quite a number of worker organized strikes in 1950s and 1960s. In any case, the Left and nationalist oppositions worked in tactical alliance and both tried to enter Solidarity in the eighties, but when Solidarity came to power it became obvious that there had to be a parting of the ways.

There was a joke about the roundtable discussions that now finally Party members were talking with former Party members: Kuron was a former

Party member, so was Modzelewski, as were a number of the others. The name Solidarity was invented by Modzelewski, but it had been used earlier in the nineteenth century by a part of the socialist movement. Modzelewski is a professor of history, albeit of medieval history, but he no doubt has a good knowledge of trade union history as well, so maybe he borrowed the name. Now Modzelewski has founded the Solidarity of Labor, the party with which I most identify, the most leftist of the groups in the Solidarity movement; Kuron is connected instead with the Center of Democratic Union, with the idea that we should build a capitalist state first and then worry about a welfare state.

To some extent the Communist Party was rooted in Polish society. I mean that it was relatively open, so one could meet within it real fascists to Maoists and Che Guevara people. In the seventies this was the conscious policy of Gierek to open the Communist Party, to create or change the Communist Party into a kind of popular or national front. The idea was like the odd prewar political movement created to support the dictatorship of Pidulski and his successor. It is difficult to translate the name, but it would be something like "No Party Bloc for Collaboration with the Government." It was organized by clerks to support the government in elections without need for any program. Gierek seems to have tried to return to this idea, and oddly for the older generation it helped, along with Gierek's opening of the borders, importing Western technology, and allowing travel abroad. For my generation, it was just further evidence of the bankruptcy of the communists, and it seemed just like the efforts in 1956 to argue for the reform of socialism. This was most militantly called for by the newspaper of the youth organization of the Communist Party called *Propostu* (Frankly Speaking): socialism needs reform, but socialism is good. Jerzy Urban (the hated spokesman of the government under General Jaruzelski) and Olszewski (prime minister, now attached to a center-right party) were connected with this paper. Urban—more Polish-style turns—now edits a very popular tabloid newspaper, *No!* that carries all the latest attacks, gossip, and slurs against Walesa and the former opposition leaders.

19 March 1992. Gierek replaced Gomulka at the time of the 1970 strikes against meat price increases (meat prices caused strikes again in 1976 and 1980). Gomulka was a communist of the generation of the 1920s who had remained active in Poland (that generation was split between those who came back with the Russian army to Poland and those who had stayed in Poland) [see Schatz 1991]. But Gierek was an entirely different sort of person: he emigrated as a child to France, had worked with miners in Belgium and France, spoke French and was proud of it, and was open to Western ideas. His dream probably was to set up an enlightened communist state, in imitation of France and Western countries. So he opened Poland to the West

and changed the passport law to make it easier to travel to the West. (Passports were used to blackmail people. I, for instance, was invited to visit my Jewish friend in Sweden in 1970, but I was refused a passport. I was 16. A couple of years later I was offered a passport if I would report back on Jewish emigration, and they told me, we know about your activity in leftist organizations. I refused. And so while most of my friends had long travelled to the West, I was first able to do so in 1985 when I went to Oxford.)

This was an important period of change. In the 1960s the only way to gain some material wealth was to be involved in some way in politics; but in the 1970s it was possible to go to the West and earn money by doing simple physical labor. So the space of private life expanded . . . In the eighties there were probably more cars in Poland than telephones . . . People began to live better. There was a big shift in ideology . . . The stress on ideology became weaker, and instead there was an attempt to create a state that could be acceptable to everybody, a kind of quiet agreement: we allow you some proper level of life and you don't interfere with politics . . . In the 1960s in comparison, Poland was a relatively closed and poor country, yet it was better-kept because people had to work in Poland. In the seventies people treated work as a necessary evil, and tried to find ways to go abroad. In the sixties there was still a stress on ideology, and there were interesting ideas and changes in Marxism, confrontations with the church, and so on; in the seventies it became more vague . . . In the seventies marxism became extinct, I mean, only something for intellectuals . . . there was a Marxist school of philosophy of science: they tried to connect Popper with Marxism . . . Another school of Marxism was hermeneutic à la Lukács. But it was all very intellectual. I was attached to an Institute for Marxist Philosophy headed by a very interesting philosopher, Ladosz, who was sincere and left wing.

The government was caught in an interesting dilemma vis-à-vis rhetorics: they tried to use three mutually exclusive rhetorics: (1) Marxist-communist authority coordinating the working class; (2) nationalism; (3) modernization. This last was the origin of the great debt of Poland because they promised to achieve Western standards of technology in ten or fifteen years, and so they began lending money to set up factories, money borrowed from abroad. Much of this money was spent on pure consumption: it was the one time under the communist government when there was plenty of food, and signs of Western influence like Coca-Cola.

It was very difficult to sustain any consistent system among these three rhetorics. So government rhetoric was very capricious and depended upon political events . . . Modernization was slower than people expected . . . Nationalist rhetoric also had obvious problems in areas associated with relations with the Soviet Union . . . It was sometimes very funny, even in films.

For instance, there was an effort to produce historical films, about the great past of Poland, about Sienkiewicz's epic novel, the period of gentry society. So it was funny that the Polish workers' government supported films that were apologetic for a gentry style of life. They tried to do a film about the last Plast king, Kazimierz the Great; he and his father had unified and rebuilt Poland, and Gierek to some extent identified with him. He lost Silesia to the Germans, but he gained territories in the east from Ukraine and Russia. What was funny was that while his battles against the Mongols and Tartars, and even to some extent Germans, were shown, the great political achievements in the East could not be mentioned given the difficult relations with the Russians . . . In the nineteenth century, Russia was the great enemy, and it was not possible to make films about the great uprisings against the Russians (although we could read about them in school textbooks!).

There is a further irony in fate of these rhetorics and ideologies, partly pointed out in a good paper I heard by the sociologist Zygmunt Bauman, who now lives in London. It is a kind of circle of ideas, because, as I said, in the sixties there was a lot of discussion about alienation from the Marxist point of view, and this discussion stops in the seventies because by then it was obvious that the real problems were in the organization of work, the organization of society, and not the problems of alienation. So Marxism became limited to intellectuals, philosophers, humanists, and people lost their belief in the role of the workers' class, but in the seventies the workers actually began to act in a Marxist way as grass roots politics. So then intellectuals in Warsaw organized a support committee, KOR, originally to help strikers in Radow, people persecuted after the big demonstrations. From then on, it became obvious that the communist government and ideology were becoming weaker and weaker. (A note on Bauman, another absurdist tale: he's Jewish of course, and was attacked as a Zionist revisionist, at which point my professor, Ladosz, defended him by saying in the 1950s he was a good guy, one of us, because he served in a section of the Ministry of Interior which supervised the secret police!)

25 Feb. 1992. I remember as a child, on the holiday of Corpus Christi, it was a state holiday, too, and the state tried to interfere with children going to church. I remember then that on TV only American films were shown, American westerns and so on, to encourage young people to see these films; it was funny, not Russian films, only American films, American westerns. It was rather rare on our TV then to see American films in the sixties, but not on Corpus Christi.

1 Apr. 1992. In 1979 I spent one year in the army . . . interesting because it was a very severe winter (1978–79), and this winter showed how ineffective our state was, because everything broke down, and people then realized that in fact the state is nothing . . . I found the army people were very criti-

cal of the social reality . . . They compared the Polish army with the Russian army. The Russian army was a war army, ready any moment to fight, but our army is nothing, the government tried to save money. And they compared the order of the army with the mess outside . . . There was a big mess in the army too, but it is different because it is hidden or covered by hierarchy and seeming order.

D. Jews and Others of Polish Identity

Growing Up with and without Jews

KOCZANOWICZ, 30 Jan. 1992. I was brought up in a small town of a one hundred thousand people in Silesia, a former German city (Legnica, or in German, Lignitz). So I and Maria, when we were growing up—she grew up in the town of Wrocław (the German name is Breslau)—lived in alien surroundings with German script everywhere. Both towns had relatively big Jewish populations, and each had a Jewish high school. Legnica was also the headquarters of the Soviet army. There were some thousand soldiers in the city (so it was nicknamed "Little Moscow"). The officers, of course, lived in a "forbidden city," but the ordinary soldiers lived in houses next door and mixed in with the Polish citizens. So as children we used to play with Russian children. There were also in this city a lot of Ukrainians who had been displaced by the war, and a significant population of Greek immigrants displaced by the Greek civil war. And there were some Jews, displaced from eastern Poland. We did not think much about this: my mother would send us shopping and say, Go buy some butter from the Jew, or Buy some sugar from the Greek. So we didn't think much about the Jews separately. Of course, we knew that Jews had been killed by Germans, but this was just part of a general image of the horrors of war. The image had no specification, if I can put it that way. My father was from a small town in Galicia, a town that was half Jewish

Compare Leninakan in the essay on Armenia.

Russian troops in Legnica are commanded by General Viktor Dubynin, an Afghanistan war veteran . . . The city is still divided by a gunmetal grey wall with gates guarded by uniformed Soviet soldiers. Rising gracefully above the stockade are some of the finest villas in the city, homes to officers of the Soviet army . . . which had 58,000 soldiers here in 1989 . . . has its own stores, schools, and municipal services . . . thousands of acres of forest used by Warsaw Pact airplanes for practice bombing runs. Some of the forest is charred by fires and the search for unexploded bombs is only beginning. [*New York Times,* 23 Feb. 1992, A6.]

and half Polish . . . My best friend in high school, as I told you, was Jewish
but did not realize it because his father . . . had kept it hidden. There were
some Jewish shopkeepers, and I remember some old people in the town
square who spoke in a strange language, Yiddish.

1968 was a turning point. You remember that was the year of the big
Communist Party campaign against the Jews. But they did not use the word
Jew: it was a campaign, they said, against "Zionists." And you know in
Polish, when written the newspapers, the word *syienist* looks very much like
the Polish word for Siam, *syien.* For many common people, who had lived
under many years of communist silence about Jews, they confused the two.
In any case, going back to my best friend in high school, one day he told me
that his father had been fired from his job. It was a high-level job as head of
the state cooperative shops. After a few days, there were some newspaper
stories about his father, that he was a Jew, that in the 1940s he had cheated
the Communist Party, and so on—even if these things were true, he had
been sentenced and punished, and it should not have come up again. But my
friend suddenly realized that he was half Jewish (his mother was Polish).
They emigrated to Sweden in 1969. Almost all Jews emigrated then. It was
then that we began to think about the Polish-Jewish question. I was only
fourteen or fifteen years old. In my city there were four high schools: two
Polish ones, one Ukrainian, and one Jewish. But there was only a small Jewish population, and many Poles went to the Jewish high school: they were
the ones expelled from the Polish high schools. Maria went to the former
Jewish high school in her town.

25 Feb. 1992. My father was a social worker and teacher in so-called social orphanages, places for children who had been abandoned or offspring of
criminals, and so on. It is said that when my mother's family first heard that
he was from Galicia, they assumed he must be Jewish, they being from
Prussian-influenced western Poland that stereotyped the eastern Poles as
lazy. During the war he was involved in the underground resistance (the
A.K.), and decided to go to Wrozcław University in the west immediately
after the war to study Polish literature, because he feared being arrested by
the Russians for political activities. Although he had been part of this right-
wing party, recruited originally through the scouts that this party sponsored,
his hero was Janusz Korczack [né Heryk Goldszmit], the Jewish physician,
famous writer of children's books, and educator, who developed a pedagogy
for children. Korczack ran two orphanages, one for Poles and one for Jews.
During the war he stayed in the Warsaw ghetto, and insisted on accompany-
ing his children to Treblinka, although offers to get him out were made.
Korczack's pedagogy was the alternative system, based on understanding
children's psychology; the official one was that of the Russian *Makarenko,*
based on discipline and work. Korczack's portrait hung in my father's office.

My father's family originally came from Lithuania, he thought as refugees after the defeat of the 1863–64 uprising, but a friend who checked out the genealogy thinks the family must have left Lithuania a century earlier, that they were small gentry [*schlachta*], and centuries earlier had some claim to be descended from one of the ten signers of the Union of Lithuania and Poland. My father said that his mother had burned the family certificates of gentry in 1920–21 when the Polish government liquidated gentry privileges (such as exemption from corporal punishment). The family, in any case, were peasants with a memory of being gentry, and my father went to vocational school before the war.

My mother's family was lower middle class and came from an area with a dialect containing many German words. She was almost killed by the Germans at Zbonszyn when the Germans tried to push all Poles out of those lands. Zbonszyn became famous because a camp was set up for German Jews with Polish passports, and it was from this camp that the young man came who assassinated the German diplomat in Paris, that served as the immediate excuse for the *Kristalnacht* rampage.

For my father and probably for Maria's father in Rymanow (where there was a big Jewish community as well), Poles and Jews lived in quite separate worlds, speaking different languages . . . This alienation of Jews from Polish culture and language can explain to some extent that Polish people, even if they wanted, were not able to help them because of language problems, lack of friendship relations, and so on. So, if my father told me about Jewish communities, it was told only about outer observances, that some days Jews live in tents (sukkah), they observed their own holidays, and I did not know what it meant.

On the other hand, Polish poetry before the war, many of the greatest poets had a Jewish origin, so much that in one of Milosz's poems there is a verse that Polish poets should each have a rabbi in their families . . . One of these poets, Slonimski, gave a memorable riposte to Gomulka's speech in 1968 when Gomulka attacked him by saying that Poles should have only one country (a clear allusion to Jews having two countries, Poland and Israel). Slonimski retorted that yes, Poles should have only one country, but why Egypt? (He's also the author of the quip that plays on a famous line from Mickiewicz that Poles should not allow themselves to be spit upon by the Germans; Slonimski: And why only by the Germans? The English, the French, the Russians, and everyone else, too.) Gomulka's speech is both famous and extremely interesting. The student riots were in response to the government censor shutting down a Mickiewicz play, *The Forefathers,* on the grounds that it stirred up anti-Russian feelings. Gomulka tried to explain the government's position in a long speech, in which he said he was not a drama critic but then spent half an hour in a detailed analysis of this play;

other parts of this speech were also devoted to literary analysis of several other authors, including a satiric poem by Slonimski, the occasion for his slur about the divided loyalties of the Jew. The poem, written in the 1960s, was about Julian the Apostate, the Roman emperor who attempted to revive paganism, set like a confession shortly before Julian's death, in which he says that his life had been wasted because he had converted. Gomulka's reading was that this was really Slonimski's confession that he had wasted his life because he had converted to Christianity, to being Polish: that is, he is not a real Pole. Slonimski was from a prominent Jewish family, somehow he escaped Poland during the war and worked for UNESCO after the war, returning in the 1950s to Poland. He was not welcomed back with enthusiasm by the state, and tried to keep his distance.

Polish-Jewish Relations

KOCZANOWICZ, 30 Jan. 1992. I have reservations about Kugelmas's general conclusion at the end of his paper . . . I was not sure that this conclusion found enough evidence in this paper. But as I said to you, probably it is true . . . This description of the mirror relation between Pole and Jew is fair. But you know some Polish people say we lost three million people, the same number as Polish Jews. In saying this, the Poles are not quite fair, there were differences: the Nazis killed Jewish children, while Polish children were able to go through the Nazi lines without being hurt. So there are differences. But still, Poles are upset about the playing down of their fate. Poles will say that every Polish family had someone killed by the Germans. And because of the long silence under the communist regime, many Poles did not realize the differences. They knew that many Poles were killed in Auschwitz, but they did not realize that there were two camps at Auschwitz, and that there was a difference in that the Poles were not killed immediately as was the case with Jews and Gypsies, but were put in another camp, and made to work first. What Poles know is that somebody in their family, an uncle or so, was sent to Auschwitz and never came back. In school, we were taught about the death camps, but not the difference between death camps and work camps.

There are a number of different points at issue in the way Poles recall the Polish-Jewish relation:

(1) When the Russians invaded Poland, many Jews welcomed them; some Poles remember this. Jews may have been sent by the Russians to camps in Siberia, but the Poles only remember that they welcomed

FISCHER: Have you seen the film *Europa, Europa,* based on the life of Solomon Perel, sent by his family to the east to avoid the invading German armies?

the Russians. Of course, there were reasons that the Jews had felt oppressed in prewar Poland.

(2) There is a common opinion among Poles . . . that in the Stalinist secret police there was an overrepresentation of Jews. A paper on the subject shows that only 5–10 percent of the secret service admitted to being Jews, but of course not everyone who was Jewish would have admitted it. Jews were alienated from Polish society and the Russians could use this alienation to establish control setting Poles and Jews against each other.

(3) The 1941 treaty between the Polish government in exile in London and the Russians. Part of this agreement was that Russia would free Poles held in the camps in Siberia. But the Russians did it so that first of all they freed Polish Jews. And so, you can understand if some of these released prisoners were not

KOCZANOWICZ: I know about the film: it was made by a Polish director (Agnieszka Holland), but I have not seen it. She is a sister of a film-school classmate of Maria. She emigrated but her sister stayed in Poland and became a successful filmmaker . . . Magda Lazarkiewicz.

FISCHER: There was an article in today's *New York Times* about a memoir of a former East German *Stasi* (secret police) agent, a young Jewish homosexual who was recruited in his early twenties, serving seven years. He kept a diary in which he tells how the *Stasi* offered him protection as a Jew and as a homosexual, but in return he had to play their game—divide and rule as you described under the Stalinists.

KOCZANOWICZ: Such things probably could not have occurred in Poland after the Stalinist period.

accepted by the Poles into the Polish resistance army. This army, you know, was evacuated through Iran and the Middle East. The future prime minister of Israel, Menachem Begin, was one of these Polish Jews released by the Russians and accepted into the Polish army, and of course when he got to Palestine he escaped from the Polish army . . . The well-known historian Krystyna Kersten . . . points out that for the Polish officers, it was obvious that if one allowed Stalin to get away with releasing 90 percent Jews from the camps in Siberia, Stalin could eventually say, "We've released enough people," and the result would be that Jews were let out, but the Poles were kept in the camps.

In the 1970s, Poland became a relatively open country. Especially many intellectuals went abroad and met Western Jews. They got to know about the accusations about Polish behavior in World War II. Kugelmas is right, but not so much about the 1980s; it was more in the 1960s that Poles had an image of themselves as heroes who fought the Germans and helped save Jews. Sure they knew that some people betrayed Jews, but mostly we heard about the Polish underground. In the 1970s, Poles faced the accusations that in fact Polish behavior toward the Jews had been inappropriate. But it was very difficult to tell how widely different kinds of behavior had occurred. Some historians began to work on the question, but we did not know the results. Open discussion began only after the rise of Solidarity. Four issues began to be explored:

(1) The history of the Jews in Poland. It is a long history that goes back to at least the thirteenth century, and maybe even earlier. It is a long common history, and this history was almost forgotten after World War II for my generation.

(2) Jewish-Polish relations during World War II, and the fact that this was one of a series of taboo subjects of discussion, along with Polish-Soviet relations, Katyn (where Polish officers were killed by the Russians), and Polish life before communism.

(3) The problem of Jews in Stalinist institutions such as the secret police. This, however, was almost a forbidden topic, because this topic was already politically appropriated and used by Polish nationalists to make accusations against the Jews. For this reason, liberals refused to discuss the issue, saying that it did not matter who was involved in totalitarian institutions because it was a totalitarian machine, and it didn't matter whether the individuals were Russians, Jews, or Poles. One should not focus attention on this issue in terms of nationalities. In my opinion, this reaction was not healthy, it was not good, because there was a lot of prejudice that came from this period [when nationalists were allowed to appropriate the issue].

(4) The Jews in Poland after 1956, their emigration to Israel, and especially the mysterious affair of 1968. The anti-Semitic campaign of 1968 probably began as a fight within the Communist Party, which used anti-Semitism as a tool. The problem is, why did they decide to use this tool? And if it worked as a tool, the problem is whether or not they knew the real attitudes of the Poles, if anti-Semitism is "inherited" among Poles, you know, Shamir's accusation that Poles suck anti-Semitism with the milk of their mothers. I think we need a real historical work on the image of Jews in our society. Recently this problem arose again in the presidential campaign of 1990. You remember, Lech Walesa expressed himself in a anti-Semitic way: he said during the campaign that he would like Jews to admit they are Jews. After all, he said, "I'm willing to admit that I'm a Pole, why should they not admit they are Jews." His former Jewish friend, Michnik, tried to defend him, that he was not an anti-Semite. He used it because there was talk that his opponent, Mazowiecki, had some Jewish ancestry. A bishop even came out to say that the Catholic church had investigated his genealogy and found that Mazowiecki was Polish all the way back to the fourteenth century. So, again, anti-Semitism had been used in political play, and the question is, did it work or not? Mazowiecki, of course, lost, but one cannot

tell if this gossip played a role or if he lost just because of his bad economic policies.

The problem is, and Kugelmas is right to some extent, that our Jewish-Polish relations are so intertwined that the strands cannot be pulled apart, so for many people the easy way is to use fixed clichés and probably many Poles in fact think in terms of these fixed clichés.

Let me make a digression here. Before World War II we had a big Jewish population, and there was strong anti-Semitism because of economic competition. There was a campaign not to buy from Jews. But this was not anti-Semitism so much as a majority-minority clash; it was not good, but it is unfair to accuse us of being hostile to Jews. It is like what goes on in Ireland between the Irish and the English, or in Belgium. But many Jews were killed in World War II. And now we have real anti-Semitism. It is anti-Semitism in the way Hannah Arendt describes in her book on totalitarianism, it has the same roots, and it is associated with the communist government. Poles tried to present this government as alien: as Russian, as Jewish, and so on, but they collaborated with it. Probably in the 1940s there was an over-representation of Jews in the secret police and in other Stalinist institutions. But in my opinion, now is the period when there is real anti-Semitism associated with a situation like that of prewar Germany, when Jews were assimilated . . . Classical anti-Semitism with vivid and vicious stereotypes.

Now, about the 1980s. In the 1980s it was fashionable to be interested in this Jewish topic. Poles discovered Jewish cemeteries, ruins of synagogues, the Jewish past. A lot of people became really interested. People collected records of Jewish songs. So we get now to these horrible things about Polish behavior and so on and so on during World War II. The image of Polish behavior, I don't think it changed in fact, the image of Polish behavior during the war, and I don't think it was necessary to change this image, but we realized more facts about this image and it became more complicated than before . . . A lot of people refused this accusation of being hostile to Jews, and I think to some extent the communist government played upon these sentiments because they liked to present in official newspapers that Jews, and especially American Jews, as very hostile to Poles. An example: when the historian Norman Davies [was denied an appointment at Stanford University] although his books were not published under the communist regime in Poland and he was not a welcome person there, nonetheless this affair was played up in the official communist newspaper, complaining that academic freedom was broken in the States. Of course many Poles who suffered terrible things under Nazis found the accusation of ill behavior towards the Jews unfair. And, of course, the common answer was, "We didn't kill Jews, we didn't help the Germans kill them, we are not guilty that they set up the camps on our soil, and so on." On the other hand, a lot of young people asked their parents what in fact were Polish-Jewish relations, they asked Jews who came to Poland, materials were published and were very popular. For instance, there was a famous interview with one of the heads of the uprising in the [Warsaw] ghetto, Edelman, who was very active in the political life in Poland, a supporter of the Solidarity movement, he ran for parliament, and so on; but he had bad relations with the Zionists.

31 Mar. 1992. Do you remember Karsky in the film *Shoah?* He was the one who informed the British government about the Holocaust after spending some days in the ghetto. I just read an interview with him in which he asks why nobody in Poland tried to find people who said things in the film, for instance in the scene with the priest where a woman says that Jews were guilty of Christ killing, and the priest stands behind her without reacting. Vatican II counts such statements to be sins. Why did no one seek out this priest to ask if he was aware of being sinful, to ask why he did not react?

IV. Conclusions

Poles and Jews lived in quite separate worlds, speaking different languages. . . . this alienation of Jews from Polish culture and language can explain to some extent that Polish people, even if they wanted, were not able to help them because of language problems, lack of friendship relations, and so on. [25 Feb. 1992]

This dialogue was suddenly broken by the Holocaust . . . we deal now only with traces . . . The interest . . . [of] young people in the '80s that we should repossess our past . . . traces of Jewish, Ukrainian and other people . . . is hopeless because it is on the intellectual level . . . intellectual work can't replace this dialogue of culture. [10 Apr. 1992]

For a lot of Poles, the Warsaw uprising is the counterpart of the ghetto uprising. The ghetto uprising was a tragic event, but is regarded by Poles to be in the shadow of the Warsaw uprising . . . The ghetto uprising, I think, for Poles, was a tragic event but limited to Jews . . . The Warsaw uprising was the biggest war experience for Poles because a lot of young, intelligent people were killed . . . among them probably the most promising young Polish poet, Barchinski, who I learned recently had half Jewish blood, his mother was Jewish . . . He was twenty-five . . . and in Polish tradition he is like a saint . . . The Warsaw uprising is like a parable of the Polish fate.

I don't think that we were very responsible for the Holocaust. We were not. The Germans killed the Jews. I don't think we should feel guilty for the Holocaust because we didn't do it. But on the other hand, they were killed on our land, so you know, doesn't matter:

guilty or not guilty . . . we have to cope with this fact like a thorn in
our body. [22 Apr. 1992]

I hesitate to end with this last quote, taken a bit out of context, for I immediately challenged it saying that the anti-Semitism he spoke of in the scene
in the film *Shoah* with the priest and the woman accusing Jews of being Christ
killers speaks to an attitude of not being unhappy that the Germans were doing
what they did; Leszek agreed immediately. His point—and hence it *is* a good
place to end, coming rhetorically full circle—is not so much a denial of guilt,
whatever that would mean for the next generation not born yet at the time of
the events in question, but rather the image of the thorn, a romantic image,
an image of suffering, a very Christian image, in all the worst and best traditions of Christian thought. But if I hear him correctly, his pessimistic insistence that intellectual cultural work is not the same as real dialogue, meaning
daily-life interactions, is a philosophical standard: it is a refusal to paper over
the past, a perfect willingness to engage however engagement is possible
again, anew, but not to forget, deny, or trivialize, or reinterpret the evil we
have lived through.

We hope that we have thrown light on two issues: (1) the complexities of
that paradoxical set of issues that goes under the label *nationalism*—the emotional investments that are both culturally constructed (not immutable or primordial) yet also resonant with layer upon layer of historical strata that give
symbolic power and historical efficacy that cannot simply be changed by good
intentions; (2) the textual difficulties of laying out these complexities, which
we have experimented with in two ways: through the dialogic collage that
follows, as a way of both marking the different positions of the two authors,
and including a variety of conflicting positions, opinions, and considerations;
and secondly through the (excerpting of) a conversation that attempts to explain the cultural resonances of a culture by an intellectual insider who is
aware of outsider perceptions to a sympathetic intellectual from another culture reacting with his own resonances.

Tools for Reflection: Ruins, Negations, and the End of Romantic Tropes

1. Silence/Dialogue, Ruins/Negations

The earliest documentary record from that [pre-Christian] part of
Europe which is now called Poland dates from A.D. 965 to 966 . . .
Ibrahim ibn Jakub, a Moorish Jew from Tortosa in Spain accompanied the Khalif of Cordoba on an embassy to central Europe . . . In
the following year, as part of the marriage agreement [with the Czech
king's daughter], he [Mieszko I, chief of the Polonaie] renounced the
pagan religion of his ancestors and was baptized.
    —Norman Davies, *God's Playground: A History of Poland*

KOCZANOWICZ: *The dialogue* be tween these two cultures—Polish and Jewish—*was* suddenly *broken* by the Holocaust so that in fact . . . we deal now only with *traces* . . . On the one side, we have *stillness,* quiet people because they were killed, so they don't speak, and on the other, we have on our side, the Polish side, we repeat the same arguments like a *broken gramma- phone record.*

FISCHER: Well *one could* argue hat the Ukraine or Lithuania as independent countries now are different from the countries of the past, and so the dialogue with them is parallel with those Poles *might have* with American Jews or Israeli Jews.

KOCZANOWICZ: *No, I don't think so.* [10 Apr. 1992]

The biblical text and the midrashic commentary are alive with the theme of silence.
—Andre Neher, *The Exile of the Word: From the Silence of the Bible to the Silence of Auschwitz*

It is only in the infinite relation with the other that God passes [*se passe*], that traces of God are to be found. God thus reveals Himself as a trace, not as an ontological presence.
—Emmanuel Levinas

II. Repetition/Mourning, Refusing Denial/Repression

What sex was to the Victorians, the question of free will is to our new *fin-de-siècle.* . . . As soon as we use pronouns with verbs—"*I* do, *she* wants, *he* desires"—we speak the language of the *cogito,* without (if Lacan is right) being one.
—Sherry Turkle, *Psychoanalytic Politics*

What is at stake in mourning is the constitution of the boundaries of the self and other: in mourning it is the world which has become poorer and empty; in melancholia it is the ego.
—Eric Santer, *Stranded Objects: Mourning, Memory and Film in Postwar Germany.*

In the Moscow of summer 1989, publishing Freud became a symbol not only of the right to repressed knowledge, but of individual economic rights in the market place of

KOCZANOWICZ: But back to Polish-Jewish relations: I find talking about this interesting. Perhaps it is a kind of psychoanalysis, exploring the unconscious of Polish culture. [30 Jan. 1992]

KOCZANOWICZ: No, it is not the same in Poland. Poland is more complicated. [27 Apr. 1992]

ideas. . . A collection of Freud's essays . . . sold 1,250,000 copies
within six months. . . Soviets *want*
to talk about repression, the unconscious, the things they feel but were
not allowed to say.
   —Sherry Turkle, *Psychoanalytic*
Politics

III. Hybridity, Difficulties of Narration, Exhaustion of Romantic Tropes

KOCZANOWICZ: This Polish identity is to some extent . . . in a constant
state of schizophrenia, you know, to show some sources of identity and at
the same time to show that the sources are exhausted or meaningless and so
on. Gombrowicz is very good for this reason.

KOCZANOWICZ: I was shocked
when you compared Poland with
Iran. Although, by the way, there
are some possibilities for a connection: the [local Polish emigré bulle-
tin] *Saramatian Review* . . .
Saramatian was the name of an Iranian tribe . . . Our gentry assumed
themselves to be descendants of
these people . . . and that they
moved here and took the land by
conquest. . . There was the idea . . .
that gentries are different folk than
peasants . . . and the gentry style
was called *Saramatian*. [31 Jan.
1992]

The Amazons whom certain
Scythian youth are said to have married and the Sauromatians who supposedly descended from this
union. . . In the wake of Greek vic-
tories in the Persian wars . . . [He-
rodotus and a Hippocratic text
identify] the Scythians as that people
who are . . . the moistest of all
Asians, which is to say the weakest
of the weak, and the flabbiest of the
mild . . . and this moistness was
therefore treated—cured with fire
. . . In contrast, the weakness and
moistness of the Amazons was located less in their environment . . .
than in their gender. [They] treated
one of their breasts the same way
that Scythians treated much of their
bodies, cauterizing it in order to dry
up its inherent moisture.
   —Bruce Lincoln, *Death, War*
and Sacrifice

KOCZANOWICZ: There is much anxiety about the purity of Polish
culture . . . there is a debate about the origin of our leading poets, because Jewish culture influenced Polish culture more than people want to acknowledge. [31 Jan. 1992]

It is hard to define Polish culture: what, for instance, is Polish cuisine? Ukrainian borscht, Lithuanian dumplings, and Jewish fish. [31 Jan. 1992] . . . the gentry dress of Poland is derived from Turkish styles. [4 Feb. 1992]

there is a very famous image in Polish history that the Pole who took this cross [in the January Uprising of 1863–64] was killed and a Jewish boy picked it up and he was killed too . . . There is a famous poem by Norwid about this event appreciating Jewish contributions to Polish culture. [31 Jan. 1992]

And so there were these three rhetorics: the rhetoric of Marxism, the rhetoric of nationality/nation, and the rhetoric of modernization, and of course, it was very difficult to sustain any consistent system among these three rhetorics. So the rhetoric was very capricious and depended on political events. . . So it was, you know, funny that the Polish Workers' government supported films that were a kind of apology for the gentry style of life.

The problem of treason in Polish culture is very important. There is a famous poem by Adam Mickiewicz called "Konrad Wallenrod" . . . And if you remember some Joseph Conrad stories, you notice that he is obsessed with the problem of being loyal to two principles. [3 Jan. 1992]

After the Second [World] War, in the seventies and eighties, Poles adopted a lot of features which before the war they ascribed to Jews . . . Poles became the most important bargainers in the Eastern bloc.

Romanticism was important when we were oppressed by the Russian power . . . Now we face other problems: confrontation with Western pop, Western popular culture, and we can lose our identity not because of power but because of being dissolved in world culture . . . Romantic symbols were very good weapons [against the] Russians but I don't think they could be so effective now in the confrontation with American action film or comics. [4 Feb. 1992]

This is an interesting methodological problem as in this book that you wrote, *Anthropology as Cultural Critique*. If I understand this book, you would like to repeat the Enlightenment project of seeing our culture through the eyes of the other, but with the difference that in the Enlightenment this other was an entire artificial construction. So now we could repeat this project but with two differences: (1) there is not an artificial construction, the other is a real culture; and (2) there is a real exchange between the cultures, because in the Enlightenment there was not such an exchange.

IV. The Ethical Face of Polish Culture

KOCZANOWICZ: It is right from the Jewish point of view to see the Second [World] War as a war of the holocaust . . . but the problem of the holocaust is for us more broadly the problem of losing any sense of Western culture, of Western philosophy, Western art, and Western values. [14 Feb. 1992]

One of the best novels about the Holocaust in Poland, Andrzejewski's *Holy Week,* is the story of a Jewish woman who unsuccessfully tried to find a hiding place, and she curses the Polish people that we should have the same situation, being turned out with no one willing to help. It is a clear allusion, since it was written after the war, to the Warsaw Uprising. . . .

The Jew after Auschwitz is a witness to endurance singled out by contradictions which in our post-Holocaust world are worldwide contradictions . . . The duty to remember and to tell the tale is not negotiable. It is holy . . . A secular holiness, as it were, has forced itself into [the secular Jew's] vocabulary.
—Emil Fackenheim

The ghetto uprising, I think, for Polish people, was a tragic event but limited to Jews, limited in space and time, limited to some days, to some people, and to some time. The Warsaw Uprising was the biggest war experience for Poles, . . . like a parable of the Polish fate [condensed] in

On the first day of Passover, the remnants of the ghetto of Warsaw rose up against the adversary, even as in the days of Judah the Maccabee.
—Passover hagaddahs of the post–World War II period.

a few days, because . . . the main experiences are unsuccessful uprisings in which people are killed. . . The other experience is of loneliness of the Polish people, because they had some illusion that the Russians, the Americans, and so on, would help, and of course they didn't.

So I think that this uprising is important for three things: it is a counterpart to the ghetto uprising in the eyes of a lot of Polish people; it is a parable of Polish life in general; and of the repeated discussion about how to fix Polish nationality through uprising and tragedy. Probably this is not only a Polish problem: there are lots of parallels between the Poles and the Irish.

References

Anderman, Janusz. 1988. *The Edge of the World.* New York: Readers International.

Ash, Timothy Garton. 1986. Introduction to the English translation of Hanna Krall (1977).

Czerniawski, Adam. 1988. *The Burning Forest.* Newcastle upon Tyne: Bloodaxe Books.

Davies, Norman. 1982. *God's Playground: A History of Poland.* New York: Columbia University Press.

Engleberg, Stephen. 1992. "Leave, But Pay Us, Poles Tell Russia" [case of Legnica]. *New York Times,* 23 Feb., A6.

Fackenheim, Emil. 1970. *God's Presence in History: Jewish Affirmations and Philosophical Reflections.* New York: Harper.

Hofstadter, Douglas. 1985. *Metamagical Themas.* New York: Basic Books.

Krall, Hanna. [1977] 1986. *Shielding the Flame: An Intimate Conversation with Dr. Marek Edelman, the Last Surviving Leader of the Warsaw Uprising.* New York: Henry Holt and Company.

Kugelmas, Jack. 1992. "Bloody Memories: Encountering the Past in Contemporary Poland." Typescript.

Lincoln, Bruce. 1991. *Death, War, and Sacrifice: Studies in Ideology and Practice.* Chicago: University of Chicago Press.

Mickiewicz, Adam. 1944. *Poems by Adam Mickiewicz.* Ed. George R. Noyes. New York: Polish Institute of Arts and Sciences in America.

Milosz, Czeslaw. 1988. *The Collected Poems, 1931–1987.* New York: Ecco Press.

Milosz, Czeslaw, ed. 1983. *Postwar Polish Poetry.* Berkeley: University of California Press.

Rozewicz, Tadeusz. 1976. *"The Survivor" and Other Poems.* Trans. Magnus J. Krynski and Robert A. Maguire. Princeton, N.J.: Princeton University Press.

Santer, Eric. 1990. *Stranded Objects: Mourning, Memory and Film in Postwar Germany.* Ithaca, N.Y.: Cornell University Press.

Schatz, Jaff. 1991. *The Generation.* Berkeley: University of California Press.

Szymborska, Wislawa. 1981. *Sounds, Feelings, Thoughts: Seventy Poems by Wislawa Szymborska.* Trans. Magnus J. Krynski and Robert A. Maguire. Princeton, N.J.: Princeton University Press.

Tagliabue, John. 1992. "Berlin Journal: Game Up, So Informers Inform on Themselves" [case of Andreas Sinakowski]. *New York Times,* 30 Jan.

Turkle, Sherry. 1991. *Psychoanalytic Politics.* 2d ed. New York: Guilford Press.

White, Hayden. 1973. *Metahistory: The Historical Imagination in Nineteenth-Century Europe.* Baltimore: Johns Hopkins University Press.

Greek Women in the Europe of 1992:
Brokers of European Cargoes and the Logic
of the West

At the end of the twentieth century, a period of monumental changes in Eastern and Western Europe, Greeks found themselves compelled to rediscover, redefine, and reaffirm their past, present, and future political and ethnic identities, despite or because of the fact that they have been full members of the European Community since 1981. The dissolution of the USSR—an event occurring parallel to the emergence of the new Europe—has intensified the exhaustion of ideas and practices once powerful in Greece (for example, the hegemony of political parties) and triggered the development of new certainties and uncertainties. On the one hand, the official dismantling of grand schemes and ideologies has brought almost to completion the communist parties' fragmentation, underway since 1968.[1] Postwar generations of Greek communists now seem to be left without coherent political identities—identities which previously had persisted hand in hand with and despite regular and predictable fragmentation—and without ready answers to questions such as, What is to be done?[2] On the other hand, the remnants of the post–civil war (1946–49) political opposition between "rightists" and "communists" became totally redundant. Props are no longer available for the Right's exclusive claims to higher national authenticity, claims once based on an expressed concern for the nation and opposed to the communists' internationalism which was considered equivalent to antinationalism. Furthermore, the thousands of Greek ethnics who came to Greece from excommunist countries during and after their disintegration tend to show indifference to the ideologies of the political parties (rightist or leftist).[3] Instead, issues such as "Greekness" (and attempts to legally affirm it) and its European/Western character appear to constitute the main poles of attraction for them.

By 1992, a tendency toward favoring nationalist (Greek/European) rather than the political (rightist/leftist) sources of identification became prevalent among most Greeks, not only because of their disappointment with political parties, but also because of another critical political event: the disintegration of neighboring Yugoslavia and the bloody reformation of new ethnic states.

This event has forced Greece to confront old geopolitical problems as well as internally and externally produced stereotypes about Greeks. The claims of former Yugoslavians to the Greek name *Macedonia*—among other identity symbols—for the establishment of their new ethnic state has revived the old disputes with "Yugoslavia" over an outlet to the Aegean.[4] In the present as in the past, most Greeks (politicians, scholars, as well as ordinary people) have met this situation by aggressive appeals to archeological and historical data and the "ancient Greek civilization" as a whole to stake their own claims to such spatial symbols.[5] This attitude has been characterized by Europeans (comembers of the European Community) as a sort of historical fetishism and "ethnic neurosis."[6] Some have even warned Greeks of the danger of a "collapse" from the status of Europeans to that of "Balkans"[7]—a term evoking the Ottoman occupation of Greece for four hundred years and implying Greeks' affinities with the Orient.[8]

External provocations and internal responses of this kind demonstrate the pertinence of the "perennial identity crisis"[9] or dilemma of Greeks with respect to their place in the international socioeconomic system—despite full entry into the "European family." Is Greece a Western/European country capable of applying Western values and institutions, or is it a special case with its own geopolitical and socioeconomic particularities (that is, "South," "Balkans," "Orient," "Third World," and so on)?

Every time this "agonizing search for a national identity and national ethics and deontology"[10] is brought to the fore, two kinds of political and scholarly discourses reemerge to address it: one, "traditional" populist in orientation, emphasizes "native," "authentic" models, ancient Greek civilization, Greek Orthodoxy, and ethnic homogeneity; the other, cosmopolitan in orientation, emphasizes development and modernization and recommends the introduction and application of Western values, institutions, and mentalities in order to "catch up" with Westerners and/or align with them.[11] Within the latter discourse, the emphasis today is on values such as rationality, planning, efficiency,[12] and the incorporation (versus the absorption) of different ethnic populations, in contrast to isolationism and ethnic insularism.[13]

Each of these two discourses appeals to different socioeconomic categories of the population in both rural and urban contexts. Yet depending on the historically specific moment, one of the two has usually dominated and been regarded as closer to Greek reality. In 1991–92 (the time of the following conversation), both discourses seemed to have a more or less equal appeal to most Greeks because of the simultaneous occurrence of two critical events: the "Yugoslavian" claims on Macedonia, and "1992," that is, the Maastricht Treaty. All political parties—with the exception of the Communist Party of Greece—adopted both discourses simultaneously, with slight differences in emphasis depending on the circumstances.

Yet these contrasting rhetorics of an idealized past (ancient Greek Civilization) and of an equally idealized future (Greece as an equal member of the European family enjoying the EC's economic and mutual aid) cannot disguise the present, increasingly peripheral, and irrevocably dependent position of Greece in the international and European systems as well as its symptoms: the puzzlement and awkwardness felt by Greeks as they confront the misfit between imported institutions and Greek reality, and efforts to transcend an agonized internalization of the causes of this misfit (labeled most of the time as Greeks' inefficiency, by Western Europeans as well as Greeks themselves).

These experiences—symptomatic of all peripheries—are not new to Greeks.[14] They had been "forgotten" though, for some time after the fall of the seven-year-long military dictatorship (1967–74). In fact, since 1974, older and younger generations of women and men, of all political persuasions, felt the urgent need to experience the new democratic opening. The succeeding conservative government undertook the reestablishment of parliamentary democracy, choosing a primarily Western European orientation (for example, reentry into the EC) to avoid total politicomilitary dependence on the United States, which was considered responsible for the establishment of the junta. Equality-oriented reforms provided for the legalization of the communists, who had been politically ostracized for the nearly thirty years since the end of the civil war. The communists promptly reorganized into parties and other organizations. The socialist government, elected in 1981 and in power until 1989, coincided with the importation of many more equality-oriented institutions from the West/EC. During this postdictatorial period of freedom, Greeks even enjoyed the luxury of becoming "Anentachti" (that is, nonaligned to parties) in the name of equality for all and liberty for each. Meanwhile, the gradual reintegration of Greece into the periphery of the European Community (through the adoption of hundreds of EC "directives" and the mindless use of economic aid) went more or less unnoticed by everyone.

In the evolution of this Greek drama, the only category of Greeks who spoke of "dependence" and "periphery" was that of women. In fact, during this period (mid-1970s to late 1980s), more than any other time, Greek women of all postwar generations and political persuasions—though mainly leftists—protested against the peripheral and dependent roles they were assigned to play by their androcentric society in the economic and political life of their country.[15] Organized variously into political parties, women's organizations (which were mostly affiliated with the parties) and "autonomous" (nonaffiliated) groups, they made various demands: the Family Law reform, equal access to employment and the abolition of occupational sex segregation, the provision of social services such as day care, and the right to control their bodies (for example, free and legal abortion on demand, birth control, and so on). For some (the liberals), the main target was state policies, for others (the socialists and communists), capitalism, and for others (the radicals), it was male power and patriarchy per se.

A few women's bookstores and research centers made their appearance as centers of theoretical development and information on the international movement. Also, a women's studies program was informally introduced at the University of Thessaloniki for instructors with a feminist orientation. Governmental bodies such as the General Secretariat of Equality were established to instigate policies related to the equality of the sexes. Finally, various kinds of magazines and journals circulated which were more or less directly attuned to the latest debates within Western and Greek feminism.

Much of the reform agenda that these women had been demanding since the fall of the dictatorship (in 1974) was actually implemented in the form of progressive legal changes and a few affirmative action governmental programs.[16] Yet by the end of the 1980s, all of these measures sounded like empty words in the context of declining Greek socialism and the debt-ridden Greek economy. The "moving" parts of the women's movement (that is, the women's sectors of the parties, organizations, and autonomous groups) shrank at the same time that political parties (and their affiliated groups) started losing their prestige as a metonym for Greece and Greekness.

At the end of the 1980s and in view of the coming "1992," many educated Greek women and men in their late twenties and early thirties turned their backs on the economic and political standards of their parties and started looking toward the European "cargoes" coming from Brussels—research programs, posts, training seminars, conferences, grants, trips—to make a living. This new cargo cult was based on a Western/European logic that was spread largely through the media: rationalization, goals, planning, and long-term versus short-term negotiations and programs. From now on, unprogrammed action in the periphery seemed to have no place in the "Western democratic logic." It would be considered a "neurosis." Greek women and men, the new stepchildren of the "European family," had to learn their lesson well if they wished to grow up some day.

This new logic seems to have permeated not only individual women's (and men's) behavior and mentality, but also the organized expressions of the movement. Women's "rational" projects and programs based on financial negotiations with the EC have replaced "visions" of equality and demands for emancipation and liberation. Networks of women researchers-trainers who have undertaken the role of brokers between Europe and the European system and Greek women are now seen as trainees.[17] According to Maria Stratigaki, our interlocutor, "these are the signs of the times." They do not include "pure" revolution, because "the revolution is not paid."

Maria Stratigaki, a longtime member of the Communist Party of Greece of the Interior (KKE-es), is a woman in her midthirties who divides her residence between Athens and Brussels. In Brussels she is working on a two-year contract as an Equal Opportunities Unit Officer at the Commission of the

European Communities. In Athens she runs, in collaboration with other women, two centers devoted to research on women's issues and technological training for women. She has been a friend of Eleni Papagaroufali since 1984, when they met through women's movement activities. They developed a mutual admiration and a teasing antagonism: Maria, who is unmarried, admires Eleni her ability to combine family with her intellectual life. Yet she's exasperated by Eleni's total rejection of all expressions of technology, even those commonly considered everyday necessities: she doesn't drive a car and refuses to learn how to operate a computer. Eleni accuses Maria of cosmopolitanism, ostentatious managerialism, and "technomania." At the same time, she admires her ability to get involved in many things effectively and on the basis of her ideological commitments. Nia Georges is a Greek-American who has been a friend of Eleni's for over fifteen years. She was introduced to Maria by Eleni for the purpose of this conversation.

Maria has a B.A. in economics from the University of Athens and has done postgraduate studies in marketing at the University of Paris IX–Jussieu, and in sociology at Paris VII–Dauphine, and attended courses in women's studies at New York University. She is now ready to defend her thesis on the effects of computerization on the division of labor by gender in the Greek banking industry. She has published articles in Greek and foreign periodicals on women's employment. During the 1980s she wrote regularly on women's issues for the newspaper and journal of the KKE-es, her political party.

Maria belongs to the postdictatorial generation of Greeks (1974 and beyond) which together with the preceding "Polytechnic Generation" believed fervently in the possibility of being both equal as free as individuals and groups of individuals. In the 1980s, like other women members of the KKE-es (mainly urbanites of Maria's age), she believed they could, should, would change the patriarchal "logic" of their party based on the principle of equality between women and men. As she puts it, she worked "within and against" her party to force the recognition of gender in class analysis and class struggle.

Yet Maria is among those Greek leftists who by the end of the 1980s "were left by their parties" as these became enervated through constant fragmentation—a fragmentation resulting from the exhaustion of socialist/communist-inspired ideas through attempts at practice. Since then, she and many of her women friends, former members of the party, "changed logic": they believed that they should and could work for women's matters on the basis of paid labor rather than "revolution," which "is not paid."

Now, in the beginning of the 1990s, Maria is still a professed Marxist. Yet, like other Greek women and men of her and the succeeding generations, she seems no longer to need the concrete ideologies and plans of the parties to provide guidelines for her/their lives. In fact, Greeks between their late twenties and midthirties are more familiar with the ideology of "equality,"[18] when compared with previous generations, to the point of taking it for granted. More or less aware of the contradictory nature of this ideology and of its Western, rather than Communist, parenthood, they seem nonetheless anxious to see for themselves and experience its maturation within Greece and the emergent schema of a Europe "without frontiers."[19]

In her conversation, Maria shows a high political awareness of her "peripheral" position as a Greek and a woman in the historically specific socioeconomic context of Europe. Also, she recognizes that Greece is largely "oriental"[20] and only a "piece" rather than a part of the EC. Despite this awareness, she shows a high degree of tolerance for the "new" transnational plans of Europe. We think it would not be too risky to claim that Maria's double, rather contradictory, positioning reflects, on the one hand, Greeks' awkwardness in the face of Maastricht-related radical changes and their unknown effects (an awkwardness shared with other Europeans as well). On the other hand, it points to the emerging determination on the part of some Greeks to oppose the country's tendency toward isolationism in the present international picture. By the same token, it conveys something of the decisiveness with which younger Greeks have undertaken to become modernizers more or less on a par with Western Europeans. Finally, though most importantly, it represents the propensity among many young Greek women today to function more as Gramsci's organic intellectuals within the transnational, pan-European power play than as instrumental members of local parties and movements.

A Woman's Movement

GEORGES: Could you tell us about how you got involved in the women's movement?

STRATIGAKI: My trajectory . . . When the junta fell in 1974, I was in my first year at the university. From my first year there, I began to be aware of illegal left organizations on campus, but I had not been particularly interested in what was going on. After that, they became legal. During that time, that is, between 1974 and 1978, everyone belonged to a party, especially students and young people, nineteen to twenty years old. There was an immense variety of communist organizations, Maoist, Albanian, Soviet . . .

My family had no Left culture, but I had a good friend whose father and brothers were leftists. Her brothers were students and older than we were, with more consciousness, and I began to understand what was going on at that time. I found myself in the theater group at the University of Athens. Every morning I worked in a family business, my uncle's. It was understood that I would start working there as soon as I graduated from high school. So

I didn't go to classes at all. I finished the university by taking exams only, in the Department of Economic Sciences at the University of Athens. In the afternoons I would go to the theater group at the university. I liked the social life. We put on plays, showed films, music, and so on. I acted in plays during that time. Within the group, like everywhere else, the parties played a dominant role. Within the theater group I entered the Communist Party of Greece of the Interior (KKE-es) youth organization, known as Rigas Ferreos.

The KKE-es was a party that had splintered from the Communist Party of Greece (KKE) in 1968, with the invasion of Prague as the pretext. The KKE-es was Eurocommunist, influenced by the Italian Communist Party. It was more national, that is, it didn't have the USSR as its model. We believed that communism, socialism, has to have some national particularities, and it should not come from foreign centers. That party had gathered many young intellectuals who opposed the KKE, the traditional Left.

In Rigas Ferreos of the theater group, I didn't get involved with the everyday syndical work, but rather with cultural politics. The politics of culture, and how culture should be. There has to be an intervention—should it take the form of a large organization or very small groups? That is, there was a dispute, a debate over culture and intervention into the cultural.

So into Rigas Ferreos came the first feminists from abroad, who had studied in the exterior during the dictatorship and who had become feminists in the European movement. Already members of Rigas Ferreos abroad, they joined the Greek branch and formed a women's group within it. I immediately joined up, too. We worked on a regular column for the youth organization's newspaper. This was around 1977–78, and I came into contact with feminism through my entrance into the party. And that happened to many women in Greece. That is, first we became leftists, joined the party, and then we became feminists. Because the priority at that time was general politics due to the dictatorship. We somehow became sensitized to social problems this way. From then on, I stayed in the party until two years ago, that is, from 1974 to 1989, but always as a feminist. We were active in various phases—changing, doing, making, putting out a newspaper column, instituting a quota for women within the party . . . for women to join.

PAPAGAROUFALI: What were the effects of these activities?

STRATIGAKI: The feminist group of the party tried to improve the position of the women members of the party. For example, during the Europarliament elections of 1989, we squeezed the men, we pressured them, to split the candidacy between a woman and a man. I was the party's first woman candidate. I would have gone for two-and-a-half years, after the man had gone first for two-and-a-half years. So I ran around campaigning in all the villages in my little jalopy.

So, I mean to tell you that of the fifteen years I was in the party, at least ten were as a feminist. In 1989, I left the party, but all that time I was a feminist. However, I wasn't in any feminist groups or organizations. You see, there were some parties that had created affiliated women's organizations, "side by side" with the party. But I, we, were opposed to forming small parties of affiliated women next to the party. Additionally, there were the autonomous groups that didn't want anything to do with either the parties or the affiliations. I wasn't in the autonomous groups, or in the affiliations. I was "within and against" the party. The intervention we wanted was as feminists in the party, to change the party, to incorporate gender in its class analysis. I do believe that our position was different.

PAPAGAROUFALI: Sure it was! It was the bravest, but at the same time, the most utopian position on the possibility of men's changing . . . Though this idea of alternating women and men for political positions was a step forward. On the other hand, the women who were simultaneously members of their parties and their parties' affiliated organizations seemed to be more compromised, yet more realistic than you in their express goal of sensitizing larger numbers of women. That is, they were able to attract new women to the party, either as followers or as members, and at the same time sensitize them to women's issues through their mass activities. The autonomous groups were the most realistic in their repudiation of the hope that men might change.

STRATIGAKI: That's why there was a dispute among the three positions. The autonomous women would say to us, "Why do you want to change the party when you know that it's an androcentric institution and won't change? What is your priority after all? For us, it's feminism." We would say that our priority is the party, but with the principles that we want. That's why we believed that we were also a part of the women's movement. We thought that within the party we could . . . That was the story.

In 1989, I left the party, or rather, I can't say that I left the party, but that the party left me. Because the party became so small after the elections of 1989, smaller and smaller, it splintered, and finally it made no sense. So I stopped going after fifteen years. Not because I left the party ideologically, but because it didn't make sense to go when it was so small. If there were elections, I would vote for the party. Or if the party doesn't participate, I will vote blank or something else. But I said fifteen years is enough, I devoted enough and nothing happened, well, almost nothing happened. I don't regret those years, though. It was a personal stand, my choice.

"Everything Is EC Now"

PAPAGAROUFALI: You got tired.

STRATIGAKI: Yes, and I changed entirely. And from 1989 to now, I'm trying to do some professional work, for example, to earn money, but always having to do with women's matters, either research or vocational training. This is a compromise, to a certain extent . . . I also left the family company I worked for in 1987. So I try not to do any other work, for example, sell toys in the morning and be a feminist in an autonomous group at night. I prefer to "water my wine" regarding my revolutionary goals. That is, I prefer to work all day on these matters. Even if these aren't terribly revolutionary. With the same logic, I'm involved with the Equal Opportunities Unit of the Commission of the European Communities right now. I understand that it's not, let us say, a matter of authentic feminist logic—rather, it's incorporation, if you will. But I prefer to do that rather than to do some completely unrelated work, and to do the feminism only as unpaid work. But I wouldn't go to any business that exploits women. I wouldn't do that . . . On the other hand, I can't say that the movement alone can be effective . . . I try, shall we say, to make some projects for women within the EC, one way or another.

GEORGES: Yet when you told me about your job with the EC, it was with an ironic smile.

STRATIGAKI: It's possible. But what can I say? I don't want to do anything else, this makes me happy.

PAPAGAROUFALI: When you say compromise and incorporation, you mean that you're not in the movement?

STRATIGAKI: Yes. You're not doing "revolutionary" work. When you say "movement," it has a revolutionary connotation, that you're doing something "contra." In going to work for the EC, in the Equal Opportunities Unit, it's not revolutionary praxis.

GEORGES: But in the women's movement, what are they doing now that is revolutionary?

STRATIGAKI: Nothing. Right now there is no group that makes me want to join. But it's not just that there's no group, but more that I want to combine women's issues with making a living. But revolution isn't paid.

PAPAGAROUFALI: I thought that the compromise you saw was that you were entering an organization, an institution like the EC, that is, the Establishment.

STRATIGAKI: Oh, no. Look, it has that dimension, too. But in this particular case, I don't have a problem with that because these organizations also have some room to make some women's programs. Take for instance the projects we made through Diotima, our center for research on women's issues, with contracts from the EC. It's a sign of the times . . . The center was formed by women like me who were in the movement, who also felt that the parties and the purely revolutionary movement had left us. So what do we do now? Our professions. We were the first to produce Equality Officers in Greece, women who work in public and private enterprises and attempt to insure the application of the equality legislation for women and promote women's projects.

GEORGES: Your center for women is maintained largely through contracts with the EC?

STRATIGAKI: Yes, EC. Everything is EC now.

GEORGES: I get the impression with what you've said so far about women's groups, organizations, and research centers, that there's a powerful impact from outside and above. For instance, in Greek feminism, from the start there has been a push from outside . . . feminists who came from abroad, and so on.

STRATIGAKI: Yes, and this can be seen in the role played by the Panhellenic Socialist Movement (PASOK) in the history of Greek feminism since 1981. Although many reforms began after the dictatorship fell, the pace picked up with PASOK's election to power in 1981. In addition to PASOK's initiative, however, passage of new equality laws was being pushed by the EC as part of our full entry into the EC in 1981. And suddenly there is bewilderment in the movement. Many of women's demands were incorporated, so to speak, into a more general policy.

PAPAGAROUFALI: Of course, feminist critiques continued after passage of the new laws because there was no indication that they would be applied. You see, they were not meant to be applied, but rather to be passed into law as rights, along the model of the ideology of human rights. But because of the historically specific moments in which these laws were passed, that is, that whole decade after the fall of the dictatorship that we call the Metapolitefsi [postregime], we Greeks took the concept out of its real, legal context, overemphasized it, and used it as a symbol each for our own reasons.

GEORGES: Have these outside influences blocked the Greekness of the Greek women's movement? In other words, are there some issues that you consider specifically Greek, that you wanted to push, but . . .

STRATIGAKI: Well, the issue that brought the most women together from all kinds of organizations was the reform of the Family Law, in effect in Greece from the beginning of this century.

GEORGES: A law that, as I understand it, provided a legal foundation for naturalized gender differences.

STRATIGAKI: But it wasn't just reform of the law; these women wanted to change their families. But then what happened? When the law passed, not only did families not change, but the movement shrank because none of the other demands had mass support—abortion, for example. Only a small portion of the women's movement held to those demands.

PAPAGAROUFALI: Yes, but that wasn't the only reason that the movement shrank. In demanding changes in the family, all of the trends of the movement were seemingly united. Once the law passed, deeper cleavages were revealed which had always been there.

STRATIGAKI: In any case, it must be said that the autonomous women's groups continue to function, in another form: a few small autonomous groups remain, small groups have been created within the labor unions, and not so much any more within the parties. Also, women's studies is gradually growing now in Greece.

Greek Coffee

GEORGES: So you consider the family issue to be characteristically Greek?

STRATIGAKI: Yes. I think that the patriarchal structure of the family is specifically Greek, when compared to Western Europe and perhaps the United States. Because there are some elements that are considerably oriental, so to speak. In other words, patriarchy has some specifically Greek expression due to its oriental origins.

GEORGES: You use the term *oriental,* a term I've heard many Greeks use in an apparently self-conscious, reflexive way as an idiom with which to discuss their similarities and differences with Western Europe.

PAPAGAROUFALI: And not simply with Western Europeans, but also with all the immigrants and refugees of Greek origin who arrive by the thousands from the former communist countries . . . All are reclaiming their Greek identity.

GEORGES: It seems to me that Greek identity is becoming problematized in a way that wasn't the case ten years ago . . . Perhaps even a sense of loss of Greek identity, particularly now with 1992 and the Maastricht Treaty around the corner?

STRATIGAKI: Oh, no. If there is something to be lost, we've already lost it. The Western, American style of life came in to Greece after World War II. But nothing is changing now. So we will lose the Drachma for the ECU. Big deal! One thing that would bother me would be if we were obligated to change, for instance, our alphabet, as happened in Turkey, where the Latin alphabet was adopted as part of modernization under Kemal Ataturk. That would bother me a lot. But there's no danger of that. For that type of difference there's tolerance on the part of the EC. What really interests the powerful of Europe is economics. Cultural differences are tolerated within the European ideology because they give the impression of national autonomy.

PAPAGAROUFALI: They wouldn't want to repeat the mistake of the USSR, when it tried to impose homogeneity.

STRATIGAKI: I would see the identity issue tied more to the Orient, to Turkey. But this link is something that the dominant ideology of Greece has rejected and denied. Here I really disagree. That is, I believe we are more oriental than we like to say officially or to believe. For example, the fact that we call Turkish coffee "Greek coffee." This kind of thing bothers me.

PAPAGAROUFALI: I remember well the time under the dictatorship when we were constantly reminded to call Turkish coffee Greek. That still annoys me, too. And this was the very regime that sold out Cyprus to the Turks.

STRATIGAKI: In other words, if there exists some threat to our identity, it comes more from inside the country. It's imposed on you to call the coffee Greek and that you mustn't have anything to do with Turkey. And yet, when you go to Istanbul you think that you are in the capital of your country. Such a policy makes you throw out something which surely exists within your country's history. We are trying to reject these similarities through various modernizing ideas of the West, so that we can appear European. But Europe sees us as more or less oriental. Third World, too. More than we think. That is, that folklore, that difference, all that appeals to the Europeans. But because we are also in Europe they're not afraid of us. When I was in Paris I was almost like an Algerian, so to speak. Not like the Arabs, who have another story and are much worse off, but almost.

GEORGES: But did you feel that in the EC, too, and in the Commission of the European Communities?

STRATIGAKI: Look, I play it European. [*Papagaroufali and Stratigaki laugh.*] No, no, look, the Equal Opportunities Unit in which I'm involved is rather marginal. In general, social matters, and in particular, women's issues, are marginal in the commission. Even the fact that I've been hired is related to my being Greek, as they want to follow a policy of respecting differences. In these painless matters, and in social matters, they respect these kinds of differences. They hire me, a woman from Greece and from a southern country, and I am supposed to tell them that their policies must change, must adapt to women of the South—Spain, Italy, Portugal—who have different needs from the women of the North. That's what I'm there for. But that's just a small piece of the picture. At the economic level, when companies come and are established here, they're not concerned with differences, the particularities of Greece.

GEORGES: I wonder what kind of impact all these new EC exchanges and programs will have for Greek women and their awareness of themselves?

STRATIGAKI: Apart from the negative effects, which will be mainly economic, I can see many good things coming out of the contact with these countries where at least the women's movement has progressed much more and both women's and men's awareness about gender, and so on, is of a higher standard, more progressive. Through contact among the countries . . . But let me tell you what pops into my mind, from my own personal experience. I had started to have sexual relations, here in Greece, when I was nineteen and a student in the university . . . I'm telling you totally personal things, but I believe they are related to this subject.

PAPAGAROUFALI: The personal is political!

STRATIGAKI: I, for instance, could definitely say that I gained a deeper understanding of my body by having sexual relations with foreigners. I had begun to gain some knowledge, as a student in 1974, when I was nineteen. Little by little, on my own, by chance . . . Three years later, I met a German man, on vacation in Greece, who appeared to have greater knowledge of the female body than I and my boyfriends did, and I was able to ask him questions. The answers he gave relieved me of some of the guilt and fears I had felt while exploring these questions myself. So what's this identity loss we're talking about? That is, if you are interested in your identity as a Greek woman, then you have to face up to the traditional, oriental nature of relations between women and men at present. Changing the name of Turkish coffee to Greek is not enough . . .

So you see, that is why I'm in favor of contacts . . . but in Greece, these only began to take place after 1974. It was only after the fall of the dictatorship that feminism and all of these ideologies came to Greece. Before then, there was no consciousness, among women or men. There were no movements, there was no freedom. The ideas of May 1968 couldn't come in. Of course, leftist discourse existed to some extent, but illegally. But discussions of feminism, the body, and all these ideas, did not exist before 1974. After all kinds of conversations, debates became public.

A Fin-de-Siècle?

GEORGES: Lately there has been much made of the changes in Eastern Europe coinciding with the end of the century, but it seems to me that for you, 1974 may have represented a "fin-de-siècle."

STRATIGAKI: Definitely. This notion of "fin-de-siècle" doesn't mean anything to me. I don't feel that something is ending now.

GEORGES: Perhaps in Greece, with the changes that will arrive with 1992?

STRATIGAKI: Sure, there will be some changes. But I have the feeling that when we say, "it ends," there is an element of nostalgia, that something good ends, and something bad begins. I don't see that. There will be tremendous changes with 1992, but you expect them, as though they were the continuation of an existing situation. Not that there is a rupture. For example, what is happening in Eastern Europe has influenced this story about change, but I don't see it that way. I haven't felt it, because I don't consider it a failure. I've always been a member of a party for which the USSR was never a model for socialism. So I don't feel that something I believed in has been lost and that values have changed. Because it never had that value, I don't find myself saying now, "Oh my God, what has happened to me?" as has occurred with many leftists in Greece.

GEORGES: That reminds me of the two men, friends of yours from the party, we talked with yesterday. I detected in them precisely this kind of anxiety you describe. Haris keeps reading all these articles in the *New Left Review* hoping, it seemed to me, to find some new unifying scheme. This was evident in his optimistic appraisal of market socialism. Kostas, on the other hand, seemed nostalgic for precapitalist forms of decentered communities.

STRATIGAKI: For the Right, on the other hand, this situation has presented a new opportunity not only to make propaganda against the previous regime, but against Marxist ideas in general. But I'm not affected by either position. I don't feel that the Marxism in which we have believed has suffered some catastrophe. So for that reason, I don't feel that something is ending. In postfeminism, too, there is a sense of change, of rupture—that equality has been achieved. But I don't believe this either. Nothing essential in women's daily lives has changed. And in many areas, it's getting worse rather than better.

GEORGES: How is it getting worse? In what areas?

STRATIGAKI: For example, in the workplace, with new technologies. I saw this in my own research on the impact of computerization on women's work in Greek banks. Once office technology is employed in the workplace, the pyramid of hierarchy becomes shortened and a large number of positions are created at the base, where computers are being used to serve clients. These positions are given mainly to women. Many of the functions of middle management are absorbed by the computer since one of its functions is output control. Thus the bureaucratic and hierarchical organization is simplified. With the reduction in middle management, the opportunities for promotion once available to women are also reduced. Jobs are polarized between the top or creative positions, which go to men information scientists, management analysts, and so on, and the other ones that go to women and involve menial work.

I have seen this in my research comparing the state-owned National Bank of Greece, which has not introduced office technology to any significant extent, with the private banks that have. Despite the traditionalism of the National Bank, with its history of a peculiar and durable form of internal labor recruitment . . .

PAPAGAROUFALI: You mean the policy that children of the bank's employees are hired on the basis of a special exam?

STRATIGAKI: Yes, that among other things. Employees at the lower levels of the National Bank are about half women and half men. Because of the presence of a large number of middle managerial positions there, women have had some possibilities for promotion up from the lower levels. In the more rationalized private banks, as in European banks, however, these positions have been largely eliminated as a result of computerization. So while women now outnumber men in the lowest levels of the private bank's hierarchy, and therefore might appear to have gained over men in employment, they have less opportunity for promotion than those who work under the less rationally organized system of the National Bank.

PAPAGAROUFALI: That's what I'm worried about . . . this notorious 1992. I'm waiting to see what will happen with all these equivalencies in work, when professionals and other workers will be able to work anywhere in the EC. That's why I have the feeling that something is beginning.

STRATIGAKI: I'm not expecting something from 1992. For me, it's a continuation of a situation which began many years ago. That all the products that circulate in Greece are imported, that won't change in 1992. It will worsen. For some, for instance, the professionals, as you point out, there may be some positive aspects—I can't say that it's all black. However, I don't see 1992 as some kind of landmark. How do you see this in the United States?

Centers and Peripheries

GEORGES: I think, and this is certainly very general and perhaps ethnocentric, that there is a feeling that there is no longer a center, that there's no longer the same kind of order.

STRATIGAKI: Well, sure, the Eastern Bloc fell, Europe is rising, Japan keeps developing. But I don't see that there is no order in all this. There wouldn't eternally be a war between the United States and the USSR. Very simply, some reordering is now taking place. After the war with Iraq, the United States came out even stronger because it became apparent that Europe could not become an equivalent pole of power.

GEORGES: But you don't see these changes you list as representing anything more fundamental than a reordering?

PAPAGAROUFALI: I guess we have this feeling that Maria describes because we are more or less certain about the prearrangement of what's happening by the big powers. This may be wrong, but we don't see these changes as monumental. Because we see them as more or less guided, not as if they were a spontaneous revolution, like the 1917 revolution: then there was an anxiety, what was to come was still unknown. In contrast now, there will simply be an expansion of some form of capitalism to Eastern Europe. So I also have a sense more of reshuffling than of monumental change.

GEORGES: How has this reshuffling or reordering been felt in Greece, and by you in particular?

STRATIGAKI: Well, we don't, I don't, think that we take it that seriously, because we have Europe to put a check on U.S. power. In other words our full placement in Europe has safeguarded us from feeling that we are expendable, the toy of the United States, which has become even more powerful. We don't have the feeling that it's over, the Americans now have seized us, because of our placement in Europe, which is a new union with its own dynamics and self-defense. If there are any direct effects on Greece, they will have their origins in what will happen in Europe. And what will happen in Europe? A huge market in which we will be a peripheral country living off of tourism. That is, I don't see any difference.

PAPAGAROUFALI: Rather, now it's sanctioned. 1992 makes official something that has been the case for years among us. But now it's much clearer.

STRATIGAKI: Yes, it's legitimated now. For instance, there always may have been the intention to industrialize Greece, because every nation's development is based on industrialization. Now we no longer have this intention. That story is over. Greece won't industrialize, because we will be a piece of greater Europe. But that doesn't worry me any more. Of course, I consider this negative, in some fashion. But I don't say, "Oh my God, what's going to happen? Our dependence on the rest of Europe will grow!" In fact, that's what's happening. But that doesn't bother me any more. I can't make the country's problem my problem. What will happen to women is what I make my problem. That's what interests me. No more than that. I don't want to get any deeper into politics, like I used to. I don't want to get into that cerebral approach I used to have. That is, that this is right, therefore that's what you should be, and then you can change your personal life to suit that ideal notion. Now I'm rather on the other side of the fence. I see that it's the personal experiences that have influenced me to become a Marxist, a leftist, a feminist. And naturally, when all this is a trajectory of fifteen or twenty years, then you can't disentangle the personal and the theory.

Notes

1. In 1968, the Communist Party of Greece of the Interior (KKE-es) splintered from the Communist Party of Greece (KKE). In 1987, the KKE-es split further into the Greek Left (EAr) and the Communist Party of the Interior-Renovative Left (KKE-es-AA). The latter was joined by the ecologists in 1992 and changed its name to the Renovative Communist and Ecological Left (AKOA). In 1989, the EAr joined the KKE in a Coalition of the Left and Progress. Since 1991, the KKE and the coalition (*Synaspismos*) constitute two separate communist-oriented parties. According to recent estimates, the percentages of voters in each of these parties ranged from well under 1 percent (AKOA) to 2 percent (KKE) to 3.5 percent (coalition).

2. On the identity crisis of he Greek Left, see Alavanos, Antenor, and Papas. See also Androulakis, member of the coalition, who proposes the formation of a "postmodern Left" as a solution to this crisis.

3. In the 1980s, Greece changed from a "sending" to a "receiving" country with

respect to international migration. Immigrants from all over the world now enter Greece by the thousands. In 1991, according to official estimates, both legal and illegal immigrants (including political and economic refugees) constituted 2 percent of the total population. This percentage includes an unprecedented flow of immigration of Greek origin from the former communist countries. There are the so-called *Pontic,* Greeks who were forced to flee from Pontus-Turkey to the USSR and then were persecuted and resettled by Stalin; the Greek minority of Albania; and the repatriated offspring of Greek communists who took refuge in the Soviet Union after the Greek civil war ended in 1949. All are reclaiming their Greek identity.

4. Greeks' dispute with Yugoslavians concerns facilities for "Yugoslavia" in the port of Thessaloniki, in the area of Macedonia. It comprises a series of agreements and disagreements—mainly since 1914—between the two countries about a free zone in the Aegean port, at the disposal of Serbian commerce but under Greek law and police administration. Yugoslavians' demand to enlarge and control this zone was never accepted by Greeks out of fear that its acceptance would encourage further demands for control of the approaches to the Aegean port. Greeks' reactions to the latest political developments have proved that this fear was never appeased despite the treaties of friendship between the two countries during the last decades (see Valden).

5. See Kofos for a summary of the Balkan controversy over the historical heritage of Macedonia and Greeks' use of the ancient Macedonian grandeur and name as testimonies of their Greekness before and after the establishment of the modern Greek state in 1830.

6. The British have accused Greeks also of constructing and misusing "ethnicist myths," thus betraying their efforts to convince the rest of the world that they constitute "a niche of Western Democratic logic" (*Eleftherotypia* 26 Aug. 1992). During the same time, 170 Greek intellectuals signed a declaration also condemning the archeological kind of nationalism and the "ethnicist hysteria" that have been cultivated and promoted by Greek politicians, journalists, and clerics "in order to make Greek people forget about" economic and other political problems (*Anti*). See also Veikos.

7. When the Danes warned Greeks of a "collapse"—from Europeans to "Balkans"—because of their ethnicist attitude, the latter reminded them of the inferiority of their past history—as opposed to their present one—compared to the superiority of ancient Greek civilization (*Eleftherotypia* 13 May 1992).

8. As Herzfeld rightly points out, Turkish forms (linguistic and other) "are associated [by Greeks] with some sort of conceptual inferiority, as well as with things that should not be disclosed to outsiders" (1986:227). In the "outside," Greeks' claim to "European" status has always constituted the most common justification to discriminate between Greek and Turkish (or oriental, or Eastern, or Balkan) identity. Yet, in a recent interview, the Turkish ambassador in Athens—a city which to him "feels like home"—claimed both Balkan and European statuses for Turks and pointed out the "many things" shared in common by Turks and Greeks, including the level of their democracy. The Greek journalist denied this last similarity and paralleled the Greek democratic regime to the British one (Kassimatis).

9. See Rozakis for a short analysis of this crisis or dilemma of Greeks since the initiation of the Greek state in the nineteenth century. In a recent short article entitled

"Uncertainties," a Greek journalist, criticizing the Europeans' ambiguous attitude towards the Greek-Yugoslavian debate, asks, "Is Greece, after all, an equal member of the European Community, or not?" (*Eleftherotypia* 13 May 1992).

10. For an excellent short analysis of this phenomenon, see Tsoukalas.

11. The analysis of this perennial problem and tactic has recently reappeared in Greek newspaper articles (for example, Mouzelis and Manitakis). That this is an old problem/tactic with a new twist is amply demonstrated by Herzfeld (1982, 1987). Also see Kyriakidou-Nestoros.

12. In a recent analysis of the relationship between Greek agricultural economy and the "European Family," Sotiris Hatzigakis, the Minister of Agriculture, made the following statement: "From my experience, the winners in the E.E.C. are those who have goals and plans, those who develop prudent negotiations by avoiding short-term positions adequate for locally based interests only."

13. On this issue see Liakos, Lithoxoou, Manitakis, Papadimitropoulos, and *Anti*.

14. The geographic location of Greece in the eastern Mediterranean, rather than its natural resources, has made it susceptible to foreign interference since its initiation as a state. For an excellent summary of the history of tutelage exercised on Greece by the Europeans (from the beginning of the nineteenth century until the end of World War II) and the United States (since the end of World War II), see Couloumbis et al.

15. See Stamiris for a summary of the Greek women's movement since the nineteenth century.

16. In the 1980s, the socialist government (PASOK)-affiliated Union of Greek Women, as well as the General Secretariat of Equality (EGE), spread their activities throughout all the cities and the countryside. In 1984, the secretariat initiated the establishment of Women's Cooperatives in many villages. To a large extent, the program was financially supported by the EC. In each case, almost all women villagers of all ages participated as members of the coops, and developed a life-style more or less oriented toward equality with men, and emancipation, for instance, through participation in seminars, travel to cities and even abroad for the affairs of the cooperatives, and so on (see Papagaroufali). During that time, events such as public speeches organized by EGE to honor International Women's Day (and reported by anthropologist Jane Cowan) had become common.

17. Herzfeld informs us that in the midnineteenth century, Greek urban sophisticates viewed educated women's "gentleness" as a means to "soften" public men's "harshness" and thus mediate "not only between male individuals and groups" (a role already known from the ethnographic literature on rural women), but also "between nations"—Greece and Turkey (1986:226). The women discussed in this article, including the most active members of village women's cooperatives, may also be viewed as "mediators" between female individuals and groups within their country as well as "between nations"—Greece and Europe. Yet contemporary women mediators do not play the role of "suitable domestic allies for the men who will conduct public affairs" (1986:227) but the role of public allies for the women who conduct domestic affairs.

18. During her fieldwork in the small town of Sohos in the mid-1980s, Cowan experienced an increased awareness of equality, in particular gender equality, among young Sohoians. She attributes this phenomenon to the historical conditions of that period in Greece, particularly the campaign for equality promoted by the socialist

government. At that time, young Sohoian women (now in their mid- and late twenties) were directly and indirectly expressing and enacting their need to be treated on more equal terms with males. If we add the cases in which women seem to have already succeeded more in this matter (for example, Cowan's village of Potamia and Papagaroufali's women's cooperatives), we might argue that this familiarity with the ideology of equality is a fact at least for younger generations of both urban and rural Greeks.

19. See Monemvasiotis for a brief but illuminating analysis of these attitudes among postdictatorial generations of Greeks and their expression in the early 1990s.

20. The discussion of Maria's sexual experiences reveals the extent to which certain "oriental" traits are, in fact, "embodied" (to use Bourdieu's term) by Greeks and that policies such as the renaming of Turkish coffee to "Greek coffee" do not suffice to eliminate the Turkishness of Greekness. At this point it might be interesting to refer to the Turkish ambassador's words with respect to coffee as a symbol of national identity: "We call it Turkish. If you call it Greek, no problem. However, when I visit the Minister of the Exterior and I am treated to coffee, we call it Greek-Turkish" (Kassimatis).

References

Alavanos, Alekos. 1990. "Let's Bury Dogmatic Marxism in Order to Resuscitate Marx." *Anti* 455 (28 Dec.): 34–35.

Androulakis, Mimis. 1992. *Meta . . .* Athens: Livanis.

Antenor. 1990. "The Hegemony of Conservatism and the Left." *Anti* 455 (28 Dec.): 4–5.

Couloumbis, Theodore A., John A. Petropoulos, and Harry J. Psomiades. 1976. *Foreign Interference in Greek Politics*. New York: Pella.

Cowan, Jane. 1990. *Dance and the Body Politic in Northern Greece*. Princeton, N.J.: Princeton University Press.

Hatzigakis, Sotiris. 1992. "In Agriculture, Maastricht Was Initiated Thirty Years Ago." *To Vima* (23 Sept.).

Herzfeld, Michael. 1982. *Ours Once More: Folklore, Ideology, and the Making of Modern Greece*. Austin: University of Texas Press.

———. 1986. "Within and Without: The Category of 'Female' in the Ethnography of Modern Greece." In *Gender and Power in Rural Greece*. Ed. Jill Dubisch. Princeton, N.J.: Princeton University Press.

———. 1987. *Anthropology through the Looking-Glass: Critical Ethnography in the Margins of Europe*. Cambridge: Cambridge University Press.

Kassimatis, Stefanos. 1992. "We Get Annoyed by the View That the Aegean Is Greek." *Epsilon* 87 (6 Dec.): 42–46.

Kofos, Evangelos. 1990. "National Heritage and National Identity in Nineteenth- and Twentieth-Century Macedonia." In *Modern Greece: Nationalism and Nationality*. Ed. Martin Blinkhorn and Thanos Veremis. London: Sage.

Kyriakidou-Nestoros, Alki. 1977. *The Theory of Greek Folklore: A Critical Analysis*. Athens: Etaereia Spoudon Neoellinikou Politismou ke Genikis Paedeias, Moraitis' School.

Liakos, Antonis. 1992. "The Balkans and Ethnic Policy." *Eleftherotypi*. 25 June.

Lithoxoou, Dimitris. 1992. *Minorities Issues and Ethnic Consciousness in Greece*. Athens: Leviathan.

Manitakis, Antonis. 1992. "Ethnic Discourse: Yesterday—Today." *Eleftherotypia*. 13 July.

Monemvasiotis, Stavros. 1992. "The Students' Movement Now and Then: 'Is King Alexandros Alive?'" *Anti* 490 (3 Apr.): 24–26.

Mouzelis, Nikos. 1992. "Greece on the Threshold of the Twenty-First Century." *To Vima* (23 Sept.).

"The '170' and the District Attorney: They Disagree with the Persecution." *Anti* 495 (29 May 1992): 44–46.

Papadimitropoulos, Damianos. 1992. "The Balkans and the New Order of Things, or in the Margin?" *O Politis* 118 (Mar.): 12–22.

Papagaroufali, Eleni. 1986. *The Greek Woman Farmer and Women's Cooperatives*. Athens: Mediterranean Women's Studies Institute (KEGME).

Papas, Tassos. 1992a. "Coalition: Looking for Alliances." *Anti* 490: (3 Apr.): 22–23.

———. 1992b. "A New-Old Schema." *Anti* 495 (29 May): 35.

———. 1992c. "Fotis Kouvelis Talks to *Anti:* 'I Don't Accept the Transition to the Other Side of the Fence.'" *Anti* 508 (27 Nov.): 12–13.

Rozakis, Christos. 1983. "Greece in the International Arena." In *Hellenism—Greekness*. Ed. Dimitris G. Tsaousis. Athens: Hestia.

Stamiris, Eleni. 1986. "The Greek Women's Movement." *New Left Review* 158 (July–Aug.): 98–112.

"The Superiors." *Eleftherotypia*. 13 May 1992.

"The 'Times' See Ethnicism." *Eleftherotypia*. 26 Aug. 1992.

Tsoukalas, Konstantinos. 1983. "Tradition and Modernization: Some More General Problems." In *Hellenism—Greekness*. Ed. Dimitris G. Tsaousis. Athens: Hestia.

"Uncertainties." *Eleftherotypia*. 13 May 1992.

Valden, Sotiris. 1991. *Greece—Yugoslavia: Origin and Development of a Crisis*. Athens: Themelio.

Veikos, Theophilos. 1992. "Ethnicism and 'Nominalism.'" *Anti* 508 (27 Nov.): 20–21.

Illicit Discourse

The interview that follows was conducted during the May 1991 plenary session of the European Parliament in Strasbourg with Bruno Gollnisch, M.E.P. (Member of European Parliament). Gollnisch was born in Neuilly-sur-Seine in January 1950. He is Professor of Japanese Literature and Law at the University of Lyon. In 1989 Gollnisch was elected a deputy to the parliament as a member of the Technical Group of the European Right (DR). The group is small with 17 of the 518 members of the parliament. It is composed of the French *Front national* and the German *Die Republikaner.* Jean-Marie Le Pen, M.E.P., is chairman of the Technical Group as well as the *Front national.* Four members of the Italian *Movimento sociale italiano-Destra nazionale* (MSI-DN) sit with the nonattached members (NI) of the parliament, though they share many of the views of the European Right. Within the parliament, Le Pen's group has been subject to various degrees of exclusion and ostracism resulting from their positions on race and nationality. The isolation of the members of the European Right frustrates their full participation in parliamentary matters as well as frames their political practice. It also renders their discourse illicit.

The interview with Gollnisch was part of a broader project that examines how cultural struggles are shaping European politics in the post–cold war era. The project has a prehistory that stretches back to the mid-1980s and the Friuli region of northeast Italy—the terrain of Carlo Ginzburg's studies of sixteenth-century agrarian cults and inquisitorial prosecutions and the grim battlefields of Ernest Hemingway's *A Farewell to Arms* (Holmes 1989). While pursuing an ethnographic portrayal of this domain, I encountered for the first time what appeared to be a rough antipolitics drawn from ethnic sensibilities and cultural aspirations. It was an antipolitics that seemed to subvert the formation of an independent political outlook and identity. In subsequent years these marginal sensibilities and aspirations insinuated themselves into the heart of European political discourse.

On the eastern periphery of the northern Italian plain I found a society that
was difficult to bound in time and space. It could be observed from a locale
but it was not confined to place. For three centuries it had mediated fundamental social transformation, yet the society itself was not transitional. The
people that inhabited this terrain were preeminently sojourners who traversed
regional and national frontiers as easily as they trespassed the conceptual
boundaries fabricated by social scientists. Their sojourns entailed long itin-
eraries crosscutting Central Europe, Australia, and the New World; yet they
maintained identities rooted in the ethnic practices of their ancient patria. I
mapped the society along the memory traces of elderly Friulani. In portraying
the intricacies of this social formation I uncovered peculiar cultural struggles
that yielded a fundamental critique of modernity.

In the rural districts of Friuli were enclaves where the metapolitics that have
dominated Europe since the late nineteenth century were reconfigured. The
great allegories of material inequality—the class struggle—that contoured
modern European politics were recast to inspire highly personal struggles
played out in obscure cultural idioms. These struggles were based on a nega-
tion of the cultural architecture of the modern world. Paradoxically, to engage
in the strugle required complex odysseys through the heart of modernity. The
terms of the struggle pitted the secularized impulses of industrial capitalism
and the nation-state against sublime orientations embedded in what social
scientists generally abstract as ethnicity or nationalism. In the rural districts
of Friuli the imperatives of rational-bureaucratic societal development pro-
voked reciprocal disenchantments that commingled premodern, modern, and,
above all antimodern elements. In the shadow of the metapolitics, played out
in opposed idioms of class struggle, intricate allegories of cultural disenchantment were fashioned. To depict the phenomenon, I drew on the poetic vision
of Friedrich Schiller by way of Max Weber.

The "disenchantment of the world" is the central theme in Weber's analysis
of Western cultural development. It refers to the progressive purging of the
authority of supernatural ideas within modern secular societies. It is thus
bound up with Weber's notion of rationalization, which traces the processes
by which "scientific" thinking displaces magical content in occidental cultures. I thought initially that the dynamics of disenchantment in Friuli pro-
voked an awareness that subverted the formation of an independent political
outlook and identity. It was only after interviewing the general secretary and
president of a tiny autonomist party, *Movimento friuli* (MF), in the summer
of 1987—when I heard a discourse on the Friulian nationhood for the first
time—that I began to recognize traces of a nascent politics. Like the numerous ethnic, nationalist, and religious groups that strive for autonomy from
Northern Ireland to the Ukraine, the program and discourse of the MF seemed

at odds with post–World War II developments in Europe. Its vision was difficult to locate along single Left-Center-Right political axis. To thwart encroachments by the secularized nation-state, the leaders of the MF seek to establish a moral order—framed in an ethnic idiom—that can bind people through language, history, religious practice, and folk tradition to a specific cultural terrain. They added to this parochial agenda a breathtaking twist entailing a fundamental reintegration of European society along ethnic, regionalist, and nationalist lines. Their vision focussed on the European Parliament as the supranational forum in which to achieve a new continental framework. It was this encounter that led to an investigation of how various cultural disenchantments were coalescing as a comprehensive historical critique which circumscribed distinctive political aspirations. In the wake of the hypermodern project of the European Community, a reciprocal politics that subverted modernist societal assumptions and sought new idioms of political struggle was emerging.

First in the spring of 1989 and then for eight months in 1991 I conducted interviews at the two major venues of the European Parliament, Brussels and Strasbourg. It was a time when the forces impelling the transformation of Europe were intensifying. The cold war ended, the Soviet Union collapsed, Yugoslavia dissolved into civil war, and the war in the Persian Gulf came and went. Cultural subjectivities of race, ethnicity, nation, religion were becoming the objective terms of political struggle. The project seeks to portray how emerging cultural fears and aspirations are translated into political idioms by various groups. The French *Front national* and the Technical Group of the European Right are committed to this form of political practice within the European Parliament.

Some of the views excavated in this study raise acute questions about how academic inquiry is depicted. The most frustrating bind posed by this study was the challenge of rendering the urgent character of various political agendas without serving as an apologist for those viewpoints. This gets at the heart of what anthropologists owe to their informants, even if they are public figures, and what the anthropologist owes the reader. In general I have erred on the side of candor, depicting the arresting character of various political aspirations while opening interpretation and scrutiny to the reader. Some of the views depicted in the interview are disquieting. The complexities of the present and the methodological challenges they pose are revealed in the interview.

I was directed to Gollnisch by Alexander Langer, M.E.P., who at the time was president of the European Greens. At the end of an interview with Langer I asked him who in the parliament articulated a political vision that he found compelling or unusual. Specifically, I asked for the names of members who expressed positions that went beyond the technocratic preoccupations of the parliament. He listed seven or eight on the back of a paper napkin, among them Bruno Gollnisch.

Licit and Illicit Discourses

The interview that follows covers a subversive form of political discourse that is illicit though not necessarily revolutionary. An illicit discourse aims at reestablishing the boundaries, terms, and idioms of political struggle. The resulting political practice is deconstructive. Its authority is often parasitic, drawing strength from the corruption, ineptitude, obsolescence, and lost relevance of established political dogmas and agendas. Its practitioners negotiate and map the points of contradiction and fatigue of partisan positions. They scavenge the detritus of decaying politics, probing areas of deceit and deception. By doing so they invoke displaced histories and reveal deformed moralities. They strive to introduce the unvoiced and unspeakable into public debate. Established political forces resist these "illicitudes," defining those who articulate them as racists, terrorists, bigots, or as some other form of essentialized pariah.

Gollnisch articulated ardently a discourse of the extreme Right with wit, vehemence, and even self-parody. He candidly analyzed the strategic aims and shortcomings of this type of politics. Significant sections of the interview dealt with issues raised by the parliamentary "Report Drawn Up on Behalf of the Committee of Inquiry into Racism and Xenophobia." Glyn Ford, M.E.P., was *rapporteur* of the committee and the document is referred to as the Ford Report. The text summarizes the rise of racism, neofascism, and extreme right-wing movements across Europe with very specific charges against the *Front national* and its chairman, Jean-Marie Le Pen. Sections of the report are reproduced below and at various points in the interview to provide an intertextual dimension for the reader to assess the counterdiscourse on racism and xenophobia.[1]

> FORD REPORT. The resurgence of the extreme Right in France can be effectively charted from 1984 when, against expectations, the *Front national* (FN) gained ten seats in elections to the European Parliament. Although the 10.9 percent vote for the anti-immigration FN was viewed as a protest phenomenon, its progress was later confirmed in March 1986, when it won more than 2.7 million votes in the election to the French National Assembly and secured thirty-five seats. [22]

> The first round of the French Presidential elections in April 1988 saw the FN's support further consolidated when, running against Socialist President Mitterrand, the FN's candidate and leader Jean-Marie Le

Pen gained 14.4 percent of the vote caused profound shock throughout France. The percentage may have masked the real scale of the
support for the FN. Analyzing the votes cast, the measure of the FN's
success can be estimated. Le Pen's total vote of 4,367,926 indicated
that his party's concentration on anti-immigration themes had gained
ground among French people. [22]

The Le Pen vote went right across the entire French social and geo-
graphical spectrum and suggested that large sections of the French
public were willing to identify with the FN policy of demanding the
removal of France's large immigrant population. [22]

Much of this . . . can be attributed to the FN's powerful organizational machine and massive resources which enable it to run heavy-
weight and relentless propaganda campaigns against immigration,
foreigners, and what Le Pen calls Marxism and the Islamicization of
France. [23]

At the same time a legacy of what were racist and nationalist policies . . . pursued by the PCF [*Parti Communist Français*] in the late
1970s and early 1980s has found an outlet now in the FN. Racism
has seduced many people in France and is there in abundance, notwithstanding the efforts of the big antiracist SOS Racisme movement. In reality it seems that this and similar movements have not
significantly dented support for the FN whose politics center on existing racism against North Africans, black people, and, from time
to time, Jews. [23]

HOLMES: I am interested in how nationalist aspirations and cultural struggles are defining European politics. Your group (Technical Group of the European Right) and particularly Mr. Le Pen have openly articulated this type
of agenda. I have also been interviewing members of the Greens (the European Greens), for the purposes of contrast, because they too are interested in
cultural identity.

GOLLNISCH: The Greens are very interesting. Yes, in a way even if they
don't realize it themselves. They go along with what we call, maybe in a
too-simple way, the cosmopolitan lobby, you know, the international lobby.
Some of them, strangely enough, are very much in favor of, how do you
say, a mixed society. For example, they advocate a culturally or ethnically
mixed society, which in a way is a bit strange because ecologists should observe nature and they would understand that species do not mix so easily and
fight to keep their own territory. Well, human beings can obviously have
different attitudes.

HOLMES: I think some of the Greens believe in extending the idea of husbandry over nature to include husbandry over culture.

GOLLNISCH: Yes, yes in this way I think the attitude of ecologists resembles our (the extreme Right) perspective, our program. But they wouldn't admit it, obviously.

HOLMES: I interviewed the Scottish Nationalists member, Winifred Ewing, M.E.P., and she asserted that the way that you can excite nationalism most intensely is by reference to the environment.

GOLLNISCH: Yes, for example, there is much resentment in Eastern Europe because people are discovering the result of the communist system in respect to the environment. It is a complete disaster, which is very strange. Theoretically speaking, a state where the rule of economy and social life is completely controlled by the authorities ought to achieve complete protection of the environment. It is absolutely contrary.

HOLMES: What motivated you to become a member of this group?

GOLLNISCH: As for me, well, there are a lot of reasons. First of all, my great uncle was a member of parliament from Algiers, though he himself was not born there. At the time of the Algerian problem, it was not so much the issue of independence. I was, by the way, very young. I thought there was some kind of betrayal, not in the fact of giving independence to Algeria, but giving it to a political movement that was authoritarian and would expel one-and-a-half million people who had lived there for six generations, who lost everything they owned. This is rather a nonhistory because history does not favor colonialism. There were a lot of massacres not just of European people, but also of Arabs who supported France. Then came a kind of distress of the political parties and political attitudes because what happened [in Algeria] was exactly the contrary [to the official history]. Again, I was very young. Then when I became a university student in 1968, at the time of the revolution, I was very surprised. I was very young; still I thought that such institutions as the university were as tough as stone and could last forever. I was amazed, because I knew them well, how a small group of activist students who used the tactics of revolution, they used Leninism . . . There were only a handful of them maybe at the beginning, forty or fifty espousing Marxism in the university. They could take control of the campus, then they controlled all the teacher and student syndicates, then they controlled all the worker syndicates . . . And the country was on the brink of civil war. You also had similar movements at Berkeley. But in France when one talks of May 1968, it was a different thing. I lived it from within. I was upper middle-class. I saw this rich businessman waiting at the bank to get just five hundred francs, that is less than one hundred dollars. All the cars were stopped because there was no gas. The whole country was completely paralyzed by strikes. Well, finally there were elections and things went back to normal. But I realized how vulnerable our democratic societies were and how pronounced political decline was. At that time I had a few student friends and they introduced me to Le Pen. I knew that Le Pen was a very

courageous man, but very much in the (political) minority with one or perhaps two seats. I was also struck that the conservative parties, the Gaullist
parties of the UDF, the Center-Right party (by the way, none of them
wanted to be classified as a right-wing party) . . . It was absolutely disgraceful to be on the Right. Mr. Chirac said himself at that time that he wanted
his party to be the French labor party. One of the leaders of the UDF, Giscard d'Estaing's party, defined himself as Center-Left. They declared their
aim to realize all that was within the common program of the socialist and
communist parties. I thought that the so-called conservative parties were refusing to be conservative. They didn't conserve or preserve anything within
society. They never talked about morals, they never talked about ethics, they
never talked about the structure of our civilization. They were just interested
in ruling the economy. In a kind of mixed society, because we were already
in a social democratic society even at the time of d'Estaing, half of GDP
was under the control of public entities whether of the state, department,
cities, nationalized industries, and so on. I had what are called right-wing
ideas, so I was in favor of Le Pen. But at that time my own belief was that
it was absolutely impossible for right-wing political success. If we had not
taken before some steps in the field of culture. I mean education, university
research, media were controlled by what you in America would call progressives or liberals. There was absolutely no way for us to manage within this
politics. If we had not first achieved something in this cultural field, and that
is why I chose an academic career.[2]

   HOLMES: It was a political impulse that led you to choose an academic
career?

   GOLLNISCH: Well, I had other interests as well and did not choose this
career simply because it would be useful for [promoting] my political ideas.
I had pure academic interests in crime and the way people think and so on,
and so far as it was useful to do something in this field instead of an active
political career . . . Well, you know better than me that it takes time to write
papers and so on, so there was not much time for politics. There was also
my military service in the navy. Then I went to Japan for research. When I
returned, I became an assistant professor of law at the University of Paris.
Finally I became a professor in the literature department, and because I had
a legal background, [the faculty] elected me as a dean. They thought I had
some administrative ability, which I absolutely do not have, by the way.
Such were things and I was in Lyon. I was not active politically. As in
America and many other places like Japan, you either have an academic or
political career. Actually it is much more common to go between the two in
France. So during this time Le Pen himself . . . and a friend of mine was
close to Le Pen . . . there was a bielection and that was the beginning of
the FN.[3]

   HOLMES: What year was that?

GOLLNISCH: It was 1983 and 1984. They came to me because they decided to have a congress in Lyon. Very simply, they wanted someone to serve as host in Lyon and since some of them knew me, they asked me. I hesitated because it was a difficult choice, especially for such a controversial group. Finally I accepted, and I do not regret it at all, and I became a member of the party. I became responsible for the Department of Rhône, that is, the Lyon area. At that time there were only maybe twenty-five members of the FN in Lyon. But it grew very, very fast; now there are more than two thousand. Still, that is not so many members, but in the recent bielection we were the third political force. Le Pen got 20 percent of the votes during the presidential election in the Rhône prefecture. It is not as much as in southern France for example.

HOLMES: Is Marseille the strongest area for the FN?

GOLLNISCH: Yes, I think Marseille is one of the strongest areas, but not only Marseille; Nice, too. Well, we also had good results in Alsace for example. Strangely enough it is the eastern part of France.

HOLMES: Has Le Pen's strength developed since the mid 1980s?

GOLLNISCH: Yes, the big development came . . .

> FORD REPORT. The size and the scale of the FN's organization and activities give the party considerable strength, especially in the south of France where in Perpignan, for example, it takes almost 30 percent of the vote and in Marseilles where it always polls heavily. [23]

> But it is not just in the south that the FN is strong. In the depressed steel and coal regions of northern and eastern France, regions suffering all the pain brought about by slow deindustrialization, it challenges the declining *Parti Communiste Français* (PCF) for the working class vote. The challenge even extends into the historic heartland of French communism, Seine-St.-Denis in the red belt around Paris. There the FN has twice won more votes than the PCF from working people who are disillusioned with the left. [23]

> By presenting itself as the voice of the working man against big capital on the one hand and red manipulation on the other, the FN has had a potent effect. The desperate crisis of the badly divided French trade union movement, to which only 20 percent of workers now belong, has helped the fascists to penetrate deeply into the most disadvantaged social layer. [23]

HOLMES: Have you seen a shift in Le Pen's thinking during the time you have known him?

GOLLNISCH: I think it has been consistent, but I must say this to an American citizen. Le Pen himself at the time of de Gaulle was much more strongly anticommunist. De Gaulle always tried to deal with the Soviet Union. He was against American policy in Indochina. He withdrew from NATO . . . At that time the FN did not exist itself, but Le Pen already had a political career. He was a Member of Parliament.

HOLMES: What party did he represent?

GOLLNISCH: It was a middle-class movement made up of craftsmen, shop-keepers, and so on against increases in the burden of taxes, and against a regime that was very weak, and the Fourth Republic. It was called Poujad-ism, named for [Pierre-Marie] Poujade, who was head of the *Union de dé-fense des commerçants et des artisans*. It wasn't violent, by the way, but the Left described it that way as they usually do when there is a movement that dares to attack their intellectual and doctrinal system. They describe it as a fascist movement. There was just a lot of protest about the burden of taxes, against the weakness of the regime, and the many defects of the political system of the time. One can say the movement succeeded in a way, but the ones who gained at the end of the Fourth Republic were the Gaullist and not Poujade himself, who had no ability to do that. At that time, Le Pen was a student leader at the faculty of law at Paris. He became the youngest mem-ber of parliament in France. He was reelected and then defeated in 1962 in the wake of the Gaullist victory and the Algerian crisis.

Well, your question was, did Le Pen change his view? In the 1960s and into the 1970s, generally speaking, the various movements, the small move-ments, the marginal movements that are part of what is called the far Right or Right activists, which are not that activist, by the way, were in favor of NATO; de Gaulle was against. In favor of stronger links with the free world, that is, with America; in favor of Israel because it was a democracy and part of the free world within a hostile political environment. Since that time, I must very frankly say, these positions have partly changed. We have not come to be anti-American. We are pro-French being French nationalists.

HOLMES: So you are against American mass culture?

GOLLNISCH: Yes, we feel that there is now some danger . . . From Israel, you know, we never received a word of gratitude. Part of the Jewish commu-nity in France, I mean part of them, and especially their leaders, were liber-als or progressives and they attacked us. They attacked us because we are right wing. If we were French nationalists, we were necessarily anti-Semitic. We stated repeatedly [that this was not the case] for years and years and decades. This charge came repeatedly on radio and TV interviews up until the time they could find a word of Le Pen that they could use against him. That came when they pressed him to say exactly what he thought about the thesis of a paper written about the history of concentration camps during the Second World War. He [Le Pen] said, I am not an historian, I am interested in how things are now. They asked if he believed in the Holocaust. "I recognize that millions of people died." "But would you like to say how they died?" "Well, it's a matter of detail." You know that *detail* can have two meanings in French, something that is part of a whole or something that is insignificant, of no interest. It is very clear when you hear the whole tape he said that the way people were killed was of little matter compared to the fact that they were killed. But they used this against him as a political weapon.[4] Very frankly speaking, we are completely fed up. We are also shocked by the fact that repeatedly the Israeli ambassador here in France speaks against us, even though he is a representative of a foreign country and, in our opinion, should not mix in French politics . . . We feel that the fate of the world should not rest on what happens between Jews and Arabs. So there has been some change in our attitudes. We are more reserved about American influence and about Israel.

> FORD REPORT The most abject in a series of desecration of Jewish cemeteries was perpetrated in the night of 9-10 May 1990 in the town of Carpentras (near Avignon), the founding place of Judaism in France. Thirty-four tombstones were damaged and the corpse of an old man who was buried two weeks earlier was removed from the coffin and mutilated. The incident caused great national and international indignation and the leaders of all political parties, excluding the *Front national,* took part in a massive demonstration in Paris on 14 May 1990. For the first time since the end of the Second World War, a president of the republic joined the silent procession in Paris composed of two hundred thousand participants . . . Although the Secretary General of the *Front national,* Mr. C. Lang, also expressed his indignation over the desecration in Carpentras, and the FN Chairman, Mr. Le Pen, reiterated that he was not anti-Semitic, publications related to the FN, especially the party's publication, the *National hebro,* and remarks made by its political leaders, including Mr. Le Pen, cannot be dissociated from the rise of anti-Semitism in France. Mr. Le Pen has already accused the "Jewish International" and freemasonry of playing "a nonnegligible role in the creation of the antinational spirit (in France)." [59–60]

> In 1989, the director of *National hebro* and member of the political bureau of the *Front national,* Mr. R. Gaucher, wrote in the November issue of his publication (with a circulation of about one hundred thousand): "We are at the start of a tremendous power struggle, a great planetary struggle between the international Jewish movement and the international Christian, first of all Catholic, one. Depending on the outcome of this combat, which will be the great religious and political confrontation of the year 2000, or of this battle, either Christianity will succeed in preserving its position in the face of the

fantastic force of the Jewish world, or else we, believers and non-
believers will come under a new religious law, that of the *shoah*."
[89–90]

According to an opinion survey of CSA published in *Le Parisien*
[17 May 1990], 55 percent of respondents considered the *Front national* to be an anti-Semitic party compared to 22 percent who held
the opposite view. Another survey carried out at the same time . . .
by SOFRES and published in *Le Nouvel Observateur* shows that
66 percent of respondents believe the *Front national* to be responsible for what happened at Carpentras. The CSA survey also shows
that 96 percent of respondents were shocked by the desecration, but
35 percent . . . considered it "normal" to make "remarks hostile to
Jews." [90]

HOLMES: You have also become more interested in the issue of French
identity and this has had an overall impact on your politics.

GOLLNISCH: Yes, yes, exactly, absolutely. Immigration is one such problem. But we never said, contrary to what our enemies claim, that immigration is the only problem of France. We were brave enough to talk about
immigration even though it exposed us to the attack of being racists. It had
nothing to do with racism. People, in my opinion, are mixing several different concepts. Racism is a theory that one race is superior to another, justify-
ing the eradication of so-called inferior races. Given this meaning, no one is
a racist in France, especially among the leaders of the FN.[5] There is something else, that is, xenophobia, which is bad, but occurs when there is a too-
strong foreign presence. You have examples of xenophobia in every country,
every culture, and every civilization; it only depends on circumstances.
There is a third phenomenon: we feel that the *policy* of immigration is dangerous. It is dangerous, for example, if you compare it to the demographic
situation in Europe. The gap in [fertility rates]. It is also dangerous because
it is coming from people who are ethnically, religiously, culturally very different. Their assimilation does not succeed.

HOLMES: This situation of new populations (coming to France) is what
causes the cultural struggle?

GOLLNISCH: Yes, that is part of the cultural struggle. But it is not the
whole problem, there is the situation with the media having movies coming
from America . . . another kind of encroachment.

HOLMES: Consumer goods like blue jeans, do you see them encroaching
on the integrity of French culture?

GOLLNISCH: Yes, but in different ways. We do not go that far . . . blue
jeans are not as threatening as could have been the Red Army.

HOLMES: Let me get back to the issue of race . . . Technically you can say that Mr. Le Pen is a racist because he advocates policies based on racial distinctions.

GOLLNISCH: Well, even this I wouldn't say. Because this could be the view of some people in France, but this is not the policy of the FN. Because our policies are based on *nationality*. For example, there are Jews and Arabs in favor of France. There are Arabs in the ranks of the FN. If a black person comes to a meeting of the FN, there will be absolutely no problem. So I won't say that race is [the basis of our policy], but we say that race exists. There are some differences between the Bantu and the Swedish. There are differences of mentality, culture, habits, and so on. Obviously, France will not be the same if thirty years from now two-thirds of the population had African origins.

HOLMES: But the implication of Mr. Le Pen's policies can lead to discriminations based on race?

GOLLNISCH: Yes, but it depends on the way you take the word *racism*. Our adversaries try to say that it is a racist policy to retain some form of identity. Obviously, it is easier to assimilate if your origins are from the same race, culture, religion, and so on, than for people from a completely different race, culture, and religion from the majority of the people in the country.

I don't know if Le Pen told you when you met him, but there was an interview of Le Pen when he went to America by a professor at an American university; I don't remember which university. Among the questions put to Le Pen was, "Why are you against immigration, because you see a country like America built entirely upon immigration?" Le Pen responded, "Yes, I know this, but remember in France I am the representative of the aborigines." American immigration policy may have been good for the melting pot, but certainly not for the Sioux, Navaho, and so on.

HOLMES: The United States now has restrictive immigration policies.

GOLLNISCH: We have one of the less restrictive.

HOLMES: How about gaining French citizenship, particularly for North Africans?

GOLLNISCH: It is even criticized by Algerian leaders. For example, according to our nationality code. It was a big political issue. You know Chirac, of the Gaullist party, when he became prime minister had promised to have a program in common with the UDF, and a revision of the nationality code. Because the lobbying against it was so strong they just appointed a committee to discuss it and nothing came from it, nothing happened. Getting back to the point, the nationality code. Someone whose father is Algerian and mother is Algerian, but born in France becomes automatically French, but is also considered Algerian by Algeria. So we have a lot of people of dual nationality. Our program, what we would like to do is to not make it automatic—either you inherit it or you ask for it. If you ask for it we would like to get a personal declaration of allegiance [to France].

> FORD REPORT. Mr. Le Pen was convicted for "provocation of racial hatred, discrimination, and violence" in two separate judgments, one for a leaflet he published in March 1983 and the other for his statements in a TV program in February 1984. With regards to the leaflet, the judge ruled that "In wanting to persuade the electors . . . that there are too many immigrants in France, that they are expensive to society, that it is necessary to reduce the number of them or else risk losing the identity of the French people, Jean-Marie Le Pen is inviting the readers to [take] discriminatory measures against them [immigrants]." On his televised statements, the judge ruled that "in attributing to foreigners a negative and evil behavior, soon to menace the French people in their liberty and future, he [Mr. Le Pen] is only inciting the latter to consider them [the immigrants] as undesirable. He is provoking the listeners to discrimination, hatred and even violence against them." [87–88]

HOLMES: Let me turn to another issue. The extreme Left has collapsed in France. This is a period of enormous political ambiguity. However successful Mitterrand has been, the Socialists do not seem to know how to position themselves. Le Pen stands out with a strong set of ideas and values. In these ambiguous circumstances he appears to know what he is doing. It that the basis of Le Pen's new strength?

GOLLNISCH: Certainly, yes. There is a complete doctrinal vacuum. The extreme Left, as you say, has collapsed with the fall of Marxism, Trotskyism, Maoism. They have been completely discredited. But this also implies the failure of socialist ideas. Because between social democracy and communism there is a difference of degree and not nature. The basic idea that dominated throughout the nineteenth century and the beginning of the twentieth century was the ideal of social justice could be achieved through control by the state over public institutions that govern social and economic life. In this sense the failure of communism is also the failure of socialism. So what remains to the Socialists in France now? It is the idea of generosity, greater equality, assistance for the poor, and so on. This agenda is collapsing too because, I do not know how closely you follow French politics, there are many scandals now. When the Socialists were in opposition they were critical of the corruption of the conservative parties. Now they [are in power] and more corrupt than their predecessors.

HOLMES: How has unemployment changed?

GOLLNISCH: Unemployment was one of the major failures of Giscard d'Estaing; there were more than one-and-a-half million unemployed at the end of Giscard's term. Mitterrand said, if he were elected, there would never be two million unemployed in France. There are now more than three-and-a-half [million]. [The Socialists] are trying to conceal it. For example there are people who are supposed to be trainees; there are young people who work on social welfare programs earning two thousand francs per month, a kind of two-year government service which has now been extended to three years. There are almost no entrance requirements for university. The universities are completely crowded with students remaining five, six, seven years [because of the employment situation] . . . Well, you know, there is . . . the Socialist mathematician, he won the Nobel Prize, said the other day in a television interview that the education system was a complete failure. But quite frankly it did not begin with the Socialists . . . As long as students are registered at university they are not counted as unemployed.

As a system [socialism] has failed. It is discredited. As a moral, ethical aim it has been corrupted. So what is left. In fact there is nothing left but to be antiracist! It is the only thing that gives them their sense of being generous [a sense of moral ascendance].

HOLMES: You also have a history of opposing taxation [by way of the Poujadism] that predates Margaret Thatcher?

GOLLNISCH: The Poujadist movement [in the early 1950s] posed a great shock to French political society. One of the shocks before the end of the Fourth Republic. It was a surprise that lower middle-class people, fed up with bureaucracy and the burden of taxation, that started as a protest, disrupting elections. People in this organization [followers of Poujade], it was a kind of a union, ran for election and they got fifty-two members elected, including Le Pen. Le Pen himself was not a shopkeeper but he was a young, brilliant, and eloquent leader. The movement was attacked, particularly by upper-class civil servants and by working-class unions controlled by the Left. If you read in *Le Monde* about Poujadism [today] it is meant definitely disgraceful. It refers to the middle class who egotistically want to protect themselves from the burden of taxation. It is kind of funny because for years and years and years, *Le Monde* has supported workers' groups that try to defend their own interests. Why should it be for shopkeepers, farmers, and craftsmen to protect their interests a crime? But intellectually speaking it [Poujadist movement] was considered disgraceful. Now, strangely enough, the burden [of taxes] is much heavier than at that time. Then it was approximately one-fourth of GDP went to public administration, now it is roughly half. That was one of the major themes of Le Pen, but he did not think it was a popular position. I am one of the people (in the FN) who wants a stronger stand on this issue. But Le Pen at the beginning of the FN in 1984 repeatedly pointed out that during the seven-year rule of Mr. Giscard d'Estaing, the amount of money taken out of your pocket [in taxation, social security, and so on] was increasing at a rate of one percent per year.

HOLMES: How did you respond to the Ford Report?

GOLLNISCH: The Ford Report is emblematic of the new trend in socialism, in European socialism. Socialism failed as a technical means to achieve social justice through public property and public management of the economy and social life. Socialism is also discredited especially in countries such as France where it was supposed to be in favor of the poor, the workers. Even for the workers the identity problem is prominent and a lot have turned to us [the FN]. Scandals and corruption have discredited their moral position. Socialists absolutely need this upper moral position. One has to understand this in European politics.

Even in Britain, I think, such is the case. For example, when we entered the European Parliament we were surprised at the attitude of the British Conservatives. We thought that the British Conservative Party was a conservative party and thus opposed to socialism. We thought that on major social issues there would be some soft criticism, even in a polite way, even in a soft way, in a British manner, of the socialist principles. Such is not the case.[6]

[The Socialists] have the absolute need for moral superiority . . . Even the failure of their social and economic system, they need an ideology of substitution and in most cases that is antiracism, antiracism. Even if it is (imposed) in an artificial way, even in a totalitarian way. For example, about the Ford Report, the regulations of the parliament state very clearly that all committees, even extraordinary inquiry committees, must be open on a fair basis to all political groups. We were excluded.

HOLMES: Wasn't the Rainbow Group also excluded?[7]

GOLLNISCH: Yes. If there is one principle that is common throughout Western Europe it is the respect of the right of defense. In this committee we were constantly attacked, criticized, defamed without the possibility to respond. Well, of course, it was an inquiry committee, but what is an inquiry committee where only the prosecutors have the right to testify? It's incredible.

HOLMES: Weren't there a large number of outside witnesses brought in?

GOLLNISCH: Yes, yes, yes, yes, and always on the same side. There were in this report, there were precise and grave accusations including against Le Pen and our group. Only the prosecutors have the right to take part in the hearings? Anyway, we clearly stated that we considered this committee was outside the competencies of this parliament. It was not legally instituted. The term of the committee was extended illegally. Very clearly [parliamentary] regulations state that a committee of inquiry does not have the right to make recommendations to permanent committees. This also was violated. But all these are technicalities; what is important is that the result was very interesting. They saw racism everywhere, everywhere. Everybody was a

racist except perhaps Mr. Ford himself and his friends. To the point that
the president of the committee, Mr. Nordmann, M.E.P., who is a Jew, a
member of the Liberal Democratic Reform Group (LDR), was against the
conclusions of the committee over which he presided. Against Mr. Ford's
conclusions! I think it is really a very important ideological matter and a
passionate one. It is symptomatic; it will be at the very center of debates
to come.

HOLMES: Didn't Giscard d'Estaing, M.E.P., have a peculiar role?

GOLLNISCH: Mr. Giscard d'Estain, you know, Mr. Nordmann, who I
mentioned before is a member of his group [Giscard d'Estaing is a president
of the LDR], and he supported Mr. Nordmann. Because there was also a
small problem when they saw that Mr. Nordmann did not vote with the majority; they deprived him of the right to present the conclusions . . . There
was a big mess, obviously, because it was absolutely contrary not to the regulations but to the customs and well-established practice of the parliament.
So, Mr. Giscard d'Estaing, who is a rather quiet man normally, came to
the defense of Mr. Nordmann. We [the members of the FN] rather laughed
because Mr. Nordmann is a very strong so-called antiracist and this fight
among antiracists was refreshing to us.

HOLMES: What is your view of Mr. Giscard d'Estaing's role in the
parliament?

GOLLNISCH: Well, he is a clever man. He is a very clever man. He is
certainly intelligent, even brilliant in some ways. In my opinion, he completely missed . . . He comes from a bourgeois family. De Gaulle used
to say, when Giscard d'Estaing was the youngest undersecretary of state
in France—nothing to do with the American secretary of state as you
know—"the problem of Mr. Giscard d'Estaing is the people." Mr. Giscard
d'Estaing wanted to be liked or loved by the people, but he did it in absolutely the wrong way. Let's give an example. Just after his election there was
a ceremony and the president of the republic goes out of the Élysées Palace
and down the Champs-Élysées to the Arc de Triomphe with the horse
guards. There is much decorum. Giscard d'Estaing thought it was more
simple and less emphatic to do it in a normal suit and to go along walking
rather than in some official car with horse guards. He thought that workers
and people of the lower classes would greet [this gesture and think] how
simple he is, how close to the people. It was completely stupid. You know,
because to the contrary, people were disappointed. He used to take the
Metro in Paris. I say he used it, I mean he took it once or twice, with plenty
of photographers. His idea was of a big center that embraced two-thirds of
France. He stated very clearly, "France wants to be ruled at the center." The
problem is the center does not exist by itself. For these reasons he followed
a kind of social democratic policy. He did not dare challenge the monopolies

the Left had acquired at the time of de Gaulle, because of the deal between de Gaulle and the communists after World War II. That goes very deep in French history, you know. He did not dare challenge the prevalence of the Left in fields of culture, education, and so on. Finally, his own policies did not succeed that well, and he even lost the backing of conservatives who viewed his policies as liberal, I mean liberal in the American sense, with increasing public expenditures. When he travelled to Moscow he put flowers on Lenin's tomb; when Mao died, he said that Mao had been one of the greatest thinkers of all time and things like that. Because he thought that the Left would be grateful; they absolutely were not. So he lost his support.

HOLMES: So what has happened since he came to the European Parliament?

GOLLNISCH: Coming to this organization, well, he is intelligent, clever, very polite, and he has stature, undoubtedly. His problem is that he wants revenge, that's obvious, for his political failure. He can play two games. He can play the French internal style, maybe to be an alternative to Mitterrand. There are some Frenchmen who believed that after his loss to Mitterrand he was utterly discredited. But after the failure of his two former prime ministers [Raymond] Barre and [Jacques] Chirac [against Mitterrand], now there is some trend to consider that Giscard d'Estaing could make a comeback.

HOLMES: Le Pen must pose a problem for Giscard?

GOLLNISCH: Oh, yes, he is, he is. He tried to avoid attacking Le Pen. Mrs. van Hemeldonck, M.E.P., who is a member of the Socialist Group, said after Giscard d'Estaing criticized the Ford Report, because she, as a socialist, thought that it was because Giscard d'Estaing had a deal with Le Pen . . . Mrs. van Hemeldonck went on to state that "Mr. Giscard d'Estaing was nothing more than shit in silk stockings." It was a big scandal here. It is typical of the way the socialists react. It is not just that they do not permit anyone to challenge them, but that someone will dare to transgress the moral line that they have fixed.

The other game that Giscard could play would be to become the first president of Europe. That is what he is obviously trying to do. His problem . . . it is very strange, in France he led in the last [European] elections a unique list with the centrist parties, the UDF, and Gaullist parties mixed together, and he was the leader.

HOLMES: How about Simone Veil, M.E.P.?

GOLLNISCH: Simone Veil had her own list against Giscard which got about 8 percent of the vote. What is very surprising is that the day after the election, as Le Pen had predicted, by the way, the members elected on Giscard d'Estaing's list split with the Gaullist followers of Jacques Chirac joining with a few Irish and Spanish members to form their own group under Mr. de la Malene, M.E.P. (RDE). So Giscard d'Estaing was left with half the French group and he became the president of the liberal group (LDR). As for Mrs. Veil, who had constantly criticized Mr. Giscard d'Estaing, most of the people elected with her, seven or so, went to the Christian Democrats (PPE), and she joined the liberal group of Mr. Giscard d'Estaing. This is the kind of thing that makes the average person fed up with politics. They understand that this election was a mockery.

What he [d'Estaing] would like is to first become the president of this parliament. But certainly this very clever man has a fault. In this parliament there is a blockade because there is a deal between the Socialists and the Christian Democrats; they rule together and follow the Socialists' guidelines. The deal is there will be a Socialist [president] during the first half of the session and then a Christian Democrat. Knowing this, Giscard d'Estaing thought that his group, the liberal group with forty or forty-five members, and he tried to take most of his group into the Christian Democrats. It is incredible, the president of a group trying to betray his own group. It was known obviously among the members of his group and he came under very strong criticism. Even a man like [Jean P. M. O. G.] Defraigne, M.E.P., former president of the Belgium national assembly, he said all of this is an unfair trick. The maneuver obviously failed.

He is a very clever technocrat. He comes from this national school of administration (ENd'A) that prepares French elites to be high civil servants. Undoubtedly they are clever, they are intelligent, they are hard workers, and so on, but this is not enough to change things in politics. It can be enough to make one's way through the establishment. Mitterrand does not come from this mold.

HOLMES: Le Pen has a different background and different political temperament.

GOLLNISCH: Le Pen is different. I have read the criticisms of Le Pen in the foreign press. It says he is a political extremist supporting violence and things like that. It is not true. Le Pen is a true parliamentarian. You know, when I was in the French assembly, we succeeded in clever games using the regulations sometimes influencing legislation. But Le Pen is much more of a democrat than the average person realizes. He is a man who began his career under the Fourth Republic with so many changes and so many combinations. Mitterrand, too [began his career at that time].

HOLMES: Did you find the French assembly an effective institution?

GOLLNISCH: I won't say that. The big problem of the French Parliament is absenteeism. It is something like that here (at the European Parliament). Some times at the debates only a few people take part, but for *votes* like today there were at least 300 members, (out of 518) and the votes are strictly private. But at the French assembly, people turn the key and vote for others. Sometimes you will have six or seven persons [present] and 400 votes. You can lend your [voting] cards to other people; this is completely unconstitutional. It is against the constitution. Article 27 clearly states that the vote (of members) is strictly personal. Against the law, against the regulations of the assembly, but it is a constant practice. I opposed the practice one night. There was a whole night of filibustering at the national assembly. I was a member of the bureau of the assembly at that time and secretary of the bureau. As secretary I had the obligation to enforce the regulation [on absentee voting].

HOLMES: Did they need a written proxy?

GOLLNISCH: They must have a written proxy, yes, and a certificate from a medical doctor that they are sick. Obviously, there is absolutely no proxy and I knew it. At 2:00 A.M. I asked to see . . . [*laughter*]. There was a big panic.

HOLMES: Did you make a lot of friends that night?

GOLLNISCH: No, No. This made the headlines. All they could do was refuse [my request]. So I ordered the civil servants [working in the assembly] to collect the [proxies] and I said it was a felony if they were not produced. It was a tremendous mess and my personal behavior was compared in the newspaper to the burning of the Reichstag, the night of the long knives, and the . . . [*laughter*]. Well, there is this problem and this is a discredit to national assembly. But I must say in terms of procedures, respect for its own rules and the parliamentary game . . . it [the national assembly] is much more of a "parliament" than [the European Parliament]. For example, you will never see in the French parliament people [blindly] voting with their [political group] without knowing for what they are voting. When it comes to the French parliament, a text of law you have a general debate and after that each article of the bill is voted on.

HOLMES: Wasn't that what Mr. Le Pen was commenting on in the session today?

GOLLNISCH: Yes, yes, but here [the European Parliament], they divide the debate and the vote. In the French parliament, it is not so. So that normally [in the French parliament] you have the debate about the article, for example, anyone who has an amendment can defend the amendment. They can take five minutes to defend it. Sometimes we only have five minutes for a whole [political group] in the afternoon here, there are so many texts. You can defend your amendment [in the French parliament], the government gives its opinion, the *rapporteur* speaks for the committee, and after the vote, paragraph after paragraph, sometimes sentence by sentence, sometimes word after word. Obviously there are many fewer laws adopted than here. It is completely different. Have you been to the French national assembly?

HOLMES: No, but I have watched the public debate on television.

GOLLNISCH: Ah, yes, but what the television shows is only the session on Wednesday between 3:00 and 5:00 P.M., which is the time for the questions of the government. So they all gather at that time. It is really a circus, you know. Because of the presence of television, everyone comes. But at 5:05 there is no one left until the following week.

HOLMES: I have heard similar frustrations expressed by Belgian, British, and Italian politicians. Do you think there is a democratic fatigue in the political institutions of Western Europe?

GOLLNISCH: I am not so sure about Italy. Because what is very surprising, Italy seems to be an entirely anarchic situation, but it doesn't work so bad. Well, it's a great mystery. They are very clever. You know we have been discussing about race. Though I am from the Germanic part of France and I have Germanic genes, I have become more and more Latin since I have come here [to the European Parliament] (*laughter*). Because I think there is a big difference in mentality between the Germans and Latins, and the Anglo-Saxons are something else.

HOLMES: But do you think there are forces encroaching on democracy?

GOLLNISCH: What we consider from our point of view, we call it "soft totalitarianism" that seems to be growing in our societies. Freedom of expression about issues such as immigration or the history of World War II, it's incredible. They [the Left] passed new laws, you know, that the position contrary to Nürnberg should not be discussed by historians.

HOLMES: I think it is an outrage that a historian would deny the reality of the Holocaust . . . The professor was fined and put in jail. What exactly happened?

GOLLNISCH: Yes, he was condemned, he was kicked out of the university. He was assessed a huge fine that he cannot pay. He was reduced to a state of slavery more or less.

HOLMES: Can you tell me more about "soft totalitarianism?"

GOLLNISCH: Yes, it is undeniable about the Holocaust and the concentration camps of course . . . The professor wrote thousands of pages and he may perfectly well be wrong. But I find it really surprising that the new law sponsored by the communists adopted in France . . . Theoretically speaking, it is illegal to say that Katyan, you know the massacre [of Polish soldiers] in the Katyan forest, the responsibility does not lie with the Germans but with the Russians. In spite of the fact that Gorbechev himself admitted it. Because at Nürnberg responsibility for Katyan was placed on the Germans.

HOLMES: So, subsequent historical inquiry cannot be taken into account?

GOLLNISCH: About Katyan you won't be prosecuted in reality, but you should be according to the new law.

HOLMES: What exactly does the law encompass?

GOLLNISCH: One can not deny or criticize the decisions of Nürnberg, nor deny the Holocaust. But there is no definition of the Holocaust. I do not remember the exact wording.

> FORD REPORT. As for the newly introduced "offense of revision-ism" aimed at taking action against those who deny the Holocaust and the existence of gas chambers, it would only concern crimes against humanity committed under the Nazi regime and recognized as such by the Nürnberg Tribunal. [86]

HOLMES: So you see this as another example of the Left trying to maintain its moral dominance?

GOLLNISCH: Absolutely, absolutely, absolutely, and also the reason why is that the communists had a deal at the time of the liberation, at the end of World War II, with de Gaulle. De Gaulle needed the backing of the com-munists so that he could enhance his legitimacy in relation to Pétain . . . So there was a kind of official history that the communists played a leading role in the Resistance, but the fact is that the Communist Party only joined the Resistance after Hitler attacked Stalin. Before that they were against the war. There was much sabotage [of the war effort]. There have been entire books written, academic books written by a former communist, for example, all of them prove [this point]. Even the general secretary of the Communist Party in France, Maurice Torres, long before the disaster of June 1940, but in October of 1939, he was a sergeant (in the French army), he deserted, he crossed German borders and he reappeared in Moscow. But I ask you, when you are on the German front in eastern France, you disappear and one month later you are in Moscow, which part [of Germany] did you cross. It is a historical fact. Everyone in France knows it. He was, by the way, con-demned for this, he claimed he wanted to prepare the Resistance. That is very strange; seven months before, he understood the [German] invasion would succeed and the fall of France [would ensue]? . . . Mitterrand is an-other case. He was decorated by Pétain.

HOLMES: Decorated by Pétain?

GOLLNISCH: Yes, he was a high civil servant, though very young in Vi-chy. Because Vichy wanted young and clever men. He claims he was work-ing for the Resistance. In fact, it is true. It was the case with Mitterrand. He was both . . . I don't think it was opportunistic, because the fact is that all around Pétain, contrary to what has been written, was a much more compli-cated situation. My grandfather, who comes from a left-wing family, he had been a volunteer against Germany during the First World War and lost an eye. So with the Second World War, though he had been a officer, he was not mobilized. But helped people in Alsace. He had been the head of the manufacturer of tobacco here in Strasbourg. It was a state monopoly. So he was a high ranking civil servant . . . He was in Paris (during Vichy) and he had many people he helped from Strasbourg. He hid young Alsatians who did not want to serve in the German army. It was very dangerous. Until his death in the 1960s, he was in favor of Pétain because he thought Pétain was right to try to buy time and hold things [the country] together. It was very ambiguous. What is certain, there were some people around Pétain who wanted to side and fight with the Germans; they were a minority, and they were more likely to be in Paris than Vichy. Some wanted to resist the Germans in some way or other. Among this group was Mitterrand. Mitterrand plays the trick first in the Vichy organization to help the prisoners because he was the head of the agency that controlled prisoners of war. This is unsurprising. But within the scope of official history, if you say Pétain was a collaborator and pro-German and everyone who worked with Pétain was, then you cannot understand the behavior of Mitterrand. But if you say [the official history] is not the case, the communists are very interested in trying to prevent any free and critical analysis of the Second World War. Because one of the main political weapons of the extreme Left, and the Left in general, [is official history] against any right-wing movement.

HOLMES: In their view the Resistance was solely a left-wing phenomenon?

GOLLNISCH: Yes, [members of] the Left were the Resistance and hence they were good, while [members of] the Right were collaborators and hence were bad. [Members of the Right] cannot be patriots, because they betrayed France . . . This is very important, it is virtually taboo to talk about this in French politics.[8] If you were against communist domination in South Vietnam, you were right-wing. So you were a fascist. So you were a Nazi. So you were in favor of the extermination of the Jews and concentration camps . . . It justifies anything.

HOLMES: So you think the cold war created an oversimplified political morality?

GOLLNISCH: Yes, you had McCarthyism, you had the same thing in America.

HOLMES: Perhaps with the end of the cold war we can escape dogma?

GOLLNISCH: Yes, we could. The problem is the knowledge of history among young people in France is horrible. Though they are perfectly normal, nicer in a way than we were. My students are wonderful. But there is this lack of political culture, lack of memory, lack of historical background.

HOLMES: Dieter Rogalla, M.E.P. [a member of the Socialist Group], wondered if younger politicians, particularly those born after the war, understood the historical imperatives upon which the European Community was founded. Schumann's and Monnet's [the founders of the European Community] motives were pacifistic and fundamentally opposed to nationalism.

GOLLNISCH: It is our [the FN's] problem, I must say, very frankly. We opposed the technocratic elitist trend in this parliament. But, I personally have the feeling that it is absolutely necessary to have some kind of system to help thwart the violent confrontation of nationalism that led to the war.

HOLMES: So the challenge for you is to promote a nationalism that does not succumb to racism and violence?

GOLLNISCH: This is the big issue.

HOLMES: The centrist parties push you [the FN] to the political margins [with the issues of nationalism and race]. Doesn't that prevent you from having an impact?

GOLLNISCH: We have to deal with more practical problems. Such as what I call the problem that conservative parties refuse to conserve. By the way it is the same in Japan. But lets say the RPR [Chirac's Gaullist party] and the UDF, though we sometimes have interesting discussions with them and we very often notice that many of them share our views, it is a little like business. You see another shopkeeper taking your customers, obviously the temptation is great to say bad things about him. It is competition. Very harsh competition.

> FORD REPORT. The so-called Le Pen phenomenon has brought about some "respectability" in racist behavior under the cover of defending Christianity against Islam, national pride, family values, and the "natural principle" of priority to French people. The congress of his [Le Pen's] party at the end of March 1990 received such support and attention that the opposition Right (UDF, RPR, CDS, CNI), who held their Congress at the same time, proposed certain policy measures on immigration which were the same as those for the *Front national*. [59]

Suspicion

It is the character of political discourse that partisan positions are asserted as claims of truth. In virtually every interview that I participated, "facts" were asserted about which I was dubious or suspicious. Often I raised my doubts during the course of the interview in order to clarify the informant's position rather than to "correct" their errors. There were political positions elicited that I found distasteful. I am concerned with truth or falsity, but more preoccupied with the fact that various political claims are "real." That is to say, they represent convictions incubated by a segment of the European electorate—convictions by which meaning is conferred on the political contestation of post–cold war Europe. Precisely because these positions have become compelling frameworks for understanding contemporary political struggles, however unsavory these positions might be, they demand scrutiny.

In the complexity of this historical moment, competing "truths," whether licit or illicit, struggle for ascendancy. Under these circumstances informants actively reframe and recontextualize political positions, they do not merely inform. When political authority is in question and intellectual consensus in doubt, the ethical imperative is to draw the reader through these complexities compelling them to render discriminations. The aim is to obstruct easy ideological resolution or escape.

Allegorist of the Right

Enfolded in Gollnisch's conversation are many voices. There is a political voice rooted in a personal biography and family history, yet what is articulated extends beyond Gollnisch's personhood. His sensibilities coalesce around aspirations that are peculiarly French, those that have come to be associated with the Old Right and the New Right. In his depiction of the present, Gollnisch invokes fragments from two hundred years of French history. There are sensibilities in Gollnisch's vision that recapitulate political configurations that span the French Revolution, the Dreyfus affair, World War II, Algeria, Vietnam, the cold war and 1968.[9] His view of the present comprises a broad cultural critique of political outlooks and practices. The critique resurrects fragments of history permitting Gollnisch to trace the fatigued ideals that dominate the political discourse of the present. It is out of this cultural critique that Gollnisch creates a moral allegory that frames a distinctive political logic and passion. The instrumentalities of democracy render his voice and his allegory of nationalism representative of a segment of the French electorate.[10]

However, to the extent that the logic and passion expressed by Gollnisch resonate with political formulations unfolding across the continent, he speaks not merely as a Frenchman but as a European. This harmonics are arresting. The simultaneous recrudescence of nationalist discourse across Europe and the former Soviet republics recasts nationalism as a transcendent political sensibility. Thus "Europe" has become a preoccupation of the extreme Right and a template of their radicalism (see Le Pen 1989).

> Above all, perhaps, attention is focused upon the future organisation of Europe. But this is the decadent, technological, crypto-Christian Europe that the ND [*Nouvelle Droite*] has always attacked. We are a long way away from the Indo-European civilisation from which Europeans have according to Alain de Benoist [theorist of the ND], sprung, especially from the cultures, the mists and forests of northern Europe. . . . He [Benoist] believes that it is the duty of the radical right, rather than the radical left, to combat accepted ideas, assumptions and values, and so to challenge the camp-followers of conformity. [Johnson 1991:243]

The allegory embraced by the extreme Right rests on a view of nature, rent by constant struggle, within which an epic cultural contestation is unfolding. It posits familiar apocalyptic consequences for those who do not awaken to this mythic engagement. The allegory generates an axis of defiance pitting egalitarianism against human freedom. "The egalitarian movement which consists of levelling age groups, the sexes and peoples, is to be criticised in my view because it masks reality, which is based on inequality . . . The theme of equality strikes us as decadent" (Le Pen, quoted in Vaughan 1991:222). The collapse of socialist regimes of Central Europe and the Soviet Union is held up as vindication of this position. The allegorists of the Right create a heroic contestation in which they and their followers must engage human nature, race, nationality, ethnicity, and religion to restore human freedom, creativity, and dignity.

At a time when extant political agendas seem fatigued, the generative power of simple allegories to delineate meaning, align fears, structure passions, disfigure histories, and galvanize political action is awesome. It is the point at which cultural subjectivities overwhelm objective interests as the substance of political engagement. Modernist agendas give way to crude certainties of race, nationality, religion, and so on, as the terms of contestation. Allegorical frameworks, under these circumstances, become the instruments for defining the historical moment, etching its contradictions, and formulating a politics to master or exploit emerging realities. It is a politics that does not yield to gradualism and compromise; it unmakes preexisting relationships between political thought and action. It is a politics disengaged from or antagonistic toward the matrix of democratic institutions that sustain rational discourse. The parochialism of nationhood has become an alternative discourse in the wake of European integration. The civil war in Yugoslavia embodies this degenerative exigency in all its mindlessness and horror. For better or worse, politics has regained a creative ascendancy in a difficult fin-de-siècle.

Notes

1. The two most important theoretical texts on the history of the French Right are Rémond 1982, and Sternhell 1983. See also the chapters entitled "Left, Right, and Temperament," "National Socialism," "Jews, Antisemitism, and the Origins of the Holocaust" in Weber 1991.

2. This intellectual and cultural development is ascribed to the *Nouvelle Droite* (ND) and particularly in the work of Alain de Benoist and his organization, *Groupement de Recherche et d'Études pour une Civilisation Européenne* (GRECE), founded in 1968. This emphasis has yielded interesting affinities with cultural Marxists. Benoist claims to draw on the work of Althusser and Gramsci. A more politically oriented organization that was associated with the ND was the *Club de l'Horloge,* established in 1974 by graduates of the *École Nationale d'Administration* and the *Polytechnique* (Johnson 1991:234–44). One of the former presidents of the *Club de l'Horloge,* Yvan Blot, M.E.P., was also interviewed for this study.

3. The FN was actually established in 1972 out of rival right-wing groups (*un*

fourre-tout ideologique) and almost immediately split in two by 1974: the PFN, headed by Patrick Gauchon, and the FN, headed by Le Pen. The former slipped into obscurity, the latter garnered 10 percent of the vote in the local elections of 1983 (Vaughan 1991:217).

4. On 28 January 1988 the Fourteenth Chamber of the Court of Appeal of Versailles confirmed the ruling rendered on 23 September 1987 by the Departmental Court of Nanterre, which condemned Le Pen to pay a symbolic one franc indemnity to each of nine associations and three survivors of the deportation who filed complaints against him. In describing the gas chambers as a "detail" of World War II, the Versailles court ruled that it was "consenting to the horrible [event]." (Ford 1990:88).

5. Sue Carol Rogers has asserted that "as far as the French are concerned there is no racism in France." Quoted in Jones 1992.

6. Euro-Conservatives are British Tories who are significantly to the left of the Conservative majority in the House of Commons. Mrs. Thatcher disparaged her Members of the European Parliament as "Euro-ninnies," and complained that in going to Brussels they had "gone native."

7. The Rainbow Group (ARC) in the European Parliament, composed of M.E.P.s representing regionalist, nationalist, and environmentalist groups, was also excluded from the Committee of Inquiry.

8. "The dichotomisation of politics into right and left is an integral part of the Revolution's legacy to republican France. The full endorsement of the organising myths which underpin the regime is held to be the birthright of the left. In contrast, the ideological credentials of the right remain perennially open to challenge" (Vaughan 1991:211).

9. The affinities with the political and cultural configurations of the late nineteenth century seem particularly relevant to the contemporary vision of the French Right. See in particular Bredin (1986).

10. The notion of "moral allegory" in political guise was inspired by Walter Benjamin's analysis of Charles Baudelaire.

References

Bredin, Jean-Denis. 1986. *The Affair: The Case of Alfred Dreyfus*. New York: George Braziller.

Buck-Morss, Susan. 1989. *The Dialects of Seeing: Walter Benjamin and the Arcades Project*. Cambridge, Mass.: MIT Press.

Ford, Glyn. 1990. "Report Drawn Up on Behalf of the Committee of Inquiry into Racism and Xenophobia." Document A3-195/90. European Parliament, Luxembourg.

Holmes, Douglas R. 1989. *Cultural Disenchantments: Worker Peasantries in Northeast Italy*. Princeton: Princeton University Press.

Johnson, Douglas. 1991. "The New Right in France." In *Neo-Fascism in Europe*. Ed. Luciano Cheles, Ronnie Ferguson, and Michalina Vaughan. London: Longman.

Jones, Stephen. 1992. "Unity and Disunity in the New Europe." *Anthropology of Europe Bulletin* 6 (Spring).

Le Pen, Jean-Marie. 1989. *Europe: Discours et interventions 1984–1989.* Limoges: Les Nouvelles Presses du Centre.

Rémond, Réne. 1982. *Le Droites en France de 1815 à nous jours.* Paris: Aubier-Montaigne.

Sternhell, Zeev. 1983. *Ni droite, ni gauche: L'idéologie fasciste en France.* Paris: Seuil.

Vaughan, Michalina. 1991. "The Extreme Right in France: 'Lepenisme' or the Politics of Fear." In *Neo-Fascism in Europe.*

Weber, Eugen. 1991. *My France: Politics, Culture, Myth.* Cambridge, Mass.: Harvard University Press.

THE OUTLAW STATE AND THE LONE RANGERS

The international media have hailed Argentina's transition from the terror of its military regime's Dirty War, 1976–83, to its current democracy as successful. But the case of Argentina's problematic and internally contradictory return to democracy is a sobering one. The backdrop, the seven-year rule of the self-denominated Process of Argentine National Reorganization, has become synonymous in the international press with modern reigns of terror. The *Proceso,* as this dictatorship is often called by Argentines, has the dubious distinction of adding the word *desaparecido* to the world's vocabulary. It represented an important ideological presence on the Latin American scene, the National Security Doctrine as disseminated by the United States especially through its military assistance from the 1950s onward. National security states have been based on the idea that the world faced an ultimate war between communist and noncommunist forces. Each would wage this battle through nonconventional warfare with subversive forces internal to each nation.

In the wake of the ouster of the military as a result of the Falklands/Malvinas debacle, Argentines now have to their credit almost a decade of civilian rule, albeit under conditions of continuing severe economic instability. Yet major representatives of the dictatorship's violence are returning to political prominence via the democratic process. This is occurring in the tragic context of aborted efforts to bring to justice those responsible for the disappearances and terror. In spite of attempts at settling accounts with the perpetrators of violence, recent Argentine events continue to produce equally dramatic gestures of condoning them. Strong military candidacies could not occur had not large sectors of Argentine society been willing to accept or ignore a violent past. Yet these candidacies have arisen simultaneously with widespread majority opposition to the presidential pardon [*indulto*] of the members of the junta most directly responsible for that past.

In this context, I returned to Argentina in 1991, now under the aegis of

President Carlos Saúl Menem and his free market policies, to continue to explore a major avenue of my twenty years of research in the Southern Cone: new perspectives on the continuing weight of the experience of authoritarian rule in a reinvented democracy. This problem has taken on increasing urgency with the end of the cold war. Argentina, like the rest of the world, is facing a reorientation of its defense strategies after the demise of the National Security Doctrine and a concomitant reinterpretation of its deeply traumatic recent experience with totalitarianism. Because these processes began a half decade earlier than similar events elsewhere, their results may illuminate the present and near future in other parts of the globe, in particular Eastern Europe and the former Soviet Union. As figures associated with an authoritarian regime reemerge in democratic politics, Argentina's present plight may have disquieting implications for other democracies also riddled with social and economic crisis and sharing similar shadows of recent dictatorial pasts.

1. Fragments and Silences: Cultural Worlds

Argentina, traditionally an export economy with resources both plentiful and relatively well distributed over its population, has until the recent past displayed a standard of living and a level of culture that seldom fails to astonish the newcomer to Buenos Aires. Other Latin Americans have long resented Argentines' pride in facts such as the wide popular recognition in Buenos Aires of currents in European literature and arts at the same time or even before these trends gained acceptance in North America. They also resented the ease with which the relatively rich Argentines travelled to and from Europe, remaining completely ignorant of the South American continent and even the interior of their own country. Argentines themselves, in an immigrant culture that had occupied an area without dense indigenous populations, retained European values facilitating a flow of communication on which Argentine identity, not only among the elites but also in the vast middle classes, came to depend.

Yet today, communication between Argentina and the rest of the world, and even communication within Argentina itself, more and more achingly speaks to frustration at a reality they never had to face before: their physical distance from centers of knowledge and power in Europe and North America. Argentines felt themselves newly cut-off from these centers of power because they lack the necessary economic resources to continue to communicate via travel or expensive technology. The daily agonies of the gradual crippling of the working and middle classes and the ongoing economic crisis in the wake of the decade of dictatorial rule find no place in official statistics concerning decreasing inflation and economic growth.

Physical distance, contrary to ideas that the onslaught of technology has caused its collapse elsewhere, is more palpable in Argentina than ever. Communications technology may have once brought Argentines closer to each other and to other parts of the globe, but its current state of collapse and prohibitive cost is gradually cutting Argentines off, both among themselves and from the rest of the world. Among urban Argentines in particular, the increasing consciousness of this is new: the Latin American country "closest" to the Euro-North American "West" suddenly finds itself continually being reminded, by the value of airfares proportional to income, the delays of deteriorating mail services, and the high cost and low quality of the telephone services, that the distance from New York to Buenos Aires is roughly that to Istanbul. The Argentine South, the Patagonia dreamed of as the land of escape and promise in the spirit of the North American wild west, is so far from anyone else on the globe that foreign interests have designated it a dump for nuclear waste. Distances stretch with every budget that fails to cover a fax machine, every telephone call truncated with the announcement that "the lines to the country you are calling are full," and with every travel plan made to or through neighboring countries because even travel within Argentina is unaffordable. They swell with every hike in utilities rates, the dreaded *tarifazos,* and with every failure to obtain that second or third or fourth job and its dwindling wages to make up for the increases. Argentines feel ever more acutely that they can receive and transmit only fragments of messages, rendering their world isolated and incomprehensible in an ever more silent universe.

The new sensation of distance from the world perceived as the one that "matters" comes on the heels of other, different distances and compounds them. A decade of state terrorism (1973–83) atomized and threw into crisis Argentine identities as the dictatorship attacked political ties and allegiances and social bonds crumbled in a climate of fear. In the face of fragmented lives and broken ties, Argentines experienced an isolating social distance which continues to affect their way of life. But in Argentina today, distance is not only a metaphor.

In the aftermath of the decade of terror, perpetrated in the main by the military, the transition from totalitarianism to democracy has been difficult and drawn out. In turn, the political transition has largely been at the mercy of the economy's slide into hyperinflation in 1987–88 and the subsequent attempts to shore it up with renewed applications of free market remedies. With increasing hardship imposed on the home fronts of the middle and working classes, social chaos—the dreaded *estallido social,* "social explosion"—looms. Internal order is all too often precarious, and debates concerning personal security as newly pitted against civil liberties grow bitter. When chaos prevails, who has the right to impose his or her idea of justice as a self-designated Lone Ranger?

Against this backdrop, I proceeded in Argentina in 1991 as usual to contact informants, colleagues, and friends. My efforts were hindered by false starts. Some encounters never happened, and many turned out to be, in the Spanish turn of phrase, "disencounters." To a greater degree than I remember at any other moment in my eight years in Argentina itself, people again and again lamented the impossibility of transmitting what they considered significant information to outsiders and, often, with each other. Fragments, they felt, lead to misunderstandings, but fragments were all they had. Some insisted on rhetorical closure as a compromise for the sake of getting through to the outside world; others repudiated it, denouncing the idea that their chaos have a story with an end.

Negotiations for an interview with a prominent member of the former government of the military junta broke down when he claimed that he did not want to tell only part of his experience. Bits and pieces, he said, had led to a complete misunderstanding of the military government and his own role in it. He needed the opportunity to recount his story in its entirety in order to make sense; fragments were worse than nothing.

At the same time, I was pursuing a group of authors with whose members I had had independent contacts, but many of whom I had recently discovered formed a network among themselves. I was struck in particular by the professional and personal relationships among an academic in Buenos Aires, a critic increasingly based in major universities abroad, and an author known for his depictions of the life in the Northwest of the country, where he had returned to live after years of exile. Of the three apparently close colleagues, I seemed able to converse at length with only one, who continually promised a meeting with others that failed to materialize. Finally my friend burst out that, given the impossibly high price of internal travel in Argentina as well as the difficulties and cost of telephone communication, the three felt that they had been virtually cut off from each other. As they felt communication disintegrate among themselves, they had little to offer me.

Argentines do introduce some order into their interpretations of this chaos. One unifying theme that does this for some, counterintuitively for foreigners, is the identification of the national security state as guarantor of free market policies. In the shadow of hyperinflation in 1987, President Raúl Alfonsín, champion of the return to constitutional rule after the terror, hurriedly divested himself of the presidency by handing over power months early to president-elect Menem. To the growing disillusion of the Peronists who had voted Menem into office on a populist ticket and to the gratification of many of those who had voted against him, Argentines watched in disbelief as Menem's government explicitly and actively began to court big business, the

United States, the International Monetary Fund, and the World Bank with their application of free market policies and brutal belt-tightening policies for the economy. In all of this he was not unlike other major figures on the Latin American scene, most strikingly President Collor de Mello of Brazil and President Fujimori of Peru.

To the particular horror of the intelligentsia, crucial posts in the ministry of culture and related organs began to fill with figures closely related to the *Proceso.* Some reassured themselves with the theory that political plums had to be handed to conservative supporters of Menem, and culture was the area targeted this time around. Others, watching internal politics, some of which smacked of lines of censorship that had driven many to swell the Argentine "brain drain," discussed protest and the threat of return to exile. Military candidates began to appear on democratic ballots—not to be disavowed by Menem for two or three years. In 1991, on New Year's Day, Menem's presidential pardon, the widely opposed *indulto,* freed the members of the junta, the authors of the *Proceso,* who had been triumphantly imprisoned for life under Alfonsín.

Some Argentines began to construct scenarios that could account for all these contradictions, scenarios pulled together in bits and pieces in short conversations, comments to newspaper vendors, and reports of overheard information. These feed into beliefs that circulate as rumor and gossip, taking on a life of their own until proven wrong. They crystallize in cafes, labor unions, or kiosks to illuminate the news of the day not only in versions discussed by the extraordinarily high number of university graduates (the highest number proportional to the population in the world in 1979), but also by members of the relatively highly educated working class.

The resulting scenarios sometimes clarified the mysterious link between Menem and the junta. It was widely thought that state terrorism of the *Proceso* had expressly facilitated an overhaul of the Argentine economy along free market lines. The person on the street had felt these policies close to home, involving excruciatingly high prices. Ordinary citizens had also watched the extraordinary enrichment of members of the government and the upper classes through speculation's the *plata dulce,* "sweet money," of speculation, a phrase that defined the era. With all this affecting their daily life, for Argentines, Minister of the Economy José Alfredo Martínez de Hoz was at least as important and as nefarious as the jailed commanders of the armed forces. As an urbane member of the highest echelons of Argentina's elites, Martínez de Hoz was believable as someone whose long-term interests and loyalties lay with the foreign partners of the rich in a traditionally export-oriented society. As Menem turned the free market screws, with prices of staples and utilities soaring and families debating matters such as whether to omit a meal a day for their children, Argentines found Menem and his free market's "adjustments" reminiscent of Martínez de Hoz and his *Proceso*'s artificially strong currency, low tariffs, and the consequent flood of imports and sky-high prices.

This rumored link was further nourished by the popularized ideas of dependency and colonization that run riot in the streets of Buenos Aires, ironically characterizing discourses of nationalism both on the Left and on the far Right. The widespread nature of such ideas makes it difficult for many to dismiss out of hand an argument constructed largely by the Left in a country that is often described as characterized by right-of-center governments but by left-of-center popular culture.[1] The argument gos that the junta's practice of "disappearing" dissenters in conjunction with Martínez de Hoz's economic policies has been continued by Menem's harsh measures to increase growth and decrease inflation. These measures are ironically accomplished by presidential decree as is the case in democracies across the continent, including Colombia and Perú as well as Argentina. In fact, the connection between free market policies and authoritarian politics has been formulated in a popular Colombian news weekly: "political dictatorship is the continuation of economic neoliberalism through other means" (Caballero).[2] In Argentina it is believed that this connection is working the other way around, with the result that a middle class that once constituted 40 percent of the population is being quickly and savagely disappeared. The sinister logic that is thought through again and again like a puzzle that never loses its intrigue is the following: the physical elimination of dissenters and the absolute marginalization of consumers reinforce each other as tactics to reconvert the Argentine economy into one totally devoted to export of both primary goods and, with both the workers and the middle classes broken, cheap labor. This will then add to another traditional Argentine export, cheap brains.

So it was that, guided by street rumor and the common experience of needing to make sense of what seemed to many the frighteningly frequent reappearance of the skeletons of terror from democracy's closets, I found myself working through the paradoxes with someone who, colleagues and friends anticipated, would embody these paradoxes himself: Major Jorge Luís Mittelbach. Now a military figure known to have put his life on the line to condemn the strategies of the national security state, Mittelbach nevertheless has not renounced his membership in the armed forces of the nation that he defended. Loyal to his identity as a military man, Mittelbach is clearly an unusual—if not solitary—voice from the armed forces, while he also does not speak for civilian Argentines. Because of his heroic story, however, he is seen by many as embodying some of the most painful conflicts of the Dirty War and therefore as holding possible keys to understanding not only the past but possibly the present and future as well. Journalists and academics urged me to talk to

Mittelbach, whose story is not unfamiliar to other Argentines, who are likely to know that such a person existed even though they may not be able to identify him precisely.

At the present time the Argentine Armed Forces have placed Major Mittelbach under sanction for having refused to participate in the torture of prisoners during the Dirty War in the important province of Tucumán and withdrawing from active duty. The commanding officer in Tucumán whom Mittelbach confronted was General Antonio Domingo Bussi, who at the time of our first conversations was the front-runner in the democratic gubernatorial race in the same province only fourteen years after his controversial intervention there as the iron-fisted military governor under the then-ruling junta.

In the discussions that I finally arranged with Major Mittelbach, internal fragmentation echoed throughout national political events. The paradox of the return of Bussi to Tucumán—the appearance of the province's former military ruler on its current democratic ballot—was at that moment on the minds of Argentines all over the republic. It was in part for that reason that I had sought out Mittelbach. While Jorge Mittelbach discussed war with me in Buenos Aires, the nation held its breath in disbelief awaiting the outcome of the elections in Tucumán. Significantly, Mittelbach asked for a set of the cassettes of the recorded interview for a record of what he had said with a view to possible inquiry from armed forces. At the same time, perhaps particularly among the military, the status of foreign researchers suddenly changed in the face of increasing incommunication with the rest of world. From interlocutors of lesser or at best equal importance, many of us became the only vouchers of credibility as conduits of communication to the outside world. In this vein Mittelbach several times dropped the names of important European newspapers that had interviewed him.[3]

In my search for keys to the problems that besiege the transition to democracy in Argentina, I was attempting to explore further the Dirty War itself. Yet the endless reverberations of distance were intruding in new ways into the luxury that research has long represented for Argentines. Again, physical distance compounded by economic crisis complicated my task. In Buenos Aires I discovered that obtaining books about the Argentine Dirty War published in Uruguay, less than two hours away by hovercraft, was a virtual impossibility in Buenos Aires. Argentines cannot import and certainly won't be publishing these books; bookstores and publishing houses are collapsing. The author of a number of works I wanted finally devised with me an elaborate strategy: since she predicted that I would not be able to get through on the faulty and crowded telephone lines between Buenos Aires and Montevideo, she suggested that I call from the provinces one way or another, despite the price of

El triunfo de Bussi en Tucumán
circuló sobre la espalda del
sistema político como un chorro
de agua fría. Hubo quienes se
golpearon el pecho y otros que
golpearon pechos ajenos, pero la
reacción fue breve y quedó
silenciada por la crisis de
colectivos y la profundización del
ajuste. Algunos poseedores de
respuestas aseguran que el triunfo
de Bussi fue una tragedia
anunciada: no podía suceder otra
cosa en una provincia en la que la
crisis ha dejado de ser hace
mucho tiempo un eufemismo
periodístico, y donde los partidos
—por intereses pequeños,
confusión, y problemas de
memoria— se han aislado cada
vez más del resto de la sociedad.

Cover illustration of special news supplement, "Bussi: Why Did He Win?" (*Pagina/12*, 12 Nov. 1989), following an initial victory of General Antonio Domingo Bussi's party.

domestic travel. This done and arrangements made, I was to return to Buenos Aires, take the hovercraft to Montevideo, and arrive in person at a local bookstore or, better still, at the author's door.

The Nation Versus the Outlaw State

In his criticisms of the armed forces and the way they fought their war against subversion, Major Jorge Luis Mittelbach challenges definitions of war and the state. Believing that his nation was in danger and needed to be defended by patriotic soldiers, Mittelbach nonetheless confronted the military, in particular in the formidable person of General Bussi. The confrontation between Mittelbach and Bussi had occurred in the most dramatic form possible, in issues of life and death in the important northern sugar province of Tucumán. Tucumán's jungle hinterland, as well as its capital San Miguel, was the sight of some of the grimmest interventions of the Argentine Dirty War. Guerrilla forces attempted to declare the "Garden of the Republic," with its lush subtropical vegetation and vast sugarcane fields, a "liberated zone" in preparation for withdrawal from the Argentine nation. The military hailed the special identity of the province as the site both of the signing of the 1816 Argentine Declaration of Independence from Spain in the past and of the doom of the guerrilla warfare in the present: the junta dubbed Tucumán "Cradle of Independence; Tomb of Subversion."

The government forces under Isabelita Perón, soon to be deposed by the military junta, launched Operation Independence with spectacular violence, culminating in the explosion of a car loaded with bodies in downtown San Miguel, plastering the city's principal buildings around the central plaza with blood and severed limbs. The history of this initiative is complex, distracting, and, for obvious reasons, not well known. Despite its brutality, Operation Independence could be grasped by observers and participants as open warfare carried out by General Acdel Edgardo Vilas (1975). Vilas's initiative seems, in the memory of the people of Tucumán, to contrast with the nonconventional warfare introduced by Bussi as military governor of the province in 1976, although Bussi's image often merges in accounts, especially in the rest of the nation, with that of Vilas. Vilas is reputed to have virtually exterminated the guerrilla forces, leaving the twenty or thirty that Bussi fought. In the course of this latter action, Bussi disappeared 380 people. The reason for the change of command from Vilas to Bussi is not clear: I was told to try to weasle this information out of other interviews. Interpretations are considered risky dealing with something this serious when those responsible are capable of reappearing in positions of power in the future.

Widespread belief exists that the province swarmed with guerrillas at the time of the arrival of Bussi, in spite of the fact that in one year's time Operation Independence had left only twenty to thirty insurgents (López Echagüe 1991; Mittelbach, personal communication). This impression could have been fed by street battles with students who sympathized with the insurgency. Further, Bussi's regime continued its disappearings, undoubtedly leading some to think that the government could only be responding to continuing existence of more enemy forces in the jungles and canefields.

So war continued in Tucumán, waged, in the eyes of Major Jorge Luís Mittelbach, by soldiers at the orders of an outlaw state.

MITTELBACH: I had the idea of *el estado delectivo* [the outlaw state] perfectly clear because when I arrived in Tucumán, I came from serving—I was serving—in *Comando Arsenales* where I ended up because previously I had been aide to the commander of the *Brigada Blindada* at the base in Tandil. When there was that assault in the *Coordinación Federal*, at the time the general in charge—a personal friend of mine and of my brother—was chief of police. He had no choice but to resign and they named my superior from Tandil in his place. He said to me, "Well, Mittelbach, you will come with me as aide." I said, "No, *mi general*, I thank you very much for your recognition of whatever degree to which I may have served you satisfactorily . . . but I don't want to go into the police. I feel uncomfortable; I believe that I will be more useful to you practicing my profession in the usual manner and not in the police. I dont like this." And so . . . they sent me off . . . to rub me out, as they say.

In the *Comando Arsenales* at that time there were assaults and they were killing people . . . In *Arsenales* they had formed groups that went out at night obeying superior orders from the Chief of Operations of the *Comando Arsenales* which in turn came, I suppose, from the *Comando de Cuerpos del Ejercito I,* whose commander was "Little Bird" Suárez Mason [one of the most notorious criminals of the Dirty War].

So you can imagine that—I refused to join these groups. I refused because I knew that they went around kidnapping people, killing people, that they rode in stolen cars without plates . . . Then they put me in quite a special situation, as I see it. I received orders—they called and said, "You get everything ready . . . because you are going to Tucumán with a contingent that is leaving soon." I supposed that they were sending me to Tucumán so that one of my own troops would shoot me at some moment and I would appear dead, a hero, no? So I wrote four letters: a letter to my brother, and three letters to military colleagues, all of them friends of mine—where I said that I was leaving for Tucumán but that I supposed that I was going because—and I detailed the motives—I believed that they wanted to eliminate me. I left them with Pati [his wife] and told her, "Deliver these letters to each person and they should be opened if I—they kill me and I turn up dead, and then they should investigate how it was and under what conditions my death occurred."

3. Definitions of War: Your War Versus My War

So it was that Mittelbach arrived in Tucumán already fearing his own demise at the mercy of the "outlaw state." This state was in the hands of a military that was divided into the bands and factions necessary for the unconventional warfare against subversion. The armed forces fought in common for national security, but the strategically determined internal splits established lines along which more or less explicit rivalries arose.

Mittelbach spelled out his own concept of war contrasted with his growing understanding of war as waged by this outlaw state. The tale of his encounter with Bussi and systematic torture was built around a series of contrasts beyond the underlying opposition of the nation-state traditionally defended by the armed forces and the outlaw state: the Dirty War and its atrocities as contrasted with "real" war within human and legal limits; battle versus torture; military order as an end in itself as against order for the ends of production; a traditional esprit de corps cancelled out by a spirit of complicity; and criminal action that could be countered only by law in a "therapy of law, *a rajatabla,* across the board." Discussing Bussi's current political campaign with me in 1991, Mittelbach used the story of their past encounter to discredit the candidate through his link with the outlaw state of the time of the Dirty War.

MITTELBACH: When I arrived in Tucumán the only guerrillas still alive were a lieutenant, MacDonald, who was a right hand man of Santucho [leader of the Revolutionary Army of the People (ERP)] and three or four more who had some military rank. And then there were still five or ten—there weren't more than twenty in all—and they were smashed, militarily speaking. Yes, a group of only twenty, but they were deployed throughout the Tucumán jungle with all the concomitant logistical and intelligence problems.

When we arrived in Tucumán . . . after a long day of travel and cold they took us to the courtyard of the *Brigada.* They made us line up by seniority. I was among the most senior . . . They told us that we would have a military review there with General Bussi. Bussi arrived and so on: he kept us waiting about forty minutes—we were very tired, very beat . . . by such an extraordinarily long trip. And I thought, "One of two things: either they will leave me here in the *Comando de la Brigada* in Tucumán, or they will send me to the tactical command in Famaillá, or they will send me to task forces—but, no, what an idea—send me to the task forces! If they send me to the task

forces at the Santa Lucía Sugar Mill [troops were billed in the sugar plantations which served as bases], what will happen is what I—what I've been
thinking all along." So they read out each of our ranks and names and the
assignment of our destination. And when they said, "Major Jorge Luís Mittelbach: Second in Command of Task Forces—ah—of—ah—the Santa Lucía Sugar Mill," I said to myself, "*Kaput—kaput.*"

"*And*"—Bussi yelled at us and he shouted at us, such a disagreeable
thing—"anyone who doesn't obey my orders, I'll kill him personally with
my pistol," and he took out the pistol—something so, so, so, so, so disagreeable, so disagreeable and I said to myself, "My god. Why do I have to
be under the orders of this imbecile, this general who uses his rank to
frighten his subalterns instead of looking for communication that might
come from respect or affection?"—because other than these there is no way
to lead a subaltern to death at least . . . They put us in a bus, they took us
down Route 38, and each person got off where they showed him to. When
we got to Santa Lucía, I got off . . . I arrived about ten at night, practically
faint with hunger and dying for a whisky or a glass of wine or something
strong . . . and the chief of the force was a *compañero* of mine, who was
leaving two or three days later because I arrived on 23 May, the 24th they
were planning the ceremony for May 25th [national holiday] for the task
force and in the meanwhile I had to learn what I was to manage, since I was
Second in Command, *Oficial de Operaciones,* and *Oficial Logístico* I was
almost all the *plana mayor* [upper ranks] rolled into one.

So I said to him, "Why don't you put me up to date?" "No," he said.
"Look, man . . . calm down, rest up, around here there's nothing happening. Get some rest. Tomorrow we'll talk. I'll take you to the operations
room; I'll show you the map, I'll show you everything, I'll show you where
the combat groups are . . . You can ask me everything; you get yourself
completely informed about what you need to know." So I take my sleeping
pill—which I have taken for nineteen years, after an accident that was serious—I go to sleep. The room of the commander of the task force was—it
was a house because it was a sugar mill, and what had been the offices had
been transformed into a house that had three bedrooms, a kitchen, a patio—a dining room, and then it had other offices next to the place that was
the officers' casino.

I was asleep, worried, nervous, anguished, and all of a sudden I wake up.
I wake up because I began to hear screams. I get up and I go out to the patio
because I was hearing those screams from that direction. So I look out—and
I see a bunch of people . . . tied up hands and feet, blindfolded, some had
fallen down, others were lying down in unimaginable positions . . . I put on
my combat jacket, because I imagined that I had to intervene . . . and I
came up against a captain, in uniform, two subofficials, a woman who was

on a cot—it wasn't a cot, it was a bed illuminated with spotlights. She was nude, and there were some buckets of water around. And then I saw immediately an electric cattle prod and I don't know what all else. I yelled out, "But what are you doing here? What is this? What is this?" A captain presented himself before me . . . "*Mi mayor,*" he said to me. "We are interrogating a prisoner." "Listen to me, Captain," I said. "This is not an interrogation. You people are torturing a human being. Period. If, on top of that you ask questions and the person responds, it could become an interrogation. But this is torture, nothing more. I order you to stop it immediately, and as long as I am here in the task force, no such procedures will be carried out. Understand?"

He stood at attention and saluted me, because he could see I had put myself into my role as a military officer. I say, "Within two minutes I want lights out, you will go to sleep, the subofficials also, and the prisoners will go to the place that corresponds to their situation." And when I said that I thought, "But does it correspond to their situation that they are like this, tied up, blindfolded?"

I go to my room, I wake up the commander of the task force—indignant—and I say to him "Listen! What—what are you people doing here? I have just watched a hair-raising session of torture, torturing an older woman about sixty or seventy years old and her husband was waiting in the line and must be about seventy years old." He said to me, "Hey man, calm down. Is this the first time you've come up here?" "Yes," I answered, "and I hope I never ever come back. On top of which I don't want any part of this. I came to fight; I did not come to torture people." "Calm down, kid. These are things that have to be done. Keep in mind that we are at war." "No, listen: war has all the human limits, all the universal legislation recognized by the whole world, and these things are outside all the customs and laws of war. It's more than that: they are on the margins of humanitarian treatment that has to be given to any human being, even though he or she is a prisoner." "Well," he said to me, "go to sleep, Go to sleep and we'll talk." I did not sleep. I pulled myself together; went over to the dining room, lit a cigarette; served myself about ten glasses of wine to see if I could sleep even if drunk . . . and I guess I must have slept some.

The next day he said, "Come on, come on, come on—let's go to the *Sala de Operaciones*. I want to show you the map; the deployment of the task force; and the deployment of the other forces, and where the *Comando de Operaciones* is, and so on, and be careful because any minute Bussi will be here because he comes every day: the helicopter lands over there fifty meters off, and we have to put on all the right clothes and put on your helmet and you have to know how to receive him correctly and you have to have the troops in formation, and I don't know what all, and you have to be in charge of all that." "All right," I said, "have people ready there, with arms and everything ready, and when the helicopter arrives they should get in formation and give a salute, I'll go forward, you go forward—I suppose that's the way it's done every day." "Yes, yes," he said. "But orders have to be given."

We got to the 25th of May, and before he left, I asked him, "Who's coming to replace you?" He said, "He's a good chap." "Well," I said, "if you don't talk to him about the incident I mentioned, I will talk to him." "No," he said, "talk to him . . . I'm off; I've done my duty . . . but don't get so nervous." I said, "I prefer not to talk about this because it calls my attention to the fact that one army major could have standards so different from those of another army major in respect to moral behavior in their profession—or outside the profession. This is ridiculous." And he said, "This is war." I answered, "it must be your war. It's not mine."

The new fellow came, and as soon as he had taken charge, I said to him, "Lieutenant Colonel, I want to talk to you." He was a tranquil, parsimonious guy with the clear and defined glance of an astute person, almost mischievous. I said, "See here: I arrived three days ago, and the night I arrived, this and this and this and this happened." He said, "this type of procedure is used in all the task forces, in all the combat units." "Lieutenant Colonel, I have ordered that those procedures, as long as I am here as second in command of this task force, no longer be carried out. If this is not compatible with your form of command I would ask you to talk to General Bussi and tell him that I will not torture the POWs, and on top of this I advise you that for the task force, as part of its mission, according to regulations it is its duty when dealing with POWs to take their name, surname, number of their ID, address, and telephone number, if they have one. And with this information, the POW has to go to the next level up, the brigade, where there are war interrogators who are specialists in interrogation and they get the rest of the information that it is permitted to take from a POW. If General Bussi is not in agreement, they can relieve me of my duties and send me to Buenos Aires. But if I stay, here in the task force, this will not be done any longer." "Well," he said, "I'll go talk to the general. I'll be back in two or three hours and will bring the reply and orders and—I don't know—you had better be getting prepared because if you have to leave, you'll have to get your things together and you'll be out of here."

So the fact was that I began to get my things together. And making a human speculation, I thought, "If they thought they were going to kill me, here their plan falls apart. Unless the vehicle they send me in has an accident and as a consequence of the accident I end up dead. But shot dead I won't be. Unless they dissimulate a guerrilla ambush and they kill me and they say that it was MacDonald who did it and I go back in a coffin covered with honors and the Argentine flag." The new guy comes back and says "You can stay. The general says yes and orders that tomorrow you have all the POWs with their necessary documents and information and two trucks are coming and they will take them off . . . The day after this incident, I go with the doctor of the task force, who was a captain, and I say to him, "Captain, I want you to give me a detailed medical report on the state of health of each of the POWs. Further, they should take off their blindfolds; further, they should have only their feet tied up and their hands should be loosed . . . And a medical report should be left."

Meanwhile, I came upon a girl, tied up. I had them take off all the bonds, and I said to her, "Stand up, daughter." She was just a little thing. "What is your name?" "María." "And you, what are you doing here?" She was frightened. "I, sir, they captured me." "What? They captured you?" "Because—a week or so ago," she answered with a country accent, "the guerrillas attacked a column of troops and they put a revolver in my hand." A revolver! So I take out my pistol and I asked her, "Is this a revolver or a pistol?" "That's a revolver," she says to me. "This is what they gave you?" "Yes, sir." "And you, what did you do?" "Well, I was with my brother, and my uncle, my family—and when the soldiers arrived, we all fired. But my gun fell out of my hand." "The gun fell out of your hand? When the shot went off, you couldn't hold it?" They had given her a .45—a .45 to a baby. "So then," I said, "what happened?" "And then they made us prisoners." "How old are you?" "I'm twelve years old." So I said to her, "Do you know how to serve *mate* [tea widely used in Argentina]?" "Yes, sir." "From now on, you will be my secretary . . . You will arrange my room; I'll show you how . . . and you'll take the *mate* gourd and fix me *mates* when I tell you."

When I spoke to my superior, I told him, "Listen, Lieutenant Colonel, among the prisoners of war that I have to hand over, there's a child of twelve years. From what I've found out in these three days, over there at the foot of the hill behind the sugar mill, a lot of people were *fusilado* [executed] and buried. I didn't see it, but people have told me so. I don't know what will be the destiny of the POWs that leave my authority and who then go under the direct control of Bussi. But I would beg of you that for this prisoner of war, you take away her condition as prisoner of war, because she is not a POW, she's a child. She should go to an orphanage, or a nuns' school, where they educate her and give her food and they let her recuperate what she lost of childhood and innocence through these experiences that aren't children's experiences but those of adults. How are they going to execute someone like this? It could be true that she had a pistol and fired; but she didn't have any other recourse. What can a twelve-year-old do? Everyone around her must have received money, food, they must have received all the things the guerrillas gave to the people of the countryside to get their support. I would like to know where she goes . . . and confirm that she is all right, that someone will take care of her, and that she will grow up as God intends for children." Later this fellow informed me, "With respect to this girl, the general said that he would send her to an orphanage and there would be no problem."

And there I stayed waiting very attentively to see what was going to happen. Because I said to myself, "I have reached the limit of the army's capacity of putting up with what could be identified as insolence on the part of a major who has been refusing to perform as expected for two or three years, and who, in full deployment already in the jungle, already in combat, demonstrates what looks like disloyalty." Time passed; the order to relieve me came; and I left. I got to Buenos Aires, tore up the letters, I talked with the people I had written the letters to . . . Really it had seemed to me that I was being sent to the firing squad under the pretense of heroic action.

One reaction to the outlaw state is a more generalized perception at present in contrast with that moment in the past—I believe we are observing more distance taken by the younger ranks . . . at the rank of captain and below, modern captains. Because some of the older captains—ten years ago, no fourteen years ago—were lieutenants and sublieutenants. They were in the middle of all this, and they were obliged to do lots of things. Remember, in our previous conversation, I told you that then, more than an esprit de corps, there had been a spirit of complicity in the armed forces, which is very different. It was a spirit of complicity that was encouraged from above by the leaders because they made everyone go to the torture chambers in their units and regiments. Each officer had to do some of the torturing so that no one could deny and so that no one could tell stories. This has had so wide a reach that it is spine-chilling and . . . denigrating for me.

4. Fragments and Silences: Security Forces from Battles to Disappearings

For Argentina, changes in armed forces themselves may reflect a fragmentation of security forces parallel to the fragmentation of cultural worlds. Nonconventional warfare, waged by counterinsurgency forces for the sake of national security, like the guerrilla warfare it combats, is carried out to a great extent by "bands," factions, vigilantes. Units and their members with such a Lone Ranger mentality can spin easily out of control.

Military action in the Malvinas (Falklands), Argentina's only conventional war in one hundred years, did not strengthen the unity of the armed forces against their external enemy in defense of national sovereignty. Conscripts reported their horror at battle in the Malvinas after being limited to counterinsurgency training and their realization that this was not the war they were taught to fight. Defeat deepened existing internal divisions within each branch and among the different forces. After the defeat, most units had to confront serious insubordination. Military uprisings occurred under the democratic regime but were mainly addressed to the Joint Chiefs of Staff. These mutinies were led by Malvinas veterans.

Meanwhile, Aldo Rico, one of such leaders and a former commando in the Malvinas, became the third political force—and, in some important electoral districts, the second—in the provincial elections of September 1991. While General Bussi lost by a narrow margin in Tucumán in what was probably his last electoral performance, Rico's first astounded the nation with its success.

Other military candidates have emerged from the Dirty War into democratic politics in the provinces of Salta and Chaco. Their popularity, along with that of Bussi and of the Malvinas veterans, may have to do with the fact that Lone Rangers are not found only in the armed forces. Several factors have contributed to the appearance of a vigilante mentality in the civilian population where its justification is hotly debated. For some, the terror of the *Proceso* left a legacy of distrust in the state's implementation of law. For most, the social chaos unleashed by the economic disarray of almost a decade of democracy has greatly undermined faith in protection provided by the law and its enforcers. When a young girl's body appeared tortured and raped in the interior province of Catamarca, a congressman, the father of the accused killer, defended his son by announcing to the news media that clearly the villain could not be someone in his family. Had the murderer been his son, the politician continued, all the evidence including the body would have disappeared. Over the next year, a nun who had been a teacher in the girl's high school led protest marches that finally resulted in the total modification of the federal police intervention and the fall of the provincial government. The lessons concerning the criminal elements harbored by the law and the nature of successful measures for obtaining justice were not lost on a nation whose attention had been rivetted by "the crime of María Soledad," the fifteen-year-old victim.

In some of the more exclusive neighborhoods in Buenos Aires, especially on the outskirts of the city, mothers struggle to explain to their children the nature of the privately hired guards: "No, darling, he is not exactly a policeman. He can't shoot anyone." "But then what good does he do?" In 1990, in a striking parallel to the New York subway shooting involving Bernhard Goetz, controversy exploded over "the case of Engineer Santos," the owner of a comfortable middle-class "chalet" in Buenos Aires who, discovering two young men about to rob the cassette player from his car in the wake of the robbery of several previous sets, pulled out a pistol and shot them both dead. Santos was fiercely defended by Argentines who felt his actions had been his only recourse, while other indignant citizens labelled him derogatorily as "vigilante" and *llanero solitario,* "Lone Ranger."

So questions remain in Argentina. To what nation do citizens owe their loyalty and is this the "nation" that counterinsurgency forces defended? The answers point toward very different Argentinas. The latter was one quite different from the community whose sovereignty soldiers thought they defended in Malvinas, but this, according to veterans, was something they discovered only through doing battle in the Malvinas themselves. They brought home from the battle for the archipelago disturbing questions that Mittelbach's protests echo. Patriotic war, as Mittelbach and the Malvinas soldiers conceived of it, may be strategically irrelevant in defense of national security. Nonconventional warfare may necessarily redefine the nation. As the cold war and, with it, national security doctrines fade into the past, their imprint on diverse communities may prove indelible in unexpected ways. Certainly, Mittelbach's outlaw state is a nation-state changed, fragmented, and devoured from within by its defense against subversion.

5. Memories of War: Tucumán Versus Buenos Aires

Disputed memories and definitions of war riddle recent Argentine history with lacunae. *Porteños* arriving in Tucumán are shocked to hear *tucumanos* refer casually to events "during the war," an understanding that implies something quite different from an identification of the same era from the point of view of the inhabitants of Buenos Aires as "under the junta" or "during the *Proceso*." Similarly, more ambiguity is allowed by harking back to the guerrilla forces rather than to the "subversives."

Tucumanos tell tales never heard in the capital of their country. They tell of witnessing eighteen-year-old army draftees who wept as their government transports ground into gear, starting on their way to battles that never appeared in the next day's newspapers. They report challenges carried down from the guerrillas in the hills to the temporary barracks of soldiers on the sugar plantations: "If you're *macho* you can find us waiting above the dam." And they remember gruesomely burned guerrilla fighters making their way from hideouts in canefields in flames to beg for medicine.

Unlike *porteños, tucumanos* have vivid memories of the initial arbitrary violence of the federal police sent from Buenos Aires to clean up the province. After the insolence and abuse of the police, provincials remember relief offered by the arrival of the army to replace them, an army that brought what by contrast seemed to be law and order with a sense of due hierarchical chains of command. Significantly, this is recalled by many as the context of the arrival of Bussi.

At the same time, the guerrilla forces had a high visibility in Tucumán where their members engaged in maneuvers in military garb with rank displayed. Many remember them as troops like any others, hierarchical forces engaged against others like them in conventional warfare. Country dwellers in Tucumán remember the army and the guerrillas engaging in identical tactics in some respects, leaving the *tucumanos* caught in the middle. To starve the guerrillas out, the armed forces rationed food to people living in the foothills just below guerrilla positions. In this way, the government troops reasoned, disloyal support for the guerrillas could be detected or prevented, as there would be no food to spare. A supporter of the insurgency would go hungry with his family if he passed food on. If he were caught, he could be attacked or taken prisoner with the guerrillas. But *tucumanos* recall that while the government threatened violent sanctions if they fed guerrillas, the guerrillas would threaten the same if they did not obtain the food they demanded.

A decade later, when I asked *tucumanos* how they handled social events where violently opposing political views were represented by close friends and relatives, they answered with a tired compassion. "We the *tucumanos* have become lost; we no longer know where we stand." Throughout the rest of Argentina, opposition of the *Proceso* often finds a voice in the famed protests of groups of mothers, originally initiated by the Madres de la Plaza de Mayo in Buenos Aires. Alone in the republic, Tucumán's mothers have been silent, unable to organize the groups brought together elsewhere to contemplate the past together. Meanwhile, the displays of Argentina's only public Museum of the [war against] Subversion appears at the elite Rural Society's annual fair, a key event in an agricultural area of an agricultural nation, where the presence of the museum's memories may all the more effectively enforce the silences of others.

6. The Phantom Regiment

On the eve of our conversation in Buenos Aires about Mittelbach's experience of the Dirty War in Tucumán, the official 1991 celebration of Independence Day was held in Tucumán and broadcast to the rest of the nation. This was ostensibly due to the desire to make the day truly "national," involving the provinces as well as the half of the population residing in the capital. The gesture also recognized the original signing of the Argentine Declaration of Independence in Tucumán itself. Widespread opinion, however, attributed the provincial celebration as a gesture of support from the government of President Menem for the opposition to General Bussi's gubernatorial candidacy.

Residents of Buenos Aires desultorily watching the hours-long parade of military contingents, folk dancers, and gaucho clubs telecast from the streets of San Miguel de Tucumán did double takes as a troop in civilian dress marched across the television screens of the capital, identified as "excombatants of the war against subversion." In Buenos Aires, eight hundred miles away, where the words *war* and *subversion* are not heard, the announcer might have been speaking a foreign language. A brief scandal ensued in the media of the capital, but in Tucumán only weeks later, I encountered silence. There had been no mention of the "excombatants" in the major news coverage, and *tucumanos* seemed barely able to remember them. But in contrast with television viewers in Buenos Aires, many of whom reacted as though they had seen a ghost, some *tucumanos* reacted in turn to the reaction in the capital in a somewhat perplexed fashion, telling me that they were sure that they had heard of or seen this contingent "somewhere" in Tucumán before. Back in Buenos Aires, still later, the episode had been forgotten.

In which war had these excombatants fought? Was there a war or wasn't there a war? Whose war is it? And how does one define the Argentina for which it was waged: nation, national security state, neither, both? As communication breaks down, these questions increasingly are answered by silence.

> THE UNFORGETTABLE PARADE—Buenos Aires, 10 July 1991. Watched by President Menem and the presidents of Uruguay, Bolivia, and Paraguay, hundreds of gauchos, Syrian odalisques, and "excombatants against the subversion paraded [in Tucumán]." . . . Behind the veterans of the Malvinas/Falklands War, the "veterans of the war against the subversion" filed in their debut in civic-military parades. Dressed in civilian clothes, which leads to the supposition that this had to do with exconscripts and not the military, they commemorated Operation Independence, the *tucumano* version of the Repression, although the person who had been their leader at that moment, Antonio Domingo Bussi, kept himself on the margins of the official acts after stating that it was only a "carnival." [*Pagina/12,* 10 July 1991, pp. 4–5]

Notes

1. Argentine sociologist Carlos Waisman of the University of California, San Diego, after characterizing this cluster of ideas as gossip of the intelligentsia in Buenos Aires cafés, went on to suggest that they would be found in publications of the Communist Party and of MAS, the left-of-center coalition that includes socialism. Further, he pointed out, these views would be found not only among students on the Left but also among young people of the Radical Party [liberals, in North American terms].

2. This parallel and the role in it of the use of the presidential decree in Colombia, Peru, and Argentina were brought to my attention by Santiago Villaveces. On *decretocracia* see Seone 1992.

3. This was an experience shared with Argentine anthropologist Rosana Guber, whose ongoing research concerns the veterans of the Malvinas War. In the course of her investigations she has interviewed informants from the entire gamut of the military hierarchy. I have incorporated insights I owe to our conversations throughout.

References

Alvarez, Chacho. 1989. "Alerta en Macondo." *Página/12,* 12 Nov., p. 17.

Caballero, Antonio. "Fujimori, modelo para armar." *Semana,* 21 Apr., p. 8.

Eliaschev, Pepe. 1990. "Nuestro Hitler cotidiano." *Página/12* (22 June): 11.

Granovsky, Martín. "El trópico de Bussi: La crisis tucumana." *Página/12* (25 Mar.): 12.

López Echagüe, Hernán. 1991. *El Enigma del General Bussi: De la Operación Independencia a la Operación Retorno*. Buenos Aires: Editorial Sudamericana.

Seone, María. 1992. "La ley del deseo." *Página/30* 3 (Aug.): 19–26.

A TERRIBLE COMMITMENT: BALANCING THE
TRIBES IN SOUTH AFRICAN NATIONAL CULTURE

At the height of the politican crisis in the late 1980s, one observer compared South Africa to a time bomb which the government had constructed in its own basement and from which it was now desperately and delicately trying to remove the detonator before it went off. An apt metaphor, but unhelpfully simplistic in an increasingly complex situation in which social identities, public perceptions, and the *terms* of political discourse are key instruments in the widening contest over wealth, power, and the public allocation of resources. South Africans have naturalized, paradoxically, the notion of *difference* in culture, affiliation, and social condition encoded in the fundamental essentialism of race as a unifying framework of collective existence. Condemned by experience and a stereotypic history to at best a working misunderstanding, South Africans (an identity which blacks have only recently been legally granted, under duress, by whites), respond to the obduracy of difference with competing urges to paper over, legitimize, and exploit it. The likely inheritors of power hope to decapitate and cauterize the hydra of sectarian murder with a nationalist vision of a color-blind, "nonracial" utopia. Others of all shades are existentially ill at ease with an abstract notion of *civitas,* perceived as foreign in every sense, and cannot imagine a community of undifferentiated "citizens," never mind how, by whom, or for what purpose difference has been created. Those South Africans, fearing the exclusion of what they most hold dear from the new dispensation, envision a multiglot rather than polyglot republic without *necessarily* greater cynicism or less idealism than their "nonracialist" (nonculturist?) opponents. But the origin and provenance of difference does have material significance, because as Renato Rosaldo observes in the final lines of *Culture and Truth,* "All of us inhabit an interdependent late twentieth-century world marked by borrowing and lending across porous national and cultural boundaries that are saturated with inequality, power, and domination" (217). This is why *nonracial* has positive valence in public discourse as a term that sets aside hierarchies of sociobiological categorization, while *multiracial* (and by extension, *multicultural*) carries the negative associations of government-sponsored subordinate subnationalisms and the "separate but equal" mystifications retailed under apartheid.

If this were all there was to it then the inventions and mystifications could be disposed of by their exposure and the excavation of the interests that lie beneath them. The efficacy of such deconstructions, predicated on a postcolonial recasting of anthropological subjects as autonomous social actors, is brought into question by the at once valorized and implicit identification people have with reified, interested notions of group culture, history, and belonging. Unavoidably, the instrumental and strategic aspects of identity are naturalized in the thoughts and feelings of those who appropriate and act upon them. This contradiction can be reconciled within an anthropology of practice by approaching expressions of ethnic identification as internalized, inextractible constituents of the self and social reality as well as resources for conscious mobilization. Naturalized and rationalized dimensions of culture do not function as a duality: *ubuZulu*, "Zuluness"; reified constructions of Zulu identity and "tradition," is the rhetorical stock-in-trade of prophets and princes, proletarians and politicians *because* it is the symbolic embodiment of an internalized, self-defining moral imagination. So these voices from a divided society in search of its selves present problems of polytranslation. Politicians invoke individual responsibility and social equality, but essentialism and opacity, what Rosaldo calls irreductible "cultural force" (2), are closely associated with popular conceptions of personal and local autonomy. Cosmopolitanism, valorized by an increasingly multiracial (hardly nonracial) elite, is inverted as deracination by ethnic loyalists who would prefer to live—and die—as Afrikaner or Zulu and not simply as the inheritors or the "wretched of the earth," thank you very much. The people in whose faces social chaos is physically exploding are suspicious of the bomb disposal squad: while rapidly gaining black and brown as well as white members, Saville Row suits seem to some an unfortunate choice of uniform (hung next to brass hats and braid in the closet?).

Problematic too is the notion of a "culture of resistance," so popular with the internationalist Left in South Africa, based on a definition of political consciousness as class identity born of common oppression and galvanizing opposition to a common enemy. As anthropology has demonstrated, consciousness is both deeper and wider, more implicit and experiential, than that. So people resist through culture whatever and whomever they perceive as devaluing their culturally inscribed humanity, as well as and sometimes more than they do an expropriative political economy and its beneficiaries: the black fellow-sufferer in the ghetto more than the white policeman, bureaucrat, or employer in the suburb. The ongoing political debate over culture-as-resistance provides the broader context for the discussion of this issue in the conversations below. The idea expressed by virtually all the participants that culture ought to function organically and not instrumentally in South Africa's process of ideological liberation has its most prestigious and forceful champion in Albie Sachs, a lawyer, liberation movement hero, and member of the National Executive Council of the African National Congress. Sachs's position paper, "Preparing Ourselves for Freedom: Culture in a New South Africa," created a raging debate in South African intellectual circles in 1990 by urging that the ANC's constitution not be applied in the field of culture, and calling for a total moratorium on the use of the liberation movement's shibboleth, "Culture is [only] a weapon of the Struggle." [1]

The final problem concerns cultural borderlands, a conspicuously dangerous territory inhabited by all the participants in these conversations, including, of course, myself. That's partly why they were chosen: each lives or has lived and worked in a cultural milieu significantly different from that in which they were raised; each is able to view the cultural contexts of self and other reflexively by virtue of having made these border crossings, many times. Which is not to suggest that any of them, with the possible exception of Bongani Mthethwa, have ever inhabited secure, bounded, systemic, self-identified cultural environments in either the first or second place. Here then, are the interlocutors:

Primary voice: Jonathan Clegg, consummate performer/composer and leader of the popular South African "Zulu rock" band Savuka ("We Have Arisen"), and former leader of the famous but now-defunct band Juluka, has been a friend of David Coplan since 1975. At that time Clegg was a young acoustic guitarist in a duo with Zulu guitarist, dancer, singer, and composer Sipho Mchunu, a migrant worker and domestic servant in Johannesburg. Clegg had learned the Zulu language as well as Zulu guitar music and male migrant Zulu dance styles in the workers' hostels around Johannesburg. By 1983, Juluka had progressed from cabaret and coffee house curiosity to one of South Africa's most successful performing ensembles, touring Europe and the United States as well as South Africa, and recording several successful albums. Clegg, meantime, had an honors bachelor's degree in social anthropology from the University of the Witwatersrand in Johannesburg, based on a thesis on Zulu migrant dance styles, and was lecturing in the same department part-time. He is the author of several rich and insightful articles on Zulu dance and "traditional" guitar music.

In the 1980s, Juluka and its successor Savuka (organized after Sipho Mchunu ended his fourteen-year musical association with Clegg) spoke for a new generation of young South Africans eager to venture across cultural and racial boundaries, and so to undermine the domination of these categories in both public discourse and personal life. With professional success came paradoxes and problems. Clegg was attacked by the government for violating the

Johnny Clegg in his office. Photo
©Karen Petersen.

spirit if not the letter of apartheid policy, and his recordings were banned from
state broadcasting, officially for "insulting the Zulu people by pretending to
play their music" (read, for embarrassing the authorities by deliberately de-
racinating himself, preferring a black culture to his own, and generally letting
down the side). Simultaneously, he was shunned by some left-wing political
activists for promoting "tribalism" and ethnic divisiveness by giving publicity and validity to "parochial" aspects of rural-based Zulu culture. Yet
when the organizers of Nelson Mandela's seventieth birthday concert at Wem-
bley Stadium in London in 1988 refused to allow any South African musicians
to perform, citing the United Nations cultural boycott, Winnie Mandela (still
a hero of the Struggle herself) vouched for Clegg's progressive bona fides and
urged Savuka's reinclusion in the event.

Clegg's conversation is a blend of profound ethnographic experience and
comprehension, engaged intellectual analysis, and a cultural politics somehow at once both worldly and naive. His description of his introduction, at
age fourteen, to African migrants' performance in Johannesburg, is an in-

genuous exposition of the ethnographic mystery and of the purpose of cultural anthropology and is among the best in the genre. The quality of his partici- pation, at that time mercifully unshaped by professional training, and his ap- plication of that participation to the practicalities of the entertainment industry in a racially stratified society, makes him both self-alienated interlocutor and organic intellectual, self-conscious outsider and habituated insider, among both his white and Zulu peers. In recent years international success has prompted efforts to explain both himself and his diverse compatriots to Euro- peans and North Americans. At the same time Clegg has involved himself in the political culture as well as the culture of politics of the liberation move- ment, helping to found and lead the South African Musicians Alliance in the mid-1980s. No one more nearly comprises in his own person the creative energy of contestation, contradiction, and conversation in South African cul- tural discourse than Jonathan "The White Zulu" Clegg.

First parallel voice: Bongani Mthethwa, a professor of music at the Uni- versity of Natal, Durban, a department which has recently added both jazz trumpeter Hugh Masakela and Zulu vocal composer and Ladysmith Black Mambazo leader Joseph Shabalala to its staff. Professor Mthethwa was tragi- cally murdered in Kwa-Mashu Township, Durban, in May 1992. I am pro- foundly grieved by the loss of this fine gentleman and scholar and present the excerpts from my conversations with him as his final intellectual and personal testament. Mthethwa's family was working class, semirural, Zulu speaking, and affiliated with the independent Church of the Nazarites, otherwise known as the Church of Shembe, after its prophet and founder, Isaiah Shembe (d. 1916). Mthethwa was a respected educationist trained in both Western classical and Zulu composition, an ex-factory worker and a self-described tribalist as well as a Christian. He was a staunch defender of Zulu ethnicity who nonetheless viewed the syncretist revelation of the Shembe church as the ideal integration of British and Zulu cultural morality and spiritual principles and practices. One is struck by the sincerity with which Professor Mthethwa asserted seemingly contradictory positions, mirrored in a life seemingly too individualistic and peculiar to be supported by the values he professed; but support him they do. He early determined to master Western classical music and pursue a musical career despite the complete lack of precedent or sym- pathy for such a course in his own community. Yet even that wayward persistence he attributed to the "Zulu stubbornness" inculcated by his "tra- ditionalist" elders. Mthethwa promoted the ethos of Western education and academic research, while subscribing to the *ubuZulu,* indigenous Zulu culture which his Anglican missionary teachers excoriated and suppressed. Mthethwa is coauthor, along with Absolom Vilakazi and Mthembeni Mpanza, of an anthropological biography and doctrinal study of Isaiah Shembe entitled *Shembe: The Revitalization of African Society* (1986). Intensely critical of the demagoguery, ethnic politics, and violent tactics of KwaZulu homeland Chief Minister Mangosuthu Buthelezi's Inkatha Freedom Party, Mthethwa still honored and supported Chief Buthelezi personally as a man who knows and practices *ubuZulu* and occupies important statuses and roles within the Zulu aristocracy. Like Jonathan Clegg, Mthethwa was intensely conscious of the mutual antagonism and cultural disjunction between rural and urban Africans in South Africa, and of their poorly developed notions of national citizenship and identity. He was dismissive of Nelson Mandela, of the African National Congress, and of attempts to cultivate the image of an "international man," a person without subnational ethnic identity. He argued instead for an "enlightened tribalism" of mutual group tolerance, since the very notion of "one person, one vote" is a potentially conflict-generating fiction in a region where the majority of the population do not think of themselves politically as individuals. He may be right, though it is unclear just how he would have accommodated South Africans such as Hein Willemse who do not see themselves as belonging to any of the subnational categories in which those who retail a discourse of "group rights" might wish to place them.

Second parallel voice: Hein Willemse belongs to that segment of the South African population officially classified as "Cape Colored" (mixed race) under the terms of the Population Registration Act (1950), a central piece of apartheid legislation repealed in 1991. Like many so-called coloreds, his first language is Afrikaans, a Dutch creole spoken by the politically dominant segment of the white population. Somewhat untypically, he was not raised in a single, close-knit, socially rooted race-based colored community, but moved about with his family a great deal as a child. At university in the mid-1970s, he attained both political and racial consciousness as a member of Steven Biko's Black Consciousness Movement, led by Biko's South African Students Organization. He is Chair of the Department of Afrikaans/Nederlands at the University of the Western Cape, a campus once reserved exclusively for coloreds under apartheid education policy, but more recently registering a student population which is over thirty percent black African (Xhosaspeaking) and whose rector has proclaimed it "the intellectual home of the Left." Willemse thus combines a passion for the Afrikaans language and its literary potential with a political commitment to Pan-Africanism and black nationalism. His chief intellectual interest is black Afrikaans writing, especially poetry and oration, and he is the author of numerous articles in both Afrikanans and English on the contemporary status of black Afrikaans language and literature. No picture of South African culture would be complete without a focus on Afrikaans, but Professor Willemse addresses it not from the point of view of its white apologists, but from the distaff side of an oppressed, client category (colored and black) who nevertheless comprise a slight majority of Afrikaans speakers. I spent 1991 teaching in Cape Town, and I was determined to include this experience in my conversations. People classified colored make up the majority of the population of the western Cape of Good Hope. Tracing their descent from indigenous *San* (Bushman) foragers and *Khoikhoi* (Hottentot) herders, Dutch and other European settlers and travelers, Indonesian, Indian, Madagascan, and Mozambican slaves, they are Christian and Muslim in roughly equal numbers. They have never historically defined themselves as colored, a residual segregationist category for the human products of a process of master-servant miscegenation that was not, by all the whites held holy, supposed to have occurred. Instead they implicitly regard themselves as the Cape People, *Kaapies*. I cannot reflect upon my own recent experience in South Africa without hearing the voices of my "colored" colleagues, students, neighbors (in the suburb of Mowbray) and friends. They were much of what I was in Cape Town.

Third parallel voice: Barbara Masakela, assistant to Nelson Mandela, president of the African National Congress, and former head of the ANC Department of Arts and Culture. Ms. Masakela has a genuine vocation for institutional support for cultural activism at both community and national levels, and her views reflect those of the likely majority party in the next South African government. She has only recently returned from almost three decades of exile. Her perspective on the possibility and desirability of a "national culture" in South Africa are revealing, and mark a sharp contrast to those of Clegg and Mthethwa. Some of her most interesting observations concern the problems of reintegration experienced by a committed exile, especially regarding gender relations and the contested uses and claims regarding African tradition among black South Africans today. Barbara Masakela is an essayist and frequent public speaker on the subject of culture in a future South Africa.

The Interrogator: associate professor David Coplan, Manhattanite, performance anthropologist, conducted fieldwork in Johannesburg 1975–77, was expelled as undesirable and worked in Lesotho in 1984 and 1988–89, and was readmitted to South Africa as a visiting Fulbright Professor at the Universities of the Western Cape and Cape Town, 1991.

The Conversations

COPLAN: Jonathan, as a boy in Johannesburg, what differentiated you from most whites was your interest in Zulu migrant workers' hostel dancing. For whites, in the city, away from mine compounds, self-proclaimed distinctive African cultural performance was out of place. You responded very differently to all this: there must have been some kind of chemistry.

CLEGG: My mother was a jazz singer, she also worked for a record company, and she was bringing back all the records as samples. My stepfather was a journalist. When I was seven, he moved into international journalism, and covered political events in Africa, from the Lumpa War in Zambia; we actually moved there for two years. I also grew up on a farm in Zimbabwe, so I went to six different schools in five years in three different countries, one a nonracial school, for two years, and I came back to Johannesburg when I was twelve. So I had already experienced being with blacks in school, I had a lot of black friends, I was living in a black area, with my personal experience up to the age of twelve, thirteen growing up in three different African countries, so I think I was chameleonlike in my ability to adapt. So I always felt myself a marginal person, because I was a marginal-ized character in my schools. Now, that is exactly what migrants are: the quintessential marginal men. But *unlike* me they have a sense of *coming* from somewhere, of coming from Zululand to the city. The city for them is an alien place, as it was for me. So we share the perception that life in the city was transient. Their hostels were a kind of Masada, a cultural Masada against the influences of the city. The dancing team, the burial society, the money collection societies were all means to encapsulate them into the *mi-grant* system and not to let them be lost to the city. All of those things reso-nate with me. The Zulu are also the most written about group of people in Africa, and they have had a huge impact on the white psyche. If you read your history at school the Zulu feature prominently; they're the reason for the Day of the Covenant,[2] they are . . .

COPLAN: The most impressive enemy . . . the major state which chal-lenged the white advance. Plus the romanticism about them . . . Even in America, there are blacks in New Orleans performing in Mardi Gras as "Zulus."

CLEGG: Yes, I had my own unique feelings about Natal [a Zulu ethnic region], and I was interested in the guitar. My entry into Zulu music was not a political statement, it was a cultural journey, an adventure in the context of a crazy political system, and politics caught up with *me*. I never wanted to be with black people to show anyone anything about politics. I went in there because I loved the music and I wanted to be there and to play it.

COPLAN: Bongani, what was your family's attitude towards cultural identi-fication? If I understand you, there was a strong cultural confidence: they said, we do need what the Anglican mission teachers are teaching, though we remain Zulu, and we are not afraid to send our young people there, not afraid that the children might be alienated . . .

MTHETHWA: There was that fear, but Shembe emphasized that you must send your children to school, to learn the skills. But they must not learn any whiteness. I had a cultural base at home and moral support, which I didn't get at school. At school the teacher would stand up and criticize our religion, or our singing at music classes. I resented them, but I had no power because I was told this was an Anglican school, and Anglican was civilization. There were also many good things that the teachers did for us, but they made us feel that we were foreigners. The schools were taken over by the government [in the midfifties] but the missionaries were still the teachers.

My father was a praise poet, he would cantillate praise poetry in the very late evening, when everything was quiet in the countryside, and then the mission people would sound cries, responses, in spite of themselves. The *imbongi,* praise poet, does it in the open air, you know, even at midnight. The mission people would sound their cries in response, showing their confusion, despising Africanness during daylight, and then at the right time it becomes their own. Shembe's dances I found very exciting as a child, and stick fighting, which was discouraged at school. I was notorious for fighting, and the missionary principal would call all the boys I had been beating and tell them to come and beat me up to their satisfaction. And he was teaching in the meantime as if nothing was happening. So these boys would beat me up, but after school, woe unto them! Because I was brought up in this tradition of fighting, that if anyone upsets you, beat him up, and don't bring in the teacher, or tell your parents. That is *ubuZulu,* Zulu tradition: you settle disputes through fighting. In fact, two of my grandfathers had fought in the Isandhlwana battle.[3] These old warriors spent time making all the Zulu regalia for me. They said, now, off with the white clothing! And I would come to them stark naked, and they would say, now, here is the warrior! They would dress me up in the regalia, and they would say, where are your weapons? So I would bring the knobkerries, and they would say, "Oh, what a magnificent warrior," and they would say, "You see those boys over there?" You must be forceful in Zulu, you must not apologize, so I would shout, "YES, GRANDFATHER, I CAN SEE THEM!" I was about seven or eight years old. So I would take my sticks and go to these chaps, and I would say my grandfather says I must come and beat you up . . . I appreciated my grandfathers, because they had been real warriors, at Isandhlwana, and they still lived that tradition. They were fearless.

It was Bantu Education that allowed the non-Christian children to come into school, since it was no longer under the missionaries, though there was still pressure that they should be given English names.[4] But every kid must now go to school . . . It diluted the divisions among people, because the Christians had been thinking of themselves as the elite, the educated, the better off, then there were the *amaxgaxga,* the "in-betweeners" who were very adaptive, they were the majority of people;[5] and then the traditionalists, who did not want their children to be educated away from them, but with

Bantu Education they knew that, "All right, son, you will go to school, you will come back home."

WILLEMSE: In 1957, apartheid hadn't had such a great impact in the remote towns. We had the development of the Group Areas Act, but people still had their own houses.[6] We lived among white people. I had white friends. As children we had no sense of recognizing racial identity. If people were different from us, it was because the ones we played with were made to be different from us. I had never met a group called *African* people. We had a friend, Johann, a white boy. And there was another one called Johnny who was, looking back now, an African. Johann, he said one day that his teacher told him not to play with us because he is the son of a *baas* and he shouldn't play with the *klasse,* with a laborer's (colored) children. In the case of Johnny, he came hone one day and said that he can't go with us any longer because he wasn't allowed into the school . . . because he was an African. He spoke Afrikaans; he had no other language. That was part of my formation of who I am. That made a hell of an impression on me.

My mother had training as a singer, we used to listen to opera. She would listen to opera, church music, and especially gospel music. She was a raconteur, could tell stories; she still can. But what also is important is what she *wanted* to be. She was about fifty-five when she wrote a short play, which I had to edit for the church sisters at Easter. Part of the family self-image was the idea of getting out of your limited circumstances. We moved from Ladysmith just when the Group Areas Act became *the* thing in Ladysmith, we got to know afterwards, and people had to move from the town to the [colored] location. We left Mosselbay for Worcester just before they started removing people to the colored and African locations. But we had to go to a school about ten kilometers away although there was a school just across the street, vacant [because it was in a white area] . . . The sense of community is something we developed afterwards when we came to Worcester, where there was much more rootedness. I never had the sense that I was a colored. Because as a child you never have any direct contact with other so-called ethnic groups.

COPLAN: Were there English-speaking people? Was there any Afrikaans/English division in the colored community?

WILLEMSE: My mother comes from Somerset West [a liberal, English-oriented town in the Cape]. She had gone to an English school. She wanted us in our first years to become English. We lost that completely when we went to Ladysmith. That was a thoroughly Afrikaans-speaking community and to be English was to ostracize ourselves. But it also tells you something about the way my mother was and what she wanted for herself and the kids . . . One also has to remember at that time there weren't any Afrikaans colored schools at all. The Afrikanerization of colored schools began after the introduction of the so called CAD [Colored Affairs Department] and BAD [Bantu Affairs Department] Acts, for Colored and Bantu Education [1953–55]. Earlier on, most of the people who went to school had English as a medium of instruction . . . in the [Cape] Peninsula area.

COPLAN: I see, then it becomes a class difference: those who go to school having English, and those who don't speaking Afrikaans, since that is the community language.

WILLEMSE: I wasn't very keen in school, because the school forced you in a way that I did not want to be forced. They were pushing students in certain [vocational] directions . . . now towards the professions. In my final year at school the principal called us in and said, "Who are the people going to teachers colleges?" Out of my class there were two or three. He said, "Why aren't you all going?" and we said that we wanted to become lawyers and doctors. He said, "Why do you want to become lawyers and doctors?" We were seen as people who could do no better than to become teachers. But there was a teacher, a white woman, who harnessed all this innovation from the students and directed it. She would invite us to her house, to listen to music and talk about poetry. She was a nationalist [Afrikaner conservative], but an enlightened nationalist, I suppose. Anyway, unlike the school, she recognized our individuality, that there were people who could become lawyers and so on, and she actually encourged people to apply for scholarships. So then I came to university, Western Cape, which was the only one you could go to [as a colored]. Nineteen seventy-six was very important for us. It was the high point of Black Consciousness [the period of the Soweto Uprising][7] . . . I became involved in the Black Consciousness Movement, perhaps because of my background. But more important, at university for the first time I had a sense of the broader society, that there were other things happening around us. Western Cape at that time was essentially a colored university, so even if we were black conscious, we were black conscious colored. We didn't have a wider sense of blackness as a lived experience. SASO was really quite strong and efficient at that time, and Steve Biko did come to see us once, and that made an impression on people. When students came from other universities to see us here, for the first time we met people who actually spoke another language, and we had to struggle using English as a common language. It was also my first time to meet whites on an equal basis. So we began to understand the world. University galvanized our political instincts to understand that there are people of a different position, and different disposition, than you. So the sense of *difference* became quite clear for me. During the protest against Afrikaans, the spark of the Soweto Upris-

ing, for about three months we didn't go to lectures, and I had to go to all
these meetings. At that time I was writing and reciting poetry, and we went
all across the cape, reciting poetry and trying to bring a political message.

MASAKELA: One of the striking things now that I'm in my fiftieth year,
culturally, is that those things I was ashamed of about my origins, are the
things I'm proud of now. One of those is that my mother is what is called
colored in South Africa. It always left you with the feeling that there was
some strange member of the family, of having someone who was not up to
the mark, and that we spoke Afrikaans as children, surrounded by people
who spoke African languages. We spoke African languages as well, but our
home language was Afrikaans. My mother was colored; her father was Scottish, her mother was Ndebele, my father is a Mopedi of the Tlokwa clan,
and we grew up in the town of Witbank (Transvaal) with my grandmother.
We were exposed to all sorts, including whites. We were lucky because from
the beginning we met whites who were very militantly nonracial. We were
able from the beginning to see white people not as bosses, but as equals. I
think that has been very helpful, coupled with my experience of having
grown up in the African National Congress.
    Right after Inanda [Seminary, a mission secondary school in Natal] I was
in Johannesburg for a year, working for *New Age* (the communist magazine), and the grip on expression for black people was really tightening in
those days (1960) and I could see the signs, so I went to college in Lesotho,
and then into exile. But at *New Age* was where I got my baptism into politics, working with people like Ruth First,[8] Joe Slovo, so it became very un-
safe, and it was clear that opportunity for black people was closing down. I
wanted to go abroad, partly because my brother [jazz musician Hugh Ma-
sakela] had gone, and we were very good friends, and we're still close. So I
went via Ghana . . . and nobody there called themselves "colored." You
saw people of mixed race but they thought of themselves as Ghanaian, no
sense of difference from the rest of the people. Those are some of the influences that one had, so much so that coming back home is a letdown, because when you are in exile you tend to embellish the past, to glorify and
romanticize. Having experienced so many other cultures, you can see South
Africa in perspective. I'm afraid you can see the limitations also of your
culture, and it puts you in your place.
    So after England I went to the States, to Fordham University in Manhat-
tan, and there I met another kind of racism, in 1964. It is the American
brand of racism, where nothing is said directly, but it's there. You feel it
every time your professor says something about "primitive people." So I
left and went to Zambia, and I studied English at the university there for
three years. I think of my generation as the first group of African people

who really went abroad, and experienced this freedom. Now we are coming back. But during our lifetimes, because it was also the period of the liberation of Africa, we've seen our classmates become ministers, become corrupted, thrown out in coups. We've lived through all the promise and disappointment of Africa, but what has kept us alive is the belief that we too in South Africa would be able to achieve freedom. That's why I take very seriously Amilcar Cabral when he talks about the culture of liberation, so that our culture was more than just your ethnic background; it was the liberation of the world.

COPLAN: So you constitute an international tribe of your own, your people . . .

MASAKELA: Exactly, and coming back home, you can no longer just easily and completely reenter. Whatever critical judgment I make, it's about myself, because those people out there are me, they are my people.

CLEGG: The funniest thing is, when I started learning the guitar music, I found I was very good at mimicking exactly what was sung, but I never knew what I was singing. Some were very tough, hard, bawdy, licentious, and downright dirty migrant worker songs. I used to go with my first teacher, Charlie Msinga, and we used to do the rounds of the shebeens [informal speakeasies] on the rooftops and I would play one of these songs, very seriously, and people would laugh and say, "Play that again! You do this so well." Later I found that I was singing about some very wild affairs. That was my fumbling entry into the culture. Then Charlie taught me how to dance, and it was the *dance* [*snaps fingers*] . . . dance was for me the most, the strongest primal recognition of something, which today I am still trying to assimilate . . . The first dancing I saw was near Number 4 [the old Johannesburg Central Prison]. I will never forget; it was a Tuesday night, we had our guitars, we had walked all the way from Yeoville, right through Hillbrow, behind the back alleys, because you could go right through to Hillbrow on the back alleys. We went down this passage and came out in a square courtyard with high buildings, and in the corner there was one light and about eighty men in a horn-shaped formation performing Bhaca dancing. They were all hunched and they were humming, and this humming, *ukugirha* in Zulu, became quintessential for me; I used it in my music and I still use it today. It is something that was so powerful for me, it has never left me. This particular group of people were Bomvu [Xhosa origin] people from Msinga [a Zulu area], and they had adapted a Bhaca [another Natal ethnic group] dancing style; they were competing against Bhacas, but not Bhacas themselves. While they were doing this, I had the feeling they knew something I didn't know; a very powerful sense of being outside a profound mystery. Not a mystery so much as sacred knowledge being enacted. As I walked up, I could feel in the concrete the stamping of the feet, and the power of the humming. I was a little bit in awe and afraid, because I didn't know these men. Each dancer seemed, although he was part of the team, to be expressing his individuality, to be separately unified. There was a fierce, terrible commitment . . . a magnificent, horrible, terrible commitment which was being divulged. I wanted to be able to do that, to know what they were feeling. And it was such a *foreign* movement. I felt I had been made privy to an important, significant behavior and a secret, as if I was being inducted into some kind of cult: you know, the young fourteen-year-old. Nobody, nobody knew that in the middle of Johannesburg in a courtyard, a traditional Bhaca war dance was being stamped out every Tuesday and Thursday night. There was a sense of being elected. This was serious shit. After the dance stopped, everybody came up and they shook my hand, because Charlie had told everybody about me. I was given a guitar to play and I played a few songs and they all laughed, they thought it was wonderful. They huddled around me and they started to sing. They put me in a team, and I started to do the movement. It was so *foreign,* and it was great because I suddenly felt like a baby. I was crawling. I wanted to walk but I was crawling. I was put between two people and I sensed that the dynamic was a tension between the torso and the legs. I learned the steps and began to work through the choreographies. I taped the dance and I listened to the stamps. When you hear them shouting on the tape, you know that the next set of movements are going to initiate the dance. I started to document these, a sort of anthropological take. I drew the dances; the shape and the different positions of the body. So I had a sense of wanting to express what I was seeing, to document it or sing about it, to live it out.

I was speaking a very rough mixture of Zulu and Fanagalo [a miners' patois] and English but I could sing fluently. It was not only my background, but the force of the culture itself, the force of the dance. There was something overwhelmingly powerful about Zulu culture, something . . . crazy, . . . the Zulu have taken the concepts of life and death to their extreme. It's expressed in the dance, in their fighting, in their aggressive and the poetic use of language. The ability to take life and give life; those two things are powerfully elaborated upon. In 1969, in a full-blown apartheid society, this amounted to an organic form of . . . "the culture of resistance," which South Africans talk about in completely incoherent ways, as if it is a conscious attempt by a group of people to create expressive forms which will resist. These people were at the bottom of the pile. Most of them were illegal here. They were considered to be backward, rural, tribal, pagan, uneducated people, even by black people in the townships [ghettos]; and here they were, saying, "We live." And when you hear the concertina being played in the street at night, and it bounces off the walls, that's what that crying concertina says: "I will be heard." The Zulu have a saying, *Inqanye mpile,* "There is nothing left except the stubborn determination to live" . . . This is not political consciousness, but a resistance to the world, a resistance to what the world throws against you. Stubborn determination, commitment, all these ideas and values are very important. The Zulu gave me those masculine values which clearly somewhere I was needing.

MTHETHWA: My grandmother felt I was musical because I could imitate any musical sound. She sang for me and she danced for me, and she taught me how to dance; that's how I learned to walk, that's how you teach any African child to walk; you dance, and as they try to dance, they learn to walk . . . But in music, it was the piano in particular. I would say that the piano satisfies our concept of music, because with us music must not be an independent melody, it must be many sounds, together, you must hear the call and the response, everything must be there, so the piano and the guitar, the concertina, these are the instruments that satisfy our musical values. Supportive instruments for the voice, so even when you play alone everything is there.

COPLAN: At this point you were determined that you were going to make a career in music?

MTHETHWA: Yes, and my family was very negative about it, and also my future wife. In those days it was unthinkable that anyone [black] could make a career out of music, but I was a strong character. I said I'm going to do music, and if you are not happy with me because of that, you can leave me and go for another man. I told my parents too; sorry, it's got to be my way.

COPLAN: So this stubborn quality they had beaten into you, it turned and bit them.

MTHETHWA: Yes! It got them; maybe those grandfathers who trained me to be stiff, this was the result. But first I worked for Alcan Aluminum, and then I was transferred to Richards Bay (Northern Natal), and there was a major strike in 1973, at that time I was doing the piano outside work, and I was studying harmony by correspondence with the University of South Africa (UNISA). But then I got fired because of that strike, where I was chief spokesman for the nine hundred strikers. I'm not a talker, but people seemed to feel that I was a very stiff-necked, resistant person, and so the right one to talk to the white people, because I would never go back on my word. When they were creating workers' committees with management, when we were pushing for trade unions, they came to me and said I had to be a spokesman, though I was not chosen officially. They said this man is a Shembe: he doesn't drink, he's always sober, he can speak English, and he's a very confident [proud] person; we want that sort of man to talk on our behalf. So

after the strike when I was fired, and "endorsed out" by the Employers Society of Natal, my *dompas* [pass] was endorsed so that I could not work for
any industry in Natal at all.[9] The best thing was to go to university, so I got
a bank loan and I went here to Natal University, doing music. I got a little
job with an African bus company, they were also scared to death to employ
me, but they were African so they gave me a chance, and they paid me minimum wages! I was really exploited! Then I worked for the KwaZulu Homeland government, but I saw I had to go back to school because they were
treating me like a boy. So I was the first African student to be accepted by
the University of Natal for [a Bachelor of Music degree]. In 1983 I got a
British Council fellowship to study in Britain, so I went to Belfast to study
with John Blacking [a world-famous African music scholar], doing music
research, 1983–84. I was working on a Master's on Shembe's hymns. Looking at the literature some writers [Coplan included] said that Shembe was
really the top hymn composer, who might be studied in future, and I said,
here I am, a member of the Shembe church, nobody has studied Shembe,
and my mother had taught me all of Shembe's hymns, and she was Shembe's
secretary: I know so much about Shembe, maybe I should do this. I felt I
should contribute towards the history of Shembe the man. Because all the
writings had been anti-Shembe propaganda, in order to frustrate the "movement," although he calls it a church. The thesis was also on the hymns of
Shembe, and I'm still working on it and I have a problem of seeing things
that I take for granted, and putting them into words; I overlook too many
things, they are in my head and I don't realize they are important for my
readers. It's a question of interpretation. I feel I must write from within.

Shembe has adopted Western hymns, especially the Methodist hymnal,
and made them sound African, and many of his dances are performed to
their music. He has taken some of the old Zulu *ihubo* styles, and incorporated them into Christianity, and even divided the whole concept of worship
into two levels: congregational worship where people are sitting and listening to a priest, and another, higher level, the African level, of expressing
worship as a dance. In the Shembe church dance is regarded as a higher
level *because* it's African; the other is foreign. To sing without the movement, and to have this one man, who is just talking endlessly, without an
opportunity to answer him back; it's an inferior type of worship. At the
higher level, we are all priests, we are all dancing . . . There is musical
polyphony, there is poetry; poetry music and dance in one, a higher form of
worship, and one you must prepare yourself for. Any thug or drunk can just
walk into a church and join the worship. But in the dance you must first be
secluded, to undergo ascetic exercises; you've got to be cleansed before you
can dance . . . Shembe was not interested in any clan but in creating unity
among Africans, especially among Nguni people.[10]

COPLAN: So Christianity works into that, becomes a resource for bringing people into a more general system of African self-identification, in opposition to other identities.

MTHETHWA: Yes, he even gave new names to people, every member of the Shembe church who is male is given a regimental name. Shembe was a very renowned praise poet. He would name anything, because that is what a poet should do, he would give you a name; it's your pride, that you've been with this person. So in that he created a new African society, with a new identity of Africanness. Shembe was a great musician, and he founded his church on hymnody. And that is African leadership, because you cannot lead people if you are not musical; ability to make music is an ability of leadership.

COPLAN: Johnny, what about your identity as the "white Zulu"? Part of what I am interested in is also the way in which popular discourse and its myths construct all of us, particularly the roles we choose.

CLEGG: Apartheid is both a racial *and ethnic* system, so race and culture, white and black, Afrikaner and Zulu, these represent its two primary features. When you can take race and culture and meld them subconsciously within an apartheid psyche, you make a very powerful statement. What you are saying is that race and culture are manifestations of the same thing, so a "white Zulu" is a complete contradiction of that. Against the discourse of apartheid during those years, it was a very hip thing: the guy is white but he is Zulu. This became a township joke; people would say *uZulu mhlope nam'*, "that white Zulu." Both blacks *and* whites would come to me and say, "What do you see in this?" and not in a nasty way, but genuinely . . . really wanting to know.

COPLAN: Did you tell them? What could you tell them?

CLEGG: I would give them descriptions of what I did and the feelings that I had when I was doing it, but it was never enough, I was just describing; I wasn't giving them *the secret,* which they want cheaply, you see . . . Yeoville [an inner-city white residential area with many African domestic servants] at that time, it had a huge rural-oriented Zulu community; street music every night. Whites never saw it. But I had the ability to see. Apartheid taught you not to see, to walk down the street and *not* see a black man coming up the street, playing the guitar. If you heard the sound it was a foreign sound. It made no sense to you, it was a garbled, distorted, sonic representation of a culture that is dangerous to you.

COPLAN: Even some urban black people might see it as such.

CLEGG: Yeah, and psychologically you cut it off, you don't acknowledge it. But when I arrived from Zambia when I was eleven or twelve, I *saw* them. That was my gift more than anything; I just saw these people.

Johnny Clegg. Photo © Karen Petersen.

At this time, Zulu guitar music was structured on two levels of accomplishment. The first level was the ability to take traditional existing songs, and to adapt them to the guitar, and that took a certain amount of understanding of the guitar and its dynamics. The next class, which was considered more important, were the original writers, writing new songs, no longer based on either traditional formats or traditional structures. They were creating original, unique music for the guitar. Sipho Mchunu [his collaborator] was already at this level at sixteen years old.

COPLAN: But in a sense his work is a cultural domestication; the traditionalizing of the guitar so that it becomes organically Zulu . . . even though what you are doing on it was not done by Zulus before.

CLEGG: The guitar became also an expression of the whole tradition of *ukubonga* [praising]; the praise poetry tradition, but in a much more common or popular sense; that is, you would sing about your own various problems in the city.

COPLAN: And praise yourself, which you are not really supposed to do in traditional praise poetry. It's the individualism of migrants. They resist praising aristocrats. It has to be bawdy and personalistic, expressed in a more popular register because you don't want it confused with *that* tradition; the chiefs—on the contrary, it's self-confidence, saying I am looking after myself.

CLEGG: Yes, that's right, saying this is *my* tradition, I am making the tradition. The compositions were often bawdy, ribald, about life in the hostel, prostitution, being arrested and so forth. Yet the most powerful aspect consists of obscure, heavy, obdurate images, song phrases like, "They have stolen the song of my child." Now it has sense for him as a composer, though he can't tell you what sense it makes. What he is communicating is a deep ability to *give* meaning. Every time the phrase comes around it is a question of whether the audience is going to understand what it means, because of the way he is singing it. Here we had a set of references or images which resonated together in a profound way, which made no sense, except when they were sung, and you were always on the verge of understanding what he was saying and you had to wait until the phrase came around again, so he could sing it again.

COPLAN: It defies interpretation.

CLEGG: You cannot interpret it and it can go on forever.

COPLAN: It defies anthropology.

CLEGG: It defies everything . . . He has created it to juxtapose multiple meanings, or tensions, in images and in references. It's these tensions which are being communicated, not the actual words or images, and the tension is in the voice and the melody. And in all those qualities making a whole, a performance. His playing is not repetitive, because every time it comes around, it's new. Can he do it the same way as last time? No. Every time it comes around, it's building up significance for him. It is a kind of formalism; a clever awareness of the tensions between words and pictures and meanings, encased in melody.

COPLAN: Even bodily movements. Like the Basotho [another South African ethnic group] say, "a song sung with the feet."

CLEGG: Yes. The other form was the humor-irony song, on the guitar, that would deal with something a migrant sees as part of his daily repertoire of life in the city. I remember hearing a song in a competition about an uncle who had come to the city, got off the train, and there was a traffic policeman directing the cars. And the uncle sang that here was an adult herdboy herding these steel cattle up and down. And sometimes they would listen, and sometimes they would bellow, "paa paa paa." Now that is daily experience, but he has put it into another, shared context. The audience loved those kind of songs, because they validated the traditional system; it says, look, it can work in the city, you can use it to understand.

COPLAN: It domesticates what is going on . . . an African pragmatics of metaphor in which everything can be a symbol of everything else.

CLEGG: It's a train, you have to couple them up.

COPLAN: And for the new couplings, of metaphor, there are no preset restrictions.

CLEGG: Yes, so it was the humor and irony above all that gave the person in the audience a sense of understanding, an illumination about his life as a migrant through humor or irony or sadness. And then the modern composers; formalists putting together these heavy strings of images and singing them in this very convincing way. You don't know why it is convincing, or what you are being convinced by, but it is very moving. You end up persuaded. And if you defeated other guitarists in a competition, there wasn't any kind of reward, it was just *ukuduma,* "thundering," the idea is, you must watch out for him, he is very famous. It's like symbolic capital.

COPLAN: You occupy a larger space in life.

CLEGG: That's the point! As a good guitarist, you then start to get invites . . . to come to a shebeen to drink up, because people like your music, your humor. We always had the upper hand because of this black-white partnership. The salt-and-pepper team, it was a winning combination . . . Every time I went into my praises, I praised myself, or I'd praise Sipho. In my own praises I would turn to Sipho and say something like, "Hey man I see you are very busy there, so let me say your praises for you." That's a very intimate thing, when one man praises another man. It's different from praising yourself, because it's an acknowledgment of that person's history and accomplishment. It changes the relationship. There's a song called "Sky People" on the first album, *Universal Men.* We found something unique, and "Sky People" [literal translation of *AmaZulu,* the Zulu] became the Zulu-Western equation, our signature. I was accused because of that album by the left wing, in the cultural politics of resistance, of romanticizing tribalism. If you look at the images in English, they are things like '*Nkosi Bomvu* [red kings]; I was trying to use the genre of the obdurate image, the image of stone that cannot be moved but cannot be understood, and cannot be brushed aside because its meaning cannot be captured. In the song "*Nkosi Bomvu*" I talk about the black bull, the image of the black bull that fights only when challenged but gives no ground. So, I was accused when the album came out of being a cryptotribalist romantic.

COPLAN: It was not understood that you can validate these images; to outsiders, even if they are Zulu speakers, it's parochial and opaque and exclusive and threatening, so they have to invalidate it; to invalidate cultural *différance* because they have internalized the fear of the race-culture equation, and so cannot honor the actual practices of the "people" whose rights they claim to be advancing. They are trying to promote the South African people and their freedom, which means you can't validate them as they are, but only in an "internationalist" guise. So, how free are you making them? They cannot acknowledge people's self-definitions, because those are inconsistent with a "nonracialist" utopia.

CLEGG: That's a big problem. What emerged from the album and from the second album, *African Litany,* was that it wasn't strictly Zulu music. If

Sipho was having a problem, I would bring in a Western solution and we would get over the problem, and if I was writing in a Western mode, he would bring in some Zulu material and reorient me to the Zulu approach.

COPLAN: It's about borderlands. It's not about replicating something that other people can do better. The point is to use the actual energy created by encountering each other.

CLEGG: The music that started to receive attention in the media, even among the migrants at some point, was this mixture, not so much the traditional material. Sipho and I both felt that we had to also function *within* Zulu, so we recorded an entirely Zulu language album, *Ubuhle Bemvelo*. Now, as to our audience, Sipho brought migrant workers and I brought students. So we really had it: intellectuals and workers! What people consider the most uneducated, rural, pagan, tribal, traditionalist, country bumpkin, and a university graduate of whatever racial or cultural background, getting sustenance from the same song. And that aspect of our project has never been properly acknowledged or understood.

COPLAN: But of course they have not been permitted in each other's environments.

CLEGG: Sure. Our first audiences were students and workers. They came together, as listeners; as people who bought our records [*laughs*].

COPLAN: An idealized unity hardly ever achieved in life.

CLEGG: [*laughing*]: And we were the ones, the "cryptotribalists," who did it. We started to see that this mixing was opening up multiple permutations that were difficult to control or structure. We created a double dualism: putting African lyrics to Western music, English lyrics to African music, and then mixing African music and Western music in the same song—three different crossovers.

COPLAN: What makes it work is that you weren't sycophantic. You were not saying, here's the "pure" Zulu material, and I'm a white person who loves it, and I can't validate my white identity in relation to it, so I'll just learn to reproduce it as faithfully as I can. Instead you said, No, my shit stinks as much as their shit, and if we pile them together it's going to fill the air, and attract butterflies. You loved yourself enough.

CLEGG: All of those tensions were around, and constant criticism coming from the so-called enlightened community. The leftists were banning me; the other side was sniffing about my "inauthenticity." But among people who were self-consciously Zulu we were making a fortune, we were a success. With them, Juluka was the biggest thing ever. The white audiences would pick up on the songs I wrote and, when we played [black] townships, it was more the dialogue, the salt-and-pepper act: I was this cute little guy praising Sipho and it had all those aspects to it. And we were singing some *very* interesting stuff. In front of mostly white audiences in Pretoria, we sang about Mandela, and people walked out, others cheered. To the African audience, concerning songs like *"Impi,"* people still say to me, "You are a musical *sangoma* [diviner], you divined that the war [between Inkatha and the ANC[11]] was coming." But I would say the song is about 1879, about the Zulu-Anglo war.

COPLAN: But that's it, the war is *perpetually* coming. The African method is to pack it all together into one image . . . Including the things you didn't like about "The Zulu." The more doors of experience with the others that you pass through, the more your romanticism fades, and you see the entangled contradictions; what works and what doesn't, inseparable from each other.

COPLAN: How did you view the Soweto students of 1976, who were protesting mainly against the use of Afrikaans as a medium in their schools?

WILLEMSE: It struck me only afterwards, that it was ironical, because my friend Andries Oliphant [well-known colored activist, editor, and poet] was writing poetry in Afrikaans. The irony never arose, since that language was still our creative medium, and we didn't connect with Soweto in that sense. For us it seemed to be a reaction against oppression and poor education, rather than against Afrikaans itself . . . During 1976, our Students' Representative Council [a radical leadership organization], was Afrikaans speaking. So distinctly Afrikaans, they came from the rural areas many of them, and they could barely get by in English. So it was against the government, rather than something against Afrikaans . . . At that time if you had to speak in any other language you had to deny yourself. If anything, English might be a "school" language, and showing yourself as being deliberately different from others. When we spoke to our new friends who spoke other languages, we used a mix of English, Afrikaans, Xhosa, just to communicate by any means. When I met the African activists in Worcester then, we spoke in Afrikaans, *about* Afrikaans, and variants of Cape Afrikaans black slang. So I got a broader understanding of my own language of Afrikaans through those encounters. In 1977 I was part of the Drama Group at UWC, led by Oliphant. We went to Lüderitz in Namibia, and we were going to perform four one-act plays, and among them was this English play. But we realized that these people speak Afrikaans, and no one is going to understand it here. It made a great impression on me in relation to what intellectuals or political people wanted, and what was happening on the ground. We got there, and we workshipped a new little play in Afrikaans just to fill up the program, and as we toured, we translated this little play, *Nkululeko* [Freedom] from English to Afrikaans. By the time we got to the third town on the tour, we could perform it in Afrikaans.

COPLAN: Yet this year Namibia has proclaimed English as their official language.

WILLEMSE: While 93 percent of the population speak Afrikaans. Politically it might be a good move, in terms of where the country wants to go, but in terms of popular participation at the local level, it's not going to work. Even in the capital Windhoek, if you speak English you must be from somewhere else. That experience in Namibia made a great impression on me in terms of my understanding of the involvement of language and the place of culture in social politics. It also made a great impact on me with regard to what people [South Africans] are. I realized what a hell of an effort it must be for someone to get themselves across in someone else's language. By my third year at university, I made a choice for literature, rather than law. I was a member of a literary group that wanted to explore other approaches to literature than those taught at university. We were influenced by political approaches, Marxist and other leftist approaches [like Paulo Friere], which paralleled the issue of culture and marginalized people, which was something I had already identified in law.

I wanted to understand how Afrikaans had now become the pariah among languages, whereas I had never experienced such a feeling in my own life. It was only when I began to meet people outside the university—in Johannesburg, for instance, there was a *thing* about Afrikaans—and I got involved in it, and I wanted to write in Afrikaans, to use it to be creative. When I got to honors year, we were studying Afrikaans literature, and my mind now had a block against *that*. Because I was not an Afrikaner, which is another kind of bind. I had an aversion to Afrikaner literature; even if you studied it from a politically subversive point of view, I was still an outsider looking in. I could never begin to share these notions of Afrikaans as a "wonderful" language, a "language of the mother," our "national language": I could never share the Afrikaans canon. I had some teachers who were critical, but not critical in terms of the *literature itself,* of *positioning* the student, in terms of our whole relationship to Afrikaans literature. It was only in later years that people like Jakes Gerwel [then lecturer in Afrikaans and now rector of the University of the Western Cape] began to investigate that relationship. I did my post-graduate studies in Afrikaans here with Jakes . . . At university, at honors level, I had a different sense of what I wanted to do, and there was no specific disciplinary approach to South African literature; this didn't exist. It was all English literature, which meant colonial literature, and there was Afrikaans literature, which meant Afrikaner literature; there was no curriculum for what I intuitively wanted to explore. For instance, it was only in later years that I heard about "oral literature," which was something that I could identify with. I realized that this was something that people can put in a book, something worthwhile. It's literature. Trying to make these things important, so that we can recognize ourselves.

COPLAN: Wasn't it a problem for you in relation to the Black Consciousness philosophy that we are blacks together, and we shouldn't pursue sectarian "colored" or other "divisive" identities within black culture?

WILLEMSE: Well at that point, in honors year, I had moved from Black Consciousness thought towards a more Marxist inclination, which recognized the importance of marginalized expressions. That was another trigger, getting to what working-class people were thinking and feeling. This made Afrikaans important. I'm still completing my doctorate, on the subject of marginalized images in black Afrikaans writing, and I'm looking at black Afrikaans writers, colored, though one is African. I still have a problem with this notion of being "colored." I lost a few friends of a more left-wing persuasion because they had problems with my working at university at all.

COPLAN: Because this was still an apartheid, "bush" college for coloreds then?

WILLEMSE: Yes, because this was "bush," and it was OK to study here as a way of finding a way out, but it was another thing to accept a job here. Anyway, it was a difficult decision for me in the first place. It seemed important to start writing about what other people, the working class, did; to understand what the role of Afrikaans literature was, the role of Afrikaner ideologues, in upholding "Afrikaans Literature" . . . That was why I had to continue studying at this university, with Jakes, because there was nothing anywhere else [at the white universities] that satisfied me. Just the straight learning of something I had very serious problems with. This is true even now. We are the first university to institute a course in the *origins* of Afrikaans, a project on black Afrikaans, and a symposium of black Afrikaans writers. To show there is more to Afrikaans than the Afrikaner idea of it, we mounted a new course in reclaiming history. Up to now there has been no systematic history of black people's contribution to Afrikaans. Until recently, whatever has been done has been derided as merely an appendage.

COPLAN: As I have understood it, Afrikaans arises from the efforts of people who couldn't speak Dutch to speak Dutch, and of the Dutch to speak to them.

WILLEMSE: It's a creolized language, encoding a clash of cultures and languages. By the early nineteenth century, it expresses class differentiation between the colored population, who spoke colored Afrikaans, this inappropriate Dutch, and the whites, who spoke in a higher register of sophisticated Dutch. The missionaries who worked among the coloreds at that time wanted to translate the Bible into this Afrikaans, to make it available to the *coloreds.* There was no consciousness among whites that this was *their* national language then. It's only later with the nationalism after the Second

Anglo-Boer War, 1902–10, that it became important to the Afrikaners to be something different, and Afrikaans was a medium for that.

COPLAN: The first translation of the Bible into Afrikaans, of course, did not appear until 1933.

WILLEMSE: Yes, for the benefit of white nationalism. There were extracts of the Bible translated into Afrikaans before that, for coloreds, but the first religious text to appear in Afrikaans, in the 1870s, by Imam Effendi, was in Arabic script, for Muslims. This clarifies the construction of history. The first slave schools, for instance, used Afrikaans as a medium of instruction. But the Afrikaner ideologues claim that the first school to use it was one of their schools in Paarl, which is not true. The ideological construction of Afrikaans is an interesting phenomenon. The changes that exist between Dutch and Afrikaans are attributed to survivals of seventeenth-century Dutch, so that it had nothing to do with this linguistic crossover, so for them it becomes a matter of a "pure" connection to Europe, and Dutch.

COPLAN: Pure because related to earlier forms of Dutch, not a modern development of its own.

WILLEMSE: For a long time that view made a great impact on literary and linguistic studies here. It's only recently that people are looking at it anew.

COPLAN: The Afrikaner ideologues now accept that the history of Afrikaans has to be rewritten?

WILLEMSE: Yes, and they want to have a stake in it, to play a more honest game if you like, but the problem with history is always interpretation; it's a matter of injecting our own vision of the future, rather than telling the truth about the past. What I feel now for *ourselves* is not to construct a history of Afrikaans that is going to be valorization of our own sectarian point of view. We had better be careful, because it will only perpetuate injustice if we do not pursue some notion of the truth. We had a long history of misguidance by the language ideologues in this country, and the position of Afrikaans for the immediate future is largely the work of language ideologues and the government. They have made Afrikaans into their own vehicle, their own possession, and neglected everything that black people contributed to it.

COPLAN: So what is your reaction to scholarly accounts of Zulu culture?

MTHETHWA: I wouldn't want to criticize any individual, but in some cases you find that Zulu culture is represented as male dominated, a concept that does not belong to Zulu culture or to *ubuZulu*. We don't have a culture of domination, we have a culture of diversity and a culture of belonging. For instance, the man is not the head of the homestead to us; the wife is, since the man is a polygamist. He must have eight wives, and all of his homesteads must belong to them. The children belong to the man. So I don't see how domination comes into it. Because the man says these are my children;

and the woman says, this is my homestead, and that includes everything including the husband.[12] If a woman is young she must sleep in her father's
homestead; the father is in charge of her; and if she is married, the husband
is in charge of her. The same is true of a man, well, a young man is a bit
free, but after you are married the ancestors watch you, so you must sleep in
your homestead all the time.

COPLAN: Of course, if you are a migrant laborer you cannot do that!

MTHETHWA: Yes, if you are a migrant laborer you are unclean, because
you don't sleep in your home, and when you come into another's home you
bring uncleanliness there, especially if you are a woman; this breaks too
many of the norms, the Christian norms.

COPLAN: This is why Shembe said you must not go and work for anyone?

MTHETHWA: Yes, especially domestic work; you must not take it up. Of
course, there are many thousands of migrants in the Shembe church; I am
one of them! I am a migrant worker because I am here at the University of
Natal.[13] It was hardly two months ago that I was allowed by the law to even
have a house in Durban [due to Group Areas regulations], or even to rent a
flat. In the townships I did have a flat, but that has come recently; before,
you had to have a permit to be in that township; to come to this university I
had to apply for two permits—one to come to the university and another to
be found in Durban at all . . . Damage is done by domestic employment,
by turning young men into garden boys, separating them from the young
women of their home district, who should be married by them with cattle
provided by their fathers. Now people are made to live like orphans, because
the fathers don't have anything, being dispossessed. The boy must pay out of
his own pocket, and no longer minds his parents. This has created very hard
people. They have been made into orphans.

MASAKELA: The question of women is a fair question. When I first came
back to South Africa I was despondent. I had forgotten all that. We struggled as women in the ANC in exile, to bring about changes that asserted the
equality of women. But we did this within an environment where women
still played a subsidiary role within the organization. The women who are
in positions of power within the movement are still very few, in a serious
minority. The Convention for a Democratic South Africa (CODESA) was
really disgusting when you looked around. You could see [the dearth of
women] . . . South Africa is really one of the most traditional countries
as far as gender is concerned . . . And because it's an attitudinal change
we are fighting for, and because it is linked with the national issue of racial
equality, there is a tendency for our male counterparts to place one above the
other, and not to recognize that democracy in South Africa will not be complete without the equality of women.

COPLAN: But people *are* saying that because we want the right to be black now, you can't be expressing attitudes that are associated with whites toward us. If we blacks have a problem to solve, we had better solve it among ourselves, not as members of an "imagined community" of nonracialism. Though there is of course a power agenda behind this; an ideology defending an unwillingness to change.

MASAKELA: Well, black people have been so oppressed for so long, that because of their primacy in traditional terms, it is men who have been mainly involved in the struggle. They have taken advantage of the traditional character of our nation. Now when they must allow competition for certain positions openly within the movement, women are vying for those positions too, and it's quite natural for men to be subjective about that. This business of using African culture as an excuse is nonsense. But this area represents the only area where black men were still allowed to have some authority, and of course they are threatened with this being taken away from them.

COPLAN: A comment was made at the University of Cape Town by a black student that what whites refer to as rape is part of black culture, and so to condemn it is racism. But I thought, this is ignorance as power, because it was never the case, and ignores the social consequences that followed from "grabbing a woman" in rural African communities, whatever the twists and distortions of "custom" historically.

MASAKELA: Well, we must face squarely the problem that women themselves also perpetuated these values, so this struggle also involves winning over women who are helping to preserve them. But the liberation movement that has led the struggle, must express and support equality publicly, and I think people will take the example. If we as a liberation movement are still equivocating about it then it can't get anywhere.

CLEGG: The male Zulu migrant value system, including its uglier aspects, is in me somewhere, I know that. It is one of the reasons why I am successful. Because I have been stubborn, and I haven't listened, and I haven't taken the shit.

COPLAN: Your enemies can choke on their own jealousy.

CLEGG: That's it.

COPLAN: But you are married to a very sophisticated woman, a professional designer.

CLEGG: Well, you see, I am a cultural chameleon. I have had a problem psychologically because culturally . . . I never knew my father; I met him when I was twenty-one for the first time. Until then I merely romanticized about being English, and of course the Zulus kept on, "Who is your father, who is your clan, what is your lineage?"

COPLAN: But they must have some of the same problems.

CLEGG: Sure. They will say, "He doesn't know who his father is," that kind of a vibe. That's very weak, you know. So I had this thing about English culture, about being accepted culturally at some point. And I married an English-speaking person who was not from my culture, but very much in that kind of mold, my first wife. The other thing is that I've had this cultural triad: Jewish, English, and Zulu. The Anglo-Zulu relationship has always been significant, symbolic in South Africa. For me it's been really a personal journey. Zulu culture didn't give me the feminine I needed, it gave me the masculine. My mother was such a domineering person in my life, almost overpowering; I had to really fight against that. But the incident that you have seen today is the height of ugliness of the Zulu male condition.[14] All these things come from a problem in this "neotraditional" image of masculinity, which is battling to haul all this old traditional baggage into a new world of taxis, guns, telephones, and communications, where assassinations are plotted from offices.

COPLAN: What about "guilt by association?" Your friend's brother was the guilty party, yet your friend will do fine as a subject for retribution— so very characteristic of South Africa.

CLEGG: It's his clan, you see. This is characteristic of any corporate society, in Africa as well. Even me, at the height of my fame in the townships, there were certain times I knew, because I was part of a corporate group, that I can't go there now. I can go there tomorrow, and some of the guys would die for me, but today they will kill me. I understand that, and the same with my friend Buff. It's a feud. I understand Mafia, I understand Sicily, because in one context I die for my brother, in another context I kill him. I don't condone it, but what I see in my life and in my country, the pressure cooker I have been in, trying to make sense of my life and to get meaning out of what I am doing is that you never ask for anything. You are born into something and you are given a set of values, a set of options. When I left South Africa at twenty-one to meet my dad, I went to England. It was like Mars. I can't overemphasize how African I realized I was. The real dilemmas I had were with the cultural dimensions of politics. I studied politics at university. They would preach, "Human rights are human rights; here we have the African delegates from Rwanda, Burundi or wherever; we condemn the tribalism and the wars and the genocide." And the diplomatic representative of the oppressing group stands up and says, "You people don't understand, this is the African way, you cannot universalize, your values are culture bound. Your 'Declarations' do not come out of Africa." Perhaps to my detriment I am saying I understand. But we really can't go forward if we keep with that idea. We are locked into the cycle of violence. That was for me a major growth point, when I was confronted *intellectually*. University for me was like a boot camp because I had simply internalized all these values through practice: I was stick fighting; I was into local-level politics. My professor, when I wrote a paper on faction fighting, said, "It's very interesting, but I don't get a sense anywhere in your paper that this business disturbs you." He was an anthropologist; he kept on saying you mustn't "go bush," we are here to equip you with *objective* models of culture.

COPLAN: Which means you'll never get to it. You'll never get to understand "The Bush" because you are afraid to be there. This has been a big problem in South African universities. Who was this, Professor [William David] Hammond-Tooke?

CLEGG: Yes, him! And that worried me and also because my [first] wife was afraid. Even now there are certain things which I understand as a man, which Jenny [his second wife] sees as indications that I am not dependable or I'm not loyal and it's not that, but I can't actually convince her. I have sometimes felt as if I had two skins, the way a spy would feel. A spy has to live out multiple personas and to pretend, to be convincing enough to deliver. I have had crises in my life: the breakup of my first marriage was because I had rejected the concept of [male] monogamy I think. I had to work that through; I *could* commit myself to many women. I am thirty-eight; only now that I have some kind of sense of purpose and dimension do I realize that a lot of what kept me out of danger was innocence. There is a part of me that is still innocent and it's the innocence of an idiot. I can go into a perilous situation and think, it's not me, I'm not involved in it; the shoe doesn't fit. And you project that innocence, as survival; it goes into your body, the way you breathe: you walk in and you convince the other . . . In Zulu it's expressed as the power to overawe or overshadow your challenger with your personality. There are medicines to achieve this mechanically, but you can do it unaided if you are innocent enough and believe in yourself. But at the same time I have to deal with local practices that are unfathomably brutal . . . like the practice of "necklacing." [15]

COPLAN: Yes, I understand about that. The idea is that informers must be publicly destroyed in a manner that will lead others to think twice before informing.

CLEGG: Sure, but . . . it makes you open to clan warfare, burnings, assassination squads, the really grubby, dirty political infighting on a local level.

COPLAN: And a lot of "crab antics." That's the title of a book by the anthropologist Peter Wilson about the Caribbean, referring to an observation by an island crab fisherman to the effect that when you are about to unpack a basket of crabs, watch out for the one on top, because the one who claws his way to the top must be one *tough* crab.

CLEGG [*laughs*]: Yes!

MTHETHWA: After Isaiah Shembe's death his younger brother, my father-in-law, J. G. Shembe, took over, and when he died, Amos Shembe, the son of Isaiah Shembe, took over, who was the last person alive whom Isaiah himself anointed as a leader. So Amos now is the last one, and we are not sure what is to happen now. And J. G.'s son Londa was murdered, and because of his involvement with the politicians, some of those politicians killed him. He was supporting the United Democratic Front (UDF), I don't know if the ANC was involved.

COPLAN: So how many members has the church?

MTHETHWA: Well, we believe about two million members, but this is always a matter of controversy, because the government is nervous about us, and would like to keep our numbers down. Although it's better since the government unbanned the ANC, because they leave us to go our own way now. They do realize that if we *were* interested in politics, we could be a very powerful force. Because we do what our leaders tell us.

COPLAN: What will be the contribution of the Shembe church to the new political organization of South Africa?

MTHETHWA: Well, we feel Shembe was ahead of his time for two reasons. One was the concept of African unity through the concept of regimental church membership, a new use for an old concept. It tended to supersede the concept of *ubuZulu,* a concept that was respected, but the members were taken beyond to a concept of Africanness. Shembe sensitized people to the context of their immediate suffering, and this is reflected in the hymns. So they became very sympathetic, and the church was in fact founded on the victims of forced removals.[16] He gathered all these people who were destitute and living on the roadsides, he gave them food and they became part of his community. The church is founded on such people, who are very politically aware.

COPLAN: But there is an effort to stay away from formal political affiliation.

MTHETHWA: Yes, to emphasize instead the unity of all Africans, and the second reason was the economic concept. In Shembe's church, to work for someone, to be employed, is a sin.

COPLAN: So is it acceptable to be a teacher [like you]?

MTHETHWA: No. It's okay to be a teacher but I can't be a teacher forever. My ambition is to work for some years, and then to get out of here [the university] because it's a sin that I should wake up in the morning and pray to God and read Shembe's hymnal, and ask God to bless the work of my hands, that I might not starve, and then I go and work for somebody else. This was Shembe's idea, and he preached it, and it's in his hymnal. He used to say, after your morning prayer take a hoe and go straight to the fields and work for what is going to sustain you. That was not from the Bible. He said refrain from begging food from people like a dog, because you are a human being. If you blame people for not feeding you, you have yourself to blame, because God has given you two hands like everybody else.

COPLAN: So he must be seen as a creator of culture.

MTHETHWA: Precisely! This is it! You find in South Africa the majority, in Natal especially, the majority of black businesses, are Shembe people. You go to the private taxis, you find that many are Shembe taxis. And it's depressing that we belong to Shembe and still have to be involved in the taxi wars. One of Amos Shembe's sons was killed recently, killed by taxi operators, because he had about five taxis. It's just petty jealousy, because it's got nothing to do with Shembe people as such.

COPLAN: How does Shembe fit into the current struggles over Zuluness in the country?

MTHETHWA: Many people will be disappointed, because when you get close, you see that Shembe did not only sanction Zulu culture; Shembe sanctioned African culture, and he happens to be in Zululand, so the concept of *ubuZulu* has an advantage over the others. But in Shembe's perception, if you are an Indian person and you join his church, you come with your sari, you keep your cultural dress, you don't dress Zulu. And the Pondos, who are dancing in the church, they come in their traditional regalia. Unless they themselves feel they are going to be stigmatized, then they would use the Zulu regalia. The Swazis, they are very culturally resilient, they use their Swazi regalia when they dance in the Shembe because the emphasis is on your traditional culture, whatever it might be. I suppose even if a Zulu man wants to wear a blanket [a Basotho trademark], he won't oppose it. Only perhaps when it comes to food. Because the Sotho, they are well known for eating any creature, and for shaving their heads. We don't approve of those. There are a lot of people who are exploiting Shembe by saying that this is the religion that has preserved *ubuZulu,* but that is not the concept of Shembe, which has preserved *ubuntu,* which is much wider, "humanity." Now that is not to say that Shembe's members do not belong to political organizations. I know from Shembe members who are ANC, some of them are even *Umkhonto we Sizwe,* and some of them who are PAC [Pan-Africanist Congress], and others who are strong Inkatha people. Nearly all the political parties are there. And many people like myself who are neutral and don't want to identify with any political party.

COPLAN: How do you feel about how Zuluness, and African Christianity like Shembe, let's say, are represented in the popular press and the media, in public debates over culture?

MTHETHWA: I think there's a lot of perversion of Zulu culture. Many politicians think that Zuluness is a continuation of apartheid, of separation. Whereas Zuluness was something that was there since before the British wars; it's over one hundred years old. It has never died; it is something that has sustained us. People are treating it as a negative aspect of our culture, but *ubuZulu* is not negative, it is the base which makes us appreciate other people. You can call it positive tribalism. It makes it possible to appreciate people like Treurnicht [the white right-wing conservative party leader]. If you have *ubuZulu* you can appreciate why Treurnicht has these feelings of white superiority. Their concept, Treurnicht's idea, could be negative, but ours is positive. It is this that makes us respect the British people, because we fought the British, and they ran short of bullets when fighting our grandparents, and so they began stabbing one another, and my grandparents who fought at Isandhlwana had great respect for the British because they could fight with spears! They said, Now, these are real men! Even though they killed us, they killed us with spears; they are not cowards who can only use bullets from a distance. And what's more they have a king [a queen in those days]. That tied in very well with *ubuZulu;* it was positive.

COPLAN: What about the Zulu feeling of superiority with regard to other African people?

MTHETHWA: We no longer brandish that sort of thing, we know it is derogatory. Even our kings could marry from another group, Swazi or Sotho or whatever. Anyway, all the groups have names they call each other on occasion. But without *ubuZulu* you cannot appreciate other people's culture, you would see other people as wrong in their ways of thinking, you wouldn't give them credibility unless you have your own credibility, you cannot have tolerance of other people unless you have *ubuZulu.* Everybody has culture, and if you don't have a cultural base you become intolerant of others, because you become these people who want to create the international man, that everybody should be molded into an international culture, which in fact doesn't exist. It's a myth created by people who go to New York, Paris, Johannesburg, and they meet similar people, and whatever *they* do they think it's an international culture. This doesn't exist. What exists are tribal cultures. All the tribal cultures put together must tolerate one another. The man with a weak identity cannot respect others, it's a unity out of diversity. That is very important for South Africa. We can listen to people such as Treurnicht, we don't have to be scared of his ideas. Because we know we also have our own ideas, which might be detrimental to him.

COPLAN: The Afrikaners took over the country by unifying themselves under the banner of culture; they didn't have unity before, until the British attacked and "oppressed" them. Of course, they have not used it only to unify themselves but also to dominate others—then what is now the result? How do you respond to that, since you say you can respect Treurnicht?

MTHETHWA: Yes, but you are not going to change them, and you are not going to kill them. You have got to live with them. If they interfere with me, then I must take action. If my neighbor in Durban North is Treurnicht, and he attacks me, then I use my *ubuZulu* and take my guns and shoot him.

The problem is that we don't have money for projects that communicate our reality. Those who do would rather give money to a white man to make a study or program about us. So my work is partly to combat that. On the politics of domination, people are unaware of how that works; they are so used to a politics of domination that when they say that domination will have to go, they still believe in a winner-take-all situation. And they are going to be very disappointed. So if the ANC says everybody should vote, but we say our two million members should not vote, then they won't vote, and whites might win an election in those areas because of that. If we do vote it will be as a unity. These politicians do not recognize the power of the church in that sense. What I am saying is that whoever wins, they will still have the other parties to contend with, there must be balance between all of them, and this is something that people have not experienced.

COPLAN: There are strong regional political affiliations as well.

MTHETHWA: Yes, if I were to vote tomorrow, I would vote for Buthelezi, not necessarily for Inkatha as a movement. If Buthelezi decided to join the ANC, then I would still vote for him, it's personal. This is the problem with African politics, it's so personal. It's not a matter of writing a constitution; it's a matter of charisma. That's what Mandela has, and so does Buthelezi. Most of us in Natal would still vote for Buthelezi, no matter what is in the Inkatha constitution. And he's *induna nkulu* [great adviser or lieutenant] to the Zulu king, so if you support the concept of *ubuZulu,* then it means you support Buthelezi, because he is the *induna nkulu* to the Zulu king, though many Zulu-speaking people might also hate him, or reject *ubuZulu.* But deep down in their hearts—I mean, I attended an ANC rally, and there was polite applause as the speakers were introduced, but one of them was Prince Ncaizeni, and when his name was spoken there was *shouting* and clapping. And I said no, this is tribalism, why didn't they respond like this to [Amin] Kathrada and Mandela? So it was very clever and strategic for Buthelezi to have the king appoint him, because if you support the king then you have to support him. It's sanctioned by the ancestors; if you pray to your ancestors, you cannot have harmony with them and with God, if you are not loyal to the *ubuZulu,* and the *induna nkulu,* and the king. They represent the ances- tors down here, and the whole cycle must be harmonious. You don't even have to think about it, it's something that you do.

CLEGG: I'm still a marginal man; I'm still incomplete culturally, and I always will be.

COPLAN: But not by default.

CLEGG: No, because of the cultural journey I have taken, which has shaped me, made me whole in certain respects, and left me unassimilated in other ways. When I travel overseas, every day there is a reaffirmation of this. Every time I go to Los Angeles [to make a recording] I marvel at the kinds of alienation that are generated there, the kinds of overcompensation that people practice. The smart-talk, all the time. You can't sit down and say to someone, "How do you really feel, man?" You can't do that like you would in South Africa even with your enemy.

COPLAN: When I first met you in the midseventies, your Anglo-Zulu bi-culturality made a powerful statement. To me, it stood for a commitment to Africanity, not to any one specific culture. Seriousness demands choice, and you chose the language that you chose, that's all. But since then it seems as if Zuluness has caught up with you in an unfortunate way, as it has caught up with Ladysmith Black Mambazo to an extent, where you are all associated with the reactionary, divisive political uses that Inkatha and Buthelezi have made of Zulu identity recently. So first, how do you respond to the ways in which Zuluness is being manipulated, and second, how do we separate what is manipulative and poisonous from what is real and organic in these identifications?

CLEGG: You don't, really, since you can't separate the inventions and manipulations from the organic. We have to go through a series of transformations because they cannot be socially engineered, they are organic transformations. It doesn't matter how many laws you pass, or how many people you kill, or whether a Pol Pot takes over; at the end of the day a transformation will have taken place. We must realize that it *could* have been the Xhosa, or the Pedi instead. The fact that it is the Zulu is the result of a complex set of interactions. There is plenty of blame to be placed on the ANC as well. Mandela wanted to negotiate with Buthelezi from the start, but the ANC hard-liners only had contempt for him, thought he could be ignored, and this was a *major* blunder. There's a hard reality in South Africa, and that is the fundamental cleavage between rural and urban in the black population. It involves jealousy, and the structural impoverishment of the rural communities. They see themselves as "traditional," carrying on the ways of their fathers. At the same time they are exploited by the political economy, and the younger generation of black people, whose fathers came from the rural areas, now look down on them. The ANC attacked the government for their massive removals, in Richards Bay, in the Natal Midlands, which they harped upon, but this was just propaganda. Because there was not and had never been any rural connection between the ANC and these people. The ANC had been under the influence of the South African Communist Party, which believed that the revolution would come only from the urban working class, trade unions and so on. So they made their choice, for COSATU [Congress of South African Trade Unions] and the "black working class," and in so doing they excluded a massive number of people. So they lacked any intimate knowledge of the people they were supposedly championing in criticizing the rural removals, who had no real idea that the ANC was fighting for them overseas or wherever. The people who were cleared off of white farms in the Natal Midlands and dumped in Msinga Reserve, they have become the shock troops of Inkatha. The ANC was just not there, and no link was made. The problem is that ANC political activists come from a certain, "internationalist" background and ideological viewpoint, and there is a generational gap as well, and they are urban and look down on those people. These are the kinds of contradictions that the present government is well aware of, and exploits all the time.

COPLAN: Applied *Boere anthropologie* [Afrikaner anthropology].

CLEGG: Yes, and it *works*. These poor people in Inkatha, they are out of work, and it gives them something they can do, to take action. And there are far larger political motivations. If you look at where the violence has been directed, it's especially the PWV Triangle [Pretoria-Witwatersrand-Vereeniging industrial area in the Transvaal], because over 30 percent of South Africans live in that area, and if you can control it, you control the board. And Inkatha is winning to some extent; Alexandra [Township, in Johannesburg] is being taken over by squatters loyal to Inkatha. That's the game. I have such a problem with this concept of [right-wing black] "vigilantes," which *is* manipulated by the government, but which ignores the reality of a core of resistance among Africans to urban black politics. They don't feel that their rural base is being served. Who are the people in Cape Town in 1986 who were called the *witdoeke?* [17] They were Xhosa migrants, and they were fighting the United Democratic Front [internal allies of the exiled ANC]. Now, who are the storm troopers of the ANC here in the PWV? It's those same Xhosa migrants, the *witdoeke!* Those same people who fought *against* the UDF. Something has happened in the interim: the ANC has now been legitimized, and a deal has been struck. In the same way, Inkatha struck deals with the removal people: "Come up [from the Cape] to the PWV, and if you are in sufficient numbers, you will have a powerful bloc vote when elections come, and be able to control the area. Squatter politics is now the dominant politics. Inkatha and the ANC are using the same methods.

COPLAN: Yes, using the workers hostels like the one in Alexandra, where the long-term migrant residents have been replaced by recent arrivals from Natal and KwaZulu, who are attacking the residents on behalf of Inkatha, a terribly real, literal "cultural Masada," if you like.

CLEGG: That's right. And this thing about a Xhosa-Zulu tribal conflict is a complete figment created by the government and swallowed by the local and Western press which calls all conflict among blacks tribal war whether it's political parties, or intradistrict rivalry or whatever. There is no history of "ethnic conflict" between Xhosa and Zulu.

COPLAN: But Buthelezi has cleverly used Zulu identity to mobilize those people. In Natal today, isn't there this division between those who acknowl-

edge King Goodwill Zwelethini [Inkatha supporters] as their own and those
who do not [ANC supporters or neutrals]? Isn't that a challenge to your own
projection of what Zuluness is supposed to be about?

CLEGG: What you are talking about is a civil war, with royalists and anti-
royalists; this wouldn't have made a difference to whether you were French
or English or not when it happened in Europe. Blacks here understand that:
they know they are all still Zulu.

COPLAN: But Buthelezi is making more and more frequent use of allegiance to the king, whom he controls, as a marker of Zulu identity.

CLEGG: Yes, but that's because he's losing the battle. So he appeals to
conservative ethnic feelings, but in the long run it is not going to work. I
came back from the States late last year, and I ran straight into a heated
conflict with my dancers, because they were being mobilized by Inkatha, by
men from the hostels. And the force around which they were being mobilized was *is'khaya* [rural home] versus *is'townshipi* [black urban areas]; we
homeboys against these city ghetto people, because they have everything;
running water, electricity, nice houses.

COPLAN: Concealed weapons.

CLEGG [*laughing*]: They carry concealed weapons. It's been going on
since 1976, with the Mzimhlope Hostel attacks on township residents during
the Soweto uprising. An Inkatha representative said to me, "Listen, we had
a meeting with these children [young ANC union organizers], and they
spoke to us in English! They failed to explain to us why we should strike:
we need to work." But, these are growing pains, dynamics that will be used
by both sides for their own political purposes.

My career has been a documenting of the situation in South Africa as it is
embodied in the culture as it passes before me. It's nearly impossible to mediate these contradictions, rural-urban and so forth. I am a living mediation,
because what used to impress black people in the old days was that I was a
university lecturer, yet I was also performing this outrageous, "tribal" war
dance; I had *isibandla* [leather bracelets] on my hands, made from goats that
had been slaughtered for the ancestors. So the subtext was, highly educated
western educator, clearly *enjoying* performing these things, and involved in
these cultural imperatives, which are considered *backward*.

COPLAN: And the statement had irresistible force because you were practicing it, not simply studying it, or *stating* your "love of Zulu culture." Because to perform is to embody culture.

CLEGG: Yes, yes. The relevance of what I do *now* is still linked to that.

COPLAN: What did you say to your dancers about Inkatha?

CLEGG: I said to them, look, do you know what Inkatha is? And they said
no, we don't know what it is or what it stands for. We [our forefathers]
fought against the Zulu king in 1879.[18]

COPLAN: Bongani, what is your opinion of culture in the township environment? For instance, one thing that concerns my friend Jonathan Clegg is the antagonism between rural and urban black people; the rural man who says that the city slickers have got no morality, you can't expect proper behavior from them, and yet they pretend to despise us because they think they are better, yet we don't know what kind of culture they have. And then the urban man says, well these *amagoduka* [bumpkins] out there, they are doing things in the old way, and we have no use for that, and it's ridiculous to try to live according to those old ways now.

MTHETHWA: Yes, but those who live in the township, the so-called city slickers, they tend to be more Zulu than those Zulu in the rural areas. When they are making marriage negotiations in the townships they are more into the details, the tradition. Because they are overprotecting the culture, more than the people in the country, who feel they don't have to. Even the Zulu who is an academic, he tries to be more traditional than the man in the street, because the man in the street is not threatened by any other culture. A person like me, I am always invaded by people who want me to behave like this or that, and then I must put my culture first, become self-conscious about it, defend it. I went to a Venda *chikona* [national dance of the Venda people of the Northern Transvaal] in 1989; there was a Venda chief there with his *indunas*. And all of my colleagues were just talking to him like an ordinary person. They wanted to get information on the *chikona* quickly. The nation comes to dance for a whole day, and it's a political rally, but it's a musical event, a thing that was started by [John] Blacking. So they wanted to get information quickly, but I said, they are not going to get anything. So when the chief greeted me I greeted him with Zulu etiquette. I did not stand, but got on my knees, and grabbed his hand, and told him I was from Zululand, and apologized for not speaking his language. Immediately they got a man who had been in Johannesburg who could speak Zulu and Venda. And when I drank his beer I used the Zulu style of drinking. So I asked them how do you drink beer, because this is our style where I am from, so they told me how in Venda tradition beer is drunk. After that I asked them just a few questions about the *chikona,* about the involvement of the ancestors. And they told me some secrets which they had not told any of my colleagues. They told me how they prepared for this dance, the prayers to the ancestors, the slaughtering of animals, the invocations against fighting at the event. They told me that they had respect for me because I was a Zulu traditionalist. So I got all the secrets of the *chikona,* in a short time, which I would not have gotten if I had a different attitude.

In Zululand a man who owns a horse and is a skilled horseman feels more important than the man who is riding in a Mercedes-Benz. That's why Buthelezi is very clever in exploiting culture. He paints himself as the defender of culture, and that makes us all very sympathetic to him. We have high respect, because he dances with the people, he carries the sticks, he does all the things that we know, and he actually knows it better than the people below him; he knows the *amahubo* [clan anthems], and so people respect him for that. And he is also a good song-leader, with the people. This is what I found frustrating with Mandela. He is leading African people, and applying international norms, which are not known to us. He should be addressing the people in song, it would make him more credible to the people. Even if he decides to use the Xhosa tradition, or Sotho, or whatever. He is a chief among his own people [the Transkei Thembu], after all. He is not going to antagonize Zulus if he does that, nor Basotho either. It would be better if he would use his own culture. All this use of constitutions and politics here in Africa, that's going to fail. There can never be what Mandela calls a "national culture." I don't believe in the New South Africa, or in international or national culture. We must present all existing culture to be credible. All these cultures must be brought to the fore, and then after that, we can live with those cultures. But singling out individuals and trying to mold a new culture from those individuals, which is neither one thing nor another, that won't work. They should link groups of people through their cultures, rather than trying to link individuals, and talking of one man, one vote. Because that is not going to work. It is never "one man" here in Africa, as with the Shembe church; we will act together. If Treurnicht says to the hard Afrikaners, vote this way, then they will all, like sheep, vote like that, and Buthelezi's people the same. This is the problem, that these politicians will kill you for saying one man, one vote won't do! Look, tribalism is not negative; tribalism is unifying. It is not intended to destroy other people; it is rather what we need, for political unity—tribalism. The notion of an international man and a culture of individualism are only notions. They must learn from both African and Afrikaner tribalism, and from British tribalism—because all these are tribalisms. My white colleagues talk of the New South Africa, whereas for the last hundred years we have been changing our culture, trying to cope with what is new, so I said to them, if you want to be new, try learning Zulu.

COPLAN: Hein, will the effort to "reclaim" Afrikaans succeed?

WILLEMSE: People need to feel the historical urge to reclaim. The elite colored people are trying to correct the history for themselves, and Afrikaans may serve as one way for them to locate themselves in history in this country. *Other* people have histories, and with the African National Congress's announced tolerance for "differences," the history of language and resistance may become a function of the group, rather than of the undifferentiated "oppressed" as a nation. That individual insertion into a group is as important as one's position as part of the oppressed.

COPLAN: I know that one of the defenses expressed by "Africans" towards "Coloreds" is that "You people of the Cape have no history, no culture of your own," whereas they have a strong historical sense of who they are, for which their languages are an important medium.

WILLEMSE: I can see, in the future, Afrikaans as a means of constructing that. But Afrikaans always, since the turn of the century, was the rural, working people's language. If you want to be classified as a *plaasjappie* [bumpkin], just try speaking English with a strong Afrikaans accent, that was a giveaway. There was always this tension, this dichotomy—the people know no other language, on the other hand they are always being told it's somebody else's [whites'] language . . . Class differences are extremely pronounced in Afrikaans, because the Afrikaans spoken by black people was not legitimated, it was completely excluded, with lexical elements which do not exist in official Afrikaans. They call that slang, but it's not slang, these words and dialects have a very long history . . . Afrikaans is really a simplified language, all the declensions from Dutch have gone; it's skeletal in construction. So it's very incorporative. In Johannesburg, someone like Don Mattera [colored street-Afrikaans-speaking author], he can speak four languages. When you listen to him speaking Afrikaans, he's borrowing from all those languages . . . Afrikaans has become completely part of black street subculture. The people who "purified" and codified the language have kept such influences out of the official language, so what you hear as Afrikaans on television is something that very few people actually speak. The language that people are writing, people don't recognize readily as theirs, and the language in which school books are written is a sort of State Afrikaans. So we have a hell of a job to get Afrikaans educationists to recognize that all the variants are part of the living language.

Cape Town is a port city, where very few people ever had the sense of being connected to the hinterland. There's a problem of geography; Cape Town is surrounded by mountains, and you actually had to cross these mountains to get somewhere else. The people just on the other side of the mountains in the Boland, they've got a different sense of what their history is from people in Cape Town. So today, District 6 in Cape Town has been historically constructed as a monument of loss, of the government's injustice to colored people, a monument to the struggle for nonracialism.

COPLAN: Like the book, *The Struggle for District 6,* which is an example of presentism: reconstructing District 6 in the terms and service of a subsequent political discourse.[19]

WILLEMSE: Yes, as in "We have a history and that history is District 6." I think we need to look at District 6 as a particular phenomenon, rather than a real lived experience as it is talked about. There are many streams of reality and constructed history flowing into "District 6."

COPLAN: One of my students here felt that coloreds are not included in the South African discourse, that when people talk about South Africa in the world, her experience is not represented. Is this reconstruction of history related to this perception, and to this attempt to insert themselves into public images and perceptions of South Africa?

WILLEMSE: Intellectually, due to my insertion, my own personal history, I can understand why it's necessary, but this is a dilemma which many people of my generation face. We have come through Black Consciousness, and through a period of connecting ourselves to a broader South Africa, trying to construct ourselves as South Africans rather than coloreds. We want to see ourselves as sharing the same experiences as Indian South Africans, as Xhosa-speaking South Africans. Most intellectuals are still in that phase, especially those of us who have had some materialist training, historical materialism. We share the perception that we need to look at some sort of overarching South Africanness, rather than individual group-oriented history. But I can understand why it's important for people to see themselves in history. One way of doing it is through language.

COPLAN: Can deeply rooted, implicit, experiential identities, which are tied up in complex ways with explicit categories such as "colored," "Afrikaner," and so on, can that kind of loyalty, that aspect of their humanity, be fed productively into the overarching identity? Must they be seen only in mutual opposition; colored *or* South African, but not both?

WILLEMSE: I can completely understand people's problems about that. I am currently working on the notion of tolerance, trying to look at our history as an overarching one: Xhosa, Zulu, Afrikaner history as part of my history. It's the only way we can become fully South African and still retain a sense that there is something particular that we have contributed. Apartheid denied people interaction with each other, any sense of sharing their humanity; of sharing what they like, for example. A friend of mine who found out that some black [African] people also like European classical music. Or that we *all* like curry and rice!

COPLAN: The odd thing that strikes me about South Africa is that it is the only African country that is a country; a unity created by an appalling history but an internalized, *felt* unity just the same. And apartheid was a deliberate attempt to dissolve this unity. How is the country going to be put together now, in a cultural sense, since to some degree people have accepted those very categories created by the state to divide them?

WILLEMSE: My answer would be neither; we should actually allow people to experience what's been done, make involvement with other people available, accessible. It is an injustice to me that I never had the opportunity to pick up Xhosa from my environment, though so many people speak it in the Cape . . . Natural, informal contact will initiate processes that we cannot foresee, that people committed to social engineering cannot foresee. A kind of fusion is happening already, partly through political struggle, though with difficulty, since Africans have always been seen as different.

COPLAN: Yet I have colored friends who take pleasure in pointing out to me, a foreigner, things that they identify as representative of them: seeing a practice or an occurrence and saying, "That's us."

WILLEMSE: Self-recognition in itself is important. But what I'm saying is that we must not legislate the movement of people in relation to themselves. The legacy of division, of apartheid, is going to last for generations. What we do have is a sense that there is a common South Africanness, and it will develop through sport, or literature, through education; that we share something, even though there is a lot of tension in that. Look, if people talk about what South Africa would look like, they would talk about Sophiatown,[20] and District 6, because those were the places and times when people had to gather together. They were not the happiest of times, of social war, gangsterism, but that is what deep down for many South Africans, and even for coloreds, is the basis of a sense that we are South African.

COPLAN: Another question, Johnny, concerns your leadership of the South African Musicians' Alliance (SAMA), the controversy over your participation in the Mandela seventieth birthday concert in England, and the personal and professional cost to you of the politics of these involvements. When I first heard of you doing this, I thought it was admirable, of course, but I also thought: quicksand.

CLEGG: My personal philosophy is that of a dancer. In a sense, life is a dance; the rhythms which are played in South Africa, although they've been orchestrated in a particular way, have been here a terribly long time. I just thought, here I am, someone who more than any other nationally known musician has tried to effect a cultural collaboration, a meeting point. I have been made suspect by certain people in the "cultural movement" [the cultural Left], and the only way I'm going to be able to walk away from this in a whole sense, is to dance with them. At the same time, in 1986, we reached a crescendo of violence, and I thought then that if one didn't dance, become involved, then one would be relegated to irrelevance. So I became a prime mover in the formation of SAMA. This threw me into a nightmare vortex of cultural politics: endless, fraught with profound contradictions and paradoxes, to this day unresolved because their solution has been limited by the way they have been *formulated* by the Left, the progressive forces. As the cult of ideology is disassembled, genuine cultural forces *will* come into play. That's why I said that you cannot engineer violence out of the political solution. Similarly, you cannot engineer a "people's culture," because there isn't a people's culture in the sense that the Left desires. What there are are varied formal expressions of three hundred years of common history, but it's been experienced in different ways, different expressions of the same reality. The commonalities, the myths, have to be reworked by performers and artists into a common or mutual knowledge of suffering and freedom.

COPLAN: What was the purpose of SAMA?

CLEGG: The purpose of the alliance was to provide a platform for musicians, who had never really been involved in politics before, to contribute to progressive cultural organizations within the UDF.

COPLAN: To make politics respond to art?

CLEGG: Essentially, but of course the opposite happened—politics leaked into art—because they [the UDF] would not register SAMA unless it was aligned directly to the policies of the UDF, to consult, and to be hypersensitive to the "necessities" of the "overriding struggle." That argument always clinched the debate, whatever reservations we might have had about our involvement as musicians. The only way we could challenge UDF politics was to say, "We will find a way to support you, but not in the direct, mechanical political way that you wish." They always felt, "Culture is a weapon of struggle"—finished. It is a tool; they had an instrumentalist conception of culture and cultural production. And the people to whom they had given cultural portfolios were not themselves successful practitioners, and virtually none were musicians. Even some of their famous writers and cultural activists had no popular public appeal. SAMA had to address these dynamics, because we had the audience, but we didn't have the right political line, as individual musicians. So SAMA became a clearing house, a place where all the politics of a nonracial democratic South Africa could be fielded, debated, and a means for musicians to participate could be created. So that our members could feel they could participate, as *musicians,* not as politicians. We had a manifesto, which I helped put together, which said that the political activists had failed to address the problems of freedom of expression, of association, of assembly, of movement for artists. These four freedoms affect musicians, so when there is an issue concerning them, we will be there, because without these freedoms, we cannot play. On censorship, or any issue of free expression, we will be there because we are fighting for music. We did their political work for them. They couldn't tie political involvement to personal concerns. So we were able to mobilize musicians; against the South African Broadcasting Corporation or wherever, so they could feel, we have a right and a duty to raise our voices because we are directly affected.

COPLAN: Performers needed a location in politics, partly because of the hostility here to performers because of their ambiguous status. Coming from the common people, they are attacked in the townships for "getting above themselves" if they succeed in the industry, go overseas and so on.

CLEGG: Yes, very much, because we were responding also to intimidation, around 1985–86, when a series of music festivals were destroyed by "comrades" [young UDF-ANC militants]. We had no one to talk to. We went to the UDF and said, whatever you might feel about "good time" music, and popular "jive," whether you feel it's politically correct or not, that's how the players, as workers, make a living; that's how they send their children to school. We feel that because we are a soft target, we're being isolated. You don't do this to boxing, or to football, because the fans there, the "people," would literally kill you.

COPLAN: They didn't do it to the "famous writers" either.

CLEGG: OK, they said, we hear you, but we can't respond to individuals. We need an organization to work with, so form one and then we'll be able to work with you to solve this problem. Our argument to them was that "traditional" African music and culture is intended to be humanizing. When you have experienced apartheid, then you don't risk going out in the townships to see a band in order to be told about that experience. You don't need that. You've gone there to be reconstituted as an individual, a human being. The weekends are for reconstitution.

COPLAN: This is the "singing revolution" argument; not as in Estonia where self-expression was their only political weapon, but in the sense that people who are singing are psychologically strengthened for the actual fight, because they have a stronger sense of self-definition as the people who are fighting.

CLEGG: Yes! "Good time" music is reconstitutive because it says, climb inside and I'll make you whole, get up off your chair, don't feel so bad, let's move together, a bit more strongly with each repeated cycle of the song.

COPLAN: African societies have in general shared a recognition that music is cathartic, and that people in a "depressed" condition cannot win. Amidst social trauma and disintegration, music provides what Laura Bohannon called the "return to laughter." But it can in any society function as an "opiate of the people" as well. As our African-American poet and playwright Imamu Amiri Baraka said about black popular music radio, "The 'soul' station is the new plantation." So, how did the UDF respond?

CLEGG: Well, SAMA became a very strong voice, added to the political struggle. There were tensions; sometimes we could not come out and support a UDF position, because we could not convince our membership that this affected them in the way they were being told. They said the issue is not "the Struggle" but us, black people, struggling to raise music up in the country, just as a man in the mines struggles for mineworkers' rights.

COPLAN: Of course, the Mass Democratic Movement calls this "workerism": a narrow concern with issues of immediate material welfare, and they campaign against this in the labor movement.

CLEGG: Our members were saying that working in a mine is not an inherently political act, so why should our work as musicians be inherently politi-

cal? Our members were basically politically illiterate, but they were trying
to find a way to fit into the movement, and to make the music they wanted to
make and at the same time be politically relevant. Of course, among all this
you had a lot of professional jealousy among musicians. The jazz artists
tended to be more politicized but less popular and successful, whereas the
commercial artists, the Brenda Fassies [a current pop star], were highly successful but not politically aware.

COPLAN: So how did it come about that Brenda Fassie and others like
her started to make political recordings? Brenda started with the album *Ag
Shame, Lovey!* and the last one was *Black President.*

CLEGG: That's because the context changed, and there was some kind of
navigational coordinate for music in general. She was responding to public
pressure for that kind of statement, and it was no longer dangerous to
make it.

COPLAN: Well, Brenda is playing a role there. When we had parties with
the black South African exiles in New York, that's all they played. Getting
worked-up to *Black President.*

MASAKELA: When I got to Lusaka in 1982 the [ANC] secretary general,
Alfred Nzo, said, "What do you want to do?" I was furious! I said, I came
here—you should know what I am to do! So then they appointed me administrative secretary of the arts and culture department of the ANC. I had to
learn how to make other people creative in the interests of what we were
fighting for. There was a growing gap between the resistance movement and
cultural movement within South Africa, and the ANC outside. There had
been an overwhelming influence of Black Consciousness in the South African artistic world. Also, the artist was *not* viewed as a part of the whole
effort for change. Attitudinally, it was a period of romanticizing and retreat-
ing into the past, but also of asserting and affirming the African aspect of
one's experience in South Africa as opposed to the Eurocentric one. The
Culture of Resistance Festival [in Gaborone in 1982] recognized that culture
had a role to play in the struggle for a free South Africa, and that cultural
workers were worthy members of the community, who were producing
something as valuable as any other, although it was not always tangible. The
artistic product was seen as an important element in the development of ourselves as a people. Although this has been decried by critics in recent years,
artists felt they had a role to play, not only to contemplate experience, but
also to participate; that art could have a political responsibility.

The most important thing is the creation of a critical audience. What wor-
ries me about our culture in South Africa is that you are only legitimated if
you have been abroad. We need artists performing here for South African
audiences, so that people here can say they like it or not. To develop our
own values in public culture.

COPLAN: Those who might come from South Africa to perform overseas had better bring something South African, because an attempt to outperform the Americans at their own popular forms will not succeed. The successes have been Miriam Makeba, Hugh Masakela, Jonathan Clegg, Ladysmith Black Mambazo, Mbongeni Ngema, and those others who have brought something of South Africa's own.

MASAKELA: But you first have to feel that your own thing is good, and that is a problem for us in South Africa . . . South African TV really is the pits. So many languages at once, it makes for such confusion . . . They are caught in the trap of having created a media culture which was meant to benefit a few of the people, and so the local industry was geared just for that limited white audience, and now what has to be done is to transform that, so that South African TV really plays a role. In addition to state broadcasting you need alternatives; it should not be a monopoly of the state. Our basic stance is that we are against censorship. You cannot legislate values. They are a by-product of democracy. Values derive from the kind of society that you establish. But there will be need for licensing. In South Africa, the key is money. I would create public places where people can go and watch whatever is available, since so few of our people can afford TV and movie tickets now. Culturally speaking, whatever we say, we still have to take into consideration that in the rural areas, people still live in the apartheid era. And it is those forces of darkness that dominate there, in the rural areas. We have to devise some sort of plan where communities who work on farms and so on will be served.

COPLAN: There are cases where people have no specific idea of what the ANC represents, and they can easily be persuaded by demagoguery or promises of immediate benefits to fight against people in the urban areas.

MASAKELA: I think that gravitates around the question of whether we will be able to create an environment of free political activity, and to remove the violence as unnecessary; whether it is the violence of the farmer toward those who are squatting on his land, or interparty violence; it's key to the creation of a new society.

COPLAN: You feel there *is* a "culture of violence"?

MASAKELA: Absolutely. Apartheid is violence from beginning to end. This society has existed and thrived on violence. The creation of this environment depends on conscious and deliberate programs for creating culture, but also on removing the violence. It's been a very short time since the ANC and other political organizations have been unbanned. What kills is that our expectations go beyond the reality. The achievements have been stunning. We never thought we could have a full conference of the ANC in South Africa, but we did. We had CODESA,[21] and Mr. Mandela being able to get up and speak his mind honestly is a vast, an immeasurable achievement . . . I don't believe that there is an ANC culture; there's a South African culture, and I think that what we as the ANC have been doing is to develop the South African culture, and allow it to become general. We all recognize, and strongly advocate the development of a strong civil society, and I think culture falls within that realm. We as the ANC will participate in that civil society, not as a political party, but as individual citizens who have a responsibility to common projects that benefit people irrespective of their affiliation.

COPLAN: There must be learning in both directions. Johnny Clegg was told by people in the movement that he was not progressive, because he was working with this "tribalistic" cultural material, and he had to say, Look, this is the music of migrant workers, and thousands of people perform and participate in it. It belongs to them, they are here, and it's part of who they are. If you don't give that recognition, and incorporate it into the general movement of the country, they are going to oppose you. They are going to remove themselves from the nationalist project saying they are not understood. There has to be room, culturally, for quite localized frameworks and contexts.

MASAKELA: Absolutely! We actually encourage our members to get involved in those things, and you can't go there wearing an ANC label all the time. It's a better way of winning people over to your movement if you show you are a person who has civic pride and wants to develop the community.

WILLEMSE: I'm not concerned about *forging* a South African identity.

COPLAN: You don't see ethnicity as a major divisive problem?

WILLEMSE: If we are not going to *make* it one; if we can refrain from reifying ethnicity all the time.

COPLAN: People will do that if the state is parasitic and weak; if social resources are up for grabs like that.

WILLEMSE: Yes, but we can start developing a set of common attitudes towards government, towards sport, social institutions, as ours. South Africanness is most likely to develop outside the politicians' domain, in the realm of common inclinations, experience, popular culture; these will play the greatest role. Coloreds would like to know what *they* have contributed toward this South Africanness. I don't deny an African the right to be president, but we need some of our own people to be there as well, and on the TV. We need to be tolerant rather than exclusive; let everybody have their place in the sun. We must emphasize common South Africanness as against the current government, which has identified Afrikaners and South Africa as synonymous. They would say, "So and so is against South Africa," meaning against the Afrikaner nationalists, the government.

COPLAN: As with the controversy as to whether the springbok should re-

main the national sporting symbol. The government's insistence that past
abuses now be forgotten necessitates the denial that the springbok is a powerful symbol of exclusion and white supremacy. Public symbols form a significant arena of reflection and contestation, because they represent and
define a political landscape.

WILLEMSE: I wouldn't deny their importance, but in twenty years we may
hope to have a common attitude toward these things. It's important for
people to undergo this process; no one is losing anything; we are all gaining
by making an issue out of it, by searching for solutions to it. Black South
Africans [Bantu speakers] have the sense they are coming into their own
now; that they are going to be the next government.

COPLAN: Which not only intimidates but is actively being used to intimi-
date members of other groups.

WILLEMSE: Absolutely. In Cape Town, on the day of Mandela's release,
after waiting in a packed crowd for three or four hours in the hot sun, a
bunch of Xhosa speakers, ruffians, began running around, grabbing people's
bags, and shouting, "We, the Xhosas, are coming now, we are going to rule
this country." People were very scared, because that was a reaction that
people there *didn't* expect. Mandela was a national symbol, a symbol of victory for a free South Africa, and suddenly you have this bunch of hooligans
masking their criminality with an ethnic label. People were scared. So a
group of us, we left and went home and watched Mandela on TV arriving,
after having waited for several hours. It was not a political statement by official spokesmen, it wasn't said on a platform; but a real life interaction and it
created an impression of the ANC for people on the scene. It undermines
official pronouncements and policies: those criminals may not have belonged
to the ANC, but they became the ANC for people.

In the Western Cape, there is a particular political history, which they
don't have elsewhere. Oldsters here will tell you that political resistance
began when the Boers first landed on the beaches [referring to seventeenth-
century conflicts between Dutch settlers and Khoikhoi, "Hottentot pastoral-
ists]; a much longer sense of time. Despite this there is no such thing as the
"colored community." I can understand the idea of community if you go up
to Bo-Kaap [an old "Malay" Muslim colored neighborhood in central Cape
Town] because they've got a real sense of common attitudes, history, relationships; they celebrate things together, there are real networks. Where I'm
living in Brackenfell [a new, distant colored suburb], you have an Afrikaans-
style, northern suburbs, not as poor as Bo-Kaap and the inner city areas, but
we have no sense of community. We bring together longtime rural residents
with recent arrivals from the city; there's no sense of having been together,
and of being as we were under apartheid, where you had networks which
functioned strongly as a protection and took a long time to develop. The

difference between rural and urban differentiates people across racial barriers. In a small town like Ladysmith, beyond knowing who is what race there was a sense of interaction, belonging, of knowing who you are dealing with. And the whole thing about the so-called colored *Volk,* colored nation, that the government tried to develop in the late fifties, what they called the "Developing Colored Nation." It's a very difficult thing for a mulatto group to suddenly find itself being forged into a "nation." Because you've got coastal people, who are the result of everything the state has been against [miscegenation] and suddenly you want to develop them into a "nation."

COPLAN: So what about the educational outlook, for us as educationists, and in relation to our research work?

WILLEMSE: I think it's important for myself as a black Afrikaans writer to bring black Afrikaans culture to the fore, and through my interest in oration, to make people see that what they have is at least as valuable as what they have received. More generally, this university has set itself the task of developing national ideals, bringing people together from across the country here, and as a young university we are interested in seeing how our people here can play a role in developing an overarching South Africanism. I think this intersects with our notions of what syllabi should look like, how should we approach literature, approach education. We have been intolerant to differences, and we need to accept that differences are not liabilities, that differences can be to our advantage. Through culture, to develop tolerance, and the sense that somehow in this country we are related to each other.

COPLAN: A national culture related to the need to relegitimate the state, since you now have an illegitimate state, but you need a strong, consensual one, and culture is an essential element in creating support for such a state.

WILLEMSE: Absolutely. Everybody talks about their expectations: "When we are free." Everyone has different definitions and expectations about what freedom is, what the "New" South Africa means. In most cases these expectations concern bridging gaps, or coming into your own, fulfilling your potential.

COPLAN: But it's always in the context of the whole South Africa; nobody, not even Buthelezi, are asserting claims within a purely regional context: the pie is South Africa.

WILLEMSE: Apartheid created certain divided identities, but it also created its opposition, in the determination to bridge those created identities. This doesn't coexist as a sort of rational opposition, it coexists in experience, and as a mental landscape. People can have an ethnic identity and a national identity, and this is not something that one should legislate about. We should create a playing field for those kinds of interactions to develop. Because attempts to legislate identity are going to create all sorts of other tensions. What would happen for instance if the ANC were to become identified as a Xhosa government?

COPLAN: People would pull back from it, and refuse to invest in it, and the problem becomes insoluble, and you can create a Lebanon.

WILLEMSE: Yes, so for the future of this country it is absolutely essential to create a state that everybody believes in, by creating elements that people can identify with.

CLEGG: SAMA was supposed to have melded into a new nonracial musicians union [Performing Arts Workers Union (PAWE)] now. But I've faded into the background. At the Los Angeles UNO Cultural Boycott conference in February [1991], we were told that we should form a nonpartisan organization, including Inkatha as well as ANC and so on, of cultural people, who could then form the basis of a proper national body for cultural issues. But that wasn't done, for political reasons. Everybody had an agenda. I felt that it was time for others to get up and run things, and I am not prepared to get involved in any more factional politics. There's been so much energy expended on that; on trying to patch together a "patriotic front" for culture. To be honest, though, culture is the last thing on the agenda of the ANC, or of anybody else, because of the level of material deprivation in the country. So let's take culture off the political agenda now, and just let it run. We are fooling ourselves if we think we are going to have a Department of Arts and Culture in a future South Africa that is going to do anything helpful.

COPLAN: Well, Wally Serote [head of the ANC Department of Arts and Culture] says, "We will reserve the right to intervene in culture."

CLEGG: I won't comment on Wally's cultural politics; he's been a stalwart in the Struggle, and when it's been darkest, he's actually helped us to weather the storm, but it's hard to not look very closely [skeptically] at someone who has had a political career based on culture. It's hard to divorce the politics of a particular party, their political view of culture, from their conception of a national culture. That's my problem with any agenda on culture. Because you can't engineer a national culture.

COPLAN: No sub-Saharan African country has succeeded in doing that, not even Tanzania, though most of them have tried. Part of what I am writing about in South Africa is the necessity of freedom of cultural expression without any assurance that such free expression will contribute to the emergence of a national society.

CLEGG: The issue of culture is a double-edged sword, useful for any political cause, a highly volatile, ambiguous arena, and that is its power: the power of the symbol is in its ambiguity.

COPLAN: Yet the essays my students wrote at Western Cape on the question of national culture all said, Yes, we must have one, because there can be no intergroup understanding, no national unity without it. Political activists are seeking policies and strategies for creating the culture they think the country needs. If you point out that it can't be done, they answer, yes, but we need nevertheless to direct our efforts towards that goal. Wally says we must all learn to speak several South African languages, and in principle I agree. I would advise any nonviolent, well-intentioned white South African who wanted to act positively to learn an African language and simply use it. That's a tall order, of course; it's more difficult in some ways than shooting the enemy. Wally, of course, he's from Alexandra where they speak *Tsotsitaal* [Afro-Afrikaans street dialect]; in fact, I think he thinks *Tsotsitaal* ought to be the national language [*laughs*] . . . And there's a part of me that agrees with that, the whole polyglot expression of South Africanity. Wally is able to carry himself with such assurance in so many contexts in this country. He's at ease in the townships, at ease in front of ANC party congresses, union meetings, academic conferences, overseas; yet he keeps his own council.

CLEGG: Well, mostly because he's lately been isolated by the recognition that culture is not important to the ANC. Culture wasn't even given its own portfolio at the Durban ANC Party Congress. His department is kept around just to humor people.

COPLAN: Yet in countries like Zimbabwe the government has officially intruded into every aspect of civil life, including cultural institutions: the schools, radio and TV, museums, art centers, community cultural organizations, publishing, the art professions, foreign scholarships, the abolition of academic freedom at the university, performance competitions; everywhere, through the Ministry of Sports, Education, and Culture. A colleague at the University of Zimbabwe wrote to me at Cape Town and said, How terrible! There's no "popular culture"; you are fooling yourself to write of any culture that bubbles up from below and challenges the status quo under such conditions. But I replied, Don't underestimate popular culture: a good deal of it has been created all over the world in response to just such conditions, though not programmatically.

CLEGG: One *naturally* does; you naturally create, express your life, in various forms. Of course, it starts in *jokes*. In the Soviet Union for example. Joking is the first essential reconstitution of the people's popular culture; it's quick, it's effective; you choose your audience; and you *communicate*.

COPLAN: Yes, like the fear of African authoritarianism expressed in the wry extension of the ANC's well-known political slogan, "One man, one vote, once." Anything can be turned against the powers, even their most "sacred" national symbols; these are often especially useful for breaking open, defamiliarizing the dominant discourse, beating them at their own game, because they cannot disavow the value and universality of the symbols they seek to manipulate. So Great Zimbabwe cannot be other than Great: especially in comparison to the country's present "nation builders." I have a lot of faith in people's ability to turn "dominant" symbols inside out.

Ironically, the increasing unwillingness of Western agencies to fund "development," which means paying the bill for repressive state bureaucracies that produce nothing but self-perpetuation, will actually assist the broadening of political discourse and popular expression. In Lesotho, the word *tsoelopele* "development," is synonymous with *'muso,* the government. So as one of James Ferguson's informants said, "Development [the government] has a lot of enemies in Lesotho" (126).

CLEGG: The issue of a common citizenship is a very abstract notion in a society that has articulated itself through racial or cultural categories, and cultural categories within racial ones. Forms of social location have been attached to group categories related to access to power. We are now saying that all this must be swept away in favor of some abstract notion of common citizenship which has no historical precedent or basis. The ANC is trying to combat group identification, and in so doing, of course, acknowledging it by saying that freedom of expression cannot be simply written into a Bill of Rights, but there must be the legal capacity to address potential *abuses* of freedom of expression, and this must be codified: a potential license for censorship.

COPLAN: As you said, this *is* an attempt to remove the expression of conflict from social process.

CLEGG: But the ANC would say that in the United States you have a judicial system whose decisions are widely regarded as legitimate. We don't have that; we can't trust the judiciary to interpret a law within a context of a general, systemic acceptability, quite apart from whether or not individuals agree with a particular interpretation. The ANC is saying that we must develop such a judicial tradition, and it must be more limiting, and more codified in detail, specific guidelines to address fears of abuse.

COPLAN: Because the current crisis of legitimacy is in large measure precipitated by the fact that those charged with keeping public order are the assassins, the reactionaries, and the fomentors of public factional violence. Yet legalized violence and destabilization by elements within the security forces is only part of the story. Even if Mandela were heading the government and, say, making policy regarding agriculture in the [Orange] Free State, the Basotho, who originally lost much of that area to the Afrikaners, and were hounded off it by apartheid land policies, will surely say, "Who is Mandela to define our land rights in the Free State?"

CLEGG: It's a tremendous task. There have always been two levels in government in South Africa. One has been the official Western system of parliament and the judiciary, and the other is the so-called tribal system, of chiefs and so on. And there was little meeting point, despite the ill-defined areas, and our Germanic [Afrikaner] and control-focussed colonial society has always been obsessed with "The Law." There must be Law and "It's the

Law," and you must follow the Law, and there has to be *mtheto* even though
it's flagrantly unjust, even absurd.

COPLAN: And both whites and blacks share this notion. This is what's
incomprehensible to an American, raised on the legitimacy of civil
disobedience.

WILLEMSE: We also have a long history, a legacy of bureaucracy and authority, whether of the state, chief, or whatever. Even the rebellion has not
been against the idea of authority itself, but against a predatory authority,
that did not recognize authorities in the community. In the new democratic
state, this will also play a role. When people start overemphasizing ethnic
identity, then it will run into trouble, but as long as it's in the context of a
common South Africanness, then conflict can be managed.

Notes

1. Responses to Sachs's paper on the part of cultural professionals and activists can
be found in the volume *Spring Is Rebellious* (Cape Town: Buchu Books 1990).

2. The defeat of the Zulu on 16 December 1838 by *voortrekkers, Afrikaner* pioneers, over the vastly larger forces of the Zulu at the Nkome River in Natal is remembered as the Battle of Blood River, and commemorated as the Day of the Covenant,
referring to the vow taken by the pioneers to serve God if He would grant them victory.

3. At the Battle of Isandhlawana during the Anglo-Zulu War of 1879, an entire
British battalion was destroyed when they were surprised by the main body of the Zulu
royalist army.

4. Under the terms of the Bantu Education Act of 1953, the government took over
all African schools, segregated all schools by race (white, Bantu, colored, Indian),
and instituted a restricted curriculum in nonwhite schools explicitly designed to educate their students for subordinate roles in the economy and society. The opening-up
of former Christian mission schools to non-Christian Africans was a rarely mentioned
"benefit" of the introduction of Bantu Education.

5. *Amagxagxa* is a Zulu coloquialism referring to people who are regarded as neither "traditionalist" nor "Western" in life-style, but who constitute a mobile proletariat who have adopted some aspects of European culture, such as dress, for strategic
reasons, without the benefit of any formal Western schooling or Christian conversion.

6. The Group Areas Act of 1950 proclaimed various areas as set aside for the
exclusive occupation of white, colored, Indian, or black African people, and forcibly
removed residents not belonging to the designated racial classification. In the majority
of cases this involved removing black residents from suburban areas newly declared
"white."

7. The Black Consciousness Movement, which arose in the 1970s under the leadership of Steven Biko and the South African Students Organization [SASO], had roots
in Pan-Africanism and proposed the revitalization and revalorization of a generalized African culture in opposition to what it saw as the irremediable subordination of

black identity within the dominant framework of settler/colonial European cultural discourse.

8. Ruth First was a noted scholar and author on African politics and a courageous campaigner against apartheid. Her husband, Joe Slovo, is former Secretary General of the South African Communist Party and commander of *Umkhonto we Sizwe,* the military wing of the African National Congress. Their story is featured in their daughter Shaun Slovo's film, *A World Apart* (1988). Ruth First was assassinated by a letter bomb in her office at the University of Mozambique in Maputo in 1982.

9. White authorities have long used apartheid pass laws to regulate the movement of black workers for both political and economic reasons, including the dismissal and "endorsing out" or expulsion from a magisterial district of anyone authorities or employers considered politically troublesome.

10. The Nguni languages spoken in South Africa include Zulu, Xhosa, Swazi, Ndebele, and Shangaan (Tsonga).

11. The Inkatha Freedom Party is the organizational embodiment of Chief Mangosuthu Buthelezi's conservative ethnic Zulu political movement, currently the chief black opposition to Mandela's ANC.

12. Strictly speaking, a Zulu *umzi,* "homestead," consists of a polygamous male head, his wives, and their unmarried children. Each wife is entitled to her own dwelling, fields for cultivation, attached livestock, and other material goods, which comprise her *indhlu,* "house." Mthethwa is playing here with the constituent autonomy of each *indhlu* within the *umzi.* Wives are often called by the honorific prefix *Ma-,* "mother/owner of," placed before the husband's clan or surname, suggesting that she is indeed the "owner" of her husband.

13. For Mthethwa to compare himself to an industrial migrant worker is a stunning statement of spiritual modesty, given that only a tiny handful of teachers of Zulu background have ever been appointed professors at "white" universities in the entire history of South Africa.

14. When I arrived for the conversation, Clegg was discussing in Zulu the problem a friend and business partner was having with members of another clan "faction," who were seeking to assassinate him in revenge for murders committed by his errant younger brother.

15. During the 1980s, Africans suspected of informing for the police were killed by "necklacing": an old auto tire was placed around their necks, filled with gasoline, and set alight.

16. Gradual enforcement of the 1936 and 1945 amendments to the 1913 Land Act, of the Group Areas Act, and of other apartheid legislation resulted in a long series of forced removals of rural black tenants from white-owned farms, among the South African government's most egregious mass crimes against humanity.

17. *Witdoeke* is Afrikaans for "white caps," and refers to the white scarves worn on the head by conservative factions armed by the government to combat young ANC "comrades" in the Crossroads squatter camp outside Cape Town in 1986.

18. The segments of the Mchunu and Zulu clans to which Clegg's dancers belong were loyal to Britain in the Anglo-Zulu war of 1879.

19. District 6 was the famous colored area near central Cape Town that was demolished during the early 1970s and designated a "white area" under the terms of the

Group Areas Act. Its population was relocated in scattered, more remote, newly constructed "colored townships."

20. Sophiatown, a black, mostly African freehold suburb of Johannesburg and informal "cultural capital" of urban black South Africa, was demolished in the late 1950s to make way for white occupation. Along with District 6 in Cape Town, Sophiatown was a focus of resistance to the Group Areas Act and a celebrated, romanticized symbol of all that black South Africans had achieved and suffered under apartheid in the urban areas.

21. CODESA was the original forum within which the major political parties debated and structured the proposed transition to majority rule in South Africa.

References

Coplan, David B. 1985. *In Township Tonight! South Africa's Black City Music and Theatre*. London: Longman.

Ferguson, James. 1990. *The Anti-Politics Machine*. Cambridge: Cambridge University Press.

Jeppie, Shamil, and Crain Soudien, eds. 1990. *The Struggle for District Six*. Cape Town: Buchu Books.

Rosaldo, Renato. 1989. *Culture and Truth*. Boston: Beacon Press.

Sachs, Albie. 1990. *Preparing Ourselves for Freedom*. In *Spring Is Rebellious*. Ed. Ingrid de Kock and Karen Press. Cape Town: Buchu Books.

Vilakazi, Absolom, Bongani Mthethwa, and Mthembeni Mpanza. 1986. *Shembe: The Revitalization of African Society*. Johannesburg: Skotaville.

A PREVIEW OF VOLUME 2:
REFLECTIONS ON FIELDWORK IN ALAMEDA

Having completed a long term project and published my book *French Modern: Norms and Forms of the Social Environment,* I was looking around for new terrain to explore, hoping to avoid that fallow period which so often follows a major project. Friends in Paris had been urging me for some time to think more about the life sciences. With the announcement, and extended debate, about the Human Genome Project, the federally funded effort to map all of our human genetic material, I decided to take the plunge and start exploring. Early on it occurred to me, perhaps if *French Modern* had been about the emergence of the category "society" as a new object of power-knowledge in the 1830s and the century-long elaboration of sciences and institutions associated with efforts to form and reform it, then perhaps we were on the verge of a parallel modernization of life.

The first step, like tackling a new language, was to accept the challenge of beginning the process of learning the basics of molecular biology and genetics. There was an immediate payoff and arousal of curiosity, the material was extraordinarily interesting. Evelyn Fox Keller kindly introduced me to the social studies of science literature. We organized a faculty dinner series on the genome project. Our first speaker was Charles Cantor, director of the genome project at the Lawrence Berkeley Laboratory, run by the Department of Energy. The DOE had been involved in biological and genetics research for a long time, concentrating on the effects of low-level radiation from the atom bomb. The genome project had, albeit under congressional pressure, committed three percent of its large annual budget to social and ethical issues. Cantor was hospitable and enthusiastic about an anthropologist working on the project. However, shortly thereafter, in a dramatic coup, Cantor was removed from his job at Berkeley. Science had its own politics and it was played for keeps.

What ensued was frustrating, certainly not uplifting, but ethnographically instructive. A large, leaderless bureaucracy lurched forward, desperately seeking a "star" to take it over. During the extended search, potential star candidates like Leroy Hood were quite receptive to including an ethical-social component to the project at Berkeley. But Hood and the other stars didn't accept the position. Those on the ground were another story. It seemed as if all of the worst qualities of the academy plus those of a governmental bureaucracy were activated. Eventually an ambitious local dog geneticist was named to head the project; high school outreach and tours of the facility to distinguished visitors were his idea of a social component to his empire. Who needed this? Very little science was being done and I was all too familiar with the other dimensions of academic small-mindedness and ambition to need to waste more time studying them.

In search of other more fertile terrains, I asked my colleague Vincent Sarich whether he knew anyone in the biotech world. He recommended Tom White, at Cetus Corporation (by that point White was working for Hoffman-La Roche but was still in the Cetus buildings) in nearby Emeryville (they soon moved to Alameda). Sarich had been consistently generous with his time as I worked through the basics of molecular biology, stopping to chat and explain details and concepts in the xerox room, whenever he was asked. He was also embroiled in a raging controversy: students had disrupted his class charging him with racism, sexism, and homophobia. The controversy had hit the press and was still swirling around during the initial contacts with White, culminating with a forum in front of five hundred students and faculty.

Who would have thought that industry, even a small corner of it in a cutting-edge field, located in the atypical San Francisco Bay Area, would be a haven in a heartless world? The contrast with the perpetual petty power plays, seemingly insatiable status lust, and insistent incivility of the academy could not have been more unexpected. No paradise to be sure, but nonetheless here was a racially and sexually diverse environment with a group of reflective people, who gave every impression of passionate devotion to their science, who seemed to take an interest in the ethical and social consequences of that science, even without any grants or congressional pressure to do so. Suspicious—appearances must be deceiving—I began my fieldwork in Alameda.

The following exchange forms part of a more extended set of interviews on a wide range of topics, especially the invention, standardization, and development of what is arguably the most important biotechnological achievement of the 1980s, the polymerase chain reaction. Tom White and I are writing a book on this relatively simple technique to amplify, rapidly and efficiently, specific strands of DNA, producing millions of copies in a number of hours. During our exchanges and through the course of interviewing other scientists at Cetus, it was striking that a number of the other senior scientists had been

politically active in their youth. The following interview explores this topic
with two of those scientists, Henry Erlich and David Gelfand.

Science and Politics: Some Spontaneous Discourses of Scientists

RABINOW: We'd like to discuss the relations of politics and science both
individually and institutionally. You were each activists during the 1960s.
I'd like to hear about that engagement and how, if at all, it related to your
scientific interests. Next, the idea that a group of former political activists
would one day have major scientific responsibility in a biotech company, one
now owned by a major multinational, and see some continuity with their
past commitments would surprise most academics. I'd like to explore that
paradox or contradiction with you. Henry Erlich, why don't you begin by
telling us about your background?

ERLICH: Well, I grew up in a family that had a socialist background—not
communist, but socialist, social democratic, really. My grandfather had been
a leader of the Bund, a Polish, Jewish, Socialist movement. I was named
after him and he was always extolled to me. I did a lot of reading about him,
so he was kind of an inspiration for both myself and my brother, who went
on to be a labor leader.

RABINOW: Was he anticommunist?

ERLICH: Yes. My dad is anticommunist, my mother isn't. What that meant
in dealing with the Vietnam War was that my antiwar mother, my brother,
and I were on one side. My father came around but he started out thinking
you had to be tough, had to be anticommunist. His dad had been executed
by Stalin. My grandmother had known Lenin and Martov and all these
people, and she was still quite left wing, and she lived in New York. Until
her late nineties she still took part in demonstrations and marches and so
forth. When I was undergraduate and grad student I was in SDS [Students
for a Democratic Society]. I was an undergraduate at Harvard, but then I
actually got more active in SDS and the antiwar movement when I was in
Seattle at the University of Washington.

RABINOW: Was there any science in your background?

ERLICH: No. I had always thought science was interesting but my father
was a professor of literature and my mother is a psychologist, so there was
no real science in my background. And my bent was always more toward
philosophy or literature. As an undergraduate I was majoring in Renaissance
history and literature. And then I took an introductory biology course from
George Wald. He later was awarded the Nobel Prize. He was a very inspir-
ing teacher; I got very excited by this and I went on to take genetics courses
and switched my major to biochemical sciences. I graduated in 1965.

Rabinow: So it's not yet a very politicized atmosphere.

Erlich: No, the late sixties were much more political. When I started grad school at the University of Washington in Seattle—I grew up in Seattle, so I kind of went back home cause I love the northwest and Seattle—I was getting my Ph.D. in the Department of Genetics. And then I got involved in the SDS and all kinds of other counterculture activities. I worked on an underground newspaper, the *Helix,* which was an exciting experience and a lively and vibrant community. And then I took a year off (1967–68) and was a VISTA volunteer in New Mexico, working with street gangs in Santa Fe, which at that time wasn't the trendy, boutiquey place it is now. It was a very poor place but interesting and beautiful.

Rabinow: My sister lives outside Santa Fe, and she was a midwife, and now she's a nurse. The other side of Santa Fe is still there.

Erlich: Yeah, well, it was a fascinating town, a lot of new age activity. There was a commune called New Buffalo—a poet named Max Feinstein was the head of it, and he was a very interesting person. And the guy I worked with was a Christian Brother, Godfrey Reggio. He left the brotherhood and became a political activist. He was the guy who made those movies, *Kayanasquatti,* produced by Coppolla and music by Phillip Glass. It's a very political film, but just pure images.

Rabinow: Was this to get out of the draft?

Erlich: No, actually I had a student deferment. It maintained the deferment; in other words, I wasn't vulnerable to the draft. I was very lucky because New Mexico was a very interesting place and it was a very good program. This was the first time I was directly grappling with problems in the community, in the world. I made a lot of friends.

Rabinow: Did your science have anything relevant to this at this point?

Erlich: No. What we were doing was trying to retain the structure of the gang with the strong leader and the cohesive group—and just redirect its activities. I liked the kids. They were basically, I'd say, with one or two exceptions, good kids. And a few of them were bad guys, like they'd try to stab you or something. Which is not very . . . not very congenial. After that I went back to graduate school, I continued to be active in SDS, but then I got my Ph.D. in 1972 and left Seattle to do a postdoc at Princeton.

Rabinow: So there are still no connections between your politics and your science? For example, I wasn't in SDS but I was certainly involved in the antiwar movement, so in anthropology, one of the things I did was learn about Vietnam, everyone knew what was wrong with the American war, but almost nobody in the antiwar movement know anything about Vietnam.

Erlich: I was very interested in science and genetics, and I was very interested in politics and wanted to maintain both of those interests. They were parallel.

RABINOW: But you didn't come out of Harvard saying, "Science for the people."

ERLICH: No, in fact, I was always a little uncomfortable by the attempts to impose politics on science. I had friends who would talk to me about bourgeois physics or bourgeois biology, and I said, "There's biology . . . you know, there's physics. I remember one of my friends showing me some article, "Is Nature Dialectical?" All those attempts to impose politics on science really didn't seem like a useful exercise to me. I thought they were getting further from the truth rather than gaining any real insight.

RABINOW: So now you go back to graduate school in Seattle.

ERLICH: Yeah I went back to graduate school and got my Ph.D., and I did a postdoctoral fellowship at Princeton continuing the kind of work I'd been doing, microbial genetics. I became very interested in immunology after taking an immunology course because it was kind of a mysterious field, very complex. The complexity and mystery that was gradually being sorted out in bacterial genetics. Bacterial genetics was starting to fit together, and while still a very elegant and exciting field, I thought I'd leave bacterial genetics and go into an area that was both mysterious and complex, but also had immediate human medical value.

RABINOW: Had those considerations weighed on you before?

ERLICH: A little bit. I thought that what I was doing was very interesting, but wasn't clear that it was really that useful or that relevant to human concerns. I did a second postdoc in immunogenetics. I was a postdoctoral fellow at Stanford from 1975 to 1979. I had met a woman with three kids—she and I got together, so I immediately had this large family to support. And she had a dance company which she brought out in a large yellow school bus from Oberlin, Ohio. And having transferred this huge dance company to the Bay Area, my mandate, as it were, was to try to find a job in the Bay Area. It had never really occurred to me to get a job in industry. I mean, I had all the standard left-wing, academic biases.

RABINOW: You assumed you'd be a professor.

ERLICH: Oh, yeah. That was just kind of assumed. But I had a friend whom I liked very much and respected at Stanford named Shing Chang, who took a job at Cetus. And his mentor was a guy named Stan Cohen, one of the developers of recombinant DNA technology, who was an adviser at Cetus. And I'd done some work with Stan. So I dropped by Cetus one day for a lecture/interview and I figured, "Well, if this is good enough for Shing, it's gotta be pretty good." I met David, I met Tom, and I really liked these guys, and it wasn't what I had expected. I realize I really didn't have a very coherent expectation . . . you know, I just sort of went. But they were very lively, interesting people.

RABINOW: So, your entry into industry was legitimated for you by the fact that people at Stanford, some of whom you had a close association with, had themselves already made a connection to working with biotech companies.

ERLICH: That's right. It still wasn't something that a lot of people did, but it was something that a few respected people had done. And basically what I realized when I got there is that in many ways this was a more congenial environment than a typical academic one.

RABINOW: Let's pause there. I want to get David's story up to the present. In sum, you came from a leftist background, you had a sort of traditional, fairly standard march through the elite schools, you maintained a strong radical consciousness during this time, but there was no sense that the science itself and the political connection were either in conflict or in harmony. You didn't see any conflict. You didn't feel ethically debased by working in immunology at a series of elite institutions.

ERLICH: That's right. They weren't in conflict and they didn't reinforce each other. I guess I had separated those parts of my life. Not that I had intentionally separated them, but they just functioned independently and that they didn't really need to interact.

RABINOW: OK. David, could you bring us up to 1978 in a parallel way. Family background?

GELFAND: I guess left of center, particularly for my father, rather than my mother. I grew up in White Plains, New York, a suburb just north of New York City. My father was an accountant, tax lawyer, by vocation. And a pro bono attorney for the ACLU, the Lawyers' Guild, and LCDC, by avocation. And so I also had a politically active upbringing in terms of Constitution law and civil rights. I don't know if my father was a true fellow traveller . . . He was an Abraham Lincoln Brigade member. In high school, the most significant political activity was in high school when we tried to get the principal to allow us to have an advanced high school biology class. I became independently, like Henry, interested in science, but was also very interested in American history. Although, while there wasn't an advanced placement course in biology, there were a few teachers who acted as mentors so that we could continue to do experiments after school in the biology labs or chemistry labs or physics labs. I was involved in high school science fairs.

RABINOW: Is that something you had, Henry? This kind of mentor relationship, because one of the things I know is going to be a theme in David's story is a series of mentors. Did you have that at all?

ERLICH: I don't think I had any real mentors, I mean, I was pretty active in high school, too, in sort of philosophy class, and I got into trouble with a lot of teachers because they claimed I was a communist.

GELFAND: He probably wanted to know why it was wrong for the Cubans to have a revolution and nationalize foreign property, but it wasn't wrong for the United States to do the same thing in the 1700s.

RABINOW: Why'd you choose Brandeis? Any particular reason?

GELFAND: Two reasons: of the places I had visited and applied to, it was one of the few that encouraged undergraduates to work in the laboratories. And because I'd done lots of experiments and taken summer courses at NYU and the University of Michigan, I was interested in doing research. I was also interested in politics and American history. I wasn't sure whether I was going to be a scientist or a lawyer.

RABINOW: Was the Jewish component a part of it?

GELFAND: No, not at all. In any event, I was involved at Brandeis in the Northern Student Movement, also in SNCC and also with SDS.

RABINOW: We're talking midsixties, early sixties, 1962, 1963?

GELFAND: Yeah, 1962 or 1963. I don't remember how I first became involved with the Student Nonviolent Coordinating Committee, but I remember one winter going into a demonstration, outside of Albany, Georgia, and had come to know people involved in SNCC, and in the fall of 1963, winter, January–February 1964, discussions on how to get more people involved in civil rights and how to get northerners, more liberals, into Mississippi.

RABINOW: Kennedy had just been assassinated and the beginnings of the escalation of Vietnam were taking place, King is moving onto the center stage.

GELFAND: Yes, we wanted to focus attention on Mississippi.

RABINOW: And while you're doing this, you're doing your biology?

GELFAND: Well, they're separate. I'm not sure we thought about it at the time, although maybe we did. A conscious political decision to get northerners involved in Mississippi in the summer of 1964, expecting that the violence that was being perpetrated on the SNCC staff people in 1962 and 1963, would also be visited on the northern volunteers, and that would carry with it the press and national attention, and hopefully the army to take over the state of Mississippi. I don't know why we thought the army would help. At the time, believe me, it was better than what was going on. Even though I had spent time with SNCC in the south, I really had not been prepared for the intensity of the violence in Laurel, Mississippi, and other parts with Michael Schwerner, James Cheney, and Andrew Goodman getting murdered, and attempts by Senator Eastland to cover it up for a long period of time until the bodies were found in August.

There were several incidents, one was at the local courthouse where I had been at court in a local proceeding because several of the other staff volunteers from the Laurel office had been attacked at a lunch group counter in Laurel. I'd been there to offer moral support and testimony if necessary. While there, I had observed the local head of the Klan attacking another volunteer as he was bringing someone to register to vote in the courthouse and had filed an assault and battery complaint against the head of the local Klan. A week or ten days later we happened to be at a lake at a farm of a

black family. This fellow and another dozen guys came out of the woods
with chains and clubs, came up to me and said he was going to kill me.
After being clubbed and shot at, I managed to get back to the farmhouse, we
phoned the FBI to come rescue us. The local FBI and northern FBI agents,
who were by this time in Mississippi, said they were not a protective agency
and they could only investigate civil rights violations. I remember saying
"Fine, could you please interpose your body between the bullets and us so
you could investigate the bullets crashing into the wall." They never came.
Eventually I was taken to the hospital in a hearse from the black community
because the white ambulance wouldn't come to pick me up. Since I knew
who had attacked me, I had lodged a complaint for assault and battery with
intent to commit murder. The following fall I was scheduled for a grand jury
hearing, and I went back to Laurel. An attorney from the New York Lawyer's Constitutional Defense Committee came with me. We had a lot of difficulty getting our own depositions and statements, made to the FBI from
August (files moved from Laurel to Jackson, no cooperation by Jackson FBI
office with Justice Department intervention), that I had made to use in this
hearing. The hearing then got moved and reassigned to a backwater county
seat rather than the city county seat where our congressman had assured us
we would have protection. After the grand jury hearing, a couple of cars
tried to overtake us and run us off the road. And at that point, I decided that
I was no longer going to pursue an American history/political science major.
I wasn't adverse to going to law school. I assumed that anyone who was
interested in constitutional law, civil rights, and civil liberties law was going
to be shot at and perhaps killed. Indeed, the lawyers who had helped us had
bricks thrown through their hotel windows. While it's fine for someone
who's a sophomore in college, it's not the way to grow up and live your life.
I thought some day I'd get married and someday I'd have kids. I had blind-
ers on. I assumed that civil rights law would always be like that. Crazy.
That's what I thought, because that's what I was living. I said, "Fine. This
is very interesting stuff, I'm going to continue to be interested in it, but I'm
going to be a biology major."

RABINOW: Did this give a shape to the biology? In other words, biology,
what biology? I mean, Henry suggested a gradual move to immunology because it was more relevant to health concerns and also was a field that was
developing. Or was it just a love for it?

GELFAND: It was just very general biology at Brandeis. Later that year—I
guess my junior year—I had begun to pester someone who was on the faculty in the biochemistry department, a cell biologist by the name of Gordon
Sato. I bugged him to work in his lab. Finally, after two years, he caved in
and said yes. He was more of a mentor than my undergraduate adviser in the
biology department. When it came time to decide what to do for graduate

school, he advised me to choose UC, San Diego. I had applied to two places: the University of Miami, Coral Gables, and the University of California, San Diego, because I was interested in scuba diving.

RABINOW: Would it be fair to say at this point that the Mississippi experience pushed you both toward a kind of privatization on the one hand and, on the other, the consolation of the republic of science. Science was going to be another kind of community, another kind of way of leading a life, that you still had faith in?

GELFAND: Yes, although I was still involved with SDS.

RABINOW: OK. On to San Diego.

GELFAND: On to San Diego! Gordon Sato told me I should go to San Diego, so I went to San Diego. One of his former postdocs was on the faculty there and arranged a summer job for me. It turned out that various people from SNCC and several folk musicians from the south lived in Del Mar. I'd played guitar in some of the clubs in Boston and Cambridge and I continued to play in San Diego. We started an off-base coffee shop in Oceanside, a folk music club, a rock place, geared to the cadets, the seventeen- and eighteen-year-old kids who had enlisted in the Marines. We hoped to try to get them to think about what they were doing, and the club was called The Sniper. It drew the fire of the local marine base, but it was off-base, and we just had folk music and a lot of Phil Ochs and Len Chandler folk music. I guess one of the most discouraging times was in 68 in L.A., the big demonstration in Century City at the Century Plaza Hotel when Johnson was there. A large number of people had been organized to protest the Vietnam War at the Century Plaza Hotel. The L.A. police, with their horses and their motorcycles, had just mowed everyone down with clubs and stuff and it was much worse than Mississippi and the fire hoses. Anyway I became less involved overtly other than The Sniper, which continued until the early seventies.

RABINOW: What are you doing in biology at that time?

GELFAND: Bacteriophage molecular biology. Classical. Heavy-duty molecular biology. I had done rotation projects in various labs, one with David Baltimore at the Salk Institute. We spent a lot of time discussing politics and an awful lot of time studying polio virus. My thesis was very intense because my thesis adviser believed that "rank hath its privilege": graduate students must work harder than the professor. He worked from 11 A.M. to 4 A.M., seven days a week. He expected graduate students to finish in three and a half to four years. No five-year theses. There were long hours all the time.

RABINOW: Who was this?

GELFAND: His name was Masaki Hayashi. There was always the competition. Once I was leaving the lab at one o'clock in the morning, and he would look up from his lab bench at me and then at the clock—really. Anne Bur-

gess, a graduate student at Harvard, was working on the same project as I.
He said, "Look. It's one o'clock. There's still three good hours in the day.
Anne Burgess had a headstart on you! Anne Burgess had a three-hour headstart on you today! That's twenty-one hours a week, eighty-four hours a
month. You must work double hard to catch up!" I said, "Hold on, I started
at seven o'clock this morning and Anne Burgess went to bed a long time
ago." He said, "Well, they're three hours ahead every day and the early bird
gets the worm. You must work double hard to catch up."

RABINOW: This is not a mentor relationship.

GELFAND: Well, actually it was. I liked him a lot. His lab was a wonderful lab in which to be a graduate student. You had to learn to do everything
yourself. It was not a very good lab for a postdoc because he was very nonpolitical. He didn't go to many meetings. He was not a part of the network.

RABINOW: Was there any talk of industry at this point?

GELFAND: *Absolutely not!* Not even a *remote* chance. I finished up,
staying on as a postdoc in the same lab because my wife had enrolled in
graduate school in the sociology department for a Ph.D. program. I stayed
for two years as a postdoc while she was going to graduate school. The draft
was affecting us also. As I recall, the draft law changed in July of 1966. So
that on 30 June 1967, the old draft law changed to the new draft law. I had
had a 2S deferment that expired 30 June 1967. My draft board had failed to
classify me, even though I was a graduate student. They subsequently sent
me a 1A classification, because you had to ask for a 2S. The first thing I did
was go to Masaki and arrange that I could complete my Ph.D. at the Pasteur
Institute. I was *not* going to Vietnam. It was either Canada or France. By
that time, it must have been spring of 1968, my wife was pregnant. I was
able to obtain a 3A deferment because of this ridiculous technicality that I
was unclassified for months. In any event, I finished my graduate studies,
stayed as a postdoc and then moved to UC San Francisco in January of 1972
to work with Gordon Tomkins. I had met Gordon Tompkins at the Cold
Spring Harbor Symposium in 1970 and thought he was just wonderful. We
had talked over the next year and a half, and it worked out that I would
come to his lab. So we came to San Francisco. And *again,* no—not the
slightest idea of ever working for industry. And three and a half years after
coming to Gordon's lab, he died tragically.

In April of 1976 I had a phone call from Ron Cape asking me, actually
first saying that he was president of Cetus, a company in Berkeley, and
heard that my future at UC was uncertain, that I was looking for a job, did I
know anything about Cetus and would I like to learn more. I said "Well,
Ron Cape, President of Cetus, my future at UC is not uncertain, I can stay
here for the next five years. I'm not looking for a job. Under no circumstances would I consider leaving before nine or ten months from now. I

thought that Cetus was doing something biological in the East Bay. Occasionally I have lunch, so if you come over I'll be glad to have lunch with you." What had gone through my mind in some flash instant was that several of us in Gordon's lab, Pat Jones, Bob Ivarie, Pat O'Farrell, Barry Polisky (who was in Brian McCarthy's lab) were close before Gordon's death, became even closer after Gordon's death, and wanted to continue to work together, if we possibly could. We realized no matter how fantastically good we thought we were, we knew the biochemistry department at San Francisco wasn't going to share that vision, and wasn't going to offer us all jobs. One way for us to continue to have potluck meals together, play baseball on Saturdays, and go sailing was if we started an immunology farm on the northern Mendocino coast. We'd make antibody reagents and purify restriction enzymes. But, of course, we didn't have any money or business experience. Here's Ron Cape telling me he's the president of this company. I happened to meet with him a month later in Cambridge at one of Miles' symposia on science and society, on the impact of recombinant DNA.

I visited Cetus for the first time in late June. I gave a seminar on the work that Pat O'Farrell, Barry Polisky, and I had been doing at UCSF on expression of heterologous genes in *E. coli*. I was struck by two things: one, the total absence of any molecular biology equipment at Cetus, and two, the very sharp questions and interruptions I was getting from the nine or ten people attending the seminar. They were asking the questions and anticipating the date for the next slide before I showed the next slide. This had never happened to me at places where I'd given talks. There were generally few, if any, comments because it was crystal clear. In any event, that afternoon Pete Farley asked me what it would take for me to come to Cetus and do genetic engineering. I said it was impossible. He wanted to know why. I told him, "Well, first, I don't like the term 'genetic engineering.' It didn't take into account what's involved: one person doesn't do 'genetic engineering.' In addition, you don't have any of the space that's necessary, you don't have any of the equipment that's necessary, you don't have any of the facilities that are necessary. It's very expensive to set all this stuff up, and besides, that's not what is important. What's important is who decides how things get done, who decides what gets done. People in industry don't have any understanding of what that takes. People who are making the decisions don't understand what's necessary, and it's just *no*." And he said I was the most opinionated, biased person he'd ever met in his life, and it might be that way at other companies, but it's not that way at Cetus. He asked if I would put down on paper what I thought it would take to organize a recombinant molecular research lab. Polisky and O'Farrell, with whom I had dinner that night, encouraged me to put down what I thought was necessary. I said, "Well, that's ridiculous. They'll never accept it." They said, "That's right,

and your biases will be validated and you can say I gave it my best shot."
Well, I didn't want to do it. So I made it as outrageous as I could think of
making it. I came back three weeks later from a meeting in Europe and a
week after that Ron Cape called me and asked when could I start. I guess
this is the end of July or August. I said "Start *what?*" And he said, "Start
the Recombinant Molecular Research Division at Cetus Corporation." I
said, "Well, this is *not* what I was expecting." And he said, "Well, look,
we considered it for the last month and the scientists believe it's a good idea,
and Pete and I think it's a good idea, and Josh Lederberg and Don Glaser
and Stan Cohen think it's a good idea, and that's exactly what we want to
do and we want you to start it up." I said, "I don't know." I hadn't *thought*
about it. He said, "Well, when do you think you'd be able to let us start,"
and I said, "I have no *idea*. I don't know. And if that's not acceptable, I'm
sorry." I just couldn't do it. "I don't know when I'll be able to let you
know." And he said, "Well, I'll be calling you periodically." I had to think
about this because it was serious. I talked with everyone I knew, who was
doing what I thought I wanted to be doing when I grew up.

The people I respected said I should take the job at Cetus. In any event,
the person I argued with most was Gordon Sato, because he had advised me
to go to San Diego, he'd advised me to go to San Francisco rather than apply for jobs at Columbia or Texas or a postdoc with Paul Berg. He told me
to do everything I ended up doing, and so I said, "Why are you teling me
this?" And he said I was crazy. I said what I wanted to do after leaving
Tomkins's lab was eventually to have a research group, have postdocs, and
do the kinds of things you're doing. Why are you telling me that I don't want
to do that. He said that he spent more than 80 percent of his time trying to
get money for graduate students, postdocs, technicians, and he had no time
to interact with the postdocs and the graduate students. When he's on campus, it's faculty meetings. If I had any *reasonable* expectation that Cetus
would be able to fulfill its commitment to me, don't hesitate for a moment.
"Because," he said, "if you stayed at UCSF on your soft-money, nonten-
ured research faculty position, you'll continue to work with people like
Barry and Pat and other people, and you'll do nice things, but where will
you be in five years?" And he said, "If Cetus is able to fulfill its commitment and you were able to attract the kind of people that you would like to
hire and expand, there's no telling what the limits are." Since I had fallen
in love with interactional science, largely through the five years in Gordon
Tomkins's lab, I accepted the position at Cetus.

Curiosity

WHITE: To me, curiosity is an extremely powerful motivating factor. You
know, food, sex, and shelter and stuff like that. Some of things we are doing

here, we don't really know where they lead, you could call it instinct or gut level, but we don't know. Henry will justify his work on diabetes or HLA, and that's right, but he just wants to know about how the whole thing works. He doesn't give a damn about whatever else is involved in it. That's why David Gelfand has boundless curiosity which takes over what he does. The elements around curiosity are what the people do to satisfy their curiosity. That brings in resource issues and external things.

RABINOW: What are the limits to curiosity?

WHITE: Well, it's probably that you just find something even more curious. Or it's just that it's boring. You'd like to go after something where you really don't have a clue what you are going to find. That's called a fishing expedition, which is not supposed to be science. I've seen curiosity end for some scientists. When it does end it's a totally recognizable element in them. They no longer have the curiosity. They go home at five o'clock. Or they say, "Well, if you want me to write up the paper I am going to have to take some time off from work" rather than write it at night or on the weekend like everyone else does. Or when some peculiar result is presented at meetings, they yawn and aren't interested. It's the strangest thing. It's like death in a scientist. They can be productive in a certain sense but the ability to solve new problems isn't there.

RABINOW: So, curiosity can die and become routine and boredom. But what about the other side, can you have too much curiosity?

WHITE: Yes, some people are so curious that they never complete anything. One idea after another, but all at a level that's not very deep so you can't determine the complexity, what's workable or not. The science fiction mode sets the limits of curiosity when humans mate with apes and meddle with God's work, that kind of thing. The limit for scientists is that scientists' visions are limited socially. Never even conceive some issues. How the family is defined. People are thinking about how to distinguish hemoglobin-S from hemoglobin-A, not these other issues. They don't think how this will affect families.

RABINOW: Curiosity is a good thing?

WHITE: It's getting the answer to your curiosity. The mouse pushing on the button to get more cocaine. There is something intensely satisfying about satisfying your curiosity. Scientists just want to know the answer to something. That's why David Gelfand is in the lab every Sunday. He just wants to know how the thing works.

RABINOW: How far down the ladder does this apply as a motivation.

WHITE: There is a range of human variation. Those who are motivated by curiosity have the problem of stopping. They ruin social occasions.

RABINOW: I've written a paper called "The Curious Patient," which was inspired by Hans Blumenberg's chapter on curiosity in *The Legitimacy of the Modern Age*. Blumenberg talks about curiosity as one of the great motive forces of the Enlightenment. He shows how curiosity has been something that has been consistently under attack by Christianity and other authority structures. But modernity faces the question of what are the limits to curiosity. There were the German medical and scientific experiments and so many others which obviously crossed the line of acceptable research. Perhaps there are no self-limiting principles within science itself to tell you not to do a particular experiment. Since curiosity and modernity combine to drive endlessly toward producing something new, the problem is the relation between the drive to newness combined with curiosity which has no internal principle of limitation. Perhaps these German scientists who worked on living patients were horrible human beings, but we now know that they were not all horrible scientists. This disjunction is troubling. The core of the distinguished German medical establishment went along with the Nazis. Curiosity has its thresholds. Perhaps it's ethics or religion which limits what one can and can not do—not science.

WHITE: That boundary where curiosity goes over into something unethical could also be an element in some aspects of scientific problems. They are always ascribed to power and priority issues, but there is an element of curiosity affecting the ability to interpret your data. It's a theme we've encountered in the history of PCF; Mullis saw the band he wanted to see, it was reinforcing his curiosity about it. Others we falsify; their experiments could be simply ignoring the data that doesn't fit.

RABINOW: And there are always data that don't fit. There is rarely, if ever, a definitive experiment which totally settles the issue.

WHITE: Curiosity does get to a point where judgment is required. One boundary to examine is when does curiosity reach a limit. How would that decision be made? Since there isn't an independent reference, what sort of process does one go through to arrive at a stopping point? What would you draw on to make that decision? Not a simple question: what to do to access resources; what you do that might be unethical; or socially advisable.

CONTRIBUTORS

George E. Marcus is Chair of the Department of Anthropology, Rice University. He is coauthor (with Michael M. J. Fischer) of *Anthropology as Cultural Critique* (1986) and coeditor (with James Clifford) of *Writing Culture* (1986). This series follows on the heels of his six-year inaugural editorship of the journal *Cultural Anthropology,* from which an anthology has recently been produced under the title *ReReading Cultural Anthropology* (1992). He is at work on a short book entitled *A Journey through the Terrain of Cultural Studies: An Ethnographic Travel Memoir, 1986–1992.*

Bruce Grant is assistant professor of anthropology at Swarthmore College. His dissertation, "Memory and Forgetting among the Nivkhi of Sakhalin Island," explores the production of Soviet culture among an indigenous people of the Soviet Far East. After almost two years of research in central Russia and Siberia, he returned to Moscow in November 1991 to interview six Russian writers for this Annual. All interviews were conducted completely in Russian; transcripts and translations were done by Grant.

Kathryn Milun was trained in comparative literature at the University of Minnesota and teaches in the anthropology department at Rice University. She is currently working on a book, *Interrupted Journeys: The Cultural Politics of Indian Reburial,* with Pemina Yellow Bird. Her article, "Hungarian Rock Music and Nationalism," appeared in the Spring 1992 issue of *Surfaces.* Milun lived for three years in Central and Eastern Europe. She returned to Budapest in the spring of 1992 to conduct interviews for this Annual and do research on Hungary's current transformation. Her interviews were conducted in English and in a combination of English and Hungarian. She did her own translations and transcriptions. Milun is a scheduled participant in volume 2 of this series.

Michael M. J. Fischer, formerly of the Rice University anthropology department and director of Rice's Center for Cultural Studies, teaches in the Science, Technology, and Society Program at M.I.T., where he is developing a graduate program in the cultural studies of science. He is author of *Iran: From Religious Dispute to Revolution* (1980), and coauthor (with Mehdi Abedi) of *Debating Muslims* (1990). His contribution with Stella Grigorian was developed from interviews conducted during a trip to Armenia in December 1991 for this project. The interviews were conducted in Armenian with translation and participation by Grigorian. His other contribution in this Annual was produced from a series of lengthy office conversations with Leszek Koczanowicz, a philosopher from Wrocław University, who was a visitor at Rice's Center for Cultural Studies (he is a specialist in American pragmatism, especially the philosophy of George Herbert Mead). All interviews were conducted in English; Fischer did the transcriptions. Koczanowicz read and confirmed both the transcriptions and the drafts of the article. Both Fischer and Koczanowicz are scheduled participants in volume 2 of this series.

Stella Grigorian is a doctoral candidate in the Rice anthropology department. For the past several years she has worked in Armenia both as an anthropologist and as the director of the Joint Distribution Committee's earthquake relief project. She was the first eyewitness to break the story of the earthquake disaster to the international press, and served as a guide and translator for a number of international relief teams. She has also been a close observer of the All-Armenia Movement for democracy and independence from the former Soviet Union. She attended all of the major demonstrations that led to the establishment of the independent Republic of Armenia. She is writing a dissertation on the several movements of repatriation of Armenians to Armenia. She speaks fluent Eastern and Western Armenian as well as Russian.

Marjorie Mandelstam Balzer teaches in the sociology and Russian area studies departments of Georgetown University. She is editor of the journal *Anthropology and Archaeology of Eurasia* and of the books *Shamanism: Soviet Studies of Traditional Religion in Siberia and Central Asia* (1990) and *Russian Traditional Culture* (1992). Using data from several years of fieldwork beginning in 1975 in Russia and Siberia, especially with the Sakha (Yakut) and the Khanty (Ostyak), she has written extensively on nationalism, religion, and gender. Interviews relevant to this project were conducted in the Sakha Republic (Yakutia) in 1986 and 1991, with confirmations and clarifications of material specifically for the project done in 1992.

Sam Beck is director and senior lecturer of urban and multicultural studies, College of Human Ecology (of Cornell University), in New York City. His book *Manny Almeida's Ringside Lounge: The Cape Verdean Struggle for Their Neighborhood* is forthcoming. He first carried out research in Romania in the summer of 1973. His chapter is based on research carried out in 1979–80 and the summers of 1990 and 1991. Interviews with Nicolae Gheorghe also were conducted in New York in the winter of 1991. The 1979 interview was conducted in Transylvania under the Ceausecuite regime.

Eleni Papagaroufali teaches anthropology at the University of the Aegean and at the American College of Greece in Athens. Her research has been on Greek women in politics and most recently on the repatriation of ethnic Greeks from the former USSR. The interviews for this volume were conducted in collaboration with Nia Georges during the summer of 1991. They were conducted in Greek, and transcriptions and translation were done by the authors with student assistance.

Eugenia (Nia) Georges teaches anthropology in the Rice University anthropology department. Her current research is on the diffusion of new technologies of reproduction and the ways in which the meanings and experiences of these technologies are culturally and politically shaped. She has done extensive fieldwork in the Spanish-speaking Caribbean and in Greece. She is the author of *The Making of a Trans-national Community* (1990).

Douglas R. Holmes teaches anthropology at the University of Houston, Clear Lake. He is author of *Cultural Disenchantments* (1989) and is currently writing two books; one examines the forces impelling integration in Europe and the reciprocal estrangements they provoke, the other probes the cultural obsessions that reanimate the discourse of extreme right-wing groups across Western Europe. His interview in this volume was conducted at the European Parliament in English during the spring of 1991. It is part of a larger corpus of interviews with European politicians spanning a spectrum of emerging positions punctuating a difficult fin-de-siècle.

Julie Taylor teaches anthropology at Rice University. She has spent a total of eight years in Argentina, returning on the average every two years. Her research has concerned the tango and political myths, as in her *Eva Peron: The Myths of a Woman* (1979). She is now working on the memory of terror following the Dirty War and its effects on contemporary Argentine society. She conducted the inter-views for this project on an American Council of Learned Societies grant in Buenos Aires during the summer of 1991. All interviews were conducted in Spanish with transcription and translation by Taylor.

David B. Coplan teaches in the Department of Social Anthropology at the University of Cape Town and has a long history of research on popular culture, music, and black township life in urban South Africa. As a result of his researches and his appearances (then illegal under provisions of the Separate Amenities Act) as a per-cussionist with the Black Consciousness African jazz group Malombo, Coplan was persona non grata in South Africa between 1977 and 1984. Until 1991 he was forbidden to work in South Africa, and spent most of 1984 and 1988–89 studying the performance culture of Basotho male and female migrant workers in Lesotho, from which several publications and a film have come. He collected materials for his contribution to this volume during his year as a Fulbright Fellow in the anthro-pology department of the University of Capetown. He interviewed Jonathan Clegg in Johannesburg on 28 December 1991 in his home music studio. Barbara Masakela was interviewed in her office at African National Congress headquarters in central Johannesburg two days later. Previously Coplan had interviewed Bongani Mthethwa in his office in the music department at the University of Natal, Durban, and Hein Willemse at the Department of Afrikaans/Nederlands, University of the Western Cape, outside Cape Town. His interviews were conducted in English, and he did the transcriptions with student assistance.

Paul Rabinow teaches in the anthropology department at the University of California, Berkeley. Known for his writings on Morocco, Michel Foucault, and the history of French modernism through the prisms of colonialism and urban planning—for ex-ample, his book *French Modern* (1989)—he has since turned to a study of the contemporary life sciences, specifically biotechnology. The full text of his discus-sions with Tom White will be included in volume 2 of this series.

INDEX

Abrahamian, Levon, 82–84, 86, 88, 122, 124
Arendt, Hannah, 227
Argentina: and affinity with Europe, 284; authoritarian rule of, and free market economics, 288; Dirty War of, 283, 288, 289, 293, 300–302; economic crisis in, 284–285, 287, 289–291; Malvinas war, 298–300, 302; state terrorism in, 283–285, 287, 291–297, 299
Armenia: and diaspora, 99, 105, 109, 115–118, 120–122; and Iran, 96, 112–113, 119; and Nagorno-Karabakh, 81, 86, 104, 110, 127 nn. 8, 9; oppositional movements in, 99–109; political reorganization of, 92–95, 104, 110–111, 114, 115, 117–119; privatization in, 87, 93, 98, 114, 115; repatriation in, 115, 117–118, 120–121; and Turkey, 82, 105, 109, 113; and USSR, 83–90, 96. *See also* Azerbaijan; Carnivalization; Ritual analysis; Sovereignty
Ash, Timothy Garton, 187
Azerbaijan, 81–82, 86–87, 111, 116

Bakhtin, Mikhail, 83
Balzer, Marjorie, 11
Bataille, Georges, 59, 77 n. 6
Beck, Sam, 9, 10, 12
Belaia, Galina Andreevna, 19–24, 32
Belov, Vasilii, 21, 22, 25
Bem, General, 207–208
Biagioli, Mario, 6
Boglar, Lajos, 54, 66–70
Borisov, Andrei Savich, 131–146, 157, 158, 160
Borowski, Tadeusz, 214

Brenneis, Don, 15
Brezhnev, Leonard, 29, 40, 88–89
Bussi, Antonio Domingo, 289, 291, 292, 296, 299–302
Buthelezi, Mangosuthu, 310, 337–341

Cantor, Charles, 359
Carnivalization: Armenian, 11, 82–84; Polish, 196; of Russia, 32, 88–90
Cetus Corporation, 360–361, 363, 368–370
Chirac, Jacques, 261, 266
Civil society, transformation of, 5, 14, 190
Clegg, Jonathan, 10, 307–312, 317–319, 321–326, 331–333, 337–340, 353–356
Colonialism, 260; Russian, 133; Soviet, 192
Conrad, Joseph, 196, 205–206
Conversational form, 6. *See also* Documentary form; Interview form
Coplan, David, 10, 12, 13
Crapanzano, Vincent, 6, 160
Cultural anthropology, 187, 190; in Hungary, 66–67, 69
Cultural Studies 1–5; and anthropology, 1, 190; Center for, at Rice University, 6, 190; critique of representation, 3; as expression of fin-de-siècle, 7; and identity, 12, 13

Dabrowska, Maria, 200, 214, 215
Davies, Norman, 229
de Gaulle, Charles, 261, 263
Democratic movements, 70, 82, 87, 92–94, 110, 114, 283, 289
Diaspora. *See* Armenia; Gypsies
Documentary form, 2, 3, 6. *See also* Interview form
Durian, Rouben, 82, 96

Edelman, Marek, 189–190

Environmental movements: European Greens, 259–260; Greens Union, 100–105

Erlich, Henry, 361–364

Ethnicity, 96, 191, 306; and ethnic consciousness, 131, 157; as form of political organization, 165, 257, 306; and history, 343–344; and intolerance, 69–70; and occupational specialization, 165; and Romanian minorities, 165–166. *See also* European Community; European New Right; Gypsies; Identity; Immigration; Nationalism; Polish; South Africa

Ethnography, 4, 6

European Community, 235, 236, 243–246, 257, 276. *See also* Ethnicity; European New Right; Identity; Greek: membership in the European Community; Nationalism

European New Right, 257, 258; as anti-American, 38, 263, 265, 266; and anti-Semitism, 263–265, 275–276; and *Den'*, 38; emergence of, 260–263; ideological fundamentalism in, 38–39; isolation of in European Parliament, 255; and the Poujadist movement, 263, 268; and racism, 259, 265. *See also* Ethnicity; Le Pen; Nationalism; Race

European Parliament, 255, 257, 272, 273

Fackenheim, Emil, 233

Fassies, Brenda, 348

Fin-de-siècle, 5, 7–8, 83, 247–249

Fischer, Michael M. J., 8, 10, 11

Folk culture, 57, 63, 123

Ford Report, 13, 258–259, 262–264, 267, 269–270

Front national, 255, 257, 259, 261–268

Galstian, Hambartsoom, 82, 99, 109–114, 122, 124

Gaulle, Charles de, 261, 263

Gazdag, Gyula, 54, 70–76

Gelfand, David, 361, 364–370

Georges, Eugenia, 10

German romanticism, 48

Gheorghe, Nicolae, 9, 165, 167–182

Gierek, Edward, 218, 220

Giscard d'Estaing, Valéry, 261, 267, 270–272

Glemp, Cardinal, 202–203

Gollnisch, Bruno, 11, 13, 255, 257, 258

Gorbachev, Mikhail, 20, 31–33, 37, 46, 50, 83, 89–90, 99, 100

Gorky Institute of World Literature, 19, 23, 24

Grandpierre, Attila, 54–66, 77 nn. 6, 8

Grant, Bruce, 10, 13, 14

Greek: androcentrism, 237–238, 245; feminist politics, 237–247; membership in the European Community, 237, 243–246, 248–249; opposition between cosmopolitan and populist identities, 236, 239; orientalism, 236, 245–247, 253 n. 20. *See also* Identity; Nationalism

Grigorian, Stella, 8, 10, 11

Gypsies: assimilation of, 167, 178, 183 n. 7; deterritorialization of, 168–171, 181; diaspora, 171; marginalization of, 169–171, 174–176, 181; oppression of, 166–167, 169; political mobilization of, 171–172, 178–181; Romanian characterizations of, 168–170, 183–184 nn. 12, 13. *See also* Ethnicity; Identity

Hacopian, Hanoush, 82, 90–95

Hambartsumian, Karlen, 82, 96–99

Harootunian, Haroot, 112

Herbert, Zbiginew, 214–215

Herzfeld, Michael, 251 n. 8

History, 67–68, 82, 343–344

Holmes, Doug, 8–9, 11, 13

Holocaust, 274–275; and the church, 201–202; Polish understandings of, 194, 195, 211, 228–230, 232–233; representations of, 189, 212–214

Holston, James, 9, 13, 15 n. 3

Human Genome project, 359–360

Hungary: "alternative" culture in, 57–58, 64–66; capitalism in, 53–54, 57–58; cultural transformation in, 55, 64–66, 68–70, 75–76; state surveillance in, 72–74; unemployment in, 53, 69, 76–77 n. 3. *See also* Pornography; Shamanism: and Shamanpunk

Identity, 13; constitution of Polish national, 11, 190–191, 195, 207–209; Greek, 235, 237, 239, 243–247; and language, 310–311, 314–316, 326–328; multiple, 167, 177; Russian, 19, 37; Sakha, 136, 144, 157, 158; symbolization of, 67–68, 136,

177–179, 192, 195, 245–247, 350–351; social and cultural categories of, 9. *See also* Ethnicity; Nationalism; Polish; South Africa
Immigration, 69–70, 260–263
Internationalism, 69, 119, 235, 306, 310, 317, 336, 339, 342
Interview form: categorical disruption in, 11, 14; and documentary, 4; engagement of reader in, 3–4, 257; fictionalization in, 10; fragmentation in, 286; framing, 13; and others' discourses, 4, 10–12, 286; and positioning, 2, 5; power dynamics revealed in, 12–13; and reflexivity, 3, 10, 14; "voice" in, 1
Ivanova, Natalia Borisovna, 28–32, 40, 45

Karp, Ivan, 15
Karp, Poel's Meierovich, 46–50
Khrushchev, Nicolae, 88
Koczanowicz, Leszek, 11, 190–233
Kondakov, Vladimir Alekseevich, 132–133, 146–159
Konrad Wallenrod, 196–197, 203–205
Korczack, Janusz, 222–223
Kozhinov, Vadim Valerianovich, 19, 23–28, 32
Krall, Hanna, 189–190
Kratz, Corinne, 15
Krauss, Karl, 83
Kugelmas, Jack, 193–194, 199, 203–205, 225

Langer, Alexander, 257
Laughlin, Kim, 15–16 n. 3
Le Pen, Jean-Marie, 38, 255, 258–264, 266–277
Levinas, Emmanuel, 230
Lincoln, Bruce, 231
Lukács, György, 53, 219

Mandela, Nelson, 310, 311, 338, 342, 349
Maroutian, Haroutian, 82, 113, 114, 122–124
Marx, Karl, 53, 84–86
Marxism, 21, 27, 38, 54, 192; in Hungary 53; Polish, 215–221
Masakela, Barbara, 10, 311, 316–317, 330–331, 349–350
Mchunu, Sipho, 307, 322–323, 325
Mead George Herbert, 190

Menem, Carlos Saul, 284, 286–287, 302
Mickiewicz, Adam, 200, 203–205, 208, 210, 211, 223
Milosz, Czeslaw, 212–214
Milosz, Oscar, 199
Milun, Kathryn, 9, 10
Mittelbach, Jorge, 10, 11, 288–302
Mitterrand, François, 258, 267–268, 275
Modzelewski, 217–218
Mthethwa, Bongani, 10, 309, 311–314, 319–321, 329–330, 333–337, 341–342
Myers, Fred, 15

Nationalism, 104, 259; 278–279; Argentine, 288; and Armenia, 104–105; and authenticity, 235; diaspora, 105; French, and the European New Right, 259, 263, 266, 277; Greek, 235, 237, 239, 243–247; Hungarian, 54, 57; Polish, 192, 195–199, 210, 229, 233; Romanian, 165–166; Russian, 26–27, 38, 49, 131; Sakha, 131, 146; South African, 311, 315, 342, 344, 352, 353. *See also* Ethnicity; European Community; European New Right; Identity
New Age, 68. *See also* Shamanism
New world order, 34
Nietzsche, Friedrich, 82–83, 191

Pamiat', 19, 27, 50 n. 2
Pan-Africanism, 310, 317, 321, 334
Pandolfo, Stefania, 6
Papagaroufali, Eleni, 10
Pasternak, Boris, 19, 20, 28, 32
Perestroika, 20, 23–24, 27, 30, 33–34, 44, 89–90, 105–107; response of the West to, 31–34; and response to Nagorno-Karabakh, 86; and rise of American globalism, 34
Poland. *See* Polish
Poliakov, Iurii, 40–45
Polish: and Armenian relations, 193; gentry culture, 196–197, 199–201, 211, 231; and Jewish relations, 187–189, 193–196, 199–214, 221–229; oppositional discourses, 192; poetry, 211–215; relationship to Eastern Europe, 197–198, 204, 211; relationship to the West, 193, 195, 197, 209–211, 218–221, 233; relations to the church, 196, 201–203; rhetorics of state legitimation, 192; romanticism and national identity, 192, 195–211; Solidarity, 217–218

Polish-Jewish relations. *See under* Polish
Pornography: in Hungary, 68, 77 n. 10; in Russia, 31
Poujade, Pierre-Marie, 263; and Poujadist movement, 268
Prokhanov, Aleksandr, 21, 32–40, 46, 47
Proust, Marcel, 61

Rabinow, Paul, 12, 15
Race, as unifying frame, 305, 321. *See also* Ethnicity; Identity; Nationalism
Racism. *See* European New Right; Immigration; Polish-Jewish relations; South Africa
Rasputin, 21, 22, 25, 48
Revolutionary processes, 83–86, 90–95, 99–110; and social movements, 86, 99–110, 126–127 n. 6; the "singing revolution," 346–347
Ritual analysis, 83–86, 88
Romania: ethnic displacements within, 166–167; as nation-state, 165–166. *See also* Gypsies
Rosaldo, Renato, 305, 306
Rozewicz, Tadeusz, 212, 214
Russia: August putsch in, 20, 29, 35, 47; and colonialism, 133; economic reform in, 24–25, 35, 39–40; political and ideological chaos of, 33–35, 49–50; reformulated identities in, 19, 26–27
Russian culture: ambivalence in, 18; division between intelligentsia and peasantry, 21, 25, 36, 40; ideological transformation of, 29–30, 35–36, 44–45, 50; and revolution, 21–22, 49; rupture within, 20, 35, 36; Slavic and Western opposition within, 18, 19, 25–26, 36–37, 40–41, 48–49
Russian nationalism. *See* Nationalism

Said, Edward, 2
Sakha, 134, 146–160; Soviet repression of, 154–155, 157
Sakharov, Andrei, 18, 22, 43, 139
Sandauer, Arthur, 212–213
Santer, Eric, 230
Science: and curiosity, 370–372; and ethics, 364; and political activism, 361, 365–367; mentoring in, 364, 366–367
Scientific imaginary, 15
Shamanism, 60, 69, 132–133; and gender,

149–150; legitimation of, 133, 146, 158; and *olonkho,* 136–137, 144–146, 160; and shamanpunk, 54, 56–63
Shembe, Isaiah, 309, 312–313, 320, 333
Shugarian, Rouben, 82, 114
Social transformation: and intellectuals, 3, 55, 82, 97, 99–100, 105, 117–118, 122–126, 140, 167, 207, 220, 238–240, 308–311, 332–333; and popular culture, 63–66, 75–76, 77 n. 7, 100, 105–106, 307–308, 311, 321–322, 324–326. *See also* Union of Writers
Solzhenitsyn, Alexander, 18, 22, 30
South Africa: and African National Congress and Inkatha conflicts, 337–342; and cultures of resistance, 306–307, 319, 324, 346–348; deracination in, 308, 310, 324, 331, 334, 336–337, 344, 350, 355–356; and difference, 305–306, 315, 328, 342, 344; and gender politics, 329–331, 333; nationalism, 315, 342, 344, 352, 353; and politics of language, 310–311, 314–316, 326–329, 342–343; tribalism in, 308, 310, 324, 332, 336–337, 342, 355; Zulu ethnicity in, 311–313, 321–323, 325–326, 329, 332–333, 335–342. *See also* Ethnicity; Internationalism; Pan-Africanism
Sovereignty: Armenian, 86–87; Sakha, 131, 140–141; of the self, 59, 77 n. 6
Soviet culture: collapse of, 21, 31, 145; as figment of mass imagination, 23, 31; opposition within, 27–28, 43; perceptions of, in West, 31; and social engineering, 17
Soviet literature: allegory in, 42; creation of, 41; declining readership of, 30, 45; political power of, 41; "secretarial," 28–29; socialist realism, 22, 41–42
Stalin, Josef, 17, 22, 24, 28, 37, 41, 46, 57, 88–89, 212–216
Stratigaki, Maria, 10, 238–250
Szymborska, Wislawa, 212, 214

Taylor, Julie, 6, 10, 12–13
Taussig, Michael, 60
Ter-Petrossian, Levon, 81, 82, 86, 92, 94, 95, 97, 105, 107, 109–110, 116–119
Totalitarianism: Argentine, 284, 285; Polish, 192; Russian, 29, 38, 43; "soft," 274
Turkle, Sherry, 230–231

Union of Writers: creation of, by Stalin, 41, 47; maintenance of homogeneity within, 28; membership and structure of, 17–18, 28, 45, 47; privileged position of, 17, 28, 29, 45; schism within, 17, 18, 23, 25, 28, 36–37, 47; in service of state ideology, 17, 18, 29

Urnov, Dmitri, 19–20, 32

USSR, 86; exhaustion of, 17, 33–34, 235. *See also* Nationalism; Soviet culture; Union of Writers

Vagtazo Hallotkemek, 54, 56–83

Voice, and authority, 3

Vsemirnoe Slovo, 46

White, Tom, 15, 359, 360, 370–372

Willemse, Hein, 10, 310, 314–316, 326–329, 342–345, 350–353, 356

Wilson, Peter, 333

Wittgenstein, Ludwig, 190

Yeltsin, Boris, 83, 100, 104, 117, 139

Zmarz-Koczanowicz, Maria, 193, 196